# THE FENS

# THE FENS

## DISCOVERING ENGLAND'S
## ANCIENT DEPTHS

# FRANCIS PRYOR

An Apollo Book

First published in the UK in 2019 by Head of Zeus Ltd
This paperback edition first published in the UK in 2020 by Head of Zeus Ltd

9 7 5 3 1 2 4 6 8

A catalogue record for this book is available from
the British Library.

ISBN (PB): 9781788547093
ISBN (E): 9781786692238

Typeset by Adrian McLaughlin

Printed and bound in Great Britain by
CPI Group (UK) Ltd, Croydon CR0 4YY

Head of Zeus Ltd
First Floor East
5–8 Hardwick Street
London EC1R 4RG

WWW.HEADOFZEUS.COM

*For Chris Evans, Mark Knight and the field team of the Cambridge University Unit for the superb quality of their excavations at Bradley Fen and Must Farm.*

# Contents

A view from the Wash sea bank at Lawyers' Creek, near Holbeach St Matthew, Lincolnshire. This is the point, at the mouth of the River Welland, where the Wash shoreline swings sharply east to head towards Gibraltar Point and Skegness, on the east coast. The sea bank is turning east on the left of this picture. This land only floods during spring tides or winter storm surges. In the foreground are tidal creeks and salt marsh. Far in the distance, over a mile away, are the tidal muds of the Wash foreshore.

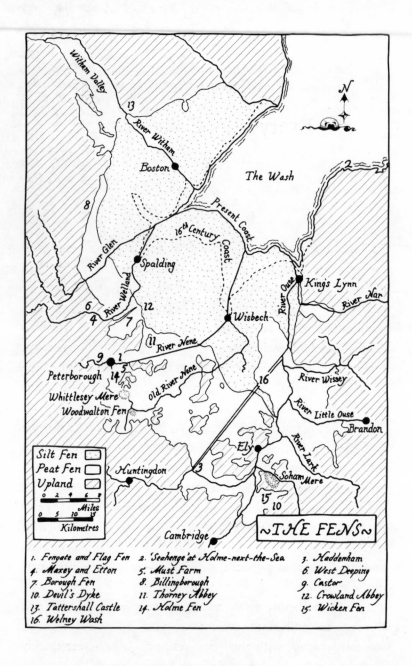

~THE FENS~

1. Fengate and Flag Fen
2. 'Seahenge' at Holme-next-the-Sea
3. Haddenham
4. Maxey and Etton
5. Must Farm
6. West Deeping
7. Borough Fen
8. Billingborough
9. Castor
10. Devil's Dyke
11. Thorney Abbey
12. Crowland Abbey
13. Tattershall Castle
14. Holme Fen
15. Wicken Fen
16. Welney Wash

# Prologue:

# Everything Comes Out
# in the Wash

Time and space are eclipsed by the sea. Nothing has greater power to transport me away from the here and now than the sight, and gently rhythmical sound, of waves breaking on the foreshore. I stood staring at the scene before me for several minutes before the scream of a low-flying jet fighter from the nearby RAF Holbeach ranges brought me rudely back to reality. I was standing on a sea bank, roughly at the mid-point of the Wash shoreline, in rural south Lincolnshire, near the little village of Gedney Drove End.

To my left, the sea lapped against the muddy banks of a flooded tidal creek and to my right was a vast expanse of water that was neither sea nor lake: no beach, no bulrushes, no water lilies – just huge tracts of silty muds dissected by creeks and covered with irregular mats of tough, springy vegetation, edged with spreads of marsh samphire. Every so often there was a patch of soft quicksand. Land birds, seagulls and waders were everywhere, and their ceaseless calls and shrill cries were an essential part of the scene.

Behind and below me the picture was very different. Beyond the concrete pillboxes, machine-gun posts and other wartime coastal defences, with their decaying pebbly concrete thickly cloaked with brambles, the land was lower lying than the Wash shores. It was intensively farmed and had very fertile pale brown soil, with a few trees and fields of vegetables, potatoes, flowers and wheat. But it was a smaller, older and more irregular landscape than the great peaty Black Fens 20 miles (32 km) to the south-west. For these were the marshland or Silt Fens, where roads often meandered and many parish churches were medieval. Huge, rounded mounds of silty soil betrayed the remains of salterns, where people in the Middle Ages had heated sea water to extract salt. In the middle distance, some 5 miles (8 km) due west, I could clearly see the magnificent ancient steeples of Long Sutton and Holbeach churches. Closer to where I stood, the larger Victorian farmhouses had an air of Georgian elegence. But nowhere could I see so much as a hint of a hill, nor a glimpse of upland – even on the most distant horizon. It was here that I first began to appreciate the vastness of the Fens' one million acres.

These two distinct and contrasting worlds were separated by the sea bank on which I stood. That grassy artificial bank was all that protected the land behind me from total and rapid annihilation by a major marine flood. It was a threatened landscape whose uncertain future seemed to demand introspection. And I wasn't struck dumb with awe at my insignificance, as happened when I first came face to face with Niagara Falls. No, this time my perception was somehow more measured, if less assured.

The views from the bank were certainly comprehensive: they extended uninterrupted to the horizon for three hundred and sixty degrees, but I was not confronting them as a puny individual, for I was standing on something created by people. Nor was I above them, looking down from a tall hill or mountain, master of all I surveyed. There was nothing obviously melodramatic or awe-inspiring about the place, like Niagara or the Grand Canyon. It was quietly sublime. It was then that it came to me that I was an essential part of it. I had acquired a profound sense of place: I now knew where I stood, not just on this sea bank but in the world and in my life. It was a feeling I have never lost and I think it explains why the Fens have become so central to my existence.

I am in little doubt that I would be a rich man if every person who told me that the Fens were 'very flat and boring' had then given me £5. Sadly, it's a widespread opinion, born of ignorance and a growing modern inability to look any further than the landscape that's flashing past the train or car window. But get people in the carriage around you to raise their heads from their smartphone screens when you start to draw into Ely station. Eyes widen and children grab at their mothers' sleeves to get their attention: 'Mum, what's THAT?'

There's no building like Ely Cathedral anywhere in Europe, and the small town that nestles around it is as charming and atmospheric as any in Britain. I shall address that often-heard 'boring' criticism as this book progresses. But what about 'flat'? Yes, the Fens are somewhat short of mountains, and indeed, the hill in Ely may seem modest compared with those beneath the great cathedrals at Durham or Lincoln, but when viewed from the low-lying plains that surround the isle, it acquires the mystical prominence of a Mount Olympus.

This is the story of my personal discovery, as both archaeologist and farmer, of Britain's most distinctive, fragile and ultimately man-made landscape. The book's structure is essentially chronological, in a historical sense, but it's also chronological in a personal sense. And somehow I want to try and mesh these two components together – as happened in real life, when I began to discover and appreciate the complex story of the Fens. And it has been a fascinating process of discovery, both of landscape, history and, indeed, of self. I sometimes wonder who, or what, triggered my thoughts all those years ago, as I stood on that sea bank overlooking the Wash. It felt somehow external, but I was almost certainly wrong. Of course, I'll never know the truth; but I'm just so grateful that it happened.

The Fens lie on England's east coast, just under halfway between the English Channel and the Scottish border, and immediately above the large bulge of East Anglia. Today the Fens comprise about a million acres of low-lying ground that forms what is essentially an inland extension of the Wash, England's largest bay. Several substantial rivers, principally the Witham, Welland, Nene and Great Ouse, flow through the Fens on their way to the Wash and thence the North Sea. Much of the story of human life in the Fens centres around the use, then the management, and ultimately the control of those rivers.

Today the Fens can broadly be divided into two areas, the Silt Fens to the north and the peat or Black Fens in the south. The Silt Fens were deposited by the tidal waters of the North Sea. By contrast, the peats, which give the Black Fens their distinctive soil colour, formed in freshwater ponds, fens and meres, fed by the rivers that flowed into the fenland basin. The Silt Fens are mostly found in Lincolnshire and around the Wash, while the Black Fens tend towards the centre and south, mostly in the county of Cambridgeshire, but extending into western areas of Norfolk and Suffolk. Parts of the central Fens, around Peterborough and Spalding, can feature successive episodes of fresh- and salt-water deposits.

Peat is composed of the semi-decayed remains of reeds, rushes, shrubs and grasses that were growing on the wet ground and which failed to break down in the soil, because of waterlogging. By and large, the Peat Fens of the south tend to be flatter and lower lying. This is largely an effect of drainage, which causes peat to shrink and blow away. Silt, of course, is a mineral whose grain size lies in the middle of the spectrum, from fine-grained clays to sands (and ultimately to gravels and shingle). So being mineral based, silt is less prone to shrinkage and wind erosion.

I have always been interested in geology; in fact I studied it for A Level at school, so I found the formation of the Fens absolutely fascinating. But in fenland research, one thought quickly leads to another: everything is so interconnected. Soon I found myself wondering how Victorian engineers managed to build railways across quaking fields of soft peat. While reading about the construction of the East Coast Main Line in the library at Peterborough Museum, I soon found I was also thinking about the draining of Whittlesey Mere, which it clipped along one side. That in turn triggered a lifelong interest in the draining of the Fens. During my twenties and thirties, I found myself pursuing even broader thoughts about Roman, medieval and modern history, and how ten millennia of prehistory had played a major role in shaping the British landscape. Indeed, landscape history is still one of my main interests. During that long journey of discovery, it slowly dawned on me that the past provides truths that can help unlock problems that we all face in the modern world. Put another way, it is relevant: it is an essential component of the present and must never be separated from it, or worse, ignored.

Once drained, fenland soils are very fertile, and the region prospered in the Middle Ages, with major ports at Boston and King's Lynn, on the north and south sides of the Wash. This prosperity was also reflected by the growth of a number of large towns around the edges of the Fens at Lincoln, Stamford, Peterborough and Cambridge. Monastic communities thrived in a region where constant drainage work required an organized labour force. The magnificent cathedrals of Ely and Peterborough are their modern legacy. In early post-medieval times, the release of lands and funds tied up in the monasteries helped foster the rapid transformation of Cambridge University from a regional centre of mostly ecclesiastical learning into an international centre of scholarship and science. These new sources of finance also encouraged drainage schemes across most of the Black Fens, from the early 1600s.

Following the arrival of the railways in 1850, Peterborough became an important industrial centre. Today, light industry still prospers, as does agriculture, and the soils of the Silt Fens grow huge crops of flowers and vegetables for Europe's supermarkets. Slowly, the region is becoming better known for its superb parish churches, which are among the finest in Europe.[1] Doubtless tourism, and I confess I say this with some reluctance, will become more important to the regional economy.

The island of Britain has a very distinctive shape that is hard to describe or pin down in a single convenient phrase. It is usually described as lying on the north-eastern fringes of the Atlantic Ocean, on the approaches to Europe, as if it was somehow different and separated from that continent. But geologically, it is part of the same land mass and continental shelf. As if to emphasize the trivial nature of that physical separation, it took place just eight thousand years ago – a mere blink of an eye in terms of geological time. But the bodies of water, the North Sea and the English Channel, that were created when we became an island have, nonetheless, had a profound influence on the development of Britain's culture and character.

If we now turn our attention in the other direction, out into the Atlantic, Britain's location on the periphery of a vast ocean is very important meteorologically. In fact, we have to step back further to appreciate that the weather systems that so often batter the western shores of Britain and Ireland ultimately owe their direction of travel to the rotation of the globe. The western approaches, to both Britain and Ireland, are characterized by sharp, rocky outcrops that seem to defy the wrath of the turbulent seas, which have ultimately, of course, shaped and formed them. The scenery is dominated by steep cliffs, defiant islands and jagged peninsulas. These are dramatic landscapes where the shades of King Arthur will linger for ever. It is the stuff of romance, and very different from the misty, fertile plains of the east coast.

Britain's eastern shores lie on the less exposed, more protected side of the island, and might be supposed to be calmer and less tempestuous. Indeed, the geography seems to back this up. A glance at the map shows a far less jagged shoreline with long, sweeping beaches and deep, protected estuaries. But all is not what it seems. The North Sea is very shallow and is exposed to the coldest winter gales from out of the Arctic Circle. Like all shallow seas, it heats up and cools down rapidly and is barely affected by the warm waters of the Gulf Stream that curl over the northern shores of Scotland. And, like other shallow seas, the North Sea is prone to fierce tidal surges that can wreak havoc along its low-lying coastline.

If the jagged shorelines of the Severn Estuary and the Cornish peninsula are the two most distinctive features of England's western approaches, they are mirrored by the smoother outlines of the Thames Estuary and the sweeping curve of East Anglia, which terminates, to the north, in the Wash. Beyond the Wash are the rolling landscapes of Lincolnshire and almost a hundred miles (160 km) further north, we encounter the wide Humber Estuary, which separates the Lincolnshire Wolds from the Vale of Pickering, and the high uplands of the Yorkshire Moors – a landscape that could not be more different from the Fens. All of this can be experienced in just a half day's drive and it illustrates well the many stimulating changes in the British landscape, which I find more distinctive and varied than any others in Europe – or indeed the world.[2]

I believe that landscapes can provide us with a uniquely balanced view of the achievements and lives of people and societies in the past. The Fens, for example, contain some of the finest churches in Britain, but between these soaring stone buildings are scattered much humbler structures: houses made from mud-and-stud and other local materials in a region where good sources of stone were hard to find. There are other, unexpected clues out in the open landscape, such as a series of structures, visible across the region, from Lincolnshire to Cambridgeshire, that were rapidly thrown together from poorly mixed gravelly concrete. These are the pillboxes, machine-gun posts and other defences that remind us that in 1940 and 1941 Britain was expecting an invasion from across the North Sea. Such signs of past conflicts can be even more subtle, such as the reddening of the stone at the east end of Crowland Abbey, where Cromwellian soldiers were supposed to have lit a bonfire during the English Civil War of the mid-seventeenth century.*

Landscapes can inspire in artists, photographers, writers and musicians feelings of wonder, fear, envy, anger and countless other aesthetic responses. And perhaps surprisingly, the Fens are no exception. I suppose the Scottish Highlands or the Lake District are more scenic and picturesque, but to my eye such landscapes lack a certain brooding quality. And if any landscape can provide darkness, with a very real hint of menace, it is most surely the Fens. This was first brought to my attention after we'd been living for two or three years near the small village of Parson Drove, near Wisbech, quite close to the Lincolnshire border. It's a very rural spot and our house had been built around 1907, on a medieval droveway, one of whose boundaries was formed by the Seadyke Bank. The area had long been famous for its huge Bramley apple trees, which were open pruned and

---

* For another, likelier, explanation, see Chapter 12, p. 272.

resembled vast, sprawling spiders, or squid, whose branches, or tentacles, seemed to reach over the Seadyke towards our house. On a moonlit night, the scene could be very eerie. Sadly, the orchard was felled in the late 1980s.

I well recall just such a night in late November. It was very cold and windy. We were just sitting down to supper, which my wife, Maisie, was dishing up from the coal-fired Rayburn that kept our small tiled kitchen warm, snug and damp-free. Suddenly, there was a sharp knock at the back door. I immediately got up and opened it. The scene was lit by the bright light that illuminated our back yard. It was raining. Before me stood a man, I guessed in his late thirties or early forties, with wet hair plastered to his head and the shoulders of his jacket soaked through. I was immediately struck by his obvious agitation: his eyes were wide and his left hand, which was holding a 5-litre petrol can, was trembling. His lips seemed to have trouble shaping words. I tried to look soothing and maybe it worked, because soon he blurted out his story – which turned out to be remarkably ordinary.

He had been on his way from Leicester to north Norfolk and was driving along the A47 when he noticed he was running very low on fuel. At that point he thought he spotted a sign for petrol, so turned left into the open fens north of Thorney Toll. But there was no garage. He admitted he should have turned back to the main road, but didn't. Instead he continued out into the open fen, along mile after mile of straight, featureless roads. By now the tank had been on reserve for some distance and he was beginning to get anxious. He didn't have a map, mobile phones had yet to be invented, and he had no idea where he might be. Then he remembered the petrol can in the boot. He stopped, got out and checked, but it was empty. He was on a long straight road. Could have been anywhere. Not a headlight in sight. So he got back in and headed towards the only sign of civilization:

a faint glow on the horizon, which I reckoned was probably Wisbech. Fifteen minutes later, the car stuttered to a halt. By now it was raining. So he picked up the can and started walking.

'I'd have stayed put,' I added, trying to be helpful.

'What,' he replied, 'alone, out there?' He paused. 'No way.' And he meant it: to him, anything would have been preferable to that stranded car 'out there' in the open night-time fen.

I gave him some fuel from the big can we use for the garden tractor and he insisted on paying me much more than it was worth. After a few more words, we shook hands and I said good-bye, but I could see he didn't want me to go. After a short pause he plucked up the courage to ask:

'Would you mind walking back with me to the car?'

I almost made a stupid joke, along the lines of: 'Of course I will, but it'll cost you a hundred quid.' I'm glad I didn't, though, because he'd have paid. He was that scared, poor man.

But the Fens are also a landscape of contrasts. Storms can come and go. Black clouds are often fringed with light, towards the horizon: signs of hope in times of despair. For many creative people, this contrast between light and dark is an integral part of the Fens. The ground may be flat, treacherous underfoot, and constantly threatened by destructive inundation, but the sky, in all its horizon-to-horizon majesty, is a constant presence too. I know it has become something of a local cliché, but fen people do live their lives in the sky. If you live and work in the Fens, you can't keep your eyes to the ground: as soon as you glance up, there's the horizon and above it the infinite dome of the sky. Gradually too, you become attuned to nature. As you live so close to the clouds you soon grow to learn the habits of the weather: how showers and storms tend to follow rivers, and when sea mists, or frets, are likely to creep their insidious way overland from the Wash. And nothing has quite the power to chill like a cold fret in March, which can penetrate to the warmest nooks of our barn, where we protect the smallest and weakest of our new-season lambs.

Our farm lies in the Silt Fens, not far from the Wash, so the landscape around us came into being mostly in post-Roman times, which is quite late in the fenland story. I will tell that story as this book unfolds, but first I want to discuss how and why this seemingly unexciting, flat area of eastern England managed to capture me so entirely. Admittedly I'm an archaeologist and the archaeology of the Fens is as rich as anywhere in Europe, but there's far more to my involvement than just professional engagement. Somehow the Fens have inhabited my soul, and I'm curious to know how and why this happened. So I will be telling two stories: one for you, the reader, and one for myself.

# Cambridge:
# My Introduction to the Fens

*The View from Afar – The Fenland Line –*
*Glimpses from Cambridge – Fengate from Canada –*
*Visits to Ely as a student*

I spent my childhood in rural north Hertfordshire and the village where we lived was typical of the time: many people still spoke with a local accent and cattle regularly crossed the road to be milked, mornings and afternoons. And nobody cleaned up after them. I used to ride my bike to the farm at the far end of the village, and then struggle along a muddy cart track, where the wheel-ruts penetrated deep into the chalk. Halfway along the track, I would abandon my bike and continue on foot for another couple of hundred yards, as far as Bush Wood, which is still celebrated for its bluebells and primroses. My route took me past an angular corner of the wood, which I now recognize as probably being the remnant of a medieval assart, where villagers had cut into the woodland to enlarge their fields.[1] Eventually I would find myself at the head of what we called Happy Valley, a deep dry gully at the very edge of the great Chalk Escarpment – Britain's largest single geological feature. Before me was one of the noblest views in England.

In the foreground, sheep grazed along the last remnants of the chalk hills. To the left was the tower of Baldock Church, surrounded by the small market town, which in those days was still cut in two by the Great North Road, or A1. Sometimes, if the wind was from the west, you could catch the far-off whistle of a steam train on the East Coast Main Line. In the 1950s, Luton and Stansted Airports didn't exist and all the aircraft overhead were military: mainly Meteor fighters and Canberra bombers, based at RAF airfields at Bassingbourn and Duxford on the vast undulating plain of south Cambridgeshire, spread out below me. On a very clear day, my grandfather once pointed out the tower of Cambridge University Library, far, far away in the distance. Like a loving and dutiful grandchild, I agreed I could see it, but I'm not sure I could. I can also remember being intrigued by what lay beyond it. What was that strange patch of grey/blue just below the far horizon? I don't know why I was sure it wasn't the sea, but it seemed to merge with the dark line formed, I subsequently learned, by the curvature of the Earth. Later, of course, I was to discover it was the Fens.

I'm going to take a rather circuitous route into the Fens because they have always been complex landscapes both to discover and to define. There are very few places where one can observe them in all their vastness – because it is impossible to see right across a million acres. Two of the best vantage points I can think of are at its geographical extremities: to the north, on the ridge of hills that fringe the fenland basin, near East Keal in Lincolnshire; and, to the south, near Warboys in Huntingdonshire (now Cambridgeshire). As a long-term resident, I tend to think of the Fens from the inside looking out, and that's the feeling you get when you take the train from London King's Cross to King's Lynn, which clips the fen-edge at Cambridge and then plunges into the deeper wetlands of north Cambridgeshire and the western part of Norfolk.

On 11 February 1952, I lined up with other young children of The Chilterns, a primary school in Stevenage Old Town, under the kind but strict supervision of the headmistress, Miss Woolley,[2] to watch a train travelling in the opposite direction, from Norfolk to London. We sat on the ground at the end of the garden that abutted the main East Coast railway line. We knew what was coming and we were all wildly excited. As the Royal Train approached on its way to King's Cross, Miss Woolley turned to us and we dutifully rose to our feet. A few of the older boys stood smartly to attention and we all lowered our heads as a mark of respect, while the train passed. I managed to sneak a quick squint at the windowless hearse coach. It was the last train journey the late King George VI would ever make, after his death at Sandringham five days previously. But for some strange reason that I still don't understand, my seven-year-old's memory of that February day includes flowers and young girls in summer frocks. It's all very odd, and reminds me that my imagination was always stronger than my memory. There is, however, a point to this digression.

Sandringham House was bought by the royal family in 1862 and the station of the nearby village of Wolferton, just a couple of miles away, was rebuilt in a suitably grand and royal fashion, in 1898. Eventually, in the 'rationalization' of the Beeching era, the line was closed and the last Royal Train called there in 1966. Thereafter, the Queen either took a helicopter direct to Sandringham, or a normal, scheduled, train to King's Lynn (which still displays its 'By Royal Appointment' coat of arms). The Royal Train no longer runs on the King's Lynn line, so Her Majesty has a seat reserved for her in the First Class compartment. When eventually she arrives at King's Lynn, I don't suppose she has to feed her ticket, correct side upwards, through the machine at the barrier (whenever I try, it invariably refuses to let me through).

The Fenland Line runs through the south-eastern Fens and sometimes clips the slightly higher ground of the Norfolk fen margins, as at Downham Market, or the edges of a fen 'island', as at Ely. I always try to get a seat on the left-hand side, when heading towards King's Lynn, or the right, when travelling south, so that I can get a good view of Ely Cathedral with the river in the foreground. I would rank it alongside the more distant sight of Durham Cathedral that you get as you draw into, or leave, Durham station.

Inevitably in Ely, one's eyes are constantly drawn up the hill, towards the cathedral, but sometimes one must look in the other direction: downhill, to the gently undulating landscapes around the approaches to the great 'island'. These were the landscapes where most people lived and which earned the money that ultimately funded the Benedictine monks who established the abbey, later to become the cathedral. We now realize that this lower-lying land holds the clues to early settlement in the southern Fens.

My father and grandfather had been students at Cambridge and they both spoke of the Fens with awe. Their memories of their student days have stayed with me. My grandfather could recall fenmen coming into town, wearing their hair in long plaited pigtails. I think it was my father, in the mid-1930s, who once saw an elderly man in a chemist's shop ask for 'a penny-worth of comfort'. He paid the money and the chemist handed him a twist of brown paper. Later he learned that it contained laudanum, a tincture of opium, which gave relief from the pains that persisted after an attack of malaria. Fen Ague (malaria) had been endemic in remoter parts of the Fens in the nineteenth century, and still gave older folk crippling aches and pains.

When I became a student at Cambridge myself, I began to be intrigued by the mysterious landscape that lay just beyond the university's threshold. Nonetheless, as far as most staff and undergraduates were concerned, it could have been on another, and very strange, planet. Or maybe I'm being a bit unfair. I read Archaeology and Anthropology and our professor, Grahame Clark, the man in charge of the department, was something of a legend.[3] He was friendly, if a bit remote, a characteristic that I attributed to his many huge achievements, but I suspect now that it was probably just shyness. As a younger man, he had excavated an extraordinarily well-preserved fenland site at Shippea Hill, whose details we were taught in mind-numbing detail. He excavated other well-known sites, including one of the first settlements ($c.9500$ BC) in Britain, at Star Carr in Yorkshire, but he also wrote more general academic books, which had a strong influence on students at the time.[4] These books broadened our horizons and our digging team was enormously honoured when he paid us a visit at Flag Fen, in, I think, 1989.*

At Cambridge, I attended a high-flying college, Trinity, but spent most of my time drinking beer, chasing women and rowing off hangovers. In the vacations, I excavated ancient sites, but I didn't then grasp that I was actually quite good at it. It was just a job and in those days the Department of Works (known since 2015 as Historic England) paid lots of money. In my third year, after organizing the music for the college May Ball, I toyed with the idea of joining the then rapidly growing pop-music business and was even offered a job by two top London agencies. Although the money was beyond my wildest

---

* Grahame Clark was knighted in 1992 and died in 1995.

dreams, for some reason I turned them both down – and I have never regretted it. After three years at Cambridge, I eventually managed to scrape a degree of 'the middling sort', a 2:2, and of course I was rather disappointed, although I acknowledged that I hadn't done enough work to get anything better.

At Trinity I discovered life, human relationships and the importance of independence. I still don't believe in the imposition of discipline by training alone, which simply limits the imagination. As far as I am concerned, focus and rigour should come from within, where they are inspired by enthusiasm and curiosity, rather than a desire merely 'to succeed'. In research, nothing, but nothing, can beat the excitement of the chase. And that, I suppose, is the story of my subsequent life in the Fens.

After leaving Cambridge in 1967, I continued to dig in my spare time, but my 'day job' was as a management trainee at the family-owned Truman's Brewery in Brick Lane, East London. I even became a qualified beer taster and have retained a delight in real ale. But deep down I felt discontent, because I knew I was doing something that didn't really satisfy me. And besides, I knew beer would soon make me very, very fat.

My life changed in 1969 when I decided, on a close family friend's advice, to look for work abroad. As he had suggested, I crossed the Atlantic and fetched up in New York. After a few months, I received notice that if I stayed in the United States, I would be sent to fight in Vietnam. I had no wish to be killed, and besides, it was a war that, like most of my contemporaries, I disagreed with profoundly. So I headed north to Canada and, after a few unhappy months selling books for a local publisher, acquired a job at the Royal Ontario Museum, in Toronto. In those days the museum had a wonderfully named Office of the Chief Archaeologist. The man himself was Dr Doug Tushingham who, for some reason, took me under his wing and in the process completely altered my career – and my life.

Doug Tushingham was writing up excavations he had directed in Jordan during the 1950s and he made me his technician. We worked together in the same office, so he kept a very close eye on me. But I have to confess I never felt even slightly that I was being used. With hindsight, his supervision was more paternal than managerial. And I don't think I have ever worked quite so hard. I had to acquire new skills, such as technical drawing and photography, not to mention the writing of clear, concise descriptions. He also suggested I should catch up with my archaeological reading and hinted that he was considering another foreign expedition. His department already sponsored digs in Iran, Israel and Belize, not to mention two in Canada. I would be in distinguished company.

In the summer of 1970 I found myself back in England. Doug Tushingham had produced a small research grant and in return I was to find him a new project.[5] I travelled around eastern England looking for somewhere to start a new research project, using Canadian funds. I decided on eastern England as that was the region I knew best, and having studied prehistory for my degree, I was looking for somewhere pre-Roman. And eventually I found it, at Fengate, on the eastern edge of Peterborough. I set about chatting up local archaeologists and the planners at the Peterborough New Town Development Authority – and by the end of the summer they all agreed that I should return the following spring with a team of Canadian and British diggers, many of whom came from Manchester University, where I had some good friends. I knew I had a very short time to build a team and it would be far simpler if I used people I already respected.

Two years previously, in 1968, the English Royal Commission on Historic Monuments had published a survey of archaeological sites threatened by the imminent expansion of Peterborough New Town. Many of those sites lay along the eastern side of the city, where the dry land merged with the neighbouring fen. The area, known as Fengate (from two Norse words meaning 'fen' and 'road'), was scheduled to be the New Town's principal industrial area. In those days it was an interesting mix of small and medium-sized farms, plus a few factories and workshops that had spilled over from the city. There was also a large population of gypsies, many of whom kept horses. After a few years we became quite friendly with some of them, who we allowed to graze their animals around the edges of our sites, over winter. There was a good deal of local prejudice against travellers, which is maybe why they viewed us migrant archaeologists as similar souls: we lived in an abandoned house and didn't seem to abide by the normal rules.

The gypsies were notorious for betting. I have it on good authority that on one occasion, at dead of night, they closed off the southbound carriageway of the nearby A1. They then raced two horses along the empty road, before moving their blocking trucks and vans to the other side of the central barrier and continuing the race back, northwards. The winner is said to have won tens of thousands of pounds. Today the area has lost its character entirely, even the name has changed. Instead of Fengate, signposts now direct drivers to the 'Eastern Industrial Area' or 'Eastern Industry'. But there is still a substantial population of travellers, now confined to a small permanent campsite right on the edge of the Fens. There was a time when I would have viewed the fly-tipped and rubbish-strewn semi-abandoned fields around the campsite with nothing but disapproval. I'm now in two minds about this blot on the landscape. Yes, it's ugly and untidy, but it's also a symbol of something else, something that's harder to define: nonconformity perhaps, maybe defiance – or just independence of spirit?

At the very start of the project, Doug had promised to find finance and he lived up to his word. So in the spring of 1971, I returned to Fengate with a substantial research grant in Canadian dollars (which was great, as the pound was then tottering somewhat). The previous winter I had done what research I could manage in the University of Toronto's excellent library, but in those pre-Internet days such work was necessarily limited. However, the previous autumn I had managed to get a good collection of prints from the aerial photography people at Cambridge University – and these turned out to be a godsend. I still have one or two of them, although now rather battle-hardened: tattered and stained with instant coffee, site hut tea and mud.

Using those aerial photographs, together with the transcriptions published in the Royal Commission's pioneering survey, I realized by the close of my first summer of excavation that we had stumbled across a series of Bronze Age fields that extended along the edge of the fen for at least a kilometre.[6] Later, radiocarbon dates were to demonstrate that the Fengate fields came into use in the centuries after 2500 BC and gave way to slightly different patterns of farming from about 1000 BC. So on this evidence, the Fens still possess one of the earliest field systems in Britain. Research over the past two decades has shown this field system (which included smaller, subsystems) to be far more extensive than I imagined back in the early 1970s. More to the point, we now realize that it formed part of a much wider network of regional farming economies, which were organized around their own Bronze Age field systems; these can be shown to have extended right across southern England.[7] But the field systems along the edges of the Fens and extending up into the lower valleys of their major rivers (principally the Ouse, Nene and Welland) were the longest lived, most complex and extensive of any in Britain. It was also a densely settled landscape, with numerous farms, hamlets and settlements. But the area lacked the stone to construct great and enduring monuments, so it will never be as celebrated as, say, Stonehenge, or Orkney.

The southern Fens have always been characterized by numerous natural 'islands'. These are formed by undulations in the underlying so-called solid, or pre-Ice Age, geology. These flood-free drier areas were a natural focus for settlement, which today takes the form of market towns, villages and hamlets – and just one small city, which has dominated the landscape for over a thousand years. I'm not a great lover of cities, but I have to make an exception for Ely, if only because it's so tiny.

I first became fully aware of Ely when I was a student at nearby Cambridge. I had inherited a very rattle-prone Austin A40 on my grandfather's death in 1960, and somehow it was still on the road, five years later. My grandfather used to sit very low in his seat, so that his head only just protruded above the dashboard, and would drive very slowly around the village and farm, glancing off buildings, tractors and gates from time to time. In those days there was no such thing as the MOT Test and the car was largely held together with bits of wire and baler twine. The cylinder head leaked pungent fumes through its cracked gasket and the exhaust pipe lived up to its name: leaky and exhausted. But it rarely broke down and carried me and my friends to various pubs outside the university bounds. Once or twice I ventured further afield, often heading south towards my family in Hertfordshire, but on at least one occasion I decided to venture north, out into the open Fens.

I generally followed minor country lanes, as even back then the major roads were dominated by impatient men in large, flashy cars who would glue themselves to my rear. This had the opposite effect on me: I would slow down and drift towards the crown of the road whenever I thought they were about to overtake. I have memories of glimpsing furious faces in my rear-view mirror, for those fleeting moments when it wobbled into the correct position, to reflect what was happening behind me. But most of all I remember seeing the black peaty soils in autumn, after ploughing. There were heaps of dried and cracked 'bog oaks' – trees that had been growing in the prehistoric peats, and which had been caught by the plough and pulled to the surface. In summertime all the dykes were lined with tall stands of reeds and rushes. And of course, the road surfaces were terrible: a mass of humps and bumps that formed and distorted every few months as the peats far below the surface dried, or were moved by slowly flowing groundwaters. One knew immediately when one had struck the edge of an 'island': the fields were paler, with fewer reeds in the dykes, and the road surface suddenly flattened out.

The slope up to the isle on which Ely Cathedral sits is slight at first, but gets steeper as you approach the town itself. By now, the great church dominates everything and it almost comes as a relief to pass below a tall ash, oak or lime tree and be screened from its towering presence. But I was enchanted. I had never come across a building that commanded its surroundings so forcefully – it was strong yet gentle at the same time. It was clearly an integral part of the landscape and I felt comfortable in its company. The great traveller Celia Fiennes, however, had a rather different opinion.

Celia stayed at Ely on her 'Great Journey' from London to Newcastle and Cornwall, and back, in 1698, the year after she had visited Whittlesey Mere, just south of Peterborough and then England's largest lake.* She was plainly a lady of extraordinary energy and with a wealth of noble and aristocratic friends who were happy to open their grand houses to her. But she was more

---

* See also Chapter 16, pp. 337–49.

*A view of Ely Cathedral from the south-east. The photo was taken from the Middle Fen Bank on Queen Adelaide Way, near the Cambridge University Boathouse. In the foreground are the seasonally flooded wash pastures, with the Great Ouse just beyond the trees in the middle distance. The cathedral can be seen on its natural 'island', behind the old warehouses and other buildings that line the river frontage below.*

than disappointed with Ely, despite the great cathedral, which then dominated the surrounding city, just as it does today. When I first visited, it was still a traditional fen town with some remarkably good pubs and fish and chip shops. Nowadays, Ely is becoming incorporated into Silicon Fen and is acquiring a new and more Cambridge-focused identity. How very different things were when Celia visited, some two centuries earlier. Here she describes her entry into the city:

> by reason of the great rains, the roads were full of water, even quite to the town, which you ascend a very steep hill into, but

the dirtiest place I ever saw, not a bit of pitching [paving] in the streets so it's a perfect quagmire... it seems only a harbour to breed and nest vermin in, of which there is plenty enough, so that although my chamber was nearly twenty steps up, I had frogs and slow-worms and snails in my room.[8]

I have to say this strikes me as a touch extreme – and, dare I say it, just a tiny bit prejudiced? The Fens have long had a bad reputation and I suspect the frogs, slow-worms and snails tell us more about the recent rains, and the standard of Celia's accommodation, than about the state of the town itself. Despite being a fen town, Ely is very dry and is built on an ancient and generally stable geological ridge, as are the neighbouring villages of Sutton, Haddenham, Witcham and Wilburton. People weren't stupid, they positioned their settlements on good dry land, rather than the flood-prone peat fens around them. It's a pattern we will see elsewhere in the Fens, although people didn't always have the luxury of an underlying geological ridge to build on. Frequently the land they chose was *drier*, rather than dry: the banks of an old creek, a coastal dune or a tidal mudflat.

It is now time to become less personal and more chronological, if, that is, we are ever to get to grips with the vast complexity of fenland history and prehistory.* I want to turn the clock back some six thousand years, to the start of our story, around 4000 BC, when the first farmers started to settle permanently in the low-lying basin that was about to become the Fens. It is the Neolithic, or New Stone Age. The people would have looked and behaved just like us, as they too were *Homo sapiens*. They

---

* I use the term 'prehistory' to refer to people and events prior to the Roman conquest of AD 43.

would have spoken languages that would evolve over the millennia to form the ancestral versions of what we would later call the Celtic tongues, which include Welsh, Cornish, Breton, Scots Gaelic and Irish.

The earliest Fen farmers still lacked metals, but their culture was far from unsophisticated. Indeed, exciting new discoveries, many of them made in the Fens, are starting to reveal just how rich and complex these ancient communities could be. I began my serious archaeological research into the Fens in 1971, when we began our first season of excavation at Fengate. And I don't think I could possibly have imagined, in my wildest dreams, what we and our successors would be revealing in our trenches, almost fifty years later. It has been such an eventful journey – although, just like the story of the Fens, not without its fair share of accidents, mishaps and lost opportunities. Good research, like human history itself, rarely runs smoothly.

## 2

# Fengate:
# Approaching the Wet from the Dry

*Mr Wyman Abbott's Finds – Early Days at Fengate*
*– Droves – 'Open Area' Excavation – Bronze Age*
*Intensive Farming – Ancient Hedges – Seahenge*

For most people, the first serious relationship with a girl- or boyfriend is an unforgettable experience that remains with them for the rest of their life. I encountered something similar with my first excavation, at Fengate in Peterborough. It took place from 1971 to 1978, while I was based in Canada, and it transformed the course of my professional life. Just like a developing human relationship, Fengate taught me much about myself, but also about the role of archaeology in the modern world. Fengate was where I discovered that I enjoyed writing and – to my huge surprise (because I had been a hopelessly poor amateur actor at school) – that I could do quite convincing interviews on radio and television. But it was a very challenging project and, of course, it didn't always run smoothly.

Although few of us were thinking along such lines at the time, it is now almost embarrassingly obvious that low-lying river valley floodplains can become very wet and eventually merge into wetlands. Soon we began to realize that those river valleys that flowed into large wetland basins, such as the Fens, could provide the much-needed explanatory context for discoveries made further out, in the wetland proper. Put another way, these drier landscapes of the river valleys were where most of the people who exploited the wetlands lived full time. As the Fengate project gathered pace, I started to appreciate that the sites we were revealing at the point where the River Nene entered the Fens were fen landscapes too.

Prehistorians working in later Victorian and Edwardian times were aware that the gravels at Fengate were important. Indeed, the first academic paper was published in a major national journal, back in 1910, by a remarkable man called George Wyman Abbott.[1] Abbott was a local solicitor who was fascinated by archaeology and used regularly to visit the hand-dug gravel pits at Fengate. I had the great privilege of meeting him. He was a charming man and I can fully understand how he won over the quarry workers. I can just remember the humps and bumps left by those pits, which now lie beneath roads, a large roundabout, a massive Pizza Hut, a garage and an industrial estate. Abbott knew the workmen in the pits and would regularly collect flints, pieces of bone and pottery, all of which are now in Peterborough Museum. Some of this material, the soft, unglazed, hand-made pottery in particular, was hard to recognize, so the men who actually dug the gravel must have known what they were doing. It would seem that most of the finds came from smaller pits, dug in prehistoric times, which may originally have been dug to provide clean gravel to go on paths or on house floors. Some of the deeper ancient pits reached down to the permanent water table, which we knew from our own excavations in the area was lower in summer than in winter, when it could be just 3 or 4 feet (1–1.2 m) from the surface. Essentially these deeper pits were wells and would have been excellent sources of naturally clean water.

The commercial gravel pits at Fengate continued to reveal finds throughout the first half of the twentieth century, particularly of pottery, which were published by leading authorities from the 1920s through to 1945.[2] When I look back on these finds I am always struck by the fact that they represent people from all the later prehistoric periods, from about 3000 BC, right through to the Roman conquest of AD 43. In the light of what we know now, we can be reasonably certain that the old gravel workings would have been the site of ancient houses, but some of the pits may well have been deliberately filled with pottery. The pre-war finds also included some burials and a large Bronze and Iron Age cremation cemetery, where the ashes were interred in pottery urns. I am in little doubt now that the gravel pit finds represented a major and long-lived settlement.

When we were working in the Welland valley in the 1980s we had *A Matter of Time* – a remarkable survey of gravel floodplains, originally published in 1960 – to guide us.* But when it came to Fengate, my crib (indeed, I still think of it as my bible) was a report on the antiquities threatened by the expansion of Peterborough New Town, which was published two years before my exploratory visit to England in 1970.[3] The archaeologist who compiled the detailed survey of Fengate (and whose name doesn't appear on the title page!) was Chris Taylor and I made several very useful visits to him for help and advice, especially in the early years of the project. Chris made it quite clear to me that the aerial photographs of cropmarks[†] along the gravel terraces where the factories and warehouses of the New Town industrial area were to be sited would repay close attention, and that I shouldn't try to work from the plans in the report. These

---

* I discuss *A Matter of Time* further in Chapter 4, p. 61.
† For a description of cropmarks, see Chapter 4, p. 65.

were accurate and very good, but only showed a tiny part of a hugely complex picture. I would have to think bigger than that. *Such* sound advice: thank you, Chris.

As soon as I returned to England in the early spring of 1971 for our first season of work at Fengate, I made several visits to the Aerial Photographic Archives at Cambridge, where I met the man who actually took the pictures, J.K. St Joseph, known universally as Holy Jo. He was a remarkable man who had the wonderful gift of being able to predict when and where cropmarks would appear at their best – and most people are agreed that nobody has ever matched him in this.

A week or so after my visits to the Cambridge archives, the prints I had ordered appeared. Carefully removing them from the stiff-backed envelope that was to remain their home (suitably reinforced with layers of yellowing Sellotape) would be a recurrent feature of the next fifteen years. They were even brighter and clearer than the prints I had seen in Cambridge, or than those that were published in the Peterborough New Town report. You could see every fence post, every bush in each hedge. It was extraordinary. But what first grabbed my attention weren't the deep, dark cropmarks of a Roman farm, but a pale flash across the corner of a modern field, which I immediately recognized as the parch mark left by a buried Roman road, known today as the Fen Causeway.

The Fen Causeway ran through Peterborough, west of the prosperous Roman town of Durobrivae, near the modern village of Water Newton on Ermine Street (the modern A1). To the east, it left Fengate and headed across Flag Fen to Whittlesey 'island' and thence, via March, to Denver on the Norfolk side of the Fens, at which point it connected with the extensive Norfolk road system. I have to confess that although I was never a great enthusiast for the Romans, the story of the Fen Causeway has always intrigued me.

Its route from Durobrivae in the west and then straight across the Fens to Norfolk is very direct and indicates that it might have been built and planned by Roman military engineers. The available evidence also suggests that it was built early in the Roman period and my own researches along the road in Fengate support this. Certainly I have never found any later material to contradict such a timeframe. Building a road across the undrained Fens was a major operation, so why did the Romans do it?

Every so often I have to visit London and whenever I'm in the vicinity of Hyde Park I look up at the statue of the warrior Queen Boudicca on top of the Wellington Arch and thank her for indirectly allowing me to crack the mystery of Fengate's prehistoric landscape. It's a strange, rather convoluted story, but it's worth telling because it shows how archaeological insights are really arrived at. Very rarely do we make insights in the correct, theoretically approved fashion, which involves first suggesting a hypothesis and then testing it against the evidence produced in the dig. Back in 1971 nobody could have predicted that a series of possibly Roman double-ditched trackways could turn out to be something very different – and much, much earlier.

The Peterborough New Town report had a section devoted to Fengate, which included Chris Taylor's fold-out plan mapping Holy Jo's newly revealed cropmarks and placing them against the possible location of the pre-war gravel pit finds.[4] The first things that grabbed my attention were four sets of paired ditches that Chris, quite reasonably, had labelled 'trackways', which ran roughly parallel across the gravel terrace that fringed Flag Fen, down towards the wetland edge, at right angles to it. One of these pairs seemed to cut – i.e. was later than – the ring-ditch of a ploughed-out Bronze Age barrow. I showed the cropmarks to several colleagues, who all agreed with me that they looked very

Roman: they seemed regular and remarkably straight and one of the ditches seemed to be cutting a Bronze Age barrow. I was also reminded by several local people that it was not unusual to find Roman pottery fragments in the topsoil. It was all very intriguing.

The timetable of our research at Fengate had to be partly dictated by the New Town Development Corporation's road, sewer and factory-building programme, and in the spring of 1971, when I returned to England for our first season of excavation, I discovered that the area they wanted me to clear for development first contained two of Chris Taylor's possibly Roman 'trackways'. So we started digging them.

New excavations don't always begin with a bang and Fengate was no exception: I must confess I was very disappointed. I wanted to report something dramatic to my friends and sponsors in Toronto: perhaps a few Roman bronze brooches, or even a nice skeleton. Frankly, anything would have made good copy for the museum's archaeological newsletter, but even after a month's work, we had revealed nothing: just a handful of rather nondescript and undateable flint flakes and a few small scraps of pottery. They were the sort of finds that would have been present in the topsoil when the Roman ditches were dug. By midsummer I managed to get my newsletter copy deadline deferred and at the same time I decided to extend the trenches. Those trackways were not going to defeat me.

I think it was in the final month of that first season that the truth about the 'trackway' ditches began to dawn on me. By this point we had roughly doubled the number of finds from them, which now included some larger and more diagnostic pieces of prehistoric pottery, which I reckoned could be Bronze Age. We also found fragments from two fist-sized fired clay loom-weights. These were distinctive and not very common and were used to tension the warps – the vertical fibres – of a frame loom.

In the Iron Age there was a technological change and loom-weights became larger and triangular. So these had to be Bronze Age and probably pre-dated 1000 BC. The trouble was, most of our small collection of finds could have pre-dated the ditches and found their way into them with topsoil and other surface debris, after their abandonment. On the other hand, we hadn't found a single sherd of Romano-British pottery, which was very unusual for a site in the lower Nene Valley, where pottery manufacture had been a major industry. Nene Valley wares occur widely on Roman sites right across south-east England. I couldn't make up my mind. My instinct was that the track-ways were indeed Bronze Age, but I desperately needed proof. And then I had to decide why on earth they had been put there in the first place.

For our first season of excavation we had rented a small flat above a solicitor's office in Peterborough's Lincoln Road. It was a pleasant, if quiet, part of town. I remember returning to the flat at the end of the day when we had discovered the first of the two clay loom-weights. I needed to look at the air photos. I wasn't quite sure why, but something seemed to be worrying me. By now the photos were less crisp and shiny, and several looked rather sad and scuffed as I tipped them out of their envelope and onto the carpet. There was a large lime tree outside the window and it cast a shifting, dappled shade as a light breeze ruffled the leaves. Maybe it was a shadow, but something caught my eye and I found myself looking down at a particular photo. I soon realized it wasn't a picture of the field where we were then digging; it was across the road, about a hundred yards away, to the north-east. I was about to put it aside as irrelevant, when I hesitated and looked at it more closely. The cropmarks were quite clear and were dominated by that parch mark caused by the dumped gravel of the Fen Causeway Roman road. Yet below the road, I could clearly see two darker cropmarks, which

I immediately identified as another pair of 'trackway' ditches. The parch mark of the road clearly concealed and overlaid the two earlier ditches. Scholars were agreed that the Fen Causeway had been constructed to move Roman troops across Britain to suppress Queen Boudicca's revolt of AD 60–61. All that happened within twenty years of the Roman conquest, so those 'trackways' were definitively pre-Roman. It was a great relief to have established their approximate age, but that still hadn't addressed the all-important question: why had they been dug in the first place?

The answer came to me the following winter, when I returned to Toronto to do what we call the post-excavation research. Again, I laid the photos out, this time on a drawing board, and decided to redraw and update Chris Taylor's plan of the Fengate cropmarks. Transcribing cropmarks onto maps is a time-consuming process and I was fortunate to have a very good base-map to work with. It took me several weeks to complete the task and I was able to add a number of new ditches, which we'd discovered in the previous summer's excavation. These new ditches set me thinking, because at least one of them was contemporary with, and appeared to link together, two of the paired-ditch 'trackways'. This ditch, and other smaller ones like it, had worried me when we were digging. I was also concerned about the lack of a dumped gravel surface along the so-called 'trackway' between the two parallel ditches.

I cannot remember a 'road to Damascus moment' when the truth dawned, but in retrospect we were working in what was still a very rural environment, albeit on the edge of a rapidly growing modern city. Fourth Drove was then little more than a rutted cart-track with tall, overgrown thorn hedges along both sides. Today it separates a large power station and a massive energy recycling plant. Dozens of heavy lorries use it every day. But I can often recall walking down it, especially when I needed to take a solitary break and reflect on what had been happening in the trenches that day. At the end of Fourth Drove, just ten minutes' walk from the site, the landscape suddenly opens up to reveal the black soil fields of Flag Fen, stretching for nearly a mile across to the brickworks on Whittlesey 'island', behind the distant flood bank of the River Nene. In those days, gypsy horses grazed in the paddocks along Fourth Drove. Long abandoned but still just discernible ditches marked the edges of the grazing. In places you could see where they joined other field boundary ditches, again long abandoned and unmaintained, but I could see this had once been part of a working landscape where drainage mattered, and where ditches would have been kept open and clean.

Those paddocks at the end of Fourth Drove made me examine fields and paddocks elsewhere in the Fens. Having spent my youth in the rolling chalk hills of north Hertfordshire, I wasn't used to ditch maintenance, simply because it wasn't needed: the chalk soils were too porous. But when I returned on weekend visits to my parents' house near Baldock, I made a point of walking up to Bush Wood, which I knew covered the top of a chalk hill capped with stiff, and very unporous, glacial clays. And there were the ditches, alongside the wood edge, fields and trackways. I still don't know why it took so long for the penny to drop, but by the end of 1971, I had realized that the 'trackways' were in fact farm droveways and that the ditches around them had been dug to mark out and drain the fields and paddocks that were, in turn, served by the parallel droveways. The droves, the fields and the paddocks formed part of a well-integrated and carefully laid-out system of land management. It had been aligned at right angles to the wetland of the nearby Flag Fen basin and it had been done so well, with straight and parallel ditches, that we all assumed it had to be Roman. I know it was never expressed as such, but I think there was more than a suggestion in many people's minds that poor old native Britons would not be capable of such things.

Handling livestock requires skill and experience. It can also be a very dangerous business, if not done properly. Good management depends on the simple fact that most farm animals are more relaxed when they are held together in a herd, flock or group. The tighter the group, the more relaxed the individuals become. Animals that become separated soon get anxious and hard to control. This principle of confinement applies to the movement of animals too. So routes used to move livestock from rural areas to towns or markets were traditionally planted with tall hedges that restricted vision and helped suppress the urge to escape. Instead of attempting to leave the droveway – as these routes became known – the flocks and herds would put their energies into moving forwards. Trained dogs were a useful means of returning escapees to the group. By the medieval period, droveways had become an integral part of Britain's road network. But some survived intact, as droveways, into post-medieval times, especially in the Fens where the raising of livestock was an important part of the economy. The old droves still survive in place names (for example, Parson Drove, Holbeach Drove, Gedney Drove End) and can often still be seen as hedges, or more usually now, as dykes that run parallel to an existing road, forming long, narrow strip fields, which often mark the edges of smallholdings around the outskirts of towns and villages.

Livestock droving took skill, if the beasts were not to arrive at market thin and emaciated after their (sometimes) long journey overland. In turn, the drovers required accommodation overnight and this was provided by specialist drovers' inns, which can still be identified by their small attached paddocks, where the livestock was held overnight. Our farm at Sutton St James is on an ancient droveway with a long disused drovers' inn, the Gate Hangs High, a few yards away.

But droveways were not confined to longer-distance routes, they were also required on farms and in the rural landscape. Very often they form ladder-like patterns where droves are seen to run parallel to each other, often at right angles to wetlands or to common land. In these instances the droves were used to take livestock to the rich grazing on the common or wetland, whenever it was available. In wetlands, such as many peat fens, this would only have been in the drier months of high summer and autumn. The existence of such droveway systems also implies that the various farms, villages and parishes that used them were in communication with one another – indeed, more than that: we know that in the Middle Ages they had committees or courts that met regularly to agree when, and how, different types of grazing could be used, which in turn would depend on rainfall, drainage, soil fertility and many other complex factors that local farmers would have understood.

So did the parallel 'trackways' at Fengate form part of such a system, but of Bronze Age date? Back in Canada for the winter of 1971–72, the implications were slowly sinking in. For a start, Bronze Age field systems were still very rare indeed in Britain – and those that were known were mostly to be found in upland areas. And these seemed so very regular and well organized that I still found it hard to be entirely convinced. Some instinct urged caution. I decided to maintain a low profile until I had some better evidence before me. I would have liked to find it in 1972, but the factory-building timetable meant that I would have to move the team to a different part of Fengate. However, the following year we were given the opportunity to examine a large piece of land that included the short length of 'trackway' that seemed to be cutting through the filled-in ring-ditch of a Bronze Age round barrow.

*

During the previous season we had realized that the complex succession of often overlapping sites at Fengate could only be satisfactorily unravelled (disentangled would be a better word) if we worked on a far larger scale than we had done back in 1971 – which already felt like it had happened a decade ago. So from 1972 we started to develop techniques of what was then termed 'open area' excavation – something that is universal on large commercial development sites today. It was an excavation strategy that people were working out in different ways at various sites. It began before the war, with archaeologists working in gravel pits along the Thames Valley, and my eyes were opened to its extraordinary potential when I worked for the whole of one Christmas holiday, during my second year at Cambridge, at a famous site at Mucking, near Grays, in Essex. I'd never been at such a site before in my life and it had a profound influence on the way my approach to excavation would subsequently evolve. Mucking was a very busy gravel pit on the Thames gravels, downstream of London. It was perched quite high on a terrace overlooking the Thames Estuary and remains the coldest site I have ever experienced. Those easterly winds that blew off the Thames in December 1966 were classic East Anglian 'lazy old winds' that couldn't be bothered to blow round you.

Mucking was remarkable in many other respects.[5] Its director was a woman, Margaret Jones, and she ran the dig tightly and well, although the funding system that operated in those days didn't allow her to write reports as she went along. She operated on a huge scale with acres of site exposed at any one time, thanks to an earth-moving agreement with the gravel company, who removed topsoil carefully and to Margaret's specifications. I went with Tim Potter, a friend from Cambridge, who had worked at Mucking before and I have to confess I joined him mostly for the money, because the Department of Works (one of many precursors of Historic England) paid the best rates then available – and somehow I had to pay college fees and a rapidly increasing bar bill.

Although I went there for the wrong reasons, Mucking opened my eyes to the benefits of opening huge areas. Margaret took us on a site tour the day I arrived and it was extraordinary. Never before had I walked through a Roman, then a Saxon cemetery (with many graves still undug), before visiting a dozen or so Iron Age roundhouses. Tim was to become a leading Roman archaeologist and although he was just a year ahead of me at Cambridge, he had already managed to accumulate vastly more digging experience. I didn't know it then, but our paths would cross again.*

Feeling far more confident about open-area excavation, we began the 1973 season at Fengate by removing layers of topsoil and quite a substantial accumulation of flood clay from the field with the ring-ditch and the short length of 'trackway'. And what we discovered was beyond our wildest dreams. What appeared to have been the ditches of a short length of 'trackway' turned out to be the boundary ditches of some rectangular fields, all of which had been entered by corner entranceways. The pottery and other finds showed that all of these features had been laid out and used in the Early and Middle Bronze Age – in the centuries around 1500 BC. Having spent my childhood on and around farms, I knew that it was much simpler to drive cattle and sheep into and out of fields if their entranceways are set at the corners. That way, the sides of the fields act rather like funnels. Gates set in the long sides cause all sorts of problems because the animals tend to bunch around them. Dogs can help sort this out, but it's far simpler to place the entranceways in the corners. Medieval

---

* See Chapter 10, p. 207.

marketplaces are invariably entered by roads that come in at the corners, and for precisely the same reasons.

The layout of the Bronze Age fields at Fengate showed they had been in existence at the same time as the barrow ring-ditch, not later than it, as the air photos had suggested. This date fitted in better with the pottery found in the ditches, which pre-dated 1200 BC. But the thing that amazed me most and caused the greatest surprise was the discovery of what sheep farmers call a 'drafting race', only this one was formed by ditches rather than the galvanized steel hurdles of the race on my farm. Essentially, a drafting race is a means of narrowing a flock of sheep down to a single-file line, or queue. Once confined in a tight, nose-to-tail line within the race, the sheep, or mature lambs, become even more docile and can readily be checked for disease, fly-strike or other problems. Udders can be checked for mastitis and teeth can be examined. Old, 'broken-mouthed' ewes – their age is indicated by the loss of teeth – can be removed for culling. So once they have been inspected and have passed along the race they must then be sorted into holding pens. Cull ewes will be sent one way, uncastrated lambs another – and so on. Today we use an ingenious, but essentially simple, three-way drafting gate that allows us to do a rapid sort out in which the animals step through it and into the appropriate holding pen. But in the Bronze Age they didn't possess such gates. Instead, and this made me wildly over-excited at the time, the ditches of the drafting race were aligned precisely on the junction of three ditched paddocks. All it would have required would have been a non-see-through woven wattle hurdle to have guided sheep into the correct paddock. Such sophisticated arrangements were remarkable for an early farming community, which was supposedly still at the 'subsistence agriculture' stage – where each family possessed perhaps a house cow and a handful of sheep and pigs.

The ditched drafting race had one further, and very important, lesson to teach us. As a general rule, the length of the drafting race is determined by flock size. For example, when I bought mine, our flock was composed of some 250 sheep and the race was 7 metres (7.5 yards) long. The Fengate drafting race was over three times as long (25 metres / 27 yards). You cannot be too specific about such things, but in the most general terms, this suggests to me that the flocks being handled would routinely have been larger than a thousand sheep – and probably two or three times that.[6] With such populations in mind, elaborate field systems, with their carefully laid-out droveways running down to the lush summer grazing of the nearby fen, suddenly make good, practical sense. We tend to think of agricultural intensification as a modern phenomenon, but I don't think it was – and certainly not in the Fens, where complex Bronze Age field systems are now known to have covered large areas of the fen margins and accessible 'islands'.

*A view of the Fengate Bronze Age field boundary ditches during excavation in 1974. This is a small part of a large field system that was in use between about 2500 and 500 BC. It is arranged around a series of parallel ditched droveways, one of which is running up the centre of the photograph.*

*

Archaeologists are very good at working out how things were done below ground: how drains were laid, walls were built or foundations reinforced, but we have always had problems when it comes to the world above the surface. Sometimes luck intervenes: a nearby volcano erupts, coating everything in volcanic dust; a wall topples into a pond, or buildings raised on a platform collapse into the muds of a glacial lake. In some ways these are exceptional conditions, because most archaeological sites are found in places that are less hostile, such as the gentle pastures along the Fengate fen margins. So in those environments the archaeologist's challenge is to think of circumstances where the chances of above-ground survival of evidence might be improved. And that was the challenge that confronted me back in 1976 and 1977, when our team at Fengate had exposed a truly vast expanse of Bronze Age fields and droveways, complete with wells and isolated farmyards with the foundations of their owners' roundhouses. It was an intact landscape, but it lacked an essential above-ground component, because those field boundaries and droveways only made sense if they were accompanied by thick hedges. I had always suspected that Bronze Age axes were not used for felling trees alone, but for other tasks such as trimming or laying hedges. The broad blades of a Middle Bronze Age (1500–1200 BC) axe, known as a palstave, would have made excellent hedging tools. I have a replica and can vouch for that. I was convinced that hedges were an essential component of the Bronze Age landscape, but where was the proof?

The east side of the field where we were excavating, which now lies beneath a massive North Sea gas-fuelled power station, was bounded by a wide dyke, dug, I think, quite recently, possibly in the seventeenth or eighteenth century. By then, peats had accumulated along the fen margins and drainage was far from straightforward. One day I was standing by the dyke at the Fengate fen-edge and looking over the peaty flatness of Flag Fen. I was standing between some straggly old trees, and thinking that the workmen who dug that dyke three or four hundred years ago had no idea of the archaeological damage they were about to commit. Their ditch was probably going to cut through a Bronze Age field boundary ditch at the very point where it joined the wetland – where preservation would be at its best. I took a few steps back to discern the lie of the land better, and then I noticed something I hadn't expected. Yes, the ground was gradually sloping down towards the drained wetland to the east, but there was a distinct rise – after years of modern ploughing it was now maybe half a metre high and 3 or 4 metres (10–13 ft) wide – along the western edge of the dyke. I walked forward and kicked the ground with my boot. As I expected, it was peaty with a few scattered gravel pebbles – typical upcast from a drainage dyke. And then the simple truth dawned: yes, that drain might well have destroyed part of our prehistoric field system, but the bank alongside it will also have protected the archaeology below from modern plough damage. All I needed was perhaps a couple of feet of dumped soil covering the buried Bronze Age ditch and the hedge issue could be resolved once and for all.

I called the digger over and explained the problem to the driver, who was used to digging out and cleaning drainage dykes. It was a job he did every autumn when the machine was hired by the North Level Internal Drainage Board. All I wanted him to do was remove the ditch filling and 'slub' (the local term for soil dredged out of a dyke) from the surface, then we would dig the rest by hand. It took him ten minutes.

I had the digger stop as soon as he encountered the old top-soil and flood clay, immediately beneath the ditch upcast, which to my surprise was almost a metre thick. That was certainly enough to have provided good protection for lower deposits.

I was optimistic when we started trowelling. In fact, I was enjoying myself immensely. One of the great delights of running a small and highly experienced team of diggers is that the director doesn't have to spend too much time supervising, they can do a bit of actual, hands-on digging themselves – and there was no way I was going to miss out on this. I was working with Bob, one of our best and most experienced archaeologists. Bob was in the Bronze Age ditch and I was working alongside him on the outer side of the ancient field, as this was where I expected to find evidence for a hedge, or bank – or both. In the end, and to my delight, it was both.

*Bob is standing in a small Bronze Age field boundary ditch, close to the edge of the main excavation at Fengate, Peterborough. Immediately beyond the excavation (and hidden) is a recent drainage dyke. This dyke's bank explains the depth of the archaeological trench at this point. This recent bank protected a far earlier, Bronze Age bank, which accompanied the field boundary ditch, to the left of the figure. Such small banks rarely survive.*

The bank showed up directly below a thin layer of flood clay, as a low mound of pale gravel, capping a layer of gravelly silt. The gravel came from the bottom of the small Bronze Age ditch. The silt below it would have been top and subsoil, also from the ditch. This covered a distinct layer of more stone-free silts, which I recognized as the topsoil that was in existence when the Bronze Age ditch was cut through it. So we had a complete sequence dating, I would guess, to around 2000 BC. I looked very carefully for traces of wood and decayed roots along the surface of the buried bank, but conditions were too dry. However, the gravels capping the bank were by no means clean and undisturbed, they could well have once have been capped by a hedge. And besides, I reasoned, why on earth have such a low bank alongside a ditch? The photograph I took for the report shows Bob standing in the ditch and the top of the bank didn't even come up to his waist. Such a low ditch and bank would certainly be no use whatsoever as a barrier to livestock, without a hedge.

Proof positive of my hedge theory, by which I remained quite convinced, especially given my alternative life as a sheep farmer, did not come until thirty years later, in 2005. By now, excavations in Fengate were being carried out by archaeological contractors and this particular development was being handled by a team from Cambridge University who were working in an area of central Fengate, known as the Elliot Site, where two of the southerly 'trackway' ditches, that we had originally examined thirty-three years previously, opened up, funnel-fashion, to form a much wider droveway, or set of stockyards. This gently tapering funnel-shape arrangement of ditches was very typical of the lead into medieval droves, both in the Fens and elsewhere. But the find that excited everyone wasn't a man-made artefact at all and it didn't come from one of the boundary ditches.

My wife, Maisie Taylor, had reported on ancient worked wood from Fengate, Etton, Flag Fen and elsewhere and this unique experience meant that she was often called upon to examine wood from other sites, including, in this instance, the Elliott Site in Fengate. One day she called me over to look at a strange piece of wood she had just seen. It came from a waterlogged pit that included some very strange (and still not fully understood) but finely fashioned thin wooden straps, made from yew wood. She showed me these first, as they really were very strange, but I could suggest nothing sensible as to their function. Then she produced another odd-looking piece of wood. It was a knobbly twig, of blackthorn, and I immediately recognized what it was, as I had seen hundreds of them when trimming the many hedges in our garden. It was a thick twig that had grown in a characteristically 'jerky' fashion with right-angled bends, where it had been cut back each year. There could be no doubt at all: somebody had been trimming a hedge in the Bronze Age. I said nothing and looked up: Maisie was smiling broadly too. She knew exactly what it was and told me there were other bits like it in the pit. It was the evidence we had been seeking for decades. Later, we heard that radiocarbon dates showed the wood must date to 2000 BC. I believe it is still the earliest evidence for hedging anywhere in Europe.[7]

Water and wet places became more prominent in religious and ceremonial life after about 1500 BC, but they were regarded with reverence for many centuries before that, largely, I suspect, because they were not readily habitable by man and were often on the edges either of huge wetlands or the biggest wetland of them all – the sea. And if ever you go to a lonely stretch of coast, especially on a winter's day with storms gathering in the distance, you can appreciate why ancient people may have imagined that beyond the distant maritime horizon lay the realms and worlds of the gods.

King's Lynn Museum deserves to be better known, if only because it houses one of the most remarkable archaeological discoveries ever made in Britain. The site in question was revealed in 1998 and was dubbed by the press Seahenge, which was a great name – and it stuck. The only trouble was: it is 100 per cent inaccurate. When first constructed, sometime between April and June in the year 2049 BC (and we can be as accurate as this, because it was dated using tree-rings), the Holme-next-the-Sea timber circle was actually erected in a back-swamp behind a band of coastal dunes, maybe a quarter of a mile inland. And it wasn't a henge because it had never been surrounded by a circular ditch and bank. It seems to have been the sort of structure you find within round barrows of the later third millennium BC, which often feature a wall-like circle, or oval, of close-set posts. The fifty-five oak posts at Seahenge had been carefully arranged into a slightly flat-sided circle of about 5 metres (16 ft) diameter, with a very narrow entranceway. I could just fit through it, sideways. This entranceway faced south-west, the direction of the setting sun in summer. But it was something else, altogether more spectacular, that caused the discovery and excavation of Seahenge to hit the headlines, both in Britain and overseas.

Holme-next-the-Sea is a sleepy village on the north-west coast of Norfolk, a short drive west of the Victorian seaside town of Hunstanton. It sits on the southern side of the mouth of the Wash, directly opposite Boston, which you could just discern on the horizon, on a clear day. I described Holme as 'sleepy', which maybe is a little unfair, but it certainly isn't a bustling hive of industry: there's a substantial retired population, many second-homers, but surprisingly few people who were born and brought up there – most of whom have moved elsewhere, to earn a living. So nobody was prepared for the fuss that was caused when it was revealed that the circle of posts surrounded a large (2½ ton) felled oak tree that had been placed in the ground upside down, so that its flared roots resembled branches. There were some very spectacular photographs that made it to newspaper front pages across the world, especially as by then we knew the date was about 2000 BC – which Maisie had estimated from the shape of the Early Bronze Age axe marks on the tree and the circle of posts surrounding it.[8]

The excavation took place in 1999 and was funded by English Heritage, but the team doing the work came from Norfolk County Council's Archaeological Unit. Maisie was a co-director and was in charge of all aspects of the ancient timbers, their excavation and interpretation. My task, which I was saddled with because of my then close links with English Heritage, was essentially to be the project's public relations and press spokesman. It wasn't an easy job at all.

*Excavation of the timber circle, known as 'Seahenge',*
*at Holme-next-the-Sea, Norfolk.*

It soon became very apparent that the soft timbers of Seahenge were being seriously damaged by the pounding of waves and by sand abrasion. So it was decided to excavate and remove them from Holme beach, then to transport them to Flag Fen, in Peterborough, where we had facilities for their storage and initial conservation. It was a fiendishly difficult site to excavate, for simple practical reasons to do with the sea and passing tides, but the work was carried out to very exacting standards; in fact, I can't think of a Bronze Age shrine that has ever been dug to such high standards, and with so much care. They were a wonderful team.

I won't describe the fuss that attended the excavation and removal of the timber circle and its central inverted oak tree, because it didn't have much to do with the Fens and was mostly organized by outsiders, for their own publicity-seeking motives. Most Fen people approved of what we were doing because they knew as well as we did that a few North Sea storms would soon destroy the site completely, whereas now it has been conserved and is on permanent display in King's Lynn Museum. Every time I visit (which I do quite often), I'm astonished by the sheer mass of that central oak tree. All the bark was removed shortly after felling and it was dragged several miles, using twisted honeysuckle ropes, to what is now Holme beach. The dig that took place in 1998–9 has quite simply transformed our understanding of the way Early Bronze Age religious sites were built and used. Maisie studied the axe marks closely and came to the conclusion that about fifty people would have been involved with the tree-felling and woodworking. If you assume that each axe-wielder came with friends and family, then maybe as many as two hundred and fifty people attended the ceremony. I was recently at a big funeral in our local village and I reckoned that was the number of people gathered in church and in the graveyard for the burial. Our village church is quite small, because the nave collapsed some time ago – as often happened in the unstable soils of the Fens.

So what would the ceremonies at Seahenge have been about? Essentially we reckon that Seahenge was probably the final resting place for an important person, who might well have been laid out on the roots of the oak tree. It's a process known as excarnation, where the flesh of the dead person was removed by carrion crows and other birds. In societies that practised excarnation until recently, it was believed that the person's soul was taken up to Paradise by the birds, as they removed the flesh. It's also quite probable that the timber circle may have been used as a shrine – maybe that was where funeral ceremonies took place – for a timber and earth barrow that we know was erected close by and at precisely the same date, in 2049 BC. Although there is no physical evidence for any later use of the site, I would be very surprised if there wasn't any: it's very rare indeed to find barrows of one period only. They are nearly always reused for several generations.

Seahenge was revealed by the sea. In effect, it was a victim of climate change. But it demonstrated something that all fenland archaeologists had been aware of since Grahame Clark's work in the post-war years: that the best sites lie far more deeply buried beneath the ground than elsewhere in Britain. But somehow one had to find the means to discover and reveal them. It was something that worried me profoundly when I started work at Fengate in the early 1970s. Ten years later, our team had come up with a fresh approach that was to reveal sites that were as well preserved as Seahenge, but which were not threatened by the sea and could be excavated in safety. It was a process that led to the discovery of Flag Fen.

But now I want to turn the archaeological clock back to the early centuries of the Neolithic, a time of immense change. Farming had been introduced to Britain shortly before 4000 BC and it triggered a period of rapid social and economic development, which has left us some truly memorable sites that are very well preserved in the damp conditions of the Fens. The process of their revelation was not always simple, nor straightforward – but it was never, ever, dull.

# 3

# Haddenham:
# Prehistory Pickled in Peat

*David Hall and the Haddenham Long Barrow –*
*'Ritual Landscapes' – The Rise of Commercial*
*Archaeology – Swiss Lake Villages and*
*Ancient Wetlands*

We used to think that the various regions of the Fens began to form at roughly the same time, but as research progresses, we can now see that certain areas became wet much earlier than we had previously expected. Often this was the result of purely local factors, such as the permeability of the surrounding geology or the effectiveness of local rivers to drain a particular area. We are also discovering that the simple pattern of dry 'islands' and wet peaty fens, which is now so characteristic of the southern fenlands, was far more complicated, especially in prehistory, when conditions were growing wetter from the fourth millennium BC. The simple wet/dry dichotomy of today's landscape didn't apply: it was often a question of 'damp' versus 'sometimes dry'. On closer investigation, many of the prominent 'islands' could be seen to have had lower-lying, subsidiary ridges that eventually became permanently flooded. I have always been intrigued by these buried and long-forgotten features that would have been so significant to the lives of people four or five millennia ago. And it wouldn't have been just a matter of rising and falling levels. All sorts of things can cause complications that require wisdom, knowledge and experience to deal with: watercourses can be dammed by fallen trees, beavers can transform streams to small lakes in a very short time and incursions of seawater can affect natural sources of grazing, such as reeds, rushes and wet-loving grasses. Local people must have understood only too well how water behaved in these intricate landscapes, because if they got it wrong, their crops might suffer and their livestock go hungry. In the worst cases, people might drown and family homes and farmyards would have to be abandoned.

Prehistoric settlements were usually placed on flood-free ridges around the larger islands in the southern Fens, near places like Ely, Sutton and Haddenham. In the early 1980s the southern Fens were being surveyed by the distinguished archaeologist David Hall as part of the larger Fenland Survey.[1] David liked to work alone, but with a large-scale map on which he would mark scatters of flint or pottery.[2] Initially, most of his discoveries were indeed surface scatters of finds, but quite soon he developed a remarkable eye for subtle variations of surface contours. And he has always been free to pass his knowledge on to others. For example, he showed me how to look along the close-set drill rows of wheat or barley seedlings in order to spot low undulations in the land surface. And he was right: the tiniest of scoops and bumps immediately became obvious. Larger rises in the ground level stood out if you looked along the so-called tramlines – the wheel marks left by crop sprayers – that are such a feature of modern agricultural fields. The largest humps and bumps were usually the remains of medieval or Saxon salterns. These are quite widespread in the Lincolnshire Fens and around the Wash and were places where people had taken scoops of mud from old or active tidal creeks and had heated them up to concentrate the salt water and eventually to extract the salt – which was a very valuable commodity.*

From a prehistorian's point of view, the most exciting of the humps and bumps that David discovered were burial mounds, or barrows. Most British barrows have been seriously damaged by centuries of ploughing and can only be spotted on aerial photographs by a tell-tale ring-ditch, which was the ditch used to quarry the rock, gravel or soil used to build up the central barrow mound. Certain landscapes, such as the Yorkshire Wolds, Salisbury Plain and the South Downs, were never intensively ploughed and here barrows can survive almost intact. Today these sites are usually protected under the Ancient Monuments Acts, which were first introduced in 1882, but came too late to prevent many barrows being 'excavated' by Victorian antiquarians. So David's discovery of barrows buried deep in the Fens caused a huge stir in the world of archaeology – quite simply because we knew they had to be intact. Not only that, but waterlogging might well have preserved ancient coffins, and possibly the fabrics that wrapped the bodies as well.

David Hall revealed one of his first group of Fen barrows on very low gravel ridges alongside one of the old courses of the River Ouse, roughly midway between Haddenham and Earith, some 9 miles (14 km) north of Cambridge. This was land that was about to be quarried and it included two low gravel ridges (with wonderful Fen names) at Foulmire Fen and Hill Row Doles. Aerial photos and David's survey had revealed three possible long barrows and three round barrows there. Long barrows were the earliest form of communal burial and they start to appear about

---

* Salt was so valuable it was even used for paying people. The word 'salary' is derived from the Latin word for salt.

a couple of centuries after the arrival of farming in 4000 BC. Most had gone out of use by 3000 BC, after which round barrows started to appear. These stayed in use until about 1500 BC, around the end of the Early Bronze Age, when there was a very profound change in British prehistory, which witnessed the rapid end of henges and barrow burial and the rise of new, more locally based religious rites that often involved water and wet places. I have described this change as a 'Domestic Revolution'.*

*An Early Bronze Age (c.1700 BC) barrow, as revealed in the freshly cleaned sides of a drainage dyke at Haddenham, Cambridgeshire. The discoverer of the site, David Hall, is standing at the bottom of the dyke pointing his spade at a Late Bronze Age (c.1000 BC) cremation (the dark patch).*

I visited the Haddenham sites with David in the spring of 1981, shortly after he had discovered them. The following autumn he phoned to ask whether I'd like to take a day off from my current excavation and take the team down to Haddenham where they had found a Bronze Age round barrow that had been cut in half by a modern drainage dyke. The sides of the dyke had a thick

---

* For more on the Domestic Revolution see Chapter 9, p. 125.

covering of grass, which David reckoned we could spade off in a day. Of course I leapt at the chance. We were fit and healthy and after a few hours' work we had removed all the grass along one side of the dyke. By the end of the day we all felt a bit sore and stiff, but it had certainly been worth the effort. The cleaned-up dykeside looked spectacular. The gravel burial mound stood out clearly against the deep peats that covered it and the ditch that surrounded the barrow was still probably waterlogged. We also found a small cremation, complete with a beautiful flint arrowhead, which had been inserted into the barrow at the end of the Bronze Age. Presumably this person would have been a descendant of the man or woman in the primary burial at the centre of the barrow. That burial is still there, hopefully intact.

One of the Neolithic long barrows was particularly clear and if you dropped to your hands and knees and looked across the freshly tilled field, from near ground level, you could clearly see the characteristic wedge-shaped gravel mound. All three possible barrows were aligned north-east to south-west, as is often the case with such sites elsewhere in Britain. The north-east end was the 'business end'. Here the barrow was wider and higher. Later, excavation would reveal evidence for a timber-revetted forecourt, where funerary ceremonies would have taken place. Similar features are known from other long barrows in Britain. But the Haddenham Barrow concealed something really unusual. It wasn't treasure – the sort of ancient bling that gets shown on television – no, it was far, far more important than that. It was a massive mortuary structure that seemed to coincide with the way I was starting to think about the Fens and the remarkable people who lived there, five thousand years ago.

The traditional picture of prehistoric life in and around the Fens was fairly low-key. A few early settlements were known on certain fen-edge 'islands', but what we believed we were looking at was essentially a continuation of the pre-farming hunting and gathering lifestyle – and that was seen as rather random and based around small bands of migrating hunters, who followed game as it moved through the thickly wooded landscape: into the Fens for the dry months of summer and back onto the higher ground of the fen margins in winter. At first it seemed that the results of the Fenland Survey supported this view. But there was something that worried me: the sheer quantity of new sites that David Hall and his Fenland Survey team were discovering was completely unexpected. In the early to mid-1970s, my own team had revealed highly developed landscapes along the fen-edge at Fengate, with tracks, field systems, farms and settlements, but these were generally seen as exceptional – something of a 'one-off'.* We had shown they were well established by 2000 BC, which was earlier than many expected, but we all failed to grasp the wider implications of this: that Fengate had never been a 'one-off' and that such landscapes were typical, not an exception, in the Fens. And now the new survey and excavation at Haddenham was proving that landscapes in the southern Fens had been cleared of trees and settled at least 1500 years earlier than Fengate – from before 3500 BC. So what lay behind such extraordinary developments in such a seemingly wet, marginal region, and how come there were no great monuments like Stonehenge, the vast stones of which were erected around 2500 BC?[3]

I didn't realize it back in the early 1980s, but we were helping to answer these questions with the work that we were doing at the time in the lower Welland valley, at sites like Etton and Maxey.† As we revealed new settlements, farms and field systems, we tended to downplay the importance of the barrows and other ceremonial sites that we were also discovering. But not for long. By the early 1980s, we realized that the Fens and the landscapes

---

*  I discussed Fengate in Chapter 2.

†  I describe our projects in the Welland Valley in the next two chapters.

around them possessed a remarkable series of henges and other prehistoric shrines – but they hadn't been made from stone, so they only survived as marks below the soil.

These were very exciting years, which I remember as being pretty harmonious ones too. By the early 1980s, David Hall's pioneering Fenland Survey had morphed into the larger and more ambitious Fenland Project, which was funded by English Heritage, with input from local authorities. The Fenland Survey was continuing in the southern Fens and had also got underway on the silts of south Lincolnshire. Excavations were in full swing around Haddenham and in the lower Ouse Valley, and new digs were beginning in the northern Fens as well. Often groups of archaeologists would get together – inevitably in a pub – and frequently these sessions would take place near Peterborough, as it was so central. For some reason, the public bar of the appropriately named Spade and Shovel pub in the village of Eye blurs its faltering way in and out of my memory. In pre-Internet times, pubs were the best way of keeping in touch – and they were *so* much more congenial than a smartphone.

Researchers and academics can sometimes squabble among themselves, but we didn't: we were all too involved with the remarkable archaeology we were discovering. Looking back, I sometimes think it must have been rather like the atmosphere in military intelligence during the latter part of the Second World War. My father had been part of the British team that investigated Hitler's two secret weapons, the V1 flying bomb and the V2 medium-range ballistic missile. Hearing him talk about the group that examined the aerial photos that revealed the launching pads at Peenemünde (a group, incidentally, that included some well-known professional archaeologists) reminded me of evenings in the pub after a day's digging, when well-thumbed and once-glossy black-and-white aerial photos lay on the table, among half-empty glasses and ashtrays with the dog ends of brown liquorice-paper roll-ups. We would argue energetically about what we had discovered and how it did, or did not, fit into the broader picture. And over the weeks, then months and finally years, the extraordinary truth began slowly to emerge. Our minds and bodies were very fit, but our lifestyle was pretty rough and ready. Discipline and restraint were reserved for where they were needed: on site.

A few years after my first visit to that field in Haddenham with David Hall, the site was excavated by a team from Cambridge University, over three seasons, from 1985 to 1987.[4] Maisie and I visited the dig frequently and I will never forget the moment when they revealed the collapsed and partially preserved oak timbers of a massive mortuary structure, buried deep within the mound. Prehistoric woodworking was done without saws, which weren't introduced until the final two or three centuries before the Roman conquest – and even then they were more like modern pull-stroke pruning saws than the more efficient push-and-pull carpenter's saw. So the planks needed to construct this huge chamber were split from the freshly felled trees using nothing but seasoned oak wedges. The massive tree that was felled to provide the timber required, sometime around 3600 BC, would have been from the primeval forest that still just survived in the drier parts of fenland, such as 'islands' and along the slopes of the fen margins. But trees of this quality were already a rapidly depleting resource and after 1000 BC, in the Iron Age, they are extremely rare. The absence of places like Stonehenge from the Fens can simply be attributed to the lack of stone. So they turned instead to wood, the strong and durable material that was readily available.


Stonehenge often appears in the news, generally because some road improvement or other development is about to destroy a neighbouring barrow or other important archaeological feature in the locality. Together with most of the dozens of other henges in Britain, Stonehenge was constructed within a special sacred area – known to archaeologists as a 'ritual landscape'.[5] These landscapes often contained dozens, sometimes even hundreds, of barrows, processional avenues, henges, mini-henges and other ceremonial monuments. It now seems probable that many of these ritual landscapes had been considered special from very early times indeed. There is, for example, more than one line of evidence to suggest that what would later be called the Stonehenge ritual landscape was believed to be sacred shortly after the Ice Age, from about 8000 BC. By 6000 BC it was still there – and probably growing in importance.

Stonehenge has been the subject of intensive survey and study, largely because of what it is: one of the best-known prehistoric sites in the world. So would it be possible to detect such ancient beginnings at other, less thoroughly studied, ritual landscapes? One clue may lie in a group of very early ceremonial gathering places, known as causewayed enclosures.* These are among the earliest earthwork monuments in Britain and date to the first half of the fourth millennium BC, just over a couple of centuries after the arrival of farming, around 4000 BC. Very often these sites are associated with scatters of earlier flints. Their careful positioning in the landscape – they rarely crown hills or dominate, say, a river meander – suggests that they respected or were even subservient to an earlier, revered space. When causewayed enclosures appeared in the landscape they seem to have triggered the erection of a series of other ceremonial and funerary sites over the following centuries, usually culminating with the construction of henges. We know of the existence of two causewayed enclosures

---

* For a more detailed description of causewayed enclosures, see Chapter 4, p. 81.

near Stonehenge, but what about the Fens? You certainly won't see any such features listed or mapped in any of the older archaeological textbooks. In the past we assumed that causewayed enclosures and henges simply weren't present in the Fens. Big monuments seemed somehow 'foreign' to the area. It was a view that I certainly never contested when I was a student in the 1960s. I don't know why, but showy ceremonial structures have always seemed somehow out of place in such a difficult and sometimes even hostile environment.

It is helpful, perhaps, to think about the role of prehistoric ceremonial structures in the way one might consider a church or other religious building in the modern era. When your daily life can be hard and at times dangerous, a large and active church can help bind communities together, and thereby perform an important social role. I first realized this simple truth when I read Dorothy L. Sayers's great detective thriller *The Nine Tailors* (1934), which is set in the Cambridgeshire Fens, near Wisbech (her 'Walbeach'), before the war. I had bought the book when I was first in Canada in 1969, and was feeling a bit lonely and homesick for England.

The action takes place in the fictional village of Fenchurch St Paul at a time when the nearby river has burst its banks. There is a memorable scene in which the vicar gathers the parishioners into the church, for safety, the distribution of blankets and, of course, for cups of tea. I too have heard church bells toll to warn of potential floods. Sayers spent much of her childhood and early adulthood, from 1897 to 1917, in the Huntingdonshire fenland village of Bluntisham-cum-Earith, where her father was rector (the fine Georgian rectory still survives). *The Nine Tailors* could only have been written by someone who knew the fen landscape and people intimately. I've read the novel several times and her affection for the place comes across vividly. Sayers, who died in 1957, would not have known about it, but a causewayed enclosure has since been revealed by the Fenland Survey near her childhood home, just across the canalized courses of the River Great Ouse, near Earith. She might well have been able to see the low gravel terrace from an upstairs window at the rectory. I'm sure she would have been delighted.

The terrace near Earith is known as the Upper Delphs and is part of that chain of low hillocks or undulations that we visited earlier, when looking at the Haddenham long barrow. It would now seem that the new causewayed enclosure is an early component of what soon became a much larger ritual landscape that included three long barrows and around seventy round barrows.[6] It is entirely possible that other causewayed enclosures and barrows await discovery beneath the later peats and river-borne deposits that lap up against the low 'islands' or terraces here. We certainly don't yet know the full extent of this remarkable ritual landscape, but what we have been able to glimpse so far would strongly suggest that we are dealing with a community that supported a substantial population of people. But is the situation in the lower Great Ouse valley unique? I think not. I won't attempt to look at all the major river valleys where they join the Fens, but take my word for it, the Nene and the Witham have revealed many sites and landscapes that are directly comparable with those in the lower Ouse. But the unassuming River Welland, which drains into the fen some 10 miles (16 km) north of Peterborough at the quiet Lincolnshire town of Market Deeping, has revealed a prehistoric ritual land-scape as rich, diverse and, more importantly, as well preserved as any in Britain. And yet, almost nobody knows about it. It kept me busy throughout the 1980s,* but first I want to explain in a little more detail how I found myself digging in the Fens. It would be nice if I could say that it was all part of a carefully

---

* See Chapter 4, p. 66.

structured academic plan, but I'm afraid my life hasn't been like that. For now, let's just say that it was the result of a series of (mostly) happy accidents.

The system of fields that we had exposed at Fengate in the early 1970s was very well thought out and showed a sophisticated understanding of a landscape that must have been difficult to farm. If you live on the edge of a wetland you must be prepared to move your flocks and herds, together with a proportion of your family, every springtime, from the safer, flood-free pastures set on higher land around the wetland edge, out into the lush, lower-lying pastures of the now drier wetland. And then, of course, you reverse the whole process in the autumn. But think of the implications of this for a moment. In the Middle Ages there were elaborate local laws that governed when and where animals could, or could not, be grazed. If you don't have such rules, disputes and conflicts are bound to arise between neighbours. But there is absolutely no indication that these Bronze Age communities were hostile to one another. All the evidence points the other way. There are positive signs, for example, in the layout of their fields and roadways that the different farming clans or families lived within the same landscape harmoniously. In other words, these people must have had firm, mutually agreed rules on land tenure and inheritance. But they could not have been written down, as writing was only introduced by the Romans, some two thousand years later. The farmed landscape must also have had permanent internal boundaries, which would have extended out into commonly owned parts of the nearby fen, the source of summer pasture. These rules would have been enforced by tribal elders and other responsible members of local communities, but they would also have had assistance from higher, perhaps spiritual, authorities.

In the modern Western world, religion is giving ground to science-based rationality. This shift is part of a longer-term, essentially post-medieval process, which has seen religion gradually confined to Sundays and a few other days, such as Christmas and Easter. In medieval and earlier times, however, religion and the morality that was associated with it influenced all aspects of life and not just at birth, marriage and death. We see remnants of this when, for example, priests or bishops attend the launching of ships or the state opening of Parliament. In early pre-modern times, religion helped to structure and parcel up the year, with memorable seasonal ceremonies.

The passage of time was seen as a series of recurrent cycles, rather than a straightforward linear progression from one numbered year to another, as we view it today. This recurrent perception of time accorded well with the annual calendar of religious observances and allowed predestiny, the spirits of the ancestors and the world beyond the grave to play a much larger role in the daily lives of ordinary people. We know, for example, that many prehistoric and Roman houses possessed family shrines or altars. Bodies, often of children or young people, were sometimes buried beneath or alongside ordinary domestic homes.[7] Bodies were also buried, it would appear, with due ceremony and in proper graves, in field or trackway boundary ditches, often near to important gateways or junctions.[8] We excavated several graves of this sort at Fengate, and I am in absolutely no doubt that they were put there as a means of invoking some form of spiritual authority to support the claim of an individual, family or clan to a particular farm or parcel of land. In other words, trespassers would have been aware that they would have risked spiritual retribution if they continued on their way.

Attitudes to death, burial and religion can reveal much about the way prehistoric societies were organized. I have already suggested that the organization of the landscape indicates that communities generally lived peacefully with their neighbours. But there also seems to be no good evidence to suggest that there was ever a powerful ruling elite that did not share the religion of ordinary people. We see such a split, for example, in ancient Egypt, where the pharaohs went to extraordinary lengths to protect their rich tombs from lower-class grave robbers who did not share their religious beliefs. Happily, for posterity, they were sometimes, but only sometimes, successful. By contrast, rich graves in contemporary Bronze Age Britain were left in peace and were respected – until modern times, when, ironically, many of the keenest Victorian antiquarian tomb-openers were Church of England vicars.

The large mounds, or barrows, in which people buried their dead in later prehistoric times, roughly from just after 4000 BC until 1500 BC, were often positioned along the tops of ridges or on hills, doubtless to make them visible from the plains and river valleys, where most of the farms and settlements were located. It seems likely that the placing of these barrows away from the areas where people lived and farmed was also seen as a step in the direction of the afterlife – the imagined realms beyond the horizon, inhabited by gods and ancestors. More recently, we have come to see the placing of barrows and other shrines in places that were near, but also remote from, the landscapes of daily life as being deliberate. These were liminal locations. The word derives from the Latin *limen*, meaning a threshold or boundary. In other words, these sites were believed to lie on the boundary between this and the next world. In the lower-lying, flatter areas of Britain, such as the Fens, where hills or steep ridges are rare, liminality had to be achieved in other ways. And this brings me to the importance of fenland's greatest threat and asset: water.

Nowadays we see water as a commodity: something we all pay for, to have in our baths and sinks, to surf or swim through, or to be restrained behind dams and flood banks. But as I have found so often in my archaeological life, the ancient perception was far more complex, subtle and interesting. Prehistoric people viewed water as the mirror and prism of life. This led to some unexpected insights.

The surface of still water is an excellent reflector and can act as a mirror. We take this for granted, but in prehistory it was of critical importance. Today there are mirrors, camera phones and plate glass windows everywhere. As a result, we know every emerging wrinkle, mole or pimple and we keep a weather eye out for double chins or damaged complexions. I suppose most of us are fairly vain when it comes to our faces, but this is only because we get to see them – and often in uncomfortable detail – dozens of times every day. But in the remote past, things were very different. For a start, glass mirrors didn't exist at all, and when polished metal ones – in bronze – appeared in Europe in the final three centuries BC they were not the handy household objects we're so familiar with today. Most of them date from the last century before Christ and were confined to the highest echelons of society. They were finely fashioned, with non-reflective backs decorated with exquisite Celtic art. This decoration may well have symbolized a high-status person's identity, which probably explains why they are often found in rich graves.[9]

Tranquil, reflective pools would have been important to people, especially younger people, as mirrors. However, there was more to them than that. Water may reflect what is happening in the world of the living, but fall through that glassy, reflective surface – and you drown. So it is not a big leap of imagination to see water as symbolizing both personal and daily reality, and the transition from life to death. Objects placed in water could be seen as gifts or offerings to ancestors who still existed, but in the afterlife.

★

In the early 1980s I took my small team of archaeologists on an undisguised 'jolly' to the Netherlands. We had just completed ten years of intensive excavation and, to be quite frank, we were all exhausted. We needed a break. By this time too, we had established some close contacts with Dutch colleagues and we were keen to learn from them. We were only too well aware that they were years ahead of us when it came to wetland archaeology. While we were over there we had an excellent and very relaxed time, largely, I recall, because the dig headquarters was within sight and smell of a large canal-side brewery, who let us have their ambrosial products very cheap. Happy days! But to return to business, during the working day I would spend much of my time walking along the edges of drainage ditches with my Dutch colleagues who were looking at the soil dredged from them, which was spread along their brinks to dry out and help build up a bank. Over winter and the following months, flints and pottery would slowly weather out of these muds. Of course, we could not be certain of the precise depth they had been dredged from, but their presence was enough to reveal lost, and buried, settlements at that spot.

The Dutch called this form of prospection Dyke Survey and I'm happy to confess that I stole the idea – and with their blessing.[10] But the big difference between our dykes and theirs was simple: the fen dykes were bone dry, whereas their Dutch equivalents were filled with water. Much of this de-watering has been blamed on the wartime 'Dig for Victory' campaign that gave rise to a huge increase of food production in the Fens; this process involved the intensive farming of many low-lying peaty areas that had previously been used for grazing alone. Today these fields – many of which can still be seen from the train between Cambridge and Ely – are where they grow vast acreages of lettuce and other salad crops. Other areas of the Fens were less low-lying and these had been maintained in a drier state, certainly since the introduction of steam and later diesel-powered pumps.

Seen from an English archaeologist's perspective, the distinction between water-filled dykes in Holland and dry ones in the Fens was depressing, quite simply because the Dutch ancient settlements would still be waterlogged, whereas ours, in Britain, would have dried out. As we saw with the creation of peat, waterlogging preserves organic materials, which on an archaeological site will include wooden objects such as bowls and tool handles, not to mention textiles and fabrics, wool and hair, even food and drink. On a dried-out site all that survives is pottery, flint and bone (if you're lucky). Our Dyke Survey* was often a depressing business. Day after day we would return after spending hours trudging along dykesides and finding quantities of flint and pottery from newly revealed ancient settlements and landscapes – but always in the back of our minds was the knowledge that if we had been working a few decades earlier all of these sites would have been waterlogged – and perfectly preserved. Occasionally, we would even find traces of burning or desiccated wood. Those missed opportunities still worry me.

By the mid-1990s there was a growing awareness that the Fens were more than a vast growbag and that something had to be done to slow down what was beginning to look like an approaching environmental car crash. I was astonished that so few people in authority in Peterborough – and by this time I had met a few people in local government – were aware of the long-term effects of drainage. In fairness to them, they shared my frustration. In the mid-1990s, in order to keep the team together, we also used to do contract excavations ahead of

---

* I will discuss some of the discoveries we made during our Dyke Survey in the next chapter.

development. This work arose as a direct result of an official change to Planning Law guidance initiated, rather surprisingly, by Margaret Thatcher, in 1989.

Essentially, the new Planning Policy Guidance* shifted the responsibility for funding the investigation of ancient sites threatened by development from English Heritage and local authorities to the developers, who were, after all, going to profit from the schemes. This new policy encouraged the rise of commercial archaeology. Often these projects were unexciting: bungalow extensions rarely reveal Roman temples; but they did provide work and much-needed cash flow. Frequently we would have to machine off half a metre, sometimes more, of sticky flood clay, before we could reveal the ancient levels beneath. Viewed under the microscope you can see how these surface clays built up in thin layers, often less than a millimetre thick. I remember once we had to remove a thick deposit of such clay from a building site in the middle Nene Valley, which I knew was intended for housing. I suggested to a group of visiting local councillors that as it lay in the river floodplain and the clay showed it had been flooded regularly for several centuries in the past, then surely it might flood in the future? But they knew better (and presumably had expensive experts to advise them). A few years later it did flood – like many others along the Thames and other lowland floodplains in southern Britain. On television I saw their confident explanations: 'unprecedented', 'a flood in a century', 'a one-off freak event'. They looked so plausible in their smart suits. And anyhow, why should they have listened to a grubby archaeologist?

*

---

* *Planning Policy Guidance 16: Archaeology and Planning.* Generally known as PPG 16.

In the past there has been a tendency to study the archaeology of wetlands in isolation, without regard to what was happening elsewhere, on the drier land. Archaeologists were, of course, aware that this was a problem, but they couldn't do much about it because thick accumulations of peats, silts and clays made any attempt to somehow 'join up' far-flung wetland sites and other discoveries impossible. Many wetland finds were remarkably well preserved and included wooden paths and trackways, boats, timber buckets (sometimes filled with prehistoric butter!), woven fish traps and, of course, bog bodies – the remains of mostly Iron Age people who had often been killed before being thrown or placed into a peaty bog, where their clothes, skin and even stomach contents were well preserved. These finds offered tantalizing glimpses into the prehistoric lifestyle of people who lived in the wetlands, but they did little to explain how, where, or indeed why they lived there. To answer these broader, but nonetheless more important questions, prehistorians needed more context: where were they living, what was the local population and how did the economy work?

In the late nineteenth century, the academic world, together with a large section of the public at large, was fascinated by discoveries made along the shores of Alpine lakes in Switzerland. These were the so-called Swiss Lake Villages, settlements raised on wooden piles to cope with the huge summer rise and winter fall of water levels in the Alps, caused by the freezing of water into ice and its subsequent melting. These new sites were uncovered at a time when Darwin's views were becoming more widespread and pioneering geologists were demonstrating the great antiquity of the ground beneath our feet. By the mid-nineteenth century, too, the subject of prehistory was becoming firmly established as an academic discipline that could demonstrate the great antiquity of human cultures and society.

Shortly after the Swiss discoveries, it became very fashionable to search for comparable sites beyond the Alps and many small man-made island settlements, known as crannogs, were discovered in lakes and wetland areas in both Ireland and Scotland. In England, two remarkably well-preserved Iron Age 'lake villages' (and the label is still used) were discovered in the later nineteenth and earlier twentieth centuries in the Somerset Levels, at Glastonbury and Meare. But then things seemed to slow down, despite a huge revival of interest in, and enthusiasm for, wetland archaeology in the 1980s and '90s, when lots of trackways and other isolated finds were made in Somerset and elsewhere. Still, however, we lacked the necessary context to satisfactorily explain how and why these sites and finds came into existence in the first place. And if ever we were to attain these broader goals we would have to expand the scope and extent of our excavations. Carefully selected small trenches can be very effective, but sometimes a larger exposure is required. And that was what I was determined to achieve. I must confess that at the time, I found it a daunting, even a scary, prospect.

# 4

# Cropmarks and the
# Welland Valley

*Carpets of Cropmarks: A Matter of Time – Maxey –
Helpston and John Clare – Causewayed Enclosures*

We live in an age of bestsellers and blockbusters. Books
and films are judged by the star-ratings proclaimed in
their publicity and by the enthusiastic praise of their quoted
reviews. Sometimes, however, the most important books receive
no publicity whatsoever, but they continue to influence and
to be read and reread for years after their publication. In the
world of archaeology, *A Matter of Time* (1960) was just such
a work.[1] It records the results of detailed surveys of aerial
photographs taken of the flat gravel floodplains of lowland
English river valleys during the immediately post-war years.
Archaeologists are sometimes accused of being out of touch
with the wider world, but the charge is an unfair one, because
those of us involved with the recording and excavation of sites
threatened by imminent destruction – what used to be called
rescue archaeology – have to be aware of the potential threats
to our national heritage posed by developers as diverse as
house builders, the Highways Agency, local authorities, gravel

pit operators – not to mention new railways, such as HS2 and Crossrail.

In 1956, a seemingly very stuffy organization, the Royal Commission on Historical Monuments (England), realized that the housing and infrastructural development that post-war Britain needed so desperately would inevitably involve the digging of vast tonnages of sand and gravel to be used in road foundations, concrete and cement. Shortly before the war, archaeologists had begun to investigate ancient sites threatened by gravel digging. It soon became apparent that these fertile river valleys were where the bulk of the British prehistoric population had actually lived out their lives. The new maps and photos in *A Matter of Time* didn't reveal single sites so much as complete landscapes covered with numerous settlements, trackways, fields, farms, barrows, henges – even camps and fortified strongholds. The dates of these new sites would have to be investigated, but based on existing knowledge they probably ranged from the first farmers (after 4000 BC) through the Neolithic, Bronze and Iron Ages, to Roman and medieval times. Places like the Marlborough Downs and Salisbury Plain, where the great barrows and other monuments survive so well, were in actual fact probably rather peripheral, especially after about 1500 BC, when land management and farming methods improved quite dramatically.

Principal among the post-war infrastructural developments were the New Towns, which in the East Midlands were built in and around Huntingdon, in the Ouse Valley, and just to the north, in Peterborough, in the lower Nene Valley. I recall the building – or rather the massive enlargement – of both. They were surrounded by expanses of river floodplain, with their characteristic flat gravel fields. These were soon quarried away to provide the aggregates needed to build roads and new housing. Today these worked-out quarries provide lakes for carp fishermen, or boating. A glance at an Ordnance Survey map shows the massive extent of gravel extraction in the 1960s, '70s and '80s. And if one thinks that was bad, it was as nothing compared with the extraction of gravel in the middle Thames Valley, around Sunbury, Staines, Datchet and, slightly further upstream, near Reading. Research before the war had shown that prehistoric settlement in the Thames Valley had been as dense as anywhere in Europe. There seemed to be sites everywhere and early air photographs were revealing hundreds more.

In many European countries, the boom in post-war gravel digging witnessed the wholesale destruction of thousands of archaeological sites, unrecorded. But thanks to the Royal Commission's forethought and the rapid production of *A Matter of Time* in a popular and accessible format, the archaeological world and local planners were given the weapon they needed to face up to the challenges posed by the rapid expansion of gravel digging in the 1960s and '70s. Soon, ground and aerial surveys were taking place across the country and local authority planning departments were starting to take notice. Things were beginning to change. The areas scheduled for gravel extraction were soon to witness archaeological excavation on a scale greater than anything that had gone before.

When I look back at those times, from nearly half a century later, I still cannot believe my luck: there I was, on the ground, with a professional team of archaeologists and in an area where aerial photographs had revealed an astonishing array of hitherto undetected ancient sites and landscapes. We knew what was happening, and we knew we had to do something about it. Before the war, many gravel quarries simply destroyed all sites and finds in their path. In those days it was largely taken for granted that they would be destroyed, simply because nobody possessed the means of doing anything about it, so the destruction was seen as a part of the gravel extraction process.

*The frontispiece of A Matter of Time (1960) showing cropmarks around and to the east of Maxey church (middle-distance, at the crossroads). The two ring-ditches of the Maxey henge are in the foreground; note also the parallel ditches of the Maxey Cursus, which run from the henge, up the centre of the photo, to the north-west.*

But not after *A Matter of Time*. Now we were determined that the many sites threatened with development would be excavated, recorded and sometimes even preserved. It wasn't just archaeologists who felt like this: local authority planners, even politicians were now agreeing with us. There were evenings in the pub when you could have cut the excitement with a knife.

Having *A Matter of Time* beside me was a great help when it came to the planning of my research into earlier prehistoric sites in the lower Welland Valley, which began when I had returned from Canada in 1979. My worn copy still falls open at the frontispiece: a full-page black-and-white aerial photo of the village of Maxey, in the lower Welland Valley, about 4 miles (6 km) north of Peterborough. It's a dramatic picture, and it revealed numerous cropmarks around the parish church.

Cropmarks, as their name suggests, are patterns that can be clearly seen from the air. They are formed by differential patterns of growth in growing crops. Lush growth over long abandoned pits, wells and ditches shows up as dark marks; alternatively, abandoned stone walls, even old roads and track-ways produce pale, so-called parch marks in the crops above them.* Marks are best seen in growing cereals, mostly wheat and barley, in late spring and early summer. The process of cropmark formation starts when abandoned pits and ditches naturally fill up with topsoil, washed in by the rain. The roots of crops growing directly over such ancient features will reach down to the less stony, finer and damp soil in the old pits and ditches. Then, as the summer weather gets warmer and rainfall decreases, they will continue to grow more lushly than the plants in the drier, undisturbed ground around them. When seen from the air, this richer growth shows up as distinctive dark marks in the field.

---

* Parch marks were a much-publicized feature of the dry summer of 2018.

*The Parish Church of St Peter, Maxey, which sits on what Pevsner describes as 'a slight eminence'. It can be seen in this view just beyond the trees, where the path comes into the sunlight. The church is surrounded by cropmarks of ancient features, including a large henge. Maybe the 'slight eminence' conceals a prehistoric burial mound?*

I was looking at those cropmarks near Maxey parish church. In the foreground were two concentric circular ditches, the outer, I read, having a diameter of some 430 feet (131 m). I recognized it at once as the encircling ditch of the then newly discovered Maxey Henge. Quickly I looked up my well-thumbed copy of Professor Richard Atkinson's Penguin book *Stonehenge,* which was in those days the only authoritative source on Britain's most celebrated ancient site, and there, on page 25, it firmly stated that the diameter of the ditch around Stonehenge was only 320 feet (97.5 m) – some 110 feet (33.5 m) smaller than the Maxey Henge!

The two circular ditches of the Maxey Henge had been placed directly over a pair of parallel ditches that could be seen to run dead straight across the landscape for about half a mile. Around them were the smaller ring-ditches that once surrounded barrows, not to mention dozens of pits, wells and enclosures, whose dates were not immediately apparent. In the body of the book was a large three-way fold-out plan of the Maxey cropmarks, which further astonished me with their richness and complexity. That fold-out was followed by four full-page maps of Welland Valley cropmarks in nearby villages, running down to the Fens near Market Deeping, where the marks dipped below and were obscured by layers of fen soils. These later deposits hid them and protected them from some of the plough damage that was so widespread in the 1970s and '80s. And then we developed techniques that allowed us to look below the later fen deposits.

I have to confess I had been ogling those cropmark plans wide-eyed, and then I returned to the text and a short paragraph that followed a description of the round barrow ring-ditches (which they called 'circles') that had been revealed in the Welland Valley. It deserves to be quoted in full:

'If all these circles were burial sites, the whole group must have been the sanctuary and cemetery of a Bronze Age population as important as any in the Thames valley.'[2]

Those words had an electric effect on me. Instantly I realized what I was now looking at: this was clear, incontrovertible evidence that the Fens had been a major centre of population in prehistoric Britain. It then slowly dawned on me that they were different in one important respect: yes, the river valleys of their fringes, like so many other areas of Britain, had been damaged by centuries of ploughing, but go just a few metres into the Fen and things would be very different. Here, layers of river flood clays and even peats will have preserved the sites below them. And of course these clays and peats would also have helped retain water, as was to be demonstrated a few years later at Haddenham – so if conditions were right, we could expect to find wood, plant material and other organic remains. It was, to put it mildly, a tantalizing prospect.

By 1979 and 1980, English Heritage were providing half the funds we needed to excavate and write up Fengate. The spending of this money was overseen by an official inspector, who was invariably an archaeologist, too. It sounds rather bureaucratic, but in actual fact it was an excellent system, providing that one got on with one's inspector, which I nearly always did. They were generally very nice chaps (female inspectors were to become more common in a few years' time) and, like all archaeologists, they enjoyed a pint. I remember sitting with our inspector in the public bar of the Spade and Shovel. I think I must casually have mentioned my fascination with the cropmarks shown in that frontispiece to *A Matter of Time*, because when I uttered the word 'Maxey' he suddenly sat up. Thinking nothing of it, I then went on to say that I was seriously contemplating leaving the Royal Ontario Museum and returning to England. I had

personal reasons for the decision, but I was also finding the transatlantic commute rather hard work. By the time I had finished
talking, the genial inspector was looking at me with what I can
only describe as a fixed stare.

The winter of 1978–79 was the last one I spent in Canada, but
shortly before I headed back to Toronto for the final time, I was
invited to attend interviews for a new job, which English Heritage
had just advertised. Immediately I understood why our inspector
had taken such an interest in what I had said in the Spade and
Shovel, a few weeks earlier. The Welland Valley Field Officer
would be a full-time appointment and the successful applicant
would be expected to monitor the expansion of gravel pits in the
Maxey area and carry out excavations when, and if, necessary.
To cut a long story short, I got the job. So when I returned to
Canada for the last time, I was feeling very optimistic about
the future. Yes, I knew I would be facing new challenges, but
I wasn't terribly worried, largely because our small team, who
by this time were experienced and very professional, would still
be together. And to lift my spirits further it turned out to be a
wonderful season in Canada and across the border in upstate
New York.

I was helping on a colleague's dig on the Niagara peninsula,
about an hour's drive west of Toronto, and the colour of the
leaves of the maples that surrounded the dig was astonishing. As
a prehistorian used to excavating unglazed sherds of Bronze Age
pottery, which often resembled pieces of coarse digestive biscuit,
I was surprised to discover pieces of blue glazed and patterned
jugs, mugs and cups, which were identical to ones hanging in my
mother's kitchen dresser back in England. Several were printed
with the maker's name and the place they were made: Stoke-on-
Trent. But in these contexts they were prehistoric finds. They
were revealed on a site where the people who used them could
neither read nor write. That set me thinking for about half an

hour, until the call came to clear up our loose earth and get in the four-wheel drive for the bumpy ride back to the main road, and thence to the museum. On the drive back to Toronto, my mind kept returning to those glazed mugs and cups and what they represented, not just in the past, but now, to me, in the present. I was beginning to realize that archaeology isn't always about past times, alone. It's also about people and the way they, and we, live, love, think – and want to be remembered. The best archaeology is timeless, because it affects the present.

My office in the Royal Ontario Museum was a hive of activity for that final winter. There were a couple of students helping me and we were busy writing up my notes and drawing sections and plans for the Third Report on our excavations at Fengate. From time to time, we would mail great rolls of paper back to Britain. But computers were beginning to appear, and I split my writing between an old IBM electric typewriter and one of these new-fangled word processors that used 5¼-inch floppy disks. I do wish they had invented email, as it would have saved us all so much time. I used to phone England every couple of weeks. Mostly we would discuss archaeological issues, but I would also listen to the BBC World Service and read the two-day-old British newspapers that you could buy in many newsagents. It seemed like the Old Country was in meltdown: everyone seemed to be on strike. The winter of 1978–79 was the so-called Winter of Discontent, and I must admit, things were pretty grim when I returned to England in March 1979.

Toronto winters may be very cold, but it's a clean, fresh and dry sort of cold. You're more likely to get frostbite than an endlessly runny nose and aching sinuses, like you get so often in England. And yes, I was sniffling and still rather jet-lagged when I entered the small office behind the weighbridge, in Maxey

Quarry. The windows were closed, running with condensation, and everyone was smoking. A door opened and I was beckoned through to the manager's office. This was smaller, but less smoky. The pit manager and the area manager were waiting for me, the former in greasy overalls, the latter in a suit. Mercifully, it turned out that the man in the suit had a secret interest in archaeology, which I determined to exploit ruthlessly. After a quick brew of tea, we went to a local pub for lunch and I managed to persuade him to lend us a shed, where we could have our tea breaks.*

Today we inhabit a better-planned and more health-and-safety-aware world, where people routinely wear hard hats, safety boots and hi-vis coats, vests and overalls. This is particularly true of places like large working gravel pits, where you have to go on a two-day safety induction course before they'll let you turn the light on. It was rather different at Maxey in 1979. The gravel pit was expanding rapidly and we were faced with the task of excavating the very centre of the great spread of the cropmarks shown in the frontispiece of *A Matter of Time*. As is nearly always the case, the marks that showed up on air photos were just a small proportion – maybe ten per cent? – of those that we revealed when we had stripped off the topsoil.

The Maxey dig lasted just three years, from 1979 to 1982, but they were very intense. We worked in all seasons and all weathers, usually for six days a week, sometimes for seven. Those years have blended together in my brain. I can clearly recall the ceaseless grind of the gravel-washing plant in the background, with the roar of dumpers and the echoing crash as four-ton bucket loads of ballast were dropped into empty lorry trailers. We rarely ventured into the washing plant, as you

---

* Much later, I featured the interior of this shed for the opening scene of my first detective thriller, *The Lifers' Club*.

didn't need a health and safety course to know that it was very dangerous. Occasionally, towards the end of the day, things did go quiet, and then we could look through the heap of the coarsest material, known as the 'wasters', for mammoth teeth, huge semi-fossilized bones, and other treasures from the Ice Age gravels. One of our team had a dog, who would occasionally escape from the tea shed. One day he vanished and was found a few hours later buried in the wasters' heap. He used to love burrowing after things, poor dog. We were all devastated. The memory of Rufus still brings a lump to my throat.

The Maxey quarry site had everything: the great henge, a Neolithic barrow, Bronze Age barrows, Iron Age barrows, and a large Iron Age and Roman settlement. The sheer density of the features we revealed was precisely what one would have expected to find in the middle Thames Valley. Just a year into the dig I was in absolutely no doubt whatsoever: the Fens were never peripheral. We were working at the very heart of what was later, much later, to become England. But one key element was still missing.

Many people will either remember the burning hot summer of 1976 from personal experience, or from hearing their parents, or grandparents, droning on about it. It was hellishly hot, so hot that at midday we closed down the dig at Fengate and the entire crew spent the hours from noon till three in a friendly local couple's disused gravel pit, which they had planted as a wonderful, tree-lined nature reserve. It had its own shingle beaches and we used to swim and rinse off the morning's sweat and grime in the deep cool water of the old pit, before eating our sandwiches and catching a quick nap. Several times I glimpsed kingfishers before I drifted away. We called it our siesta and we made up for it by working well into the evening. A few of us even lost weight, as we drank less beer.

The sunshine of 1976 did more than merely contribute to my current skin problems. The dry summer followed upon a damp late spring and the transition was sharp. This caused vigorously growing crop roots to seek ever-deeper sources of water and meant that fields of wheat and barley with thick topsoils, and even places with a surface layer of flood clay, started to reveal cropmarks that had never been seen before. Aerial archaeologists, as the growing number of air photographers were then beginning to style themselves, took full advantage of the situation and tens of thousands of new photographs were taken. Many of these were along the fen margins, especially in those places where the known and massive spreads of cropmarks started to vanish beneath later deposits. One of these places was the tiny village – hamlet would perhaps be a better word – of Etton, about a mile south-east of Maxey.

Etton, like Maxey, only more so, is one of those fen-edge vill-ages that are built of essentially the same limestone that gives the now over-gentrified villages of the Cotswolds their special charm. In the Middle Ages, the main limestone quarries were at Barnack, on the south side of the Welland Valley. Those old and long-abandoned quarries, known as the Hills and Holes, are now a wonderful nature reserve, with a rich collection of orchids.[3] The neighbouring village, a couple of miles east, on the fen-ward side of Barnack, is Helpston, and it was here, in the old village school, just across from the church, that we established the new head-quarters of the Welland Valley Project. I now wanted the project to take a wider, more balanced view of prehistoric settlement in the Welland Valley, so we did ground surveys and field-walking, rather than excavation alone. We also did research into earlier digs and aerial photographs. I'm glad we took such a broad approach, because it put our most exciting discovery, the earlier Neolithic causewayed enclosure at Etton, into its context at the very start, and heart, of that spectacular ritual landscape around Maxey.

Maxey had been so full-on and all-consuming, because the gravel pit's deadlines were very pressing.[4] But I wasn't altogether happy: I felt strongly that there was a real danger we would end up knowing a vast amount about a relatively tiny area of land, whereas what really interested not just me, but all the members of our team, were the wider questions: Was Maxey unique? How many other sites like it were there in the Welland Valley and along the fen-edge, and how had these changed over the centuries?

By the early 1980s we knew quite a lot about the fen-edge around Fengate and the new site that was beginning to emerge at Flag Fen, and we were discovering more and more about the pre-Roman Fens. In my experience, if somehow you manage to keep your mind open and flexible, and don't become obsessed with minutiae, you can better identify the really big opportunities for exciting research. I've been told many times that our discoveries in the Welland Valley were 'lucky'. Maybe they were, but we created the chances for them to happen. You don't reveal fresh insights if you endlessly pursue particular avenues of research.

By the time we were setting up the Welland Valley Project, I had fallen helplessly in love with the Fens, and in some respects it was like a human relationship: hard to understand and pin down. Sometimes you can visit a landscape and immediately be gripped by its appeal: how can anyone, for instance, fail to fall in love with the Lake District? As if the steep hills plunging into mirror-like lakes weren't enough, there was Wordsworth (plus his underrated sister, Dorothy), hosts of golden daffodils and later, of course, countless other poets and painters, not forgetting the redoubtable Beatrix Potter. But what about the Fens, who was there to sing their praises? I felt I needed somebody to propel me to higher, to greater things, if only in my own mind and imagination. I knew only too well that I was no poet and I paint bathroom doors better than pictures. But then something remarkable happened.

★

I decided to house the new Welland Valley Project in the Old School at Helpston, a short distance south of Etton, where we would then be digging. I can't remember precisely, but I think it was a couple of weeks after we had moved our stuff into the Old School and were beginning to settle down. Being a bit of a churchaholic, one sunny lunchtime I excavated my copy of Pevsner from deep within a packing case in the loft, and walked the few yards from the Old School to the church. Whenever I call at a new church, I like first to stroll around the outside, seeing what I can deduce about its date and phases of modification from the shape of the windows, the stonework, and so on. I know it sounds a little obsessive, but treating every church visit as a search for clues helps me remember the main points about each building. It also turns up some amazing surprises. Sometimes the surprises are architectural – a seemingly over-restored Victorian exterior can hide a superbly preserved medieval interior. But the treat that Helpston had in store for me was altogether different.

I was staring up at the windows, when my gaze was caught by a glimpse of something bright and shiny on the ground. I hate litter in churchyards, and if it's not too smelly or soggy, I generally pick it up and dispose of it. So I can remember being slightly annoyed by the interruption, as I was starting to understand the building sequence of the church. I was frowning with irritation as, not really concentrating on the task, I bent down to pick up whatever it was. Then I stopped. It wasn't litter that had caught my eye, and it wasn't lying on the ground, but was leaning against a low tombstone. It was a small bunch of roses, mostly in bud, with their stems wrapped in shiny kitchen foil. Normally one sees flowers on the graves of young children or people who have died recently. But there were no new graves in this part of the churchyard and this one looked Victorian, albeit in very good condition. I read the epitaph before seeing the name:

## A POET IS BORN NOT MADE

I had stumbled across the final resting place of the poet John Clare (1793–1864).[5] Today Clare is ranked alongside Keats, Wordsworth and Byron as one of the greatest English poets of the nineteenth century. I'm aware that it's a profound meditation about what it means to be a human being in the natural landscape, but I cannot read the final stanza of his best-known poem 'I Am' without thinking about the open country around Helpston and the people who still live, and once lived, there:

> I long for scenes where man hath never trod,
> A place where woman never smiled or wept,
> There to abide with my Creator, God,
> And sleep as I in childhood sweetly slept,
> Untroubling and untroubled where I lie,
> The grass below – above, the vaulted sky.

*The poet John Clare's grave in the churchyard of St Botolph's Church, Helpston (foreground). The low, 'raised ledger' tomb carries the inscription 'A Poet is Born Not Made'.*

There is something so sad and wistful about those lines, which were written late in his life, when Clare was confined in Northampton General Lunatic Asylum. In my opinion he was the greatest poet of the English landscape. I don't think anyone, and this includes even Wordsworth, has captured better what it means to be alive in the countryside. It's a vision completely without sentimentality, but suffused with passion and always conscious of human dignity.

I loved poetry at school, where we had to learn it by heart, and I can still remember my favourites, particularly some of Keats' Odes, Coleridge's 'Kublah Khan' and Gray's 'Elegy Written in a Country Churchyard'. With the possible exception of 'Kublah Khan', all my old favourites were about the countryside. But Clare's name was never even mentioned. It wasn't until the late 1960s, when my younger brother, Felix, went to Cambridge to read English, that I first heard his name. Felix enthused about him, but it was a few years before I got round to reading some of his poems. As soon as I started to work in Peterborough, I discovered that Clare was very highly regarded locally. And now I understand why. He was born and raised at Helpston in a rural community and had a deep and abiding love for the tranquil landscape of his childhood. But he was destined to live through a time of massive landscape change, including enclosure and the construction of the railways. Although the landscape did eventually recover, albeit in a much altered and certainly more controlled state, he resented the changes bitterly. The local impact was substantial. The railway line from Peterborough to Stamford, for example, was opened in 1846, with a level crossing at Helpston, which today causes huge delays, as it also includes the much busier East Coast Main Line from Peterborough to Grantham and Retford – which was extended north in 1852.

But by far the biggest agent of change in rural areas of the Midlands and eastern England during the eighteenth and first half of the nineteenth centuries was the movement known as enclosure, which essentially involved the abandonment of earlier and less formalized patterns of land management, to be replaced by closely defined holdings controlled by local landowners and their agents. Essentially, the landscape was rationalized: roads were straightened, their verges and boundaries were defined, hedges were planted along both roads and fields, areas of woodland were assigned and common lands were formalized – usually shrinking in the process. Enclosure saw the rise of a new rural social class, yeoman farmers who owned their holdings and often supplemented their income by marketing their produce in the area. The peasants of medieval times became tenants of the larger landowners. It was a pattern of rural land use and tenure that was to survive into the present. Today, of course, things are changing again: tenant farmers are under threat and most landowners pay contractors to farm their land.

Clare detested the changes that enclosure brought about. As a farmworker's son, born and raised in Helpston, he felt that the landscape, his landscape, had been taken away from him. You can certainly sense the raw emotion in some of his writing. One collection of manuscript poems in Peterborough Museum, which was never published in his lifetime, is known as *The Midsummer Cushion*. It includes a poem ('The Fallen Elm') addressed to a familiar great elm tree that has just been felled as part of enclosure. Having watched so many noble elm trees die following the avoidable introduction of Dutch Elm disease to Britain from North America in the 1970s, I can share his almost palpable fury:

> With axe at root he felled thee to the ground
> And barked of freedom. O I hate the sound!
> Time hears its visions speak and age sublime
> Had made thee a disciple unto time.

It grows the cant term of enslaving tools
To wrong another by the name of right;
It grows the licence of o'erbearing fools
To cheat plain honesty by force of might.
Thus came Enclosure – ruin was its guide
But freedom's clapping hands enjoyed the sight
Though comfort's cottage soon was thrust aside
And workhouse prisons raised upon the site.

I always find that final line particularly poignant. Clare was to suffer from deep and profound depression for much of his life, and he wrote the poems of *The Midsummer Cushion* after a particularly bad two years. He was certified insane in 1837, but still struggled to write. Eventually, in 1842, he was confined to Northampton General Lunatic Asylum. He died twenty-two years later, of a stroke – and as a final, unthinking irony, his body was transported back to Helpston by train.

I owe a great deal to John Clare. He opened my eyes to the subtle yet enduring beauty, not just of the fenland landscape but of 'the vaulted sky' above. It's a world whose inhabitants aren't confined within surrounding hills and valleys – because there aren't any. So they do indeed live part of their lives as it were in the sky. I'm a farmer, too, and whenever I meet my neighbours, or see a group of them standing by the edge of a field discussing the slow germination of the winter wheat, or something similar, someone will gesture towards the sky. Others will do so too. Many will look up. The thing is, they take its presence for granted: the Fens are nothing without winds, rain, frosts and sunshine. You can watch while storm clouds develop and you can follow their progress across the landscape. A big, black hammerhead storm cloud was approaching us the other day, when I was chatting to a neighbour, leaning on the bonnet of his Land Rover. I looked up at it anxiously. He glanced up, too: 'No,' he dismissed it, after scrutinizing it in silence for a couple of seconds. 'That'll follow the river.' And it did. In fact, it seemed to be veering north-east, away from us, just as he spoke. I think there's more than a bit of John Clare in many fen farmers.


John Clare loved his wife, his family and his children, some of whom died while he was still quite a young man. Doubtless this must have added greatly to his mental torment, but the point is that families are the principal element of stability in most people's lives. This applies as much today as it did in Victorian times, or indeed in prehistory. Put succinctly, the family is the basic building-block of human society. Everything else follows from it. Even religion, which is usually structured to enhance and strengthen existing family ties. Viewed from a pragmatic, Darwinian perspective, families are about propagation of mankind and the survival of our species. Although I would hesitate before stating this as a proven fact, it is my experience that the importance of family ties increases in situations where people are under stress, or are separated by long distances. Family ties have always been important in the Fens. And I also think they may partially help to explain why most of the great religious, or ritual, monuments were built in prehistory.

In the early fourth millennium BC, the British landscape was still in a relatively early stage of development: large areas of woodland were being cleared to provide fields for grazing and cultivation, settlements were beginning to appear and a country-wide informal network of roads, tracks and animal droveways was being established. We know that a raised timber walkway, called the Sweet Track, was built to cross part of the Somerset Levels wetlands in the winter of 3807–06 BC. So it is quite likely that similar things were being erected in the Fens.

Archaeologists are very adept at inventing descriptive but

extremely non-memorable names for the sites they discover, and 'causewayed enclosure' is a classic example. Essentially, cause-wayed enclosures were built in the centuries around 3600 BC. Their boundaries were marked out by one or two parallel ditches that often formed a rough circle or oval, surrounding an area of a few acres. Some of these sites were quite large – maybe the size of Regent's Park, while others were smaller – more like town marketplaces. The 'causewayed' bit of their name comes from the fact that the encircling ditch or ditches weren't dug in continuous stretches but in short lengths, separated by gaps, or causeways. From the air, the interrupted ditches sort of resemble strings of sausages.

Widely separated communities must keep in touch. At a very basic level, regular contacts are needed simply to prevent inbreeding, both of the human and animal population. Until very recently, some areas of the Fens have had a reputation for inbreeding, which simply reflects the isolation of certain families and communities. Nobody wants to be solitary, but sometimes it just happens. Farmers quickly become aware that their flocks and herds are becoming inbred. In my experience, the appearance of certain conditions in lambs, such as cleft palates, inturned eyelids and incipient deafness, often mean that it is time to introduce new blood – which is best and fastest done by buying in some new rams. So where does one look for the new, and entirely unrelated, bloodlines? I could go to local farmers, but over the years we have all bought and borrowed from each other, so there are no guarantees that our sheep are unrelated. Normally, I would take my trailer to Melton Mowbray Market. In actual fact, the last time I needed two new rams, I went all the way to mid-Wales. But what did farmers do in prehistory?

Many medieval market towns, like Melton, were established at points where major communication routes crossed. Very often these places had origins that extended back to the Roman period, if not earlier. We are not completely certain where this tradition began, but I suggest that the causewayed enclosures of the earlier Neolithic are pretty good candidates. There is, moreover, some evidence to suggest that they were erected in special places, which probably had much earlier origins, maybe extending as far back as post-Glacial, hunter-gatherer times, some ten thousand years ago. These were the sites that later gave rise to ritual landscapes. Clearly then, causewayed enclosures were very important places and we know they occurred in the Fens. But when we started to dig at Maxey in those perishing cold winter days, early in 1979, I little suspected that in three years' time, our team would be excavating the best preserved causewayed enclosure yet discovered. And it lay, still deeply buried beneath layers of flood clay, just four large fields away, at the edge of the little village of Etton.

# Etton:
# Perfect Preservation

*Aerial Photography – Etton Revealed – Ceremonial*
*Centres – Prehistoric Religion – We Build our Own*
*House and Farm – The Etton Causewayed Enclosure*

We all love big discoveries. We would not be human if we didn't. People outside archaeology assume that it's all about those moments in a trench when there's a glint of gold or your trowel scrapes the bones of a skeleton. But nine times out of ten, the really exciting finds aren't made on excavations at all. The process of revelation can be far more humdrum – but still just as exciting.

In its early days, aerial survey was quite a slow process. Aeroplanes took shorter flights and early cameras held less film. But everything speeded up during the Second World War and by the 1970s aerial photography was fast, efficient and sophisticated. It was especially exciting in, and in the months after, a good year, such as the hot, dry summer of 1976, when the results of aerial surveys began to emerge. Suddenly we were inundated with information and some of it took quite a long time to sink in. We knew that the summer had been so very dry that the air photos were likely to be good, but what began to emerge over the following two to three years was little short of sensational. To go back to that frontispiece in *A Matter of Time,*\* the henge in the foreground seems to be sitting on two parallel, dead straight ditches, which resemble those you'd find on either side of a road. Similar features are found within other ritual landscapes and they were given the name 'cursus', after the Latin word for a racecourse. We're still far from certain how they were used, but most people think they were processional ways – a third millennium BC equivalent of The Mall.

The ritual landscape at Maxey developed on a low gravel 'island', where the floodplain of the lower Welland Valley joins the Fen. The name Maxey comes from an old Scandinavian form of 'Maccus's island', Maccus being a Viking man's name.† The henge, the modern village and the church are located on the highest part of the low gravel 'island', which is traversed diagonally by the ditches of the Maxey cursus. At its south-eastern end the ditches seem to quickly fade away, as they are covered by layers of flood clay deposited by the two ancient courses of the River Welland that flowed past Maccus's island, to north and south. Today, these strands of the river are confined between the high banks of the canalized Maxey Cut.

I must confess I had always thought that the ubiquitous flood clays that you find all along the fen margins were as old as the Fens themselves, but our soil scientist, Dr Charles French, was able to show that they actually began to form in the second millennium BC, and only started to accumulate to any thickness in the Iron Age, a few centuries before the Roman conquest. We

---

\* See p. 65.

† A.D. Mills, *A Dictionary of English Place Names* (Oxford University Press, 1991), cites a reference of c.963 to *Macuseige*, meaning 'Island or dry ground in marsh, of a man called Maccus'.

now realize that the bulk of the clays around Maxey may have started to form over a millennium earlier, but the process was rapidly speeded up by the introduction of winter wheats in the Iron Age. This happened when farmers a few miles upstream (in what is now northern Northamptonshire and Leicestershire) started ploughing their fields in the autumn, in order to sow the more productive and recently introduced hardy varieties of wheat. The bare fields where the crops now grew were soon eroded by rain and frost – a process that has continued ever since. The fine silts found their way into fast-flowing streams and rivers. These particles were then carried downstream and were naturally deposited as the pace of the river slowed down when it encountered the wide, flat floodplains of the fenland basin. Many man-made environmental problems are as old, I suspect, as mankind itself.

The clearest of the aerial photographs taken in 1976 revealed what we had all been waiting for: the unmistakable, if faint and slightly blurred, outline of the string-of-sausages ditch of a causewayed enclosure. Although it had clearly been an integral part of the Maxey ritual landscape, to avoid any confusion with the Maxey henge we named the new site after the nearby village of Etton. The precise sequence of events has become slightly unclear in my mind because we were so very busy. We began work at the Maxey quarry in the spring of 1979, and very shortly thereafter we heard about the new site at Etton. By this point, Peterborough was expanding rapidly and the gravel pits all around had to be extended to keep up with the huge demand for ballast – and of course we were working full-time just to keep up with them. So, much as I would have liked to excavate Etton then and there, we already had far too much on our plates.

In 1981 the Maxey dig ended and we learned that the quarry planned to expand eastwards in the immediate future. The new site at Etton was now under direct threat of destruction. When the timetable emerged, we learned that we had a maximum of two summers to start our investigations. If the quarry expanded even further east we would have another three to four years to excavate the rest of the site. I immediately transferred part of our team from the now running-down dig at Maxey, across to Etton, some three large fields of wheat to the east. The gravel quarry also lent us one of their newest excavators and a superb, highly experienced driver. In the following three weeks they would both prove indispensable.

We knew from the air photos that the causewayed boundary or enclosure ditch of the new site was overlain by the high flood bank of the Maxey Cut, a major canalized tributary of the ancient braided system of the River Welland. It was simply a matter of measuring along the bank to determine precisely where to start digging – or at least, that was the theory.

It was a foggy morning when I watched the digger trundling down the farm track from the quarry towards the new site. I've always enjoyed large machines and for ten years I held a digger driver's official licence. But this was one of the smart new Swedish Ackerman machines that were far more powerful than the rather creaky Hy-Macs that I was used to. It had wide bog-crawler tracks and I remember the sound of Radio 1 floating across the field from the driver's cab. This amazed me: the old Hy-Mac cabs were far too noisy for such things. As if to make his point, the driver was sitting back in his well-padded contoured seat, his arms behind his head, puffing on a cigarette, his steel-toecap boots protruding through the front windscreen. It was the picture of leisurely, luxurious travel. As he approached where I was standing, beside the two red-and-white range poles that marked the presumed edges of the Etton enclosure ditch, I pointed to an imaginary line between the poles. And that's where he began digging.

I knew before we started that the enclosure ditch was quite deeply buried beneath layers of sticky flood clay, known as alluvium. During surveys I had even bored holes through it with a hand-held auger. But seeing the stuff in handfuls is not the same as standing alongside a rapidly growing spoil heap. I hadn't appreciated how clay, when freshly excavated, occupies such a vast volume; you can roll and compress it subsequently, but when first dug from the ground, the stiff, sticky clay stacks up in piles that are mostly composed of air pockets. Soon, clay was tumbling across the area we were trying to work in, so I had the machine go round to the back and claw the spoil heap away from the excavation. While he was doing this, I jumped into the trench and had a poke around with my trowel.

I have to confess I felt ill at ease surrounded by so much clay. This wasn't at all like a normal gravel site: it looked, felt and even smelled different. There was dampness everywhere, even in the air. When I knelt down to trowel the ground, it was soft beneath me and soon I felt the cool damp penetrating through my jeans, to my knees. But the thing that struck me most was the lack of texture and colour differences in the trench. Yes, there was a dark and a little more crumbly layer of topsoil covering the clay, but that was it. Thereafter, the walls and even the floor of the trench were the same homogeneous browny yellow. If you looked at the clay walls very closely you could see they were actually very subtly banded, but this wasn't visible everywhere. I knew these bands represented individual, and usually annual, flooding events, so presumably those very slightly darker bands were years when the floods had been particularly bad: the river water had flowed faster, so the material deposited had been coarser, and darker. But those tiny colour and texture differences aside, there was nothing to scrape. So I put my trowel in my back pocket and stood up. By now the digger had pulled the spoil heap back and had returned. The driver was waiting for instructions.

If a trench won't tell you anything – and this one was as blank as any I had ever encountered – there are two things an archaeologist can do: go down or go sideways. Normally I favour going down, but in this instance I felt that we were now well over a metre below the surface and if I wasn't careful I would come across archaeology, but would be unable to relate it to anything – and excavating anything 'contextually blind' is to be avoided at all costs. It is, after all, what treasure hunters do. So I selected the sideways option: I jumped out of the trench and had the digger track to the side. Then we started to dig down again, the machine taking long steady scoops, each one about 3 or 4 inches (7.5–10 cm) deep.

I stood outside the trench as the digger started to go down, as I was once nearly trapped when a trench side that we were enlarging collapsed. The bucket was now about 6 inches (15 cm) from the bottom of the original trench and I was about to jump back in when I heard something that made every nerve tingle. Immediately I raised a hand and the bucket froze. I'd worked with this driver many times before, and we had agreed a set of our own hand signals. I could see he was looking at me for instruction and I was aware that the digger driver can't see through his bucket and often can't hear noises from the trench because of the engine (I'm glad to say he'd turned off Radio 1). So I made a sort of curling sign with my hand and wrist. As soon as he saw it, I watched as he slackened off the engine revs and slowly curled the bucket forwards, to reveal what lay below its cutting edge.

That noise was so distinctive: it was the sound made by gravel pebbles scraping against the metal of the bucket. And it had been music to my ears. With two hands I signalled that he should very gently continue drawing back. By now – and I honestly can't remember when I had jumped back in – I was standing next to the bucket (something modern health and safety rules wouldn't permit), with one hand resting on it, and I could feel the vibration of the gravel at the cutting edge. Then I looked behind the bucket at the freshly scraped ground and there it was: the edge of the causewayed enclosure ditch, where it had been cut into the pristine gravel subsoil of the river floodplain, some five and a half millennia ago. I think the driver knew I'd been a bit anxious, because when I looked up I could see that he, like me, had a grin as wide as a Cheshire Cat. It was a great moment.

If there is anything that archaeologists hate, it's not being able to fix their trenches in either time or space. The discovery of the edge of the ditch not only provided us with a fixed point of reference, but also allowed us to make some important predictions that would profoundly affect the way we were to carry out five subsequent seasons of excavation, from 1982 to 1987. For a start, we knew it was going to provide problems with the earth moving, as about a metre of topsoil and flood clay had to be removed and I was determined to reveal the entire site before it was destroyed by the quarry. In the end, our trenches covered an area of just under 190×120 metres (208×130 yds) and I did a lot of the machine driving myself, ably assisted by our soil scientist, Dr Charly French, on a Drott (a type of earth-carrying bulldozer).* In those days we turned our hands to many things! In other respects, too, I think Etton was the most challenging dig of my life, because it combined many of the best features of both wet and dry sites. Preservation of organic materials was superb, especially in the enclosure ditch, where wood, leaves, twigs and even tree bark were preserved in peaty muds. Meanwhile, the entire surface of the enclosed area had been protected from modern and indeed medieval plough damage by the thick accumulations of flood clay.

Somehow, we had to combine an open-area, large-scale approach, but with a concern for detail, which is why we recorded

---

* Charly is now a professor at Cambridge.

the precise location of everything we found: every twig, every sherd of pottery, every bone, every flint tool and all the tiny fragments that were revealed in the ground and in the sieves. In those pre-digital days, when everything had to be measured with tapes and optical levels, it was a truly Herculean task, but our wonderful team of diggers rose to the challenge. As a result, the site has been subject to some major reassessments, in which the basic data was re-examined to provide further insights.[1] I'm proud to say that our detailed records and those later studies have helped give Etton a sort of second life; I don't regard it as having been completely obliterated by the quarry.

In 1981 we would have loved to have taken time off to write the Maxey report, but the pressure to expand the quarry was relentless, so we had to do it whenever we could, which was mostly on weekends and evenings. We were well aware that Etton would make no sense unless readers could set the new site within the complex development of the ritual landscape right across Maxey 'island'. In the event, the report appeared in 1985 – and I'm still not quite sure how we found the time to do it so quickly. Many candles were burned at both ends. Then, in November 1982, at the end of our second season of excavation at Etton, we discovered the sensational new site at Flag Fen, some 8 miles (13 km) to the south, in Peterborough.* It was the busiest period of my life.

The remarkable preservation at Etton gave us glimpses into the way people regarded and used causewayed enclosures. These insights made it easier to understand how and why these early ceremonial centres had given rise to the henges, barrows and other sites that comprised the ritual landscapes of the later Neolithic and earlier Bronze Age, from about 3500 to 1500 BC. There were all sorts of ideas and theories that had been put

---

* I discuss Flag Fen in Chapter 6.

forward over the past hundred or so years to explain how and why causewayed enclosures had come into existence and some of them, I think, still stand – although not as single or sole causes for these sites, which are far more complex than was once supposed. The principal idea that I liked (and decided to retain when I began our own investigations) was that these enclosures were neutral meeting places where sometimes far-flung and widely separated communities could come together, probably at regular intervals, to trade and exchange things. I now think these gatherings were about far more than trade and exchange alone. We can be in little doubt that regular get-togethers would have been essential to the growth and prosperity of any farming community, but just like markets in medieval and later times, they were about far more than the movement of goods. I know of several people who met their wives and girlfriends at markets. Pubs and bars around the market sales rings still provide a vital social service to local communities. I can remember Westminster politicians in Tony Blair's time urging all markets to go online, because the Internet was so much more efficient. Certainly, it is, and was; but markets do more than just sell things, as any rural person could have told a Westminster politician, had they been asked, which they weren't.

The more we investigated what might have been happening in earlier Neolithic times at Etton, the more I became convinced that causewayed enclosures were more about social organization and the family than even religion or trade. Indeed, all three were closely linked in prehistoric times: goods weren't simply bought and sold, as the market economy had yet to develop. Instead, grain and livestock were exchanged to cement family ties and obligations. We see this survive in the recent anthropological record in the form of 'bridewealth' where marriage partners' families were linked together by mutually agreed exchange arrangements: one family, for example, providing the other with a supply of pork in exchange for oatmeal and good potting clay. Religion, ideology and families were also united by a belief in another dimension (in effect, an afterlife, or realm of the ancestors), from whence the dead were thought to enforce and oversee agreements – for example, field and property boundaries – in the here and now. That may well have been one of the reasons why skeletons from earlier Neolithic chambered tombs were removed from their resting places and taken out into the community. We know this, because quite frequently the bones of different individuals had been muddled together, probably in the decades following burial.

Causewayed enclosures seem to have been some of the earliest of the large ceremonial monuments to be constructed in ritual landscapes that then continued to be used for some two millennia. So they can perhaps be seen to be setting the tone for what was to follow. Radiocarbon dates showed that the main period of Etton's use was from 3775 to 3650 BC.[2]

As our examination of Etton progressed, it became increasingly clear to us that families and clans had been of fundamental importance. It had long been known that the soil that filled the lengths of causewayed enclosure ditches often contained 'offerings' of some sort: complete pots and quite frequently human and animal skulls, too. Excavators elsewhere in Britain had noticed that these offerings very often occurred in the ditch butt-ends, on either side of the undug causeways that separated the individual ditch segments. The standard archaeological approach to such sites would be to dig a series of quite narrow slots across the ditches to investigate the sequence of layers in some detail. But I thought we'd try something a bit different, and to my amazement, it worked.

I determined to trowel out long lengths of ditch very carefully in the hope that we could discover more about those strange offerings at the butt-ends. The filled-in ditch segments that we had first tentatively revealed in the previous season were now more fully exposed, to reveal complete segments of ditch, together with the causeways that separated them. We knew from the 1981 investigation that the upper fillings of these ditches were partially waterlogged, but we had no idea whether the preservation improved further down into the ditch. It was also quite possible that the deep de-watering that had been required to operate the nearby quarries for so long had dried our deposits out, but from the bottom up – in which case the few scraps of semi-desiccated wood that we had revealed earlier would be all we would find.

On the day when we began to excavate the ditch filling, everyone on the dig was tense. Would the site be as great as we all hoped? Normally it takes some time to dig down to the wet levels, but at Etton we were already very deep. I was worried because the natural gravels did indeed seem surprisingly dry – and that, we were later able to prove, was due to the nearby quarry's de-watering. But it wasn't long before we realized, to my huge relief, that the clays filling the ditch had retained nearly all of the moisture and, as a result, the clay-rich ditch fillings were still wet. Consequently, organic remains within them were well preserved. We could all relax. I still find it sobering to think that if we had begun excavating Etton in 1992, rather than 1982, we would only have found a few dry sherds of pottery, the odd flint tool and fragments of bone.

As soon as we saw that the ditches were still waterlogged and that wood and organic material would be preserved, my wife, Maisie, began to get very excited. Maisie is a specialist in prehistoric woodworking and I knew this would be a golden opportunity for her. She immediately insisted that we should excavate the ditch in long lengths because you can't expose and unravel a complex tangle of twigs, branches and brushwood in a conventional narrow slot. I was delighted to hear this, because that was what I wanted to do anyway.

*Recording the wood and other finds revealed in the waterlogged*
*layers of the Etton causewayed enclosure ditch (c.3700 BC), in 1982.*
*Some of the long, straight pieces of wood were probably the*
*by-products of coppicing.*

The long trenches were started and it took several weeks
before we began to reveal signs of coherent patterning. The
upper layers were disturbed by water, but about half a metre into
the ditch, we started to find signs of more deliberate behaviour.
Quite close to the butt-end, alongside one of the causeways, we
came across an intact pottery bowl, but there was something very
odd about it. I can remember when the archaeologist working
on it called me over to have a look. My first reaction was that
it was a human skull – which is what I would have expected in
such a location. But I couldn't have been more wrong. Luckily I
didn't say what I was thinking, and as soon as I had knelt down
to have a closer look I understood that it wasn't bone at all. It
was fine, smooth pottery: a round-bottomed bowl, in a well-
known early fourth millennium style of decorated hand-made
vessel, known to prehistorians as Mildenhall Ware, after the site

in Suffolk where it was first recognized. It was a stunning piece, and I knew it would delight the curators at the British Museum, who were our sponsors for that first year.

Over the next couple of days, we carefully excavated around the upside-down pot and discovered it had been placed rim down on a sheet of birch bark – in effect, a mat. I can't remember if it was before or after we found the pot, but that trench also revealed two other extraordinary waterlogged finds. Each one was organic, which explains why they are still unique. The first was a large sheet of birch bark, which had been deliberately peeled off a tree and measured about a metre and a half by half a metre. This is very much larger than the small pieces of bark I sometimes find in my garden, which become detached by natural means. It had also been cut square and folded in half. Repeated beating and soaking are part of the process of softening birch bark for use as waterproof containers, shoes and boxes. Its position in the wet deposits at the bottom of the ditch suggests that it was either in the process of being made into a pliable sheet that could then be used to make boxes or basket-like containers, or had been deliberately left in the ditch, as an offering. Its size and location both suggest that its loss had not been casual. I'm fairly sure it was a deliberate offering, like the bowl on the smaller mat, a short distance away.

Not far from the sheet of bark we found a complete (i.e. uncut) length of fine twine made from two spun threads of flax fibres, plied together. It was just over half a metre long and on close inspection Maisie came to the conclusion that it had just been made and had never been used – a suggestion that was confirmed when it was examined in the British Museum. So was it coincidence that two recently made artefacts were left in the ditch, or was something else going on? Given that we found no further evidence for either birch bark or flax working in or around the ditch, I think it's reasonable to conclude that both items had been placed in it, or left there, deliberately. But that doesn't answer the all-important question: why?

The Etton dig lasted seven years and we excavated about three-quarters of the site. The remaining quarter lies beneath the massive banks of the Maxey Cut, where I hope the ditch deposits have been kept wet for posterity by the river water. As the seasons passed, we began to notice consistencies in the way that finds were distributed through the fillings of the individual ditch segments. The first thing that struck us was that the layers of soil, sand and gravel that filled each ditch segment had been put there (i.e. dumped or back-filled) in a series of quite distinct episodes. It was impossible to correlate precisely what was happening from one segment to another, but in general there were three quite distinct phases of ditch digging and filling.

The initial digging out of each ditch segment would have left it with banks of gravel on all sides, including the causeways (which were therefore probably not routes or paths). Very shortly indeed after its digging, and probably as part of the same process, the first offerings were placed on the clean gravel exposed along the flat bottom of the ditch. These included human and animal skulls, the inverted pot on a mat, the birch bark mat, many neat heaps of animal bones and fragments of querns, or corn-grinding stones, which had been broken and set on edge. Each one of the offerings was quite distinct and separated by spaces of about a metre or half a metre. The offerings were then covered over with gravel from the surrounding banks and the ditch was filled up, probably to the top.

A few decades later – maybe after a generation or two – the ditch was re-excavated but only as far down as the top of the lowest offerings, which were left undisturbed. A new set of offerings were then placed in the recut ditch, but these weren't quite as large or carefully separated as the first set. Again, the new offerings were buried under gravel. After another gap of a decade or two, the ditch was dug out for a third time, but now the offerings were placed in a continuous and quite narrow line along the base of what was more a shallow trench than a big ditch.

*The latest, usually final, set of offerings at Etton were placed high in the filling of the ditch. By this time the separation between individual deposits had been replaced by a continuous line of material, where larger items can be seen to occur at regular intervals. This suggests that the deposit was placed in the ground during a series of separate actions, rather than as a single homogeneous event.*

I believe that what we are looking at here is the evolution of rituals and ceremony, in which big formal occasions become smaller and simplified, maybe as the emphasis of the gathering itself shifts. So if we assume that the original purpose of causewayed enclosures was to provide a place where separated communities in the region could come together, then it is possible that each ditch segment represents a family or clan, and that the whole enclosure was identified with, say, the people who lived in and around what would much later be called Maccus's Island, or Maxey. We now know of three other causewayed enclosures nearby in the lower Welland Valley and another two not far away in the Nene Valley, which would have been centres for their own districts. Etton and the enclosures around it form one of the largest concentrations of these early ceremonial sites known in Europe.[3]

If each ditch segment represented an individual family or clan, then it is not unreasonable to see the offerings as somehow illustrating, or recalling, individual episodes in a family's history. Some, such as the skulls or the inverted pots, may even have represented individual men or women. There is also evidence that a proportion of the later offerings were arranged into sub-groups, separated by clearly identifiable objects, such as broken querns. Maybe this represents the natural tendency of families to break up into separate groups of cousins, over time. There is also evidence to suggest that these later offerings became somehow miniaturized: in one case, a tennis ball-size round fossil had been carefully positioned on a flat stone, much as the earlier skull-like complete pot had been placed on a mat. I could imagine what lay behind these actions: those heaps of bones were often the remains of meals that had included butchered meat. Did the complete pots celebrate the passing of the person who cooked, or the setting-up of a new kitchen? It would always be difficult to be more specific, but we were beginning to glimpse what had been going on in their minds. And some of it felt strangely familiar to me. We were seeing reflexions of family life, five thousand years ago.

In prehistory, and later in Saxon times, most young men and women would probably have experienced what it was like to have built and furnished their own homes. In Britain, the appearance of bricks and readily available quarried stone from later medieval times meant that houses became more durable and longer lived. More and more people would buy or inherit their new houses, rather than build them. Today even fewer people get the chance, or more importantly, have the time, to 'self-build'.

In 1993 we put our first house on the market. It was a typical four-bedroom brick farmhouse, built in 1907, on the edge of the villages of Parson Drove and Murrow, in what was once the Isle of Ely, but is now Cambridgeshire. For several years we had kept a handful of sheep in the old farmyard alongside the house, which we enjoyed so much that we decided to expand the enterprise. We looked around for a farmhouse with an attached smallholding, but these were very expensive, especially anywhere near a town, where developers were looking for plots of land to build new, 'executive' dwellings. To make matters worse, in 1994 house prices fell sharply, which meant that our old house simply wasn't selling. We had to drop the price we were asking and at this point we discovered that the cheapest option was to buy a plot of land and 'self-build'. So that is what we did.

To find anywhere affordable we had to cross the county boundary into Lincolnshire and eventually came across the land we were looking for: a 17-acre field on the edge of the parish of Sutton St James, in the Silt Fens, a few miles from the towns of Holbeach and Long Sutton. Our old house still wasn't selling, but we did have enough money to purchase the land and erect a timber barn, which would provide winter housing for our sheep and their hay, but which now also sheltered a temporary kitchen and shower unit. We slept in an old caravan. Our barn was the most spacious dining room in the county, even if the chairs were straw bales and the folding table was a bit wobbly.

Eventually our old house sold and we could start work on the new one. I remember I was driving a mini-digger, laying the new water main, when a Land Rover drew alongside me and one of the local farmers got out and introduced himself. I told him about our plans to keep sheep and plant a small wood. He listened attentively, smiled broadly and headed off. A man of few words, but I knew that by nightfall the whole village would know what we were doing. And I was right. Over the following weeks we were greeted cheerfully in local shops, pubs and markets. It was then that I realized that building your own house is a way of establishing yourselves in the local community. And then there were the rites of passage, which as an anthropologist I was very familiar with – except that these were often not the usual ones. Yes, we did have a big house-warming at the end of it all, but we also celebrated the completion of the roof, the arrival of the Aga, the erection of the staircase, the laying of the upstairs floor, the delivery of our bed and the turning-on of the shower. I'm sure that archaeologists in the future will find many sherds of Prosecco bottles in the flower beds surrounding the house.

Had we not built our house, I think it would have taken at least another five years to have fully become a part of the local community. It also taught us the importance of belonging somewhere and the confidence that can inspire. In fact, there were times I rather regretted not being a believer, or otherwise I would have attended the village church. As it was, I supported, and still support, church fetes and other local activities. But while we were experiencing the process of being taken into a community, we were also excavating at Etton and I have to say I found both worlds had begun to mesh together. I was also starting to understand that farmers have never operated alone: not only are there networks of supply and marketing, but being involved with the land somehow fosters deeper relationships. Several times Maisie and I have helped out neighbours who were having lambing problems and often at ungodly hours of the night. Since we started our small sheep farm, sheep have become more popular in the region, in part, I suspect, because the heavy clay-silt soils grow such a lush crop of grass. We all know when our neighbours are planning to lamb and we're all on standby to help out, when needed. Frequently, neighbours will turn up with bottles of unused medicine, bags of feed or dietary blocks, when their lambing is over. We none of us like to see anything go to waste, but in reality we are also keeping an eye on each other, in case anything should go wrong. Put another way, we are part of a community and we care for the members of that community. Were things different in prehistory? Life would have been much harder then, and I strongly suspect that, as a result, communal bonds would have been tighter.

I don't want to give the impression that Etton was just a religious or ceremonial site, because I think it was more complex than that. For a start, it was divided neatly in half by a ditch and fence line, which ran straight across the middle of the enclosure from the south (where its start was hidden beneath the huge earth bank of the Maxey Cut) to a point just short of the main ceremonial entranceway, midway along the curved causewayed ditch, at its most northerly point. To the left (west) of the fence the ditch was wetter and there seemed to be more evidence for what one might term domestic life. A few animals were probably kept there and I suspect families would have established temporary homes there, too. On the other (eastern) side of the central fence there was much more evidence for ritualized behaviour, both in the layers of the enclosure ditch and in pits and other features of the interior, which featured carefully placed items, such as wild cattle skulls and a complete, lightly used quern, or corn-grinding stone, positioned on-edge but on top of the stone that was used to rub it. In other words, it had been symbolically placed out of reach to mere humans. I suspect that this was the side where most of the feasting and other activities, such as cremations, would have taken place.

*The scale of the Etton enclosure suggests that it was sometimes used by quite large numbers of people. This view of the interior of the enclosure was taken in 1986. The photographer is standing just outside the enclosure, with the segmented ditch curving to the right. The two ditches in the foreground extended from the main northerly entranceway and divided the interior into two halves.*

When we started work at Etton we were inclined to follow current ideas about causewayed enclosures, which tended to emphasize their religious and ceremonial side. Indeed, they were viewed as large, shrine-like sites. Most people saw them as places that were used temporarily, or perhaps episodically would be a better word, and probably at certain times of the year, such as autumn and midwinter, which were quiet periods in the farming calendar. I would imagine that the ground at Etton might be a bit wet for midwinter gatherings, but groundwater levels are at their lowest in autumn. Recent studies have suggested that ordinary domestic life played an important role at Etton, along with the known ceremonies, and a new reassessment of the bone assemblage has drawn attention to the abundant evidence for routine butchery (for meals and feasts), together with human cremations.[4] Recent research at Star Carr in North Yorkshire, a very much earlier site (*c*.9500 BC), has revealed a similar mixture of ceremonial or ritualized behaviour, which seems to have taken place alongside the ordinary activities of daily life.[5] It is not until very much later, say 3000–2900 BC, that we see some of the rituals being moved out of daily life and into special shrines, at places like Stonehenge. It's interesting that Etton is linked to the main, central henge at Maxey by the parallel ditches of the Maxey Cursus, a ceremonial monument that was constructed in the centuries after Etton went out of regular use.

So what would the seasonal use of Etton have involved? For a start, I don't think we're looking here at mass migrations. Whole communities did not 'up sticks', abandon their villages and come to Etton. I strongly suspect we are looking here at (probably) selected members of the community who were given the privilege of representing their clan or family at the autumn gathering. They would have established temporary homes there for a few days or, at most, a few weeks. There was absolutely no evidence for permanent dwellings, although we were able to detect a few log-built structures around two of the entranceways. We could identify three (to north, east and west) main entrances into the enclosure, and I would guess there would also have been one to the south (now hidden beneath the bank of the Maxey Cut), which may have included provision for boats to be moored beside the nearby stream.

The symbolic representation of events and individuals is not always easy to identify, but I think it reasonable to suppose that the inner ring of the much smaller Bluestones at Stonehenge may well have symbolized certain important ancestors, just as the numerous carvings of bronze axe heads on the larger stones around them may have recorded individual ceremonies such as funerals, where the bodies were carried out to one of the many barrows on Salisbury Plain. Both Etton and Stonehenge reveal a remarkably rapid evolution of ceremonies and the monuments where they took place. This suggests to me that prehistoric society of the third and fourth millennium BC was very dynamic and in a constant state of development and change. And of course this helps to explain the role of both sites: the earlier, Etton, was what we might call today a regional hub; Stonehenge was to grow into something very much larger and more important. But the fundamental role of both places was essentially the same: they were all about social cohesion and stability, in changing times.

I imagine John Clare would have been appalled by the state of the landscape around Helpston today and he would have detested the sprawl of modern Peterborough and the new roads that have appeared with it. I suspect he would have disliked the ever-expanding gravel pits too, and the vast 'grain plain' fields that are such a feature of modern arable farming. So what would he have liked? Maybe one or two nature reserves (although I think he would have found them too small and too controlled) and a few remaining ancient woodlands, especially further north, along the Lincolnshire Fen margins. I imagine that little would have pleased him about today's physical landscape. But he was also a dreamer and a man of ideas, and although I have absolutely no evidence to back me up, I think he would have been delighted by what we understand today about prehistoric religion and society. I am quite confident that Clare, as an intelligent and gifted farmworker's son, would also have been fascinated by what we know about pre-Roman farms and farmers along the fen-edge. We now have fresh evidence that covers almost every aspect of the subject: from their four-thousand-year-old history, their development and their changing role in the national and regional economy. It seems to me that the big challenge facing us is somehow to make these people and their way of life relevant. They must come alive and be appreciated by new generations and a wider public. If we cannot do that, then all our exhaustive research will have been in vain. Clare highlighted the importance of the lives of ordinary farming folk and their concerns by linking current changes to higher truths. Yes, his anger shone through, but so also did his humanity. How dearly I would like to have asked him for advice.

In our broad, flat fenland landscapes we have glimpsed ancestry, ideology and aspiration. Now I want to turn my attention to the practical and the ordinary. This does not mean, however, that the story the next chapter tells will be less high flown and more down-to-earth. Quite the contrary, because don't forget that although a fenman may appear to be ploughing a field behind a team of oxen, heavy horses or within the air-conditioned cab of a high-powered modern tractor, his mind is actually half in Clare's 'vaulted sky'. You cannot remove imagination from even the most humdrum of farming chores. We will discover shortly that taming the prehistoric fenland, at a time of rapidly rising water levels, was to prove a daunting task. It would certainly have changed the landscape profoundly, but also, and perhaps more importantly, it would have transformed peoples' lives.

# 6

# Flag Fen:
# Wetlands Revealed

*A Dragline Jib – Flag Fen Discovered –
Prospection and Exploration – The Post
Alignment – Pattern and Purpose*

In 1982 our team was working in the Welland Valley, but in 1981 I had persuaded Geoff Wainwright, the chief archaeologist at English Heritage, that it would be a good idea if we could be allowed a small sum of money to do a pilot season of dyke surveys out in the open fens downstream of the Nene and Welland valleys. By now I was convinced that close inspection of the layers revealed along exposed dykesides would be the only way to discover those deeply buried sites I was so keen to examine, before they all dried out. I don't think Geoff thought it would be a success, but he was always up for a challenge and decided to fund us for one season. In the event, the project lasted until 1986 and only stopped because we were too busy with various other excavations to do any more.[1]

It was mid-October, 1982 and I was returning to our base in Helpston. As I had done hundreds of times before, I turned the Land Rover away from the River Nene, and headed northwards, towards Peterborough. I knew that twisty old road well. We had just crossed the Roman Fen Causeway, which was showing up quite clearly in the freshly ploughed fields to my left, and we were now heading down to the edge of Whittlesey 'island', into Flag Fen, at Ha'penny Toll. I won't say that the edge of the 'island' is exactly hilly, but it must stand 4 or 5 metres (13–16 ft) above the surrounding peaty basin, and even on a dampish autumn afternoon, the view to the north-west was spectacular, with Peterborough Cathedral magnificently visible on the horizon (today it is hidden by the power station). Then something caught my eye.

I have to confess I am not always the most attentive of drivers and I have only been saved from several nasty accidents by Maisie's terrified screams from the passenger seat. The trouble is, I have always enjoyed working out landscape history, and

*A view of the dyke close to the spot where the Bronze Age timbers of Flag Fen were discovered, in November 1983. The water in the dyke is approximately at sea level. In the background is the dry land 'shoreline' of Fengate, a district of eastern Peterborough.*

sometimes clues glimpsed from the road can be very telling. Or at least, that's my story. On this particular day, I spotted something that actually made me pull over into a field gate, which I did suddenly and without any warning for the white van who was following far too closely behind me. He missed me, but I suspect not by much, for all my attention was taken by what I'd seen out there in Flag Fen.

Today, all dyke maintenance is done by hydraulic excavators, which in the Fens are usually fitted with long-reach digging arms. But in the late 1970s, a few drainage authorities still used draglines. Essentially, this was pre-war technology. I've never actually driven a dragline, but they consist of heavy-duty tracked cranes fitted with a digger bucket instead of a hook. The bucket gathers soil by being dragged back towards the machine by a powerful winch near the driver's cab. Hence the name. Being interested in all manner of earth-moving machines, I immediately recognized the jib out in Flag Fen as belonging to a 22RB, a popular middle range dragline built in Lincoln by Ruston Bucyrus. But what was it doing out in the middle of Flag Fen? By now, the mini-rush hour, when shifts changed at the huge Perkins Diesels factory at Fengate, had just begun, and the first workers were racing home to Whittlesey. Somehow I managed to turn the Land Rover around without an accident, and headed back towards the River Nene, where I could drive up onto the high bank and get a better view of Flag Fen. When I got there, I could see the dragline was working along the brinks of the deep engine drain (as dykes leading up to a pumping station are known) that serves the Padholme Pumping Station, which pumps floodwater from eastern Peterborough and Flag Fen up into the Nene. At this point, the embanked river flows high above the surrounding landscape.

I got back into the Land Rover and drove down to the pumping station, where I climbed the fence and started walking along the engine drain. It was beginning to rain, but I pressed on.

I arrived at the machine just as the driver was finishing his tea-time docky (a sandwich).[2] He was an old fen boy and he looked at me quizzically, as if I was slightly mad to be wading through damp slub on a wet afternoon. Later, Arthur was to work for us and then he let it be known that he knew immediately who I was, because he had keenly followed our exploits at Fengate. But he wasn't letting on now. Arthur had a fenman's sense of humour, which is very dry, and he was enjoying the situation. He had been cleaning out the bottom of the dyke and as I looked back along the drain I could see the edge profile of Whittlesey 'island', sloping down to the water at the bottom of the drain. I couldn't conceal my excitement: this was precisely the sort of buried, wet environment I'd been looking for.

I know it was silly of me, but I had to ask: 'Have you found anything interesting?'

He didn't reply, but pointed with his thumb to a twisted, rusting bicycle frame that he'd dumped behind the machine.

For a moment I was lost for words. It wasn't what I meant at all. Arthur's face was all innocence, with just the merest hint of a twinkle in his eyes. But I still didn't realize he was having me on.

Frowning, I tried another, more sensible, question. I asked him who was employing him on this job and he replied it was Anglian Water, as they were responsible for upkeep of the engine drain. That made sense. The next day I went to their offices in Wisbech, told them I wanted to look along the sides of the Padholme Engine Drain and they were more than happy to help. They even offered me the use of a small boat, which came in very useful later on.

The basic principle of all good archaeology is to work from the known to the unknown. In dyke survey this isn't always easy, because some dykes out in the middle of open, deep fens are slow to reveal their secrets, but an explanation for their presence can usually be found. In the case of the Engine Drain – or Mustdyke, to give it its medieval name – that crossed Flag Fen, the obvious starting point for our survey was at its southern end, by the Padholme Pumping Station. Here, the drain had been cut through the underlying glacial gravels that fringed the margins of Whittlesey 'island'. Those gravels gave us our securely 'known' (as opposed to 'unknown') starting point, to extend from.

We began recording profiles along the dykeside, which hadn't been left quite as clean by the dragline bucket as we would have liked, but we had spades and were prepared to use them. Meanwhile, Arthur and the dragline were still working their way steadily north. By early November he was approaching the clear, straight gravel line of the Fen Causeway in the ploughed field, which had now been drilled with winter wheat. So I took a couple of members of the team with me to record what Arthur revealed when he reached the Roman road.

I'd dug a couple of sections through the Fen Causeway when we were digging at Fengate and it hadn't been wildly exciting, then: basically, just a dump of gravel on a pre-Roman land surface – and no finds. Sadly, it was just as boring out in Flag Fen – and again, no finds. It took us a day to clean the section exposed on the dykeside for drawing and a few photos, and the following morning to record it all. So it was early afternoon when we decided to head to the Dog in a Doublet for lunch and a well-earned pint. My colleague, Dave, was walking ahead of me, carrying the dumpy level and tripod, I was following with my camera case, tripod, a range pole and a spade. Then it started to drizzle, as so often seems to happen in the Fens around lunchtime. My spirits rose: if it stayed wet, we'd have an excuse to extend our lunch in the pub. We had only walked for a short distance when my foot caught against something hard buried in the wet slub that Arthur had earlier spread out to dry along the top of the dykeside. Normally, I might well have ignored it, but something made me stop and put down the camera case. I reached into the slub and pulled out what looked like the sharpened tip of a disused fence post. Immediately I knew this was different. Even when covered with slimy, smelly slub I could see that it wasn't modern. By now I couldn't hide my excitement and I suspect my hands were shaking as I started to wipe it clean.

Clear axe marks had shaped the pointed end of the post. All modern fence posts are sharpened with circular saws, not with axes. But the marks I began to reveal beneath the mud hadn't been made with a modern, broad-bladed steel axe. During the previous summer I had taken our team to the Netherlands, where we had worked on wet prehistoric sites and I had learned to spot the distinctive narrow and slightly spoon-shaped marks left by a Late Bronze Age socketed axe. And that's what I was staring at now – wide-eyed. I was sure of it. I looked at the other end of the post, where it had been broken by the dragline. Like most wetland archaeologists, I had long known how to spot the distinctive pale medullary rays that run at right angles to the growth rings and give oak its great strength. Again, the use of oak was what one might have expected in the Late Bronze Age. And there were no trees, let alone oaks, growing in Flag Fen today.

By now, Dave was halfway back to the Land Rover and hunched against the gradually increasing rain. He was too far away to call back. Somehow I had to discover where that post had originally come from, before the dragline had dumped it on the brink. So, what the hell, I scrambled down the wet dykeside, using the spade as a break, but my inevitable slide into the cold water was suddenly stopped when my boot snagged against another piece of wood that had been caught by the dragline. Again, I could see instantly it was oak. There were other pieces too, all in a rough line about a metre below the bottom of the Roman Road. We knew that the peats around Flag Fen had accumulated at the rate of, very roughly, one millimetre a year, so if the Roman road had been built in the middle of the first century AD, then that meant the wood had been deposited, dumped or put there about a millennium earlier: say, 1000 BC, or just before – which would fit in very nicely with the date of those Late Bronze Age socketed axe marks. All in all, I was chuffed! I can't be certain, but I think Dave had to drive our Land Rover back from the Dog in a Doublet after lunch.[3]

Over the two months between the discovery of that first piece of wood and Christmas, we all worked on the dykeside of the Padholme Engine Drain, because it's one thing to find ancient wood, but quite another to explain how it got there, three millennia ago. The first thing we had to do was to determine the size of the deposit and to characterize it. Was it, for example, continuous and of the same thickness? Could it have been washed there by an ancient stream, or was it a deliberate deposit, by man – or indeed by beavers? With these questions in mind we began two months of intensive investigation.

In an ideal world I might have chosen two warmer months than November and December, but in retrospect it was the perfect time of year to excavate a waterlogged site: the days were cool and damp, but without the extreme winds and thunderstorms of spring and autumn; ground frosts had begun, but the far more damaging air frosts of January and February were still to come. The dampness of the atmosphere was to prove a huge bonus. Waterlogged wood isn't wood as we know it. After millennia of lying in wet ground it loses most of its strength and all of its flexibility – you can break thick logs across your knees.

These changes are due to complex chemical reactions brought about by soil acids and other natural agents in the groundwater. So although the preserved wood has lost its strength, flexibility and 'woodiness', its shape, size and surface appearance usually remain largely unaltered. I say 'usually' because certain factors, such as the weight of overlying deposits or episodic drying out, can lead to a degree of flattening or compression, where round logs, for example, become oval in section. The main problem facing anyone excavating waterlogged wood is how to keep it wet. In summertime I would strongly recommend a shelter to provide shade and protection from drying breezes. And then of course you must find a way of delivering dampening sprays, using either a watering can fitted with a fine rose or a garden sprayer. By the time we finished excavating at Flag Fen we had bought the local garden centre's entire stock of five- and ten-litre sprayers.

The first three weeks, almost to the end of November, were very exciting for all of our small team of about half-a-dozen people, because our initial task was simply to define the extent of the spread of wood along the dykeside. And it was to prove difficult, because the dragline had only dug out the bottom and the lowest sides of the dyke. The rest of the steep, V-shaped profile remained covered in matted grass, which had to be spaded off, by hand. They were a great three weeks: hard work, but exciting. Every day we discovered something new and unexpected. For a start, it took us at least a couple of weeks to find the edges of the spread of wood, which was an extraordinary 72 metres (78 yds) wide, or long (we didn't know which dimension we were measuring); it revealed about 500 pieces of wood. All the wood seemed to have been brought there and none was growing in situ. This would strongly suggest that the spread was not a natural deposit. Later, when she was examining the wood more closely, Maisie found very few pieces that had been felled or chewed by beaver, who leave very distinctive ripple-like tooth marks. However, the vast majority of the wood had either been felled, split or modified by the hand of man. Whatever this strange structure might have been, it was never a huge beaver dam.

Quite a high proportion of the wood was oak, which wouldn't have grown in such wet conditions, so it had to have been brought in from outside. The width of the growth rings suggested it had probably been grown and felled in reasonably dry conditions, perhaps in the gently rolling limestone hills of nearby Northamptonshire, or on higher ground away from the River Nene floodplain, which we knew had been cleared of tree cover at least two millennia previously. Other trees they used for timber included alder and willow/poplar (the two are very hard to distinguish under the microscope), plus some ash – all of which will grow around the edges of the Fens. Only the alder and willow will tolerate actual waterlogged conditions.

The northerly edge of the 'platform' (as we named the spread of wood) had clearly been constructed, with planks and split pieces of wood laid out on top of larger logs that had been sunk into the muds. I still think of this rather strange structure as the 'walkway'. Maybe boats were moored there? We just don't know. But the timbers that excited us most consisted of five quite distinct rows of posts, each one about a metre apart. The spaces between the rows of posts looked like they had been trampled: the pieces of horizontal wood were quite flat and some appeared to have been dusted with sand and fine gravel. I had never seen anything like it before, but I had to come up with some form of explanation: even in 1982 'We don't know what it is' would have sounded very lame. So I said that I thought the posts were part of a rectangular structure, possibly a house, that had been built (and subsequently rebuilt many times) on a timber platform. I'm fairly certain I had those Swiss Lake Villages in the back of my mind. Anyway, the news media loved it and we were featured on Radio 4's *Today* programme, and all the national newspapers and television news.

The following year we returned for a first season of excavation, which would be accompanied by an exploratory survey, using hand-held soil drills, or augers, which would attempt to pin down the size and extent of the timber platform. This survey was carried out by our soils specialist, Charly French. Charly was never a weightlifter, nor a big man, but somehow he and an assistant managed to twist the handles of that auger so that it penetrated down through over a metre of flood clays and peaty silts, until it struck either gravel or, more likely, wood. He did this hundreds of times, recording the position and depth of everything in each borehole. I was his assistant on a few days and on each occasion I would get home in the evening with my shoulders throbbing. After about six weeks' work, Charly's auger survey revealed that the platform covered an astonishing 5.46 acres (2,21 ha).

In the main excavations, of 1986–95, we focused our attention on the five rows of posts and more particularly on the floor-like surfaces between them. The outer two rows still retained evidence for a wattle wall or revetment, but there was no evidence that this had ever been coated with 'daub', the clay-and-manure prehistoric precursor of plaster (which wasn't introduced until Roman times). The house theory was further supported over the following three seasons by the discovery of worn and fragmentary pieces of Late Bronze Age pottery – on a dry land settlement they would have been described as 'domestic debris' – plus several pieces of animal bone. We also learned that the sand between the posts had certainly been brought there, because Charly was able to identify that it was probably from the Nene gravels. He was quite certain that it could never have been moved into Flag Fen by flowing water. So by the end of the 1987 season, when we opened Flag Fen to the public (about which more in a moment), the house hypothesis was beginning to look very plausible. But, contrary to the Indiana Jones view of archaeology, the biggest revelations often happen when the picks, shovels and trowels have been laid aside.

*

Archaeology is generally classed with the humanities, like its co-discipline anthropology, and most people regard it as having more in common with social sciences, such as sociology, than with the so-called hard sciences. But my personal background was in botany, geology and zoology and I have always tended to favour such evidence. I try never to miss an opportunity to see what science can tell us and during that first season at Flag Fen our excavations were visited by numerous specialists in everything from pollen grains to seeds and beetles. So it came as a great shock when, in the winter of 1987–88, our beetles expert made an unexpected phone call to tell me that he could find no evidence at all for the presence of woodworm in or around the supposed 'house'.[4] 'Woodworm' is the general term for many species of beetles, whose larvae bore their way into wood, leaving the distinctive small, round holes. The trouble is that prior to modern chemical treatment, woodworm was endemic in all domestic structures and farm buildings in Britain. Woodworm-free houses simply didn't exist and older buildings were often riddled with it. They thrive in the warmer, drier conditions of the roof space of thatched houses.

I discussed the problem with Charly and other members of the team and we all agreed that there was quite a lot about the 'house' theory that we didn't like: the floors were very rough and uneven, there were no clear partitions or doorways and abso-lutely no signs (nor space for) a hearth, or hearths. So the lack of woodworm, that unavoidable component of all early houses in Britain, came as the final nail in the theory's coffin. So if it wasn't a house, what was it?

I had long had an ambition to run a dig that people could visit and our site huts at Fengate in the 1970s had even featured a small museum. But I wanted Flag Fen to be different: more professional and better organized. Ultimately, I wanted the admission fees to pay either for running the dig or for a substantial proportion of it. I was also very concerned that Flag Fen was drying out (which is something we were later able to prove). So before we opened the site to the public in 1987, we decided to construct an artificial lake to keep the platform and its timbers wet. We did this by inserting a waterproof membrane 'skirt' through the 3 metres (10 ft) of silts and peats that overlay the glacial clay into which the Bronze Age posts had been driven. Once the membrane had been inserted, we started to pump in water from the Mustdyke. It took several weeks before the shallow lake formed.

We decided to make the most of the lake to enhance Flag Fen as a visitor attraction, because it didn't have much going for it. Most people's initial reaction on first visiting the site was, to put it mildly, unenthusiastic. The land had been used until very recently as a sewage settling ground and there was still a background smell. The view towards Peterborough was blighted by factory construction and the open Fens to the south and east were concealed by the bank of the Nene, the embanked Whittlesey road and a disused gravel pit. Finally, the southern skyline was dominated by the massive chimneys of the Whittlesey brickworks, whose smoke would add a wine-taster's 'sulphurous notes' to the sewage-tainted air. And this, as I started to say, is where the lake came in.

We knew we would have to have a visitor centre and a site museum, and we were also aware that any construction out in Flag Fen would probably damage the buried timbers and other remains. So we decided to build a semi-floating structure in the lake – which we did with help from Ove Arup, a major firm of consulting engineers, who happened to have an office in Peterborough. We also thought it would be a good idea if we could make a model reconstruction of the Bronze Age platform, as a small island complete with fibreglass houses, which might draw peoples' eyes from the realities of the modern landscape around them.

To provide soil to build up the model's surface we scraped a few inches off what would later be the lakebed. To our amazement we exposed the tops of several dozen semi-rotted posts, which had survived far higher than we had anticipated. At the time we assumed these posts belonged to another house. And now the plot begins to thicken.

We had inserted the plastic sheet around the lake in July 1987 and while we were doing the work we kept a close watch for ancient posts and other timbers, which we found in several places. The following winter we plotted the location of everything we had found and discovered that the rows of posts in our main excavation along the Mustdyke lined up with those along the artificial lake-edge and around the model island. So we didn't have a house at all, but something more like a barrier, a road or a causeway. But what should we call it? I hesitated. It wasn't only that I had got it very wrong when I had labelled it a 'building', I was also aware that names in archaeology could cause problems and sometimes be very misleading. In some respects I had sympathy with the people who called those early social and ceremonial centres 'causewayed enclosures'. It wasn't a very appealing name, but it wasn't loaded with other meanings, either – unlike a term such as 'hillfort'.

Hillforts occur widely across highland and lowland areas of Britain. They were often settlements and sometimes more than that: centres of population, and not just for people – some were probably intended to enclose and protect herds of cattle or flocks of sheep. They are defined by one or more deep ditch with an accompanying internal bank (henge banks were external), which together form a physical barrier, known as a rampart. These were often further strengthened by walls, fences or palisades. The trouble is, the more we investigate and learn about hillforts, the more complex they become and it is now quite clear that the name is very misleading: they were often far more than mere forts placed on hills – and as if to emphasize this, we know of two substantial hillforts in the heart of the Fens.*

So what was I to call the new site at Flag Fen? I rejected all names that included functional terms that implied a particular purpose, such as road, causeway or barrier – although it may well have been used as all three of these at various times. Instead, I opted for something simpler and more descriptive, even if it isn't very sexy: I labelled it a 'post alignment'. It's a term that seems to have stuck, although I now see it has been dropped from the current Flag Fen visitors' guide, in favour of 'causeway', but I can't say I'm too worried: the name I chose was aimed more at archaeologists and other specialists than the general public. Its aims were modest and it serves its purpose, still.

The reason I was determined not to call the post alignment by a more usual name was quite simply that I didn't believe that, as a site, it was at all straightforward. Indeed, during the summer of 1989 we could confirm that it was a great deal more complex than just a road or causeway. Our excavations in the mid-1980s revealed that it had been actively maintained for some 400 years, but continued to be used and visited for double that time – right through to the Roman period, to judge by the many Iron Age finds we discovered along its length.

In its initial phase, shortly after 1300 BC, there seem to have been just two rows of posts, which were separated by quite a wide gap. At the same time there was some evidence that the route of the alignment was subdivided by screens of brushwood or larger logs into a series of short segments, of about 5 or 6 metres (16–20 ft) long. Special offerings of metal objects or pottery had been placed into the water or damp ground around these screens.

---

* See Chapter 8, pp. 155–179.

*Bronze Age timbers at Flag Fen, as first exposed by excavation in 1987. Note the large split oak plank and the long, pencil-like sharpened tip of an unused oak post. Both are resting on the surface of slightly raised paths or walkways that ran between parallel rows of posts.*

*The same area three years later. The large horizontal timbers have been removed, as have at least two layers of wood chips and other debris that served to build up the causeway's surface.*

This pattern recalls the segmented ditches of the much earlier causewayed enclosures, where most offerings were concentrated at the causeways. I'm not suggesting for one moment that there was any kind of direct link between sites that were separated by over two millennia, but I think they both might be reflecting a common underlying theme of clan and family. Maybe the segments at Flag Fen, too, were visited by members of a particular family, who commemorated their ancestors, the recently deceased and other family history with their offerings.

We saw at Etton how the offerings in the ditch segments often symbolized domestic life. The same could be said for those at Flag Fen. I would suggest that the many bronze and bone weapons – including swords, daggers and spearheads – had been placed in the ground to commemorate the passing of male ancestors. Similarly, brooches, pins and even jewellery (we found a small gold ring, probably part of quite an elaborate, Swiss-made earring) would have celebrated the lives of women. But when, in 1989, we did a much larger-scale excavation of the posts at the point where the alignment reached dry land at Fengate, we found offerings that suggested that some of the rites were more diverse. We also acquired some fascinating insights into the nature of the ceremonies – I am tempted to call them services – that took place there.

We did a complete metal-detector survey before we began to machine through the higher silts that covered the posts. Removing these deposits would have been impossible by hand, as we needed to expose just over 50 metres (55 yds) of the alignment in a single year. This was because the area was threatened by the construction of the new Fengate, North Sea gas-fired power station. In the end, I was delighted by the results and I also realized that digging the site entirely by hand would ultimately have led to its destruction, because many of the posts were already in an advanced state of drying out and would soon have crumbled to dust. I think we got there in the nick of time.

The metal-detector survey revealed that offerings had been placed directly over the posts and in a wide band along their southern side. The post alignment ran across a narrow 'strait' of wetland that would have linked the Flag Fen basin to the open Fens. If we imagine that the people who lived and farmed around the margins of the basin would have regarded Flag Fen as somehow theirs to graze, fish and, ultimately, to control, then the relatively narrow (about 1,100 metres/1,200 yds) 'strait' between the dry land at Fengate and Whittlesey 'island' would be the only access into their essentially enclosed landscape from the broader Fens to the north and east. So it came as no surprise when we discovered that some of the posts had originally been quite substantial and would have formed a tall barrier or screen across the access to Flag Fen. That would explain why the offerings revealed by the metal detectors were only found along the south, Flag Fen, side of the posts. Finally, and as if to prove the 'inside/outside' theory, we briefly revealed the much-decayed remains of a human skeleton on the north, or 'outside', of the posts. None of the bones survived and the body was revealed as a pale stain in the overlying flood clays. When we compared the depth or level of the body with that of finds revealed above the posts, he or she was probably buried in the early Iron Age – sometime in the centuries around 600 BC. Had the ground not dried out, this would probably have been a so-called Iron Age bog body, many of which have been shown to have been sacrificed.

The offerings in the waters around the posts at Flag Fen are part of a far wider, north European phenomenon in which wetlands were regarded as being spiritually and symbolically important places: on the boundaries between the ideological worlds of the gods and the ancestors. In Britain, there seems to have been a major shift in prehistoric religious attitudes in the centuries around 1500 BC. This was the time when we see henges and many other features of the older ritual landscapes being

*A selection of bronze swords, daggers and spearheads found at Flag Fen. Many of these objects have been deliberately damaged, such as the sword (top), which has been broken along a casting flaw at the widest part of the blade. These weapons mostly date to 1200–900 BC.*

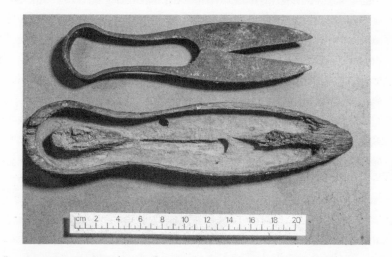

*A pair of bronze shears, found with their carved wooden box at the Flag Fen Power Station excavations of 1989. These shears are unique in Britain and date to the early Iron Age (c.600 BC). They were probably used to cut hair and beards, rather than to shear sheep.*

abandoned in favour of the new river and wetland-focused rites. These new rites were far smaller in scale and were more locally based. We also see a return to less centralized and more family-focused ceremonies, which is why I have described the change as the Domestic Revolution.[5] It was a revolution in terms of speed – maybe two or three centuries – rather than violence, for which there is no evidence at all. It would have been encouraged, if not enabled, by the development of the landscape, which might be considered as developed by the mid-second millennium BC: in other words, large areas of trees and scrub had been cleared from most lowland areas and a network of roads and tracks now linked the many settlements of Britain together. At the same time, man-made routes, streams and rivers would have provided the barriers that separated the territories of local communities. I described the changes around 1500 BC as being domestic, but I could also have said that these were the years when local government, which of course had been present from earliest times, became more formalized. As time passed, and most particularly in the later Iron Age, after about 300 BC, larger tribal groupings began to emerge, eventually giving rise to the pre-Roman tribal kingdoms, such as that of the Iceni of northern East Anglia and their rebellious queen, Boudicca.

But what did Flag Fen reveal about the rites themselves: why and how were people making offerings to the waters? The trouble is that Hollywood and Arthurian Romance have coloured our view of ancient water-based rituals, which we imagine involved throngs of people, grand gestures and much cheering, when the hand of the Lady of the Lake grasps the flying sword Excalibur and carries it down into her watery realms. Sadly, I don't think that's what actually happened at all.

Swords certainly played an important role in these ceremonies, indeed I have suggested that the Excalibur legend dates back to the Late Bronze Age, when swords were not beaten out by iron smiths, but were cast in stone moulds – hence Arthur's removal of the sword from the stone.[6] But when we plotted the exact location of the swords that had been broken, we found that the various pieces of blade, hilt, rivets etc. were invariably close together – maybe spread over a couple of square metres. That does not suggest big gestures: warriors hurling weapons far out into the waters. Rather, it implies a more intimate gathering, of perhaps a few dozen people, standing together in a family group. We saw this particularly clearly when we excavated the blade and hilt of a bronze dagger, where the two had been pulled apart and then carefully positioned in the shallow water, so that the blade lay on top of the antler hilt. Inside the socket of the hilt we found two very thin but finely fashioned oak wedges. Again, this suggests the careful but deliberate breaking of, perhaps, a much-loved grandfather's prized possession, rather than the ritualized destruction of an enemy's weapon in front of a huge crowd.

I love it when archaeological finds speak to us so directly. When our metalwork specialists examined a couple of the broken swords they noticed that they had broken across casting flaws. This was hardly surprising, because cast bronze swords require deep, narrow moulds where air blocks can readily happen. We also know that many recent societies that employed similar metalworking techniques often treated the day when castings were to be made with special respect. Sometimes the clay moulds and furnaces were fashioned to resemble the bodies of pregnant women. Often women were barred from workshops during casting. So the casting of metal objects was seen as a form of birth. If something similar applied in the British Bronze Age, which seems highly probable to me, then it is not surprising that newly cast but flawed swords were consigned to the waters in a special place. They had been 'born', and most probably named, too, and therefore required appropriate disposal, with due reverence. Although it wasn't their intention, it's also worth adding here that such practices would have helped retain the value of bronze for the smiths and merchants who produced and traded it.

The finds from Flag Fen also provide glimpses of the impact the new technologies must have had on contemporary society. Finds that intrigued us included two groups of two miniature lead anvils and no fewer than fourteen tanged awls – small, sharp etching tools the size of two-inch long nails. The anvils and the awls were both metalworkers' tools. At the time of the excavation, we were very much thinking in terms of death: that so many of the items would have been offered to the ancestors and the next world to accompany somebody who had just died. But one day I was chatting with the team about what we had done as vacation jobs and after leaving university. I can't remember if we were in the pub, but I suspect we may have been, because I was holding forth about my time working at Truman's Brewery.* In those days the brewery still had a coopers' workshop, where the thousands of oak barrels (with wonderful names like tun, firkin, kilderkin, butt and hogshead) were made, maintained and repaired. It took years of training to become a qualified cooper and the ceremony that marked the transition from apprentice to skilled craftsman was elaborate and involved being rolled around the workshop in a barrel made by the newly qualified cooper himself, which was filled with all sorts of nasty solids and unmentionable liquids. The apprentice's barrel had to be fashioned with the tools he had made – and this set me thinking. Maybe those miniature lead anvils and tanged awls had been placed in the sacred waters of Flag Fen as part of metalworkers' apprenticeship ceremonies?

But there were other clues as to the nature of those long-forgotten rituals. The site revealed dozens of pins, rings and brooches, which might well have been offered to the waters during wedding or betrothal ceremonies. There were also four complete

* See p. 6.

quernstones, three of which came from unidentified quarries in Wales or the west, but one could be identified to a small area of Kent. These must have been very valuable items indeed and had to be made from the right sort of rock – otherwise the flour they made would be contaminated by sand and grit. We can only speculate as to how the querns from the west reached Flag Fen, but the one from Kent was too heavy for a man to carry and must surely have been transported along the east coast, by boat. Again, we don't know why these useful and expensive items were offered to the waters, but it was probably to mark an important event, such as a marriage or the completion of a new house.

While we were excavating at Flag Fen we would sometimes be visited by the dean, and even by the bishop, of Peterborough. They knew my views, or rather my non-views, on religion, but were very nice about it. I remember once greeting one of them with something like: 'Welcome newcomers, to the cathedral's prehistoric ancestor.' A bit corny, I concede, but that was how we thought of Flag Fen in the last two decades of the twentieth century: like the great Cathedral of St Peter in the middle distance, it was the place where most rituals and ceremonies had to happen. I now realize that this was a very ethnocentric view: we were imposing our Western concepts of religion and ideology – where ceremonies take place in churches and chapels on certain days – onto a pre-modern society. I no longer believe that Bronze Age people compartmentalized their lives to the extent that we do. Distinct, defined entities, such as employment, worship, relaxation, domestic life or the dreaded 'me time', simply didn't exist. Instead, their outlook was suffused by elements of work, religion, family and history to provide what we would now see as a rich and all-encompassing view of the world. By the mid-1990s we were just starting to glimpse these things. But even then, I don't think we could possibly have anticipated the extraordinary developments that were about to overtake us.

# Must Farm:
# At Last, a 'Lake Village'

*Discovery – Contract or 'Rescue' Archaeology
– Prehistoric Populations – West Deeping – The
Southern Fens – Bradley Fen – Bronze Age Boats –
The Must Farm 'Lake Village'*

It was the turn of the millennium. The writing of the large Flag Fen report, which was published in 2001,[1] was in its final stages. Life was getting very busy. In the late 1990s several publishers wanted me to write more popular books and a television programme that I didn't think would ever get off the ground had become a huge success: *Time Team* had arrived on the scene and, for better or for worse, I was very much a part of it. They even filmed an episode at Flag Fen in the summer of 1999. Amidst all this frantic activity, a local friend and colleague, Martin Redding, came to us with some unusual and potentially very exciting news. Martin had been with our various Peterborough projects for many years during his school and student days and he had always been mad keen on archaeology. His family lived in Whittlesey, just 3 miles (5 km) from Flag Fen, and on weekends Martin liked to patrol the local brickpits, on the lookout for anything archaeological. One day he thought he'd found something very interesting and he phoned Maisie and me to see if we'd care to pay a visit. Of course we said yes.

We had to make our way through quite a dense growth of seedling bushes and sapling ash and willow trees, which had grown up around the deep brickpit since its abandonment many years previously. We walked around the edge of the old brickworks for about five minutes, before Martin led us down the sloping clay sides of the pit. It was hard to be certain precisely where the modern land surface was, or had been, because the ground was so disturbed, but Martin reckoned we were probably 2 or even 3 metres (6–10 ft) into the flood clays that capped the underlying grey Jurassic Oxford Clay, which was what the brickmakers had been seeking. It was then that I spotted what he had discovered.

Immediately below where we were standing, and protruding between tufts of coarse grass and dock seed heads, was quite a dense scatter of wooden post-tops. At first glance they resembled the posts revealed along the dykeside at Flag Fen, but we needed to do more than just guess. On closer inspection, they proved to be quite dry and flaky and Maisie snapped a bit off one to look at it more closely. I could see her frowning as she examined it. Then she announced it was oak, and split – just like the posts at Flag Fen. We were all pretty certain that it was another post alignment, but it didn't seem quite as wide as Flag Fen. So maybe it was a bit simpler: either a barrier or a causeway. We couldn't be at all certain about the date, but the use of split oak and its likely depth below the surface suggested it was probably prehistoric – and perhaps roughly contemporary with Flag Fen. Future events were to show our guess was broadly correct, but hopelessly unambitious: Must Farm, the site it revealed, was to prove far, far more exciting.

★

The last decade of the twentieth century was a time of momentous change in British archaeology, due entirely to the introduction of the new principle in planning law – that the developer pays. It signalled an end to the old hand-to-mouth way of doing things, where small teams of archaeologists (often amateurs) grappled with the excavation of huge housing estates or massive gravel pits, paid for by a cash-strapped English Heritage, an even more impoverished local authority or, in my case, a Canadian museum. By 1995 a system of contract archaeology had come to replace the earlier informal way of doing what we used to call rescue archaeology. The work was now done by limited companies of professional archaeologists, generally known as excavation units, who won the new projects that their survival depended upon through a system of competitive tendering. Individual projects were overseen and regulated by local authorities. Although I rather regretted the passing of the older, cheery and somewhat hit-and-miss way of doing things, we now lived in a world where projects had strict timetables and many of the people involved were highly litigious and employed top lawyers. Everyone and everything, it seemed, had to be fully insured. I can see now that archaeology had at last come of age and was ready to compete in the twenty-first century.

The Fens are surrounded by deep deposits of gravel, laid down by glacial action during the Ice Ages. As we saw previously, these had been exploited earlier, but by the 1990s a single survey in a slim volume, like *A Matter of Time*, would not be adequate to meet the new demands. So a series of computer-based archives of aerial photographs, maps and finds records was established by county councils, known today as HERs or Historic Environment Records. Of course, there was a downside to all of this standardization and competition: some of the excavations were, to put it very kindly, minimal.

Many of the people actually doing the work came from outside our region and had no experience or knowledge of fenland archaeology. Sometimes I would be called in to advise if a site presented problems. I was once being shown 'a linear', as ditches were then known in the jargon. Did I have any idea what it might be? I took a quick stroll around the site and saw that the 'linear' was running at right angles to the nearby wetland. There was another one, parallel to it for some distance, and others could be seen joining it. It was plainly part of a Bronze Age field system. I told the excavator, who looked at me blankly: he had no idea there were prehistoric field systems in the area. Later, over a cup of tea, I discovered that his background and experience was in Roman archaeology. He had never worked on a prehistoric site before.

I had many other, similar experiences in the 1990s, most of which were very disheartening. But sometime around the turn of the millennium, locally based units became better established and standards started to improve. Developers also began to realise the good PR potential of archaeology and were prepared to provide much better funding – and over a longer period. This allowed top-quality research projects, with outside and academic contributors, to be established. Today, some of the most imaginative and technically advanced excavations in the world are taking place in the Fens.

Although they were far from perfect, even the poorer-quality developer-funded excavations of the 1990s provided plans and information on finds, which could be used to build up a bigger picture. They were much better than the unrecorded total destruction that was so commonplace both before the war and throughout the 1950s, '60s and even into the '70s and '80s. We must never allow our unique treasury of archaeological sites to be treated with such ignorance and, yes, contempt, ever again.

The picture of later prehistoric life in the Fens that emerged as a result of developer-funded excavation is, to say the very least, extremely complex. By and large, the impression one gains is of prosperity combined with social flexibility, resulting in successful adaptation to constantly changing environments. And notice here that I refer to environments, plural, because the way that fields, settlements, barrows and boundaries were arranged differs quite widely around the areas we know were farmed and settled in the Bronze Age. There has recently been quite a lot of discussion about the extent to which people living around the edges of the Fens also exploited higher and better-drained land. My own feeling is that this was quite limited, because most of it was open and not parcelled up into fields.

It is evident that both sheep and cattle farmers in the most densely populated fen margins went to great lengths to ensure that their animals didn't mix with those of other farmers around them. Speaking as a livestock farmer myself, I can readily understand this, because inbreeding can cause many problems throughout a herd or flock – some of which can prove very hard to remove, even with modern medicines. We also know from analyses of cattle teeth that new bloodlines were introduced to the Flag Fen area from farmers as far away as the Peak District and even eastern Scotland.[2] The prevailing academic view would see such long-distance exchange as being about elites demonstrating their power and influence. That might apply too – but farming common sense would suggest that the acquisition of fresh breeding stock from far away was more important – especially in these developing regional economies that depended so heavily on livestock.

The great expansion of excavation that followed the planning changes of 1989 may not always have been perfect, but it did produce a huge amount of additional information, much of which lay hidden in the so-called grey literature of clients' reports in the various county Historic Environment Records. Most archaeologists knew about the research in their areas of interest, but few attempts were made to draw this mass of new material into a coherent story, until 2007. In that year two books were published, both of which drew attention to the large number of new Bronze Age field systems and other sites in the Fens and the rivers draining into them.[3]

Those of us who had been active in research were aware that there were differences in the way that fields, farms, settlements and ceremonial areas were arranged in each region, but the subtleties that were now revealed were remarkable. First inspection of the new material confirmed what many of us had long suspected, that organization of the landscape was essentially based around the natural drainage pattern of rivers flowing into the Fens. Although clear when mapped out, the geography of the fen-edge didn't determine how and why people came to live and work in a particular area; this was because out in the open floodplains of the Fens, boundaries became far less distinct. I suspect these would have been areas where communities were able to mix and exchange ideas. This may well help explain the economic vigour that seems to have been such a feature of the Fens in the Neolithic, Bronze and Iron Ages. It also became clear that long-cherished rules of prehistoric behaviour simply didn't apply in these areas: burial mounds, for example, were not necessarily confined to those less accessible, more liminal, areas away from the fields and settlements. Like all of my colleagues, I was forcibly struck by the enormous complexity of the pre-Roman landscape and by the pace and subtlety of the way it evolved through time. Sometimes this evolution was in response to environmental change, but often it was a result of factors that were harder to pin down and probably reflected social, political or economic influences. It's worth remembering that in Tudor times the Dissolution of the Monasteries had a profound effect on the fenland landscape and there must have been equivalents of it in prehistory as well.

The new picture of the prehistoric Fens was also important because it provided a coherent context for later Roman, Saxon and medieval developments that used to be thought of as dramatic impositions on a nearly blank canvas. The economic upsurge that took place in Roman times can be explained better if the size of the pre-Roman Iron Age population was very much larger than was once believed. Similarly, the major changes that happened after the Roman period, in early Saxon times, need not necessarily be attributed to waves of incoming Germanic invaders, for which there is no physical evidence. Instead we must look to the substantial indigenous population of the area as the agent of these innovations, many of which were inspired by new ideas from overseas and the evolving political identities of post-Roman Britain. I suspect that the complexity of the many prehistoric Fen landscapes was probably just a faint reflection of the regional and wider political worlds that shaped and modified them. It would be a huge mistake to assume that life was somehow simpler in prehistoric times.

Most of the extensively settled and well-organized prehistoric landscapes of the Fens are preserved in two areas: around the rivers Nene and Welland, to the west, and from the Great Ouse, north of Huntingdon, eastwards as far as the River Lark, downstream of Mildenhall (Suffolk), in the south. The north and north-western fen-edge does not (at present) appear to have any substantial prehistoric field systems, but the current construction of the new south-eastern bypass to the City of Lincoln may well reveal them in the upper reaches of the Witham Valley. I suspect that some may well lie below the thick accumulations of later silts that are such a feature of the northern Fens.

In the mid-1990s I visited, for the first time, a site just outside the village of West Deeping in the lower Welland Valley, about a mile to the west of the charming town of Market Deeping, which is just sufficiently distant from Peterborough to retain its local character. When we were working at Maxey and Etton we would often visit its pubs, butchers, open market and fine fish and chips shops. I visited the site only a few times, because it was being dug under great pressure so that gravel extraction could start on time. I knew only too well what that was like and didn't want to delay things, so my visits were short – and I hope sweet.

Air photos of the land about to be quarried for gravel at West Deeping showed a great expanse of Bronze Age fields, covering, or rather surviving, across a huge area, of some 630 acres (255 ha). Despite being quite close to the large Bronze Age ritual landscape at Maxey, the field system at West Deeping included some barrows, which had clearly been integrated into the field system and formed a part of it. Doubtless the presence of the ancestors would have helped to maintain long-lived farm and property boundaries, as we found at Fengate and elsewhere. This was a good example of the way that in prehistoric times belief and religion were integral components of daily life.

At Fengate, the parallel droveways ran down to the fen-edge at right angles, which is what happened at West Deeping, except that the wetland was now the floodplain of the River Welland. The West Deeping droveways were about 250–400 yards (229–366 m) apart and were quite narrow, like those at Fengate. But I was forcibly struck by the presence of four, and possibly five, quite distinct livestock handling yards. I examined the air photos closely and I could detect indications that these had been subdivided into smaller yards and pens. It was just as if I had been looking at a modern livestock handling system, where the yards and pens would have been of decreasing size, as animals were sorted into various groups for different purposes. Again, I was in no doubt that this fragment of a larger Bronze Age field system had been used to handle substantial flocks and herds.

But there was one new factor that fascinated me: the stockyards had all been placed on the same, roughly westerly, side of each droveway. I was delighted to see this, as it supported the idea I had floated at Fengate – that the droveways separated individual family holdings and had been arranged to cause the minimum disturbance to other farmers.

If you have ever taken sheep or cattle to a market or county show, you will know only too well that when people are handling livestock nearby, it will make the animals you are trying to groom very restless. So stockyards are best kept well apart, which can best be achieved if everyone agrees to follow the same guiding principles. And that is clearly what was happening at West Deeping. The regular and careful layout of Bronze Age field systems around the Fens, and indeed elsewhere in Britain, such as the Thames Valley, Dartmoor and across huge tracts of downland in southern England, suggests that local communities were in close contact with each other and also possessed formal systems of local government, probably on tribal grounds.[4] There would also have been the informal arrangements between neighbouring farmers that we had discovered when we established our own small fenland sheep farm. These enclosed and controlled local landscapes would provide an ideal basis for agricultural expansion, and with it population growth during the first millennium BC, and into Roman times. The Fens were an integral and important part of this larger story of increasing prosperity; although low lying and at times very wet, these productive landscapes would certainly not have been seen as either peripheral or marginal.

I want to turn my attention briefly to the flat river floodplains of the southern Fens, before returning to the landscape around Flag Fen and the extraordinary discoveries that have been made there.

By now it must be quite clear to many readers that I have very warm feelings towards the Bronze Age and this is partly because we have taken so long to appreciate the period as more than a source of beautiful metalwork or glorious monuments such as Stonehenge. This would be rather like trying to understand life in the Middle Ages by looking at cathedrals and illuminated manuscripts alone. To get a more rounded picture you need to research into the houses, farms and workshops of ordinary people, as this was where the wealth that paid for the fine buildings and great artworks was generated. In archaeology, it was the expansion of contract-based research in the 1990s that opened our eyes to the true extent of Bronze Age farming and the influence it gave people on their landscapes and environment.

Cambridge has long been one of the most prosperous cities of England, in part due to the presence of a great university at its heart. In the 1970s we began to see the appearance of science parks and high-tech industrial areas where small companies could expand rapidly in the new realms of biotechnology and microelectronics. When I was at Cambridge in the mid-1960s, everyone was talking about the potential impact that Watson and Crick's discovery of the molecular structure of DNA would have on the economy. Things were very slow at first, but began to happen in the 1970s. The expansion of what some still call Silicon Fen, and with it the accommodation of people who worked there, required new roads, buildings and services – all of which relied heavily on a good supply of sand, aggregates and gravels. The result was a massive expansion of the gravel pits in the lower valleys of rivers draining into the Fens near Cambridge, principally the Great Ouse, Cam and, to a lesser extent, the rivers Snail, Lark and Little Ouse, across the county boundary, in Suffolk.

Haddenham, in the Ouse Valley,* was one of the sites affected

---

* See Chapter 3.

by the expansion of gravel pits and in the early 1980s we enjoyed countless mugs of tea at our farmhouse near Parson Drove, in Cambridgeshire, with their discoverer David Hall. David's surveys were fundamentally important because they covered not just the known archaeologically rich areas of the fen-edge, but extended out into the deeper fen, where conventional air photography was less effective. Today there are new aerial survey techniques, such as LiDAR,* which can detect any buried features, especially barrows that protrude even a few inches through the later peats and flood clays covering them. Back in the 1980s, David's approach was all we had, but it was a technique that also allowed finds to be collected. If it hadn't been for David's surveys, many of the barrow fields and other large sites that were excavated in the 1990s, and later, would never have been discovered.

A comprehensive description of the Bronze Age landscapes recently revealed in the southern Fens would be quite a major undertaking, because the newly discovered fields, settlements, farms and houses varied a great deal and many of the more shallow-ditched field systems appear to have been quite short lived.[5] The resulting complexity can sometimes seem rather overwhelming. But a few general observations can be made. Fences seemed to have been employed, along with hedges, and there is evidence that rows of single post screens were used to link different parts of the landscape with areas that were religiously significant and contained barrows and other monuments.

The use of so many posts, all of roughly the same diameter, would strongly suggest that large areas of woodland were being carefully managed, by regular coppicing and pollarding, to produce good, straight poles that could be cut into posts. By the second millennium BC, not many areas of woodland in lowland

---

* Light Detection and Ranging.

Britain would have been 'wild', in the sense of unexplored virgin forest. Again, the use of these wooden screens seems to have been an attempt to further integrate the realm of the ancestors and other religious beliefs into people's day-to-day lives. There is also some evidence in the later Bronze Age (in the final two or three centuries of the second millennium BC) for the rise of an elite class who lived in a remarkable rectangular hall-like building that echoed contemporary Europe, and would certainly not have been out of place in Britain in the early Middle Ages. Again, as we saw at Fengate, livestock farming was far more intensive than mere subsistence farming. These people understood their complex landscapes well and managed them very effectively.

I love it when new information comes to light, but it's even better if it appears at a time when you really need it. After Martin's discovery of those posts in the Whittlesey brickpit in 1999, everything went quiet. The next thing I knew was that the Cambridge University Unit were digging a site quite close to them in the same brickpits on the far (southern) side of the Flag Fen basin. The site in question was called Bradley Fen and, lo and behold, they had Bronze Age fields and settlements that very much recalled Fengate, but were far better preserved, because they were lower lying, wetter and covered by many thick layers of protective flood clays. It was a fascinating site and I visited it frequently.

By the year 2000 I was no longer running full-time excavations. This was in part because I was rapidly approaching sixty, but I also felt very strongly that archaeology had to reach a broader public if it were to survive into what seemed to me to be a very uncertain future. I have never thought of myself as an economic forecaster, but from the early years of the new millennium I sensed that a banking crisis was approaching – although I have to confess that I thought it would arrive before 2007/8.

In 2002–2003 I was writing *Britain BC* and was preparing to film its mini-series for Channel Four; I was also filming more and more programmes for *Time Team*. Research for the book and subsequent filming took me right around Britain, where I met all sorts of people, rich and poor. These encounters did nothing to remove my profound feeling of impending doom, which was getting steadily worse.

All of these things were occupying my thoughts when I made those first visits to the Cambridge Unit's Bradley Fen excavations in 2001. I knew that I could continue to write about my own team's researches at Etton, Maxey, Fengate and Flag Fen, but I was also aware that I needed something new to enthuse me. Ideally, this would be something that could be related to the earlier work and reveal it from a different angle. And that was what the new excavations, first at Bradley Fen, then more recently at nearby Must Farm (from 2005), were able to do. Looking back on it, they gave my work, but also my own career, which was now shifting into the broader world of public archaeology, new impetus. Their discoveries were so important that nobody could possibly ignore them. At least, that was what I hoped.

Many members of the Cambridge team were old friends and colleagues, who invariably welcomed Maisie and me when we turned up on site. That meant a lot to us – and still does. On our early visits to Bradley Fen, the archaeology resembled what we had been excavating at Fengate, some twenty years previously. There were the familiar foundations of roundhouses and field boundary ditches, all cut into a very similar-looking gravel sub-soil. But as time passed and the excavators moved ever closer to the wetland-edge, the story grew rapidly more exciting. The first results of the new wetland-edge excavations came to light just in time for the publication of *Britain BC* and the unit very kindly sent me a plan of what they had revealed.[6] It showed that the change from wet to dry was very significant to those Bronze

Age farmers. Their shallow field boundaries ran right up to the wetland-edge, where another shallow ditch marked the precise wet/dry division. On the 'dry' side were all the usual signs of settlement: pits, post-holes and the foundations of roundhouses. But immediately along the 'wet' side of the boundary were a series of features that were carefully positioned to line up with the different fields or landholdings, just across the boundary ditch on the 'dry' side. These included three pairs of watering holes alongside so-called burnt mounds, which consisted of heaps of fire-reddened stones and gravel. Burnt mounds are quite often found on excavations along the Fen margins and they almost certainly had a ceremonial or semi-ceremonial purpose. Sometimes the burnt stones covered a wooden trough, and one example at Bradley Fen contained part of a large oak dug-out boat. Various explanations for their use have been suggested, ranging from sacred sauna baths to ritual breweries. You pays your money and you takes your choice, but either way, some Bronze Age ceremonies could be remarkably relaxed.

The 'wet' side of the Bradley Fen boundary ditch also featured offerings of metalwork, including single bronze spearheads and a small group (known as a hoard) of swords and other weapons. Many of these had been placed in the wet ground close by the property boundary ditches, which might suggest they had been put there to cement agreements between neighbouring farming families. Although we had found hints that such rites may have been taking place at Fengate, this was clear, unambiguous evidence for them. It also helped place the rituals that were happening at contemporary Flag Fen into a new context: no longer was the post alignment the only focus for religion and ceremony in the region – just as Peterborough Cathedral was never the sole place of worship in the Middle Ages. I think it was the appreciation of the inter-relatedness of life in the many communities along the prehistoric fen-edge that brought home to me the close parallels between the Bronze Age and our own times. I have often been asked if these ancient communities were 'civilized'. When I was starting my career I might well have deferred my answer, or changed the subject. But not now, not after so many years of research. I am absolutely convinced that they were civilized and although they lacked written laws, they lived together in law-abiding, peaceful settlements, as part of a wider community, where people shared the same language and beliefs – and that, surely, is the definition of civilization.

You cannot write an account of life in an ancient wetland without considering boats. I have the faintest recollection of somebody once telling me about a prehistoric boat that had been found in Peterborough. Maybe it was a newspaper account, I don't know, but somehow that Peterborough boat managed to lodge itself in my subconscious. It was found in October 1950 when the foundations for a new power station were being excavated on the edges of the River Nene, a couple of miles upstream of Flag Fen, towards the centre of the city. I would have been just five at the time, so I doubt if my memory is about its discovery. Later, I came across a remarkable photograph in Peterborough Museum, and published it in my Third Fengate Report.[7] When I first saw the picture I was astonished: I had no idea that boats hewn from the trunk of a single tree (usually, but not always, oak) could have such thin sides and appear – there is no other word for it – 'boatlike'. I had a mental picture of something rounded, thick-walled and tree-trunk-shaped, as you might see being enthusiastically paddled in *The Flintstones*. It now seems likely that the boat dates to the later Bronze Age – sometime in the centuries around 1000 BC.

Our knowledge and understanding of prehistoric ships and boats have come a long way since the 1950s. It used to be believed that dug-outs, so-called logboats, were the only type to be used in early times, but now we know that coracle-like craft and lightweight boats of sewn-together thin planks were also used. Then our view of ships, boats and communications in general was profoundly changed in 1992 by the discovery, deeply buried beneath a street in Dover, of a substantial, plank-built sea-going vessel that could be dated, with some certainty, to *c.*1550 BC. It's now on permanent display in Dover Museum and I would strongly urge anyone to see it. The upper part of the sides are missing, but we know there must have been at least one additional plank. Experienced sailors have suggested that with this plank in place, the boat could have weathered strong winds, and possibly even light gales. I sailed in a scaled-down replica of the Dover boat off the south coast for a *Time Team* documentary, and didn't find the experience even slightly worrying: if I hadn't known the design was Bronze Age, I would have assumed it was the product of a skilled Viking shipwright.

Some twenty years before the discovery of the Dover boat, sports divers swimming off the coast of Devon started to find groups of objects that they thought came from ancient ship-wrecks. These were soon seen by specialists in prehistoric metal-work, who pronounced them to be Bronze Age. The best known of these shipwreck sites was discovered somewhat later, in 2009, at Salcombe.[8] It consisted of 320 bronze objects, including 30 ingots of tin and 258 of copper. These objects originate on both sides of the English Channel and clearly demonstrate active trading in commodities such as raw metal. This is precisely the sort of cargo the Dover boat might have carried and it shows us how some of the exotic foreign products might have reached Flag Fen. It would be a mistake to think of Bronze Age boats like Viking longships; they would certainly have been less able to cope with long-distance voyages. It seems likely that most of their sailing would have been closer to shore: a series of long loops, rather than straight-line voyages. This would neatly explain how the quernstone from Kent found its way to Flag Fen. All the evidence now suggests that from at least 2000 BC, Britain was in regular contact with continental Europe. By the time the Dover boat was built (c.1500 BC) I would imagine that if the weather was reasonably quiet, there would probably have been daily crossings of the Channel.

Our knowledge of the smaller canoe-like vessels of Bronze Age Britain came from chance finds in rivers, or occasionally from beneath barrow mounds. Few had yet been found in situations where they had been used in ordinary, daily life. Then in 2011, Mark Knight and the team working at Must Farm made a very bold decision. In most situations, archaeologists and

*One of the old channels of the River Nene at Must Farm, near Whittlesey, Cambridgeshire. The muds filling the channel have been excavated, but leaving high walls (known as baulks), which show the succession of layers. The bed of the channel starts just beyond the tarpaulin in the foreground. The scaffolding in the channel beyond surrounds the remains of a prehistoric boat. Excavation by the Cambridge University Archaeological Unit.*

geologists investigating extinct river channels normally cut narrow slots, whose sides can be reinforced with piling and braces. Anyone who has ever escaped from a collapsing trench wall (and that includes me) will have glimpsed a horrible, slow death through suffocation, and will go to any lengths to avoid a repeat. So Mark decided on another approach entirely. With the help of the brickpit operators, Hanson UK, large excavators were moved in and a length of about 250 metres (273 yds) of the ancient riverbed (part of the original Nene system) was exposed down to its archaeologically interesting layers. The length exposed meant that there was no danger of collapse and the end walls, or baulks, could be stepped, for extra strength.

The extraordinarily bold decision, in effect to strip a Bronze Age river, paid off handsomely. It exposed what can only be

*Two boats in the Must Farm river channel. The boat on the left lies lower in the river muds and is several centuries older than that to the right. Note the walls of mud left in place by the excavators to support the boats' fragile sides. Excavation by the Cambridge University Archaeological Unit.*

described as a busy, thriving waterway complete with some eight boats (together with pieces from at least one more), which ranged in age from about 1300 BC, when the river channel first formed, to about 700 BC, in the early Iron Age. It is the largest assemblage of prehistoric boats ever found in Europe. If that one stretch of preserved riverbed is at all typical, then many hundreds, possibly even thousands of prehistoric vessels still lie buried out in the Fens. Their existence is yet another reason why the de-watering of so many fen landscapes has got to stop. The Must Farm boats are currently being conserved at Flag Fen, where eventually they will go on display. And they will be well worth seeing, not least because they are so varied in form, size and shape.

*Close-up of one of the Must Farm prehistoric logboats showing its near-perfect preservation. Excavation by the Cambridge University Archaeological Unit.*

Some of the Must Farm boats are undoubtedly canoes, intended to be paddled, with high sides, which in one case was decorated (we assume) with lightly carved lines. Other boats are very shallow indeed and were probably built to be punts. Many of the vessels show clear signs of repair, with carefully fitted wooden plugs, often made waterproof by sealing with clay. All the boats appeared to have been deliberately sunk, because their watertight transom boards, which fitted into vertical slots at the stern, had been removed. This sinking may have been done as some kind of offering to the gods. But I doubt it, because no effort was made to split them or make them permanently non-seaworthy. I think it more likely they were stored underwater to keep the wood wet. A hollowed-out, thin-walled boat, especially if made from oak wood, would soon start to split if it was allowed to dry out for a few weeks in the hotter months of summer. But boats were not the only discovery in that long-lost river channel.

When I was excavating the Fengate fields, back in the 1970s, it became clear that many had been abandoned sometime in the centuries around 1000 BC. This is a time when we know the climate became wetter and it was also when water levels in the wider fens began to rise quite quickly. At the same time, many fen-edge communities broadened their farming base from a one-sided reliance on cattle and sheep to a more balanced regime, where cereals, such as wheat and barley, played a larger role. I used to see this change as something of a retrograde step and I assumed that many people moved inland to higher ground and that the fen-edge population declined. In hindsight, I suspect this view was also conditioned by my own love of sheep farming: how could anyone in their right mind choose to give it up? But whatever my reasons, I now realize that I had got it wrong. Badly wrong. My main sin was one I have accused others of committing: I had underestimated the intelligence, strength and adaptability of people living in the remote past. And the truth was revealed to me, not so much by those superb boats, but by the structures that Mark Knight and his team from Cambridge found on the banks of the river beside them.

The riverbed had been traversed in several places by a succession of V-shaped weirs or dams made from quite closely set vertical posts, which were woven together by strands of willow to form a fish-proof barrier. The base of the V pointed downstream and was towards the centre of the river. At the centre there was a small gap in the dam, which was blocked by a highly sophisticated two-chambered trap made of tightly woven basketry. Fish and eels, funnelled in by the weir, then swam into the trap's outer chamber, which was not easy to exit; this encouraged them to pass down a short funnel into the inner chamber, from which there was no escape. Every day or so, a fisherman would pick up the trap, replace it with a new one and empty the catch. To judge by the size of fish bones from Flag Fen and Fengate, fish such as pike and eels could be very big – which also suggests a large population. Some of the fish were quite exotic and included sturgeon – so one must imagine local families enjoying the occasional dish of caviar.

The presence of so many fish weirs, complete with their traps, whose design seems to have been universal across northern Europe and which continued, virtually unaltered, into Victorian times and later, was very revealing. As with the droveways and field systems along the fen-edge, they showed that fishing did not take place at a so-called subsistence level: it was far more intensive than that. The proteins and oils from fish would have been an important part of people's daily diets, especially during the normally very lean months of winter. I also think it likely that some fish was cured by smoking and rubbing with salt, which may well have been done in purpose-built wooden smokeries, or simply by hanging fillets in the roofs of roundhouses, all of which lacked chimneys. I know from experience that the roof space of a roundhouse can be very smoky. And maybe those burnt mounds could have been used in this way too? But the final evidence that clinched the case for continued, or even growing prosperity during the years of wetter climate and rising water levels in the Fens, was far more substantial than a few boats or fish weirs. It is time to return to those posts on the edge of the Whittlesey brickpit.

For nearly five years, the cluster of posts that Martin had discovered remained undisturbed, very slowly drying out, because the local water table had been lowered by the nearby brickpits. Then in 2004 it was decided that the old pit should reopen as a quarry and the Cambridge University Unit won the contract to excavate the archaeological remains, before the big machines of the brickworks took over.[9] In 2005, they opened a series of evaluation trenches that revealed the river course, where the boats were later found. They were also able to demonstrate that Whittlesey had never been a true 'island', as I had supposed for so long, and was actually on a peninsula, joined to the main land mass of the fen-edge. But their most interesting discovery was made in 2006, when they put another evaluation trench across the edge of the quarry, close to the spot where the posts had been found. And what they discovered there, on the very edge of the fen and river floodplain, was to have an international impact. At last, Britain had its own 'Lake Village', but one that has revealed more about life in the Bronze Age than even the great sites of Switzerland. This may sound like an exaggerated claim, but I make it because the Must Farm platform settlement ('Lake Village' is a misnomer, as few villages consist of just five houses) was only occupied for about a year. Most of the great Swiss sites had been settled for many decades, and even centuries.

This meant that although preservation was just as good as at Must Farm, it was very difficult to pin down precisely when and where various activities had taken place. The accumulated debris of many years had obscured things.

The 2006 trench revealed that the posts we had seen in 1999 belonged to a causeway, which tree-ring dates showed had been built between 1290 and 1250 BC, more or less the same time that the first posts were erected at Flag Fen. But that first trench also revealed good evidence for settlement, including pots with food still inside them, many animal bones and other domestic debris – all of it superbly preserved. Despite the fact that this new settlement was actually in the wetland, much of the food they ate, and the animals they kept, came from the dry land. These wetlanders either had close links with dry land communities or farmed land themselves on the nearby fen-edge. Personally, I think that more probable.

I could write at great length about the Must Farm settlement because I find it so exciting. In fact, I'm so glad to have visited the dig many times and have climbed the scaffolding tower inside the great plastic-covered shelter that protected the dig from the elements. From the top of the tower you can look down on the perfectly preserved remains of a collapsed Bronze Age roundhouse. Everything is there: the roof timbers have collapsed onto the floor and the external walls are broken, but it is still there to see. Lying on and below the floor are the pots, wooden tools, implements and everything used to prepare food and eat it. Some of the vessels have even been stacked inside one another, like porridge bowls on the draining board after breakfast, waiting to be washed up. The settlement was dug in 2015 and 2016 and consisted of five roundhouses. Originally there would probably have been eight, but three were lost before the site was discovered. Much to Maisie's and my surprise they appear to have been built on stilts, which supported a platform above the waters of the nearby fen and stream. The platform was undoubtedly built as a defensive structure, as it was protected along its landward side by a substantial palisade of posts. The earlier causeway (the one Martin found), which had been abandoned for a couple of centuries when the platform was built, runs below it, in a dead straight line.

*Ten of the ash poles that formed the palisade around the Must Farm Late Bronze Age settlement. Note the sharpened tips. This work was done with a bronze axe. Excavation by the Cambridge University Archaeological Unit.*

The settlement was erected and occupied sometime between 1000 and 800 BC, although that date will probably be refined more closely in the final report, which is due to be published in 2019. After it had been occupied for about a year, disaster struck: the entire settlement and platform caught fire. One of the excavation team is a forensic fire expert who told me that the surviving evidence for the fire – the charring and suchlike – was actually far better preserved than on many of the modern fires he had attended. All the buildings show the same degree of burning, which does suggest the blaze may have been intentional. But we must await the final report to be certain. Objects lying on the collapsed house floors all follow the same basic pattern. The front doors face eastwards, towards the rising sun, and the eastern, better lit side of the houses produces all the domestic material: the pots, utensils and implements. This was where food was produced and eaten; this was the social side of the house. The western, darker side was where people slept.

*The collapsed roof, floor and wall timbers of a Late Bronze Age roundhouse at Must Farm. The posts that supported the roof and the floor are vertical. The long timbers that formed the rafters of the roof can be seen to radiate out from the centre of the building. They are now lying where they collapsed, below floor level, in the waters beneath the house. A few posts of the palisade can be seen, top right. Excavation by the Cambridge University Archaeological Unit.*

My final visit to Must Farm took place late in the excavations when the collapsed floors were being excavated and the last few complete pottery vessels were being lifted. We had observed the same east/west pattern in the way Bronze and Iron Age houses were used, in our own excavations at Fengate. Then, as I drove home, I couldn't help thinking about those families, at the ghastly moment when the fire struck. No bodies had been revealed in the dig, so I assume the blaze happened during the day and that everyone escaped. But how did they then cope with the loss of everything they possessed? Did they become outcasts, forced to move away, or were they helped by friends and relations? I suspected the latter, but I couldn't be certain. My anxiety was real: I cared about those nameless fen folk four thousand years ago. And I still do.

# 8

# Borough Fen:
# A Hillfort Lurking Beneath
# the Surface

*The Iron Age – Invaders and Natives – Cat's Water,*
*Fengate – Houses and Byres – Duck Decoys – The*
*Borough Fen 'Hillfort' – Wetter Times: The Fen-edge*
*in the Iron Age*

Iron and iron-working arrived in Britain during the eighth century BC, an event that marked the end of the Bronze Age and the start of the Iron Age. But in human terms, almost nothing changed: people didn't wake up one morning and declare they were now living in a new age – the ages of stone, bronze and iron were invented by museum archaeologists in the first half of the nineteenth century to help them make sense of their collections. Life for folk in the early Iron Age was almost precisely the same as it had been in the closing decades of the late Bronze Age, but the clock of prehistory was still ticking. Progress may have been relatively slow by modern standards, but it was happening, quietly and steadily, in the background. And the greatest engine of change wasn't the arrival of a new metal, but the steady growth of the British population.

By 1500 BC the British landscape had become 'developed' –
not a very good term, I concede, but the only one I can think of.
It had settled down. Localities and regions had become clearly
defined. It hadn't become static, but the dynamic of landscape
development was taking place in regions where people knew
who they were, and who their neighbours were. Daily life was
becoming increasingly structured. The landscape evolved around
a growing network of roads, lanes, rivers and waterways. The
population continued to grow during the second half of the
second millennium BC and with it came new field systems and
settlements. Some of these were entirely new, others grew from
pre-existing farms and communities. The point to bear in mind
is that this ever-growing population had to be fed.

By about 1000 BC we can start to identify the beginnings of
a new class of site or settlement, which were to be labelled 'hillforts' – a term I have already discussed.* Some of these were
not on hills and many weren't forts, in the sense of a castle-like,
inhabited strongpoint, at all. But they were something new in
the landscape and with their readily identifiable surrounding
bank and ditch, or banks and ditches, they could easily be spotted. Many, but not all, were placed on the tops of hills. So what
were they, these hillforts? I think the simplest way to think about
them is as an expression of local and regional identity. Towards
the end of the BC centuries, some of the larger hillforts became
major tribal centres, but unlike modern capital cities they were
rarely actual centres of population, although some enclosed very
substantial settlements.[1] Most of the people lived down on the
plains, close to the crops, water, transport, farms and fields they
needed simply to stay alive.

The centuries on either side of 1000 BC was a period when the
climate grew somewhat wetter – and in the Fens this coincided

---

* See Chapter 6, p. 119.

with a natural rise in groundwater levels, ultimately brought about by encroaching sea levels. As the high tide line crept relentlessly inland, tidal sand bars and dunes would impede river outfalls. Increases in rainfall, coupled with the inability of rivers to discharge their waters into the North Sea with any reliability, meant that water draining into the Fens from northern Norfolk and the East Midlands would overflow and pond in the lowest-lying fens, especially in the south and west, around the floodplains of the rivers Great Ouse, Nene, Welland and Witham.

When we look back on these centuries it is almost impossible not to think in terms of catastrophic change. I have had to live through a few severe tidal surges myself and I have witnessed the damage done at first hand, with buildings along the sea front damaged and boarded up and flood banks breached and washed away. It is almost impossible not to transfer one's own experiences and knowledge of recent history directly back to the distant past: to see the natural changes of the later Bronze and early Iron Ages as prehistoric parallels for the terrible fen floods of 1947 and 1953.[2] But that would be a mistake, for the simple reason that the prehistoric Fens remained undrained, and could thereby dissipate the effects of flooding gradually, giving people time to adapt or move elsewhere, whereas the twentieth-century floods happened suddenly and dramatically, with great walls of water being released when massive river flood banks were breached. I think this historical bias and oversimplification has led many of us – and I must plead guilty of this myself in the past – to equate wet with bad and dry with good. As some-body who lives at, or close to, sea level, the fear of flooding is never far from my thoughts and I now realize that I must have allowed it to colour my thinking about the prehistoric past – and indeed the future, where too much dryness, or drainage, is doing serious environmental and ecological harm.

So 'wet' doesn't have to be bad. In fact it can be very good, as the current excavations at Must Farm are demonstrating so well: those fen-edge communities had adapted to their gradually changing environment and were exploiting it very efficiently. Those V-shaped fish weirs made a huge impression on me when I first saw them. One glance was enough to tell me that this was no part-time amateur enterprise: these people knew exactly what they were doing and they did it very well. The fish and eels they caught must have been a major component of the local and regional economy. But there were other changes, too.

Many of the livestock-based field systems, with their stock-yards and droveways, that were such a growing feature of the fen-edge during the Bronze Age, go out of use around the start of the first millennium BC. In the past I had assumed that this change was directly linked to the shrunken size, or even the unavailability, of wetland fen pastures, during the usually drier months of summer. This may indeed have played a part in what happened, but I was missing the bigger point. 'Wet' didn't equate with 'bad': it was far, far more complex than that.

My own excavations at West Deeping on the fen-edge in the lower Welland Valley in 1996 and '97 had shown that during the middle and later centuries of the Bronze Age, fields were being spread with manure and domestic refuse (hearth sweepings, food debris etc.) to act as fertilizer for growing crops. At about 1000 BC we see the widespread introduction of the more productive and easier-to-grow winter wheat, which may well have played its part in influencing farmers to move away from a heavy reliance on livestock to a more balanced form of mixed farming, which would have been better adapted to the new conditions. And of course the wetter fenlands had resources of their own, of fish and wildfowl, which provided plentiful sources of protein, especially during the hitherto rather lean months of winter. These factors may help to explain why there is no evidence for a decline in population along the fen-edge in the early centuries of the first millennium BC. Indeed, as Must Farm has demonstrated so clearly, fen communities adapted, prospered and may well have grown in size.

I sometimes wonder how I could have allowed myself to suggest there might have been a decline in the fen-edge economy at the end of the Bronze Age, especially when I think back to our excavations at Fengate in the second half of the 1970s. So I'm absolutely delighted I got it wrong. That's one of the joys of archaeology, when unexpected discoveries turn your ideas upside down – and the truth edges ever closer.

The part of Fengate we were digging back in 1975 was called the Cat's Water sub-site, after the dyke that bounded it to the east. That, in turn, was possibly named after, or as a folk memory of, the Iron Age tribe, the Catuvellauni. At least, that's the theory I'd love to believe – and while it's never likely to be proved, it won't be disproved, either. One suggestion is that the old rivals of Queen Boudicca's Iceni, the Catuvellauni, expanded out of their home base in Essex (their capital was at Camulodunum, or modern Colchester) and that the Cat's Water marks the northern, and maximum, limit of their enlarged kingdom. The Cat's Water originates in Fengate as a catch-water drain, probably based on a natural stream, that skirts the fen-edge, where we were excavating in the 1970s; it then turns out into the open fen, and heads north-eastwards, towards Thorney 'island'. Thereafter, its course to the Wash is largely speculative, as the dyke changes its name several times, but recently Maisie drew my attention to the fact that a road near where we live, which follows the deep ancient dyke (Lady Nunn's Old Eau) that forms the Lincolnshire/Cambridgeshire boundary near Tydd St Giles, close to the (modern) Nene outfall, has always been known as Cat's Lane.[3] There are lots of Dog Droves in the Fens, partly because 'dog' referred to a dyke filled with dock plants; it was also a word used to describe somewhere that was a bit rough, wet or unpleasant. But I know of no other Cats. Coincidence? Perhaps, but historical speculation is always good fun.


The first four years of our excavations at Fengate were largely taken up with those Bronze Age fields and farms. It was very exciting work, as we were revealing highly sophisticated landscapes whose existence had previously been unsuspected. I soon found myself championing Bronze Age farmers, who had generally been ignored in favour of the metalwork, pottery styles, henges and barrows of the time. It had become a period dominated by objects and monuments. People didn't seem to get a look-in. So I saw the landscapes that we were exposing at Fengate as a means of drawing the different aspects together. And as we did this, we discovered that the lives of Bronze Age people slowly began to emerge. Finally, the discovery of Flag Fen seemed to complete the job and we could now view Bronze Age communities, in the round.

The Iron Age, on the other hand, has had a very different archaeological history. It's also a period that has tended to be seen in a historical perspective from the most recent back to the beginning, whereas archaeologists tend to think the other way round: starting at the beginning, then moving forward. The reason for the historical approach is undoubtedly the arrival of the Romans, which has, I think, both coloured and distorted our view of the period. So while the Bronze Age used to be interpreted through its barrows, henges and metalwork, the Iron Age was viewed as a series of invasions or migrations – doubtless reflecting the Roman conquest, which ended the period. Something as minor as a change in pottery style was attributed to an incursion of new people. Of course people *did* settle in Britain from the continent from time to time, but these folk movements were small in scale and the incomers soon adapted to local ways.

The Celts were also believed to have played a critical role in the culture of Iron Age Britain. It was widely accepted that they came to Britain, ultimately from central Europe. We now realize that the major pre-Roman invasions never happened and that the Celts didn't come here from overseas. So today the word 'Celtic' is used to describe the indigenous and very distinctive insular cultures of Britain and Ireland during the Iron Age.

I had read a paper, published as long ago as 1962 in the learned journal *The Proceedings of the Prehistoric Society* – known throughout the archaeological world simply as PPS – that questioned the existence of so many supposed Iron Age invasions.[4] I confess I was completely won over by the non-invasion hypothesis. So it came as no surprise when I began work on the Cat's Water site, part of the Fengate complex, in 1975 to discover that there was absolutely no evidence that the fen-edge had ever been abandoned for any length of time in the first millennium BC. Yes, field boundaries changed and settlements had come and gone, but all of this happened as an integral part of longer-term landscape change, evolution and development. Indeed, we now know that the rotting, abandoned posts out in the waters of an increasingly wet Flag Fen were regularly visited throughout the Iron Age and even into early Roman times, when objects – some of them quite precious – were offered to an ancient site that was already as old as many early medieval churches are today. The people who made those Iron Age offerings at Flag Fen clearly knew about the place's importance. I think it more than probable that they were directly descended from the men and women who built it.

The Cat's Water Iron Age settlement was a wonderful excavation. I have fond memories of warm summer days and a happy team of by now highly experienced excavators. The site we had been asked to clear for future factory development showed up on air photos as a series of ditched yards at the end of a wide ditched droveway. But this time the droveway ran inland from the fen-edge, but at an angle – closer to forty-five degrees, or a diagonal, than a right angle. This layout marks a complete change from that of the Bronze Age and shows that the emphasis was now on dry land, rather than on seasonally available wet pastures. The droveway is also heading towards the known area of prehistoric settlement that was destroyed by the hand-dug gravel workings before the last war.

*A model of part of the Cat's Water, Fengate, Iron Age settlement, c. 250 BC. Model by Eric Ricketts and David Rayner, 1976.*

When the Cat's Water site was first assessed in the report on sites threatened by the building of Peterborough New Town, it was considered to be Roman, for the very good reason that there was a dense scatter of locally made Roman pottery lying in the topsoil directly above the farmyards at the head of the droveway. So I prepared myself for a couple of seasons in which we would dig a Romano-British farm. I can't say I was wildly enthused with the idea, because sites of that period can produce such huge quantities of finds that all the team's efforts are spent washing and marking tens of thousands of potsherds – which ultimately don't provide much information, given all the time spent on them. On the other hand, by the mid-1970s not many farms of the period had been fully exposed, because most Roman digs of the 1950s and '60s had been of villas, urban or military sites. We still knew remarkably little about the Romano-British countryside. Incidentally, I'm aware the term 'Romano-British' is rather cumbersome, but most of the archaeological sites of the Roman period in Britain were actually built, used and maintained by British people. There were very few true, Latin-speaking Roman citizens in the province of Britannia. So we generally use the term 'Roman' just to refer to the period of time (AD 43 to 410) when Britain was under Roman rule. Everything else was Romano-British.

I also have to confess to a slight anti-Roman bias. I never enjoyed learning Latin at school – in fact I loathed it. But in the 1960s it was still required if you wanted to go to Oxford or Cambridge. So I was lumbered. And then when I began working on archaeological sites I soon developed a dislike of Romano-British pottery. It was produced in workshops on the outskirts of certain Roman towns, including Durobrivae, the prosperous small town to the west of Peterborough that we encountered earlier, when discussing the Fen Causeway. It may have been produced in what today we would call artisan workshops, but it all looked the same and there were a limited number of vessel types, shapes and sizes. To my eye, it looked like something from a factory. Even the very fine Samian tablewares imported from France and Italy looked mass produced. I have to confess, Roman pottery left me cold. The hundreds of coins weren't much better, either – and some of the experts, the numismatists, who knew all about them, could be on the geeky side of obsessive.

So I was delighted when our supposedly Roman farm turned

out to be mostly Iron Age. In this instance the term Romano-British is, if anything, an overstatement, because everything about the farm, and the people who lived there, was British. But having said that, identities have never been static. The presence of Roman culture and the long-term effects of the towns and roads they built during their short stay in Britain did undoubtedly affect British society quite profoundly, as we will see in the next chapter.

To describe the Cat's Water Iron Age site as a 'farm', as I have just done, is probably an oversimplification. Today, most farms are still family enterprises. Some fen farms, especially in the more prosperous vegetable-growing areas, are run by limited companies; very often these are enterprises that were set up by the family who owns the land. But the Cat's Water farm was run by a number of households – maybe half a dozen at any one time. Knowing rural communities, I would be prepared to bet good money they were related, but that cannot be proven. It's also interesting that the size of the farming settlement at Cat's Water is broadly comparable with the earlier platform settlement at Must Farm. Fen-edge landscapes require quite a workforce to clear ditches, lay hedges and do the other routine jobs of maintenance so it does not surprise me that farms were in fact farming settlements of perhaps twenty to sixty people, including children and old folk, which would have had an active workforce of around ten to thirty individuals. As community sizes go, this is much larger than one would have found on contemporary upland areas, such as Dartmoor or the Yorkshire Dales or North York Moors, where single-family farms were, and still are, the norm. Larger populations of people and animals would have had a detrimental effect on the landscape, causing yards, field gates and droveway surfaces to become areas of permanent mud over winter. Although the horrible disease of sheep known as foot rot did not arrive in Britain from Australia until the nineteenth century, sheep and cattle can catch nasty fungal infections if they are forced to stand in mud for too long. Overcrowded farms never prosper.

Cat's Water revealed evidence for some fifty-six round buildings, which were distributed across the northern part of the site, mostly within the largest ditched yards.[5] Buildings were notably absent from a series of much smaller ditched yards close to the head of the droveway, which must surely have been used for sorting livestock. As we saw in the Bronze Age stock-handling areas, these smaller yards were generally entered at the corners. You may have noted that I was at pains to say that the site revealed fifty-six round buildings. I deliberately did not say 'houses', because while we were excavating their foundations we noted that some buildings revealed pottery and other domestic refuse around their doorways. These buildings often had evidence for central hearths too. Nearby buildings, on the other hand, were almost finds free and did not have hearths. We also carried out a series of soil phosphate tests, which were kindly done for us by Dr Paul Craddock, a friend at the British Museum Research Laboratory, and the results were fascinating.

Heavy concentrations of manure can leave permanent traces in the soil by raising phosphate levels, which stay high long after the manure itself has rotted away. Earlier in the project, Paul had demonstrated that the Bronze Age droveways must have been running with manure. It even dripped down the sides of the two bounding ditches, with higher concentrations along their inside edges. Paul described the conditions on the drove using colourful Cornish rural slang: a 'piss-mire'. Those 'piss-mire' droveways show that the field system was heavily used and adds further support to the idea that Bronze Age farming was about far more than mere subsistence.

Paul decided that the Cat's Water site would require a two-pronged approach: first a general grid-based survey of the entire site, followed up by samples taken from individual buildings. The general survey showed that higher levels of phosphate tended to occur around the outer part of the site, with lower levels at the centre, over the large yard. This area also revealed higher levels of soil magnetic susceptibility, which is measured in the field and indicates the presence of fires or burning. Presumably in this case, the fires were in fact domestic hearths and their sweepings, which may well have been spread along paths to combat mud. His analysis of phosphates in individual buildings revealed that those structures that had hearths and produced many finds had low phosphate levels – which confirmed our suspicion they were family homes. By contrast, the buildings with high phosphates and few finds are best seen as animal byres or shelters. But what amazed us was the fact that animals were housed in buildings that were as large and well-built as the family homes alongside them. Taking all the evidence together, we reckoned that about half the buildings were used for people, and half for livestock.

From sometime around the middle of the first millennium BC we start to see evidence for social differentiation. Now I'm not saying that suddenly elites appeared on the scene and that villages were ruled by powerful chiefs. The reality seems to have been far more subtle. Two of the Cat's Water houses, for example, were slightly larger than the others, and three had been positioned within their own ditched yards, or enclosures (gardens perhaps?).[6] This suggests that certain families, or individuals, were starting to play a more prominent role in the running of each community's affairs. As time passed, this tendency towards growing social stratification increased, culminating in the tribal kings and queens of the generations that grew up after Julius Caesar's invasions of Britain, in 55 and 54 BC. The most famous of these tribal rulers was our friend Queen Boudicca of the Iceni. I shall have more to say about the Iceni in the next chapter.

The Cat's Water settlement thrived in the later Iron Age, perhaps starting around 350 BC, and there was absolutely no indication of a break when the Romans invaded in AD 43. Everything continued as normal, except that the day-to-day pottery slowly became more Romanized, albeit made locally. But some aspects of life were starting to change: farmhouse kitchens began to employ heavy-duty mortars (*mortaria* in Latin), which were used to grind herbs and spices. This implies that some meals were becoming more exotic – perhaps spicy (using garlic?) and more Mediterranean. Some of the tableware included more up-market, shiny-finished red Samian wares, imported from southern France. Again, this would suggest that traditional Iron Age ways were becoming increasingly Romanized. But no coins were found, which must indicate that these families did not spend much time, for example, in the markets of nearby Durobrivae. So in this part of rural Britain, the process of Romanization had only just begun to catch on by the time the settlement was abandoned, in the late second century AD.

Fen drainage can produce some vivid contrasts between wet and dry. It was while we were carrying out the dyke survey in the early 1980s that we came across a particularly striking example. It had been a hot, sunny spell and we were exposing a small group of buried Bronze Age barrows out in Borough Fen, a short distance east of Peterborough. The barrow we were working on had been cut cleanly in half by a dyke and everything was superbly preserved, but sadly, very dry: pieces of wood in the Bronze Age ditches were crisp and flaky. Twenty years previously they would have been very different. I can remember showing the farmer the extent of the gravel mound and some ashes from a probable cremation. He smiled and pointed to his bungalow a few metres behind us. Then I saw what he was telling me: the house had been built on another barrow, presumably because it was dry, firm ground. He asked about the cremation and whether there'd be any more like it beneath his bungalow. 'Yes,' I replied. 'And probably some burials, too.' He paused, with a slight, dry smile: 'Better not tell the wife. She'd never sleep again.'

While we were working at Borough Fen we would often take our lunch break in the Decoy pub at the crossroads on the edge of Milking Nook. A short distance to the south-west was the then thriving wetland nature reserve and Wildfowl Centre at Peakirk, together with a hermitage for solitary nuns – and another pub, although you hear less about that. One day after lunch I decided to knock off early and head down the small lane – a 'road less travelled', if ever there was one – that formed the northern arm of the Decoy pub crossroads. It was to prove a journey of discovery.

I mentioned contrasts, and Borough Fen was full of them. The open drained areas were spectacularly dry. This was because the ploughed peaty soils were so crisp and crumbly at the surface and most of the field drains were empty. Grass fields seemed to fare better and retain more moisture. But then there was wetness, too. The Peakirk Reserve had its water levels maintained high and the place was bursting with life. You could hear the splashes and quacks from the various ponds as you walked by on the road from Newborough. But now I was driving the Land Rover along a very narrow road, on a low bank with ditches on either side, and heading towards the actual duck decoy that I knew was at the end of the road. Of course, it was this real decoy that had given the pub its name.

Duck decoys are probably best thought of as the avian equivalents of the fish weirs and traps we saw at Must Farm. They are, however, very much later, because to work effectively they depend on large quantities of fine, strong netting, which did not appear until early modern times. They were introduced in the seventeenth century by the Dutch and were first described in 1678. Previously, ducks and geese had been caught, trapped or shot by driving them in a certain direction. This of course was labour-intensive and not always very effective. The Dutch system was both more subtle and successful and worked by enticing the birds towards the traps. The central lake, of only a few acres, was the initial attraction: from the air it was surrounded by innocent-looking bushes and trees and it must have seemed like an ideal spot to get out of the wind and spend the night. It was made even more attractive because the decoy man had thrown feed out into the lake and there was also a welcoming group of tame ducks. It must have seemed like heaven to any unsuspecting visiting birds.

From the air, a duck decoy resembles a spiked wheel with a central pool and the spokes of the wheel formed by wide-mouthed but sharply tapering channels, known as pipes, which were covered over with netting to form tunnels. The ducks were enticed into the tunnels with bait and by the trained ducks who would lead their wild brethren into them. A set of woven-wattle screens was placed along one side of the decoy pipe, behind which lurked the decoy man, who would also deploy a highly trained dog who would appear from behind the screens and then vanish again, but always in the direction of the traps at the end of the pipe.

Today we think of undrained wetlands as an abundant source of fish and eels, which we saw at Must Farm were being exploited in a very thoroughgoing fashion. But we tend to forget that wildfowl also inhabited the Fens in very large numbers, especially over winter when many birds from colder climes in the north migrate to Britain for food and protection. In the seventeenth, eighteenth and nineteenth centuries, wildfowl were trapped in decoys in huge numbers and sent to markets in London. Geese and ducks may be shot by bows and arrows, or caught in nets, either concealed or thrown by hand. In the eighteenth and nineteenth centuries they were blasted out of the sky by massive guns, which were mounted in punts to absorb the huge recoil when the gun, filled with old nails, shot and other shrapnel, was fired.

I think I must have been at Cambridge when I saw my first punt gun. Punting was a skill I was still struggling to acquire, but I was getting better at it: not exactly graceful, like those third-year students with their languorous girlfriends, but at least I could go in a straight line. So I had visions of the wildfowlers sneaking up on their prey, while standing elegantly at the stern. Of course, all the ducks would immediately have taken flight at the approach of an upright man. In reality, the punt-gunners lay flat in their punts for the final approach, paddling as quietly as they could. Punt guns were used very effectively across the Fens, but especially in the tidal basins and marshlands closer to the Wash. This was also the region where most of the duck decoys were built. One or two, however, were placed further inland and one of the earliest and largest of these was constructed in 1640 at Borough Fen, just 6 miles (10 km) north of Peterborough.[7] The proximity to a major city with excellent links to London was no accident, because in their heyday in the 1720s, some individual decoys were sending up to six thousand birds to the markets in the capital city. The record year for Borough Fen was the winter of 1804–05, when 458 dozen birds (5,496 individuals) were caught and sent to market. It continued to operate intermittently until 1959.[8]

When I visited the Borough Fen decoy it had long since ceased to be used to catch ducks for the table and was now employed by the Wildfowl Trust to net birds for ringing and various surveys. It was a wonderfully peaceful place in the summer and the warden of the Wildfowl Trust gave us a demonstration of his decoy dog, jumping and weaving his way along the side of the netted pipe. Somehow the dog seemed almost too active, given the tranquillity of the lake and the silent hovering of hundreds of dragonflies.

My drive along the road leading to the Borough Fen decoy had been eventful in other ways, too. I was very struck by the subtle surface topography. At the time I was discovering how to 'read' the surface of the ground. Now this may sound like an essential attribute for any archaeologist, but in fact most of us, particularly if we work from remote sources such as aerial photographs, LiDAR images or geophysical surveys, tend to think in two dimensions. It was only after I'd been digging at Fengate for three or four seasons that I began to be able to identify, for example, the cultivated banks of drainage dykes, or the flattened remains of plough headlands – the low banks cast up when the plough is turned around at the end of a row of furrows. David Hall, who had spent most of his early life surveying the medieval field systems of Northamptonshire, had a sharp eye for such subtleties in the landscape, which I knew I would never match – and he taught me a great deal.

It was also so unusual to see unploughed fields in this part of the Fens. So I slowed the Land Rover down and made a mental note of the various ditches and banks I could see in the pastures on the west side of the narrow road. Normally, I'd have hopped out and had a look, but the field was being grazed by young bullocks who were looking very flighty. The other side of the road was marked by a deep dyke that had cut through an earlier bank. I looked out into the field of wheat, which was nearly ready for harvest, and I thought I could discern a gently curving bank and ditch. The topsoil in the side of the dyke was dry, but it flaked and cracked like river-borne flood clay. So whatever that bank was, it was probably earlier than the clay – which could make it prehistoric. I continued along the road, past the farm with the livestock sheds for the cattle, and turned sharp right for the decoy.

I had really enjoyed my visit to the decoy and had forgotten about the humps and bumps in the fields alongside the road leading up to it. But as I drove back, something was different. Maybe the angle of the sun was lower, I don't know why, but suddenly I could see that the banks and ditches in the cattle pasture formed the outside of a huge roughly circular enclosure. In retrospect, I should have been aware of the site, but one cannot know everything, and besides, I had had my hands more than full writing up Fengate and managing big digs at Maxey and Etton. At least that's my excuse, because when I visited the County Sites and Monuments Record in Shire Hall, Cambridge, I was astounded to discover that the curved ditches were thought to form part of a medieval enclosure. I ran this past various members of the team when I got back to Peterborough and the news was greeted with hilarity. Everyone was aware that the area would have been under water for most of the year in the Middle Ages. We all agreed that it had to be prehistoric and we were also unanimous that its shape was remarkably like an Iron Age hillfort, albeit on one of the lowest, flattest hills in Britain – a low-lying, rounded gravel 'island' that would have been dry land in later prehistoric times. A new, unploughed and potentially waterlogged hillfort? The prospect was very exciting indeed. In our enthusiasm we dubbed it a 'Fenfort', but it never really caught on.

However, I did learn something useful on that trip to Cambridge. I had wondered why the banks and ditches in the field to the west of the road were under what was plainly permanent pasture: from the road you could see the grass was mixed with clover, patches of creeping buttercup and the occasional thistle. These are not plants you'd expect to find in a field of newly sown ryegrass (the non-native grass that is generally used in short-term sown pastures). One glance told me: this was very old pasture and very distinct from the field on the other side of the road, which I guessed had been arable for a long time. And the reason for the contrast? Quite simple: the ditches and banks of the supposedly medieval enclosure had been protected under law as a Scheduled Ancient Monument. This meant that the farmer had been legally prevented from ploughing them. And by the same token, I knew that we too would be unable to carry out any excavation there, without a huge amount of red tape. And if there's one thing field archaeologists loathe, it's red tape and those who purvey it. But what about the other side of the road, where the ancient ditch and bank were clearly exposed in the roadside dyke – surely we could investigate that, as part of our dyke survey? It was a tantalizing prospect.

I approached the farmer and he willingly gave us permission to enter his field and investigate the roadside ditch as soon as the crop had been harvested. This meant I had time to go to London to discover the precise boundaries of the protected (scheduled) area. Although I detest red tape, I do rather enjoy legal language, so I was pleased to discover that the edges of a Scheduled Monument are still described as its curtilage. Delightful. While I was in London in the offices of what is today Historic England, I also got the chance to have lunch with the inspector who supervised our region of the East Midlands. Inspectors were not career civil servants, most had, and have, archaeology degrees and their sympathies are with archaeologists and archaeology. They were never willing purveyors of red tape.

Over a pint and crisps, but no lunch, I explained to our inspector what we had discovered about the date of the Borough Fen enclosure. He immediately grasped its importance and said he could lay his hands on some money to fund a small investigation, and the writing up of what we found. Result! He also insisted that I should take him out to a 'proper' lunch when he came to visit.

*A drainage dyke runs through the centre of an Iron Age fortified site in Borough Fen, just outside Peterborough. In 1982 we cleaned back the dykeside in two places to expose the archaeological layers. The near exposure, which is being worked on, is through the ditch surrounding the site. The far exposure revealed the occupation layers.*

As soon as the harvest was safely gathered in, I took the team to Borough Fen, where we cut a series of sections up the sides of the roadside dyke. And what we found surpassed our wildest dreams. We never discovered the bottom of the hillfort ditch, which was so deep it passed well below the groundwater table, so its entire filling would still be waterlogged. The flood clays had also sealed the original prehistoric soils in their entirety. I'm in little doubt that this is one of the best-preserved 'hillforts' in Britain – if not in Europe.[9] Normally you don't reveal many artefacts when you clean up dykesides, simply because the sample of earth you are revealing is so tiny: maybe a few bucket-fuls, at most. But not here. We found four rim sherds of hand-made pottery made from clays that had been deliberately gritted

*The occupation layers of the Borough Fen Iron Age site
are stained black (mostly by charcoal). The pale band
beneath formed at the base of the topsoil.*

with crushed fossil shells. This type of pottery fabric was very
common in the older layers at the Cat's Water farm at Fengate,
and occurs widely across the East Midlands. One of the sherds
had been decorated with lightly scored lines across its outer
surface. This decoration, together with the shelly fabric, left me
in little doubt that the sherds belonged in the Middle Iron Age,
sometime around 350 BC – a date that is absolutely spot-on for
hillforts, too.

The potsherds had broken from ordinary domestic vessels. They were quite soft and showed little evidence for weathering or erosion, which might imply that they came from a house floor, or maybe from a rubbish pit close by a dwelling. We also found many fragments of animal bone that had been finely broken up, suggesting they were the remains of actual meals – probably stews or soups. The meat bones were of beef, pork and lamb/mutton. So people were living well. But even more important, all the evidence for life in the settlement still lies out there, in Borough Fen, waterlogged, buried and intact.

In the past, some archaeologists preferred digging to writing up their results. I used to sort of understand this: it was all about the excitement of the chase. Discovery and revelation – and let's be honest, media coverage and with it, a fair bit of personal glory. But as time passed, I realized that this view of archaeology and archaeologists was actually a distortion. Yes, some very eminent people dug sites, including such key monuments as Stonehenge, and failed to write them up. But things have changed. Speaking for myself, I think this is because writing up is now an integral part of the excavation process. And I find it hugely rewarding – and often just as exciting as work out in the field. For example, when we started to examine the aerial photographs and other evidence for the landscape around the Borough Fen enclosed settlement – perhaps a better term than a 'hillfort' – we discovered it was part of a carefully laid-out landscape that made the very best use of its rather difficult and increasingly wet fen-edge location.

Our dyke survey had shown that the Borough Fen Iron Age site had been positioned quite close to the southern edge of a very low gravel 'island' that would have grown smaller, as water levels gradually rose, towards the end of the Iron Age. Then, in

Roman times, fen water levels probably fell, perhaps as a result of changing tidal conditions around the southern edges of the Wash. This led some archaeologists and historians to suggest that the Roman authorities undertook drainage projects – for which there is still no good evidence. More likely, they were opportunistic and made the most of the new, drier conditions. We discovered one example of this at Borough Fen, where a small settlement of the second and third centuries AD had been positioned just 300 metres (328 yds) east of the 'hillfort', at the edge of the buried 'island'. We can be reasonably certain that people were living in this settlement (and for about a century), because of the quantities of domestic pottery found and the increased levels of soil magnetism, brought about by the spreading of ashes from hearths and fires.[10]

The really exciting part of the project came when we started to trace out and reconstruct the prehistoric field systems around Borough Fen, which had been revealed by aerial photographs. As we checked geological and other maps, it soon became clear that the slight rise in land beneath the Borough Fen ditched enclosure was part of a natural promontory, or peninsula, that ran into the Fen from a north-easterly direction. At its tip was the later monastic settlement of Crowland, a spot that many believe would have been chosen for its remoteness. The Borough Fen enclosure was positioned at the root of the Crowland peninsula at the point where it joined the slightly higher land of the lower Welland Valley. The aerial photographs clearly revealed a series of parallel ditches that ran north–south on the western, or land-ward, side of the Borough Fen enclosure. Had these been something to do with farming they would have had other ditches running up to them and would have been principally orientated east–west, to use the available dry land more effectively. So I am in no doubt they were defensive outworks, intended to protect the main enclosure from attack from the west.

As things currently stand, the Borough Fen fortified enclosure – for that surely is what it was – seems to have stood on its own in a landscape without any fields. I strongly suspect, however, that this will prove to be an illusion caused by the blanketing effect of later peats and flood clays. I would not be at all surprised to discover that there were a series of earlier, Bronze Age, settlements along the centre of the peninsula, on either side of, and maybe also beneath, the Iron Age fortified enclosure. The edges of the peninsula were bounded by two zones of Bronze Age field systems, which appeared to have been laid out slightly differently. The system to the south, around gravel quarries at West Deeping, seems to have followed the Fengate model, with parallel droveways running down to the wetland-edge at right angles and stockyards spaced at regular intervals between each of the boundary droves.

I was able to excavate the system to the north, at Welland Bank, and it proved to be somewhat more complex, with clear evidence for livestock, but also for manuring and the growing of crops in clearly defined fields. There was also evidence for the extraction of salt from the tidal waters of the Welland.[11] But the contrast between the landscapes of the Bronze and Iron Ages does seem quite marked, with fields and farms appearing to give way to a solitary, central, defended site. On the ground, however, it wasn't so simple. There was no evidence that the landscape of the Bronze Age fields was ever abandoned and allowed to revert to trees and scrub, as would have happened quite quickly in such a fertile area. And we also recovered quite a lot of Iron Age pottery at Welland Bank, where many features could be shown to have continued in use until about 600 BC. At this point it seems likely that rising water levels caused the abandonment of the field systems and led to the construction of the fortified enclosure. But we must be careful not to paint this change as some kind of disaster, because the construction of the substantial earthworks of the enclosure would have required massive manpower and our investigations further suggested that the interior was the scene of a sizable, and probably long-lived settlement. So the changes were about adaptation, rather than retreat and collapse. As we saw at the more low-lying site at Must Farm, people took advantage of the wetter conditions, using their boats and fish traps. We must also imagine that they worked out ways of trapping wildfowl and there is good evidence that in the Iron Age and early Roman period, communities were also extracting salt in semi-industrial quantities from the rising waters.[12]

So people adapted their ways of life and became more economically diverse. I am also sure they would have established close contacts with the farming communities on drier land, as well as maintaining their own farms on the less flood-prone parts of the growing wetland. Of course it's entirely speculative, but I wonder whether the Borough Fen fortified enclosure was constructed when the neighbouring communities on either side of the peninsula, at West Deeping and Welland Bank respectively, decided to come together – to pool their resources. Doubtless they were aware of the richness of their environment and had pride, too, in their new, enlarged community. So I see Britain's lowest 'hillfort' not as a statement of deterrence – keep away, or else! – so much as a symbol of local pride: look what we have achieved together. I can also see clear parallels between the Borough Fen defences and the town walls and imposing gate towers of the Middle Ages.* Those walls were as much about the display of wealth and success, as mere defence. For me, the Borough Fen enclosure is very similar: it is all about hope, identity and aspiration. I'm so pleased it has survived – and is now protected by law.

---

* A good fenland example is King's Lynn's South Gate (see Chapter 13).

# Billingborough Iron Age: Salt and Farming in the Northern Fens

Rapid social and economic changes are things we tend to associate with our own times. I'm writing this in the year 2018, when we celebrate the one-hundredth anniversary of votes for women. Two hundred years before that, we were sorting out the mess left by Waterloo and the end of the Napoleonic Wars. Midway between these two historical events comes the Great War of 1914–18, and fifty years ago, the start of the digital-electronic technological revolution. Epoch-changing developments seem to be happening every half-century. But surely this pace of change cannot be paralleled in the past? That depends on how you view and define your criteria. Yes, I concede that women's suffrage, modern warfare and microchips are huge steps (I hesitate to say 'advances' for warfare), but only when seen from our own times. Had I been living in the Neolithic, I would have viewed the arrival of metalworking as something that was just as important – and it would have taken many half-centuries to have absorbed the various steps of its social and economic consequences. It would have transformed how we cleared and farmed the land, built our houses and expressed our wealth, power and prestige.

We must never underestimate what Neolithic societies had achieved in the first one and a half millennia of farming, which was truly remarkable. In effect, they had opened up the land-scape. The arrival of metal, sometime just before 2500 BC, gave them far greater control over their surroundings, allowing com-munities to expand, and that, in turn, led to an elaboration of social networks across larger areas of the country. The new material wasn't a direct cause of change, but it allowed it to happen faster. The processes of economic and social change were, if anything, gathering pace when iron-working arrived in the seventh and eighth centuries BC – and like earlier technological advances it, too, played a role in the huge social and economic developments that happened during the five or so centuries prior to the Roman conquest of AD 43.

Britain has been an island for at least eight thousand years and there are some who clearly cherish our insularity. They view the past through red, white and blue-tinted spectacles. But archaeology and modern genetic science is showing that the reality was often far more complex. We saw in Chapter 7 that earlier Bronze Age ships were very seaworthy and that cross-Channel voyages must have been commonplace. Indeed, the many finds of imported continental metalwork, together with at least one of the heavy stone querns, from Flag Fen, prove this. But of course boats can carry people as well as objects, and recent genetic studies of prehistoric DNA from Lincolnshire have shown that there were a small, but significant, number of people who grew up in Africa and who were resident in the county during the Bronze and Iron Ages.[1] Dr Caitlin Green's study went on to show that the percentage of African migrants increased suddenly and dramatically in Roman times. In other words, migration is nothing new.

I have just outlined some of the reasons why I have never shared the popular view that somehow life in prehistory was slow to change. I also shy away from one of the alternatives: that people were constantly fighting and squabbling as they struggled for political supremacy. Such social instability invariably causes problems in the food chain, which results in hunger. Although the move away from barrow burial has probably meant that a smaller proportion of the growing Iron Age population can be studied as skeletons in graves, the Iron Age burials that have been recovered show good levels of nutrition, and the sort of wounds that are caused by hand-to-hand conflict are rare. Yes, of course there were periods of instability, but these were relatively short-lived. Economies that depend on the efforts of their young men to run farms and increasingly specialized crafts, such as wheelwrights and boat-builders, cannot afford to waste such skilled labour on something as destructive as internal warfare.

It would be a mistake to view any period of history or pre-history in a contextual vacuum and this certainly applies to the mid- and later Iron Age. The last five centuries BC were undoubtedly years of rapid change, but they were firmly based on advances made since the arrival and spread of farming across Britain, in 4000 BC. These changes can clearly be seen in modern excavations, through details of settlement arrangement and building modification – especially in the Fens, where preservation is often so superb. Some of the finest Iron Age sites anywhere in Britain are to be found in the southern Fens, especially in the lower reaches of the River Great Ouse, where they have been ably excavated by teams from Cambridge University.[2]

The extent of Iron Age settlement around the lower Great Ouse is still quite hard to assess comprehensively because of thick layers of blanketing flood clays, but sometimes we are allowed glimpses, especially around the edges of buried 'islands' and in gravel quarries, where the upper layers of topsoil and flood clay can be carefully removed by machines. In these situations occupation can be very dense, with a succession of substantial roundhouses, very often in their own individual ditched enclosures. There is considerable evidence of prosperity, with quantities of fine pottery, metalwork and domestic rubbish. Preservation is so good that it is often possible to detect changes in the way that buildings were used: sometimes ordinary houses appeared to become upgraded to shrines. Again, as we saw at Cat's Water, there was increasing evidence for social stratification, as shown by the range of house sizes. Livestock numbers do not appear to have been quite as high as around Fengate but there was far more evidence for ploughing – including, for example, large areas of plough scratches* still present in the subsoil, close to the settlements near Haddenham. It was a well-balanced pattern of classic 'mixed farming', which was able to reap the benefits of both wetland pasture and dry land arable.[3] And following the discoveries at Must Farm, we must also include fish, eels and wildfowl (bones of geese, duck and pelican were recovered, too), as another substantial source of winter protein.

The evidence for large Iron Age populations in the Greater Ouse Valley extends inland from the Fens to St Ives, Huntingdon and even St Neots. In population terms we must be looking at numbers comparable with parts of the Thames Valley – certainly thousands, not hundreds. Broadly similar levels of population can also be detected in the lower Nene and Welland Valleys, although these sites do not extend anything like as far upstream – and of course the floodplains themselves are narrower.

---

* Iron Age ploughs, known as ards, lifted, but did not turn the soil over, because they lacked a mouldboard.

\*

About halfway through the Fengate project, in the mid-1970s, I was becoming increasingly excited by what we were discovering, but I was also feeling frustrated. It seemed to me absurd that we were working in isolation. To be quite honest, I was itching to widen our keyhole glimpse of life on the prehistoric fen-edge, and see it as part of a broader canvas.

So I would try to get out and about as often as I could, and would drive around on the lookout for any development with possible archaeological potential. My old Land Rover, with the memorable first three letters of its number plate – ONK – which sounded exactly like its distinctive horn, was great for this task, because it was high and gave me an excellent view above most roadside walls and hedges. Inevitably, given the rural nature of the region, most of the places that interested me were gravel and stone quarries. Much of my time was spent in the Welland Valley, where most of the ballast used in the construction of Peterborough New Town was being excavated, but sometimes I would turn north at the Market Deeping crossroads and take the A15, where it follows the line of the Roman King Street, from Durobrivae, a few miles to the south, ultimately towards Lincoln. It was always quite a relief to leave the A15, as the Land Rover was a bit slow and lumbering and even back then, lorries and large vans would breathe down my neck, often forcing me to pull over into lay-bys. I've always hated having to delay traffic and rarely take my aged tractor (a 1964 International B414) onto the roads near my farm, because nowadays I find I'm delaying other tractors – which may be vast, but can still move like greyhounds.

Just north of Bourne comes the junction with the B1177 (the Donington Road), which veers slightly to the east, to follow the precise edge of the medieval fen. I like that road a great deal –

it is so rural and atmospheric. Somehow it has escaped the 'bungalow blight' that is such a sad feature of many parts of the Fens. Maybe this reflects the fact that, here, much of the land along the fen-edge still belongs to large farming estates. The villages along the Donington Road are evenly spaced and are all set back just over half a mile (a kilometre, say) from the fen-edge. This is a safe, flood-free distance, but it is also the geological spring line and of course springs would always have been a vital source of fresh water – which would have been important in a region where some watercourses were likely to have been slightly salty.

Many of the villages have Viking names, ending in the characteristic '-by', the Norse word for a farmstead or village. Dowsby is a good example and the road passes a short distance east of the fine, if slightly altered, seventeenth-century country house Dowsby Hall, which was the ancestral home of the Burrell family.[4] It was bought by my old Cambridge college, Trinity, in the 1920s and they let it to Henry Burtt, who was the largest grower of blackcurrants in Britain, mostly in nearby Rippingale Fen. In 1947 the BBC Radio producer Godfrey Baseley made a programme there, called *Farm Visit*, which gradually evolved into *The Archers*, and Baseley was the soap's first editor. He is reputed to have modelled Dan Archer on Henry Burtt, the blackcurrant grower. Old houses can sometimes tell some unusual tales.

Once you have driven through Dowsby and the smaller hamlet of Pointon, you come to Billingborough, the principal village in the area. Like other villages round about, the older buildings are made from Lincolnshire limestone, the best of which – and probably used at houses like Dowsby Hall – was from quarries begun in Roman times, at Ancaster (a Roman name, of course), a few miles west of the fen-edge, roughly midway between Grantham and Sleaford.

I knew the village of Billingborough partly from my exploratory Land Rover trips, but also because I used to travel to Sleaford once a week to rehearse with the Kesteven morris side. Now, I'm fully aware that I am not the most coordinated of people and in my younger days my dancing was charitably described as 'energetic' and 'enthusiastic', but never 'rhythmic', nor 'graceful'. But energy and enthusiasm is what drives morris dancing and gives it its charm and excitement. Beer helps, of course. We used to rehearse in a Scout Hut behind a Batemans pub in the centre of town – and nothing tastes quite as good as a pint or two of Batemans Beer, after a couple of hours of vigorous skipping about.

We danced in the classical, Cotswold tradition of morris dancing (the word morris is supposed to derive from Moorish,

*The Whittlesea Straw Bear Festival, January 2005. This shows various morris and molly dancers, together with the Straw Bear and the Baby Bear, beneath the canopy of the late seventeenth-century Butter Cross in the Market Place.*

which was another way of saying 'exotic' or 'foreign' in the Middle Ages) and the leaders of our side, Ray Worman and Ada Turnham, had close links with the increasingly popular electric morris movement. They had danced on the classic album *Morris On* (1972);[5] many of the musicians on this album had been associated with the famous folk-rock band Fairport Convention.

Through my interest in folksong and dancing I learned that the Fens had once had an active tradition of morris, which was known as molly dancing. The main event of the molly dancing year was the Whittlesey Straw Bear, which used to happen every winter, although it lapsed in 1909, to be revived in 1980.[6] The revival is based on actual memories and I reckon is remarkably accurate and captures the earlier tradition very well (without some of the violence that often went with it). Again, beer is involved and the festivities conclude with a parade in which dancers from all over the Fens accompany a man wearing an extraordinary thatched straw suit. He is the Straw Bear and his costume is made afresh, every year.

It used to be thought that the Lincolnshire fen-edge was only lightly populated in later prehistoric times, but from the 1970s, a number of excavations have shown that substantial sites are waiting to be discovered. The dig at Billingborough was one of the most remarkable of these.

I had heard on the archaeological grapevine that there was a very exciting dig at Billingborough, a place I knew from my weekly journeys to Sleaford. The excavation lay on the fen-ward side of the village in open, flat country. Air photos had revealed a series of yards and fields that ran down to the wetland-edge and many of these were threatened by a proposed new drainage scheme. The Billingborough dig took four seasons, from 1975 to 1978, and revealed extensive evidence of settlement from the middle of the Bronze Age through to the later Iron Age. It also became famous in archaeological circles for producing debris, known as briquetage, from salt-making, which we now realize was a major industry in the Iron Age Fens. At Billingborough, the salt extraction lasted some 400 years, from the eighth to the fifth centuries BC. But again, the main feature of the prehistoric and Roman landscape along this part of the fen-edge was the intensity of land use and the continuity of settlement. There do not appear to have been any breaks from the mid-second millennium BC until the first century AD. These were plainly well-inhabited landscapes.

The Billingborough excavations revealed a series of ditched enclosures, which came into existence in the middle of the second millennium BC, although there was some indication for later Neolithic and earlier Bronze Age activity (from, say, 2500–1500 BC), close by.[7] The excavators were able to prove that the water in the nearby wetland would fluctuate between fresh and salty, which would fit with the evidence for salt extraction, beginning in the first two or three centuries of the first millennium BC and ending sometime, perhaps, in the third. The evidence shows how settlements were surrounded by ditches – presumably mostly for drainage – and that a linear field system came into being during the Iron Age. This was aligned at right angles to the fen-edge, which suggests it was rather different from the fields that we excavated in the lower Nene Valley – which were positioned along the wetland margins. I suspect that the main reason for this was that the farmers in this northern stretch of the Fens were aware that the nearby wetlands were salty and influenced by tidal waters. So they laid out their fields in a way that made it easier to access the higher, flood-free grazing that skirted the wetter ground.

The Iron Age field system was followed by another in the early Roman period, and again, there are no reasons to suppose

that these new fields were constructed and occupied by incomers. These fields were also accompanied by several Romano-
British settlements, including one of slightly higher status. This
produced tiles and building materials that would not have been
used in the timber dwellings of most ordinary early Romano-
British communities.[8] It has been suggested that it might have
been an early 'villa-like' site. Most true Roman villas were
built during the third and fourth centuries AD, which was when
Roman Britain was enjoying its greatest prosperity.

With Billingborough we are entering the world of the Lincolnshire Fens, which are far less well known than their southern
counterparts. In some respects I am loath to correct this bias,
because part of the appeal of the Lincolnshire Fens is their
remoteness and the fact that so few people know about them.
I first discovered them not when I was scouting around in my
Land Rover looking for new sites, but almost two decades later,
in 1993, when I made the significant eight-mile shift from a
farmhouse near the Cambridgeshire village of Parson Drove, all
the way north, across the county boundary, to the Lincolnshire
village of Sutton St James. Although I am still registered with
the Parson Drove surgery, I sometimes think I might have moved
not 8 miles, but 80, to another country, not county.

I suppose an outsider might think that nothing much has
changed between our old and new locations: the dykes are still
deep and straight and the farms are distributed evenly across
the landscape; many of them include the old houses, built in
the earlier to mid-nineteenth century, with characteristic long,
sloping 'catslide' roofs, giving space for a corridor along the rear.
But nonetheless, everything is different. Parish churches are in
the Diocese of Lincoln, not Ely, and locals tend to look north
and east for their market towns: places like Boston, Spalding,

Holbeach and Long Sutton, whereas people down in Parson Drove tended to look south and west, towards Wisbech, March and Chatteris. This difference is also reflected in the way people speak: to the north you can hear the influence of the Midlands, whereas to the south of the county line there is a hint of Norfolk. Wisbech has its own unique accent, possibly born of the isolation that preceded the town's great prosperity in the seventeenth and eighteenth centuries. You can always tell a Wisbechian (pronounced 'Wisbeckian') by the way they pronounce the word 'right' as 'rate'.

So when I made the monumental 8-mile transition from Cambridgeshire to Lincolnshire I found that I too was now looking towards the north and east. The first place we discovered was Boston,* but I was soon forced to widen my outlook. It happened one day when I was out in our newly planted wood, spraying circles of weedkiller around the growing trees. I've always had 'green' leanings and hoped this would be a job I wouldn't have to do, but I hadn't bargained on the fertility of the soil, which encouraged fast-growing weeds, such as docks and nettles, to completely dominate the young tree seedlings. I can remember concentrating hard on what I was doing, because I didn't want to squirt any glyphosate on the wrong plants. Suddenly there was a deafening noise in the skies above, and the sun seemed to go in for a second. A Lancaster bomber roared over, banked left and headed back towards its base in Lincolnshire. Today the Battle of Britain Flight is based at Coningsby, close to the fen-edge, just south of Woodhall Spa – about an hour's drive to the north. That set me thinking, so the following weekend we went exploring.

The northern fen-edge has a character of its own. For a start, it isn't always very easy to determine whether one is in drained fenland or the flat 'skirtland' around the edge. In the southern

---

* See Chapter 13.

Fens the big giveaway is the black, peaty soil. But here the silts are less flat and low lying and the pale colour is not always very easy to distinguish from the limestone-rich gravels around the edge. The most northerly fen-edge is formed by the slopes of the southern Lincolnshire Wolds, which appear quite suddenly after an initial, relatively brief, gradual gradient. The main road north out of the Fens, the A16 (Boston to Louth road) climbs steeply up to the village of East Keal, and there are some stunning views across the Lincolnshire Fens if you pull over, about half a mile before you enter this village. I was busily photographing the view when I couldn't help noticing a van turning left towards the village of East Kirkby. Then I spotted that the turning also included a cream-and-brown sign to the Aviation Heritage Centre. I have loved old aeroplanes since I was a boy and that was too good to resist.

I've spent enough of my life working for 'official' institutions, such as local authorities and national museums, not to develop quite a strong liking for amateur organizations. Indeed, when we set up Flag Fen as a visitor attraction, that's how we organized it: an amateur-run charity, staffed by professionals. That way, we managed to tap the best of both worlds. So I was delighted when we turned into the East Kirkby Aviation Heritage Centre to see that the place hadn't been over-branded. I couldn't spot the dead hand of the consultant: everything struck me as amateur, but in the best sense of that word. The place was run by, and for, people who loved what they were doing and believed it was important. Almost everything seemed to carry a name; seats, information panels, photographs, displays: 'Given in loving memory of my dear husband, Flight Lt. Jacob Smith, late of 333 Squadron, Bomber Command'.*

I won't attempt to describe the museum at East Kirkby, but

---

* Not a real name.

it's sited on an old airfield with wartime buildings, including a control tower, NAAFI canteen and hangar.[9] It was founded by two Lincolnshire farming brothers, Fred and Harold Panton, in memory of their elder brother, Christopher, who was shot down and killed on a raid over Germany on the night of 30/31 March 1944. At the centre of the project is a Lancaster Bomber, known to everyone in Lincolnshire by her wartime name *Just Jane*.* Sadly, *Just Jane* isn't airworthy because her main spar (which unites the wings to the fuselage) is broken. So visitors can pay for rides when the aircraft is taken out to test its engines on the surviving runways of the old airfield. And of course all money goes towards the restoration of *Just Jane*, and recently there have been some exciting developments: modern technology will now allow the main spar to be repaired and there is the very real possibility that three Lancasters will be airworthy. One flies with the RAF's Battle of Britain Flight, but many Lancasters were built on the other side of the Atlantic by Avro Canada – and one is still airworthy, over there.

You might suppose that the airfield at East Kirkby is the only link between *Just Jane* and the local landscape, but there is another – and it's very unusual. In the past two or three decades, Lincolnshire cheese-makers have gained a growing reputation and you can buy their products right across Britain. One of the new cheeses was a cylindrical, black-wax-coated hard cheese sold as *Dambuster*, because of its striking resemblance to Barnes Wallis's famous 'bouncing bomb', used in that raid. The Dambusters, 617 Squadron, were based at RAF Scampton, about 5 miles (8 km) north of Lincoln. Then somebody had the bright idea of producing an identical, but smaller, black-wax

---

* *Just Jane* was a wartime cartoon strip in the *Daily Mirror*. Jane rarely remained clad for very long. She is depicted on the nose of the eponymous bomber.

cheese, which was named *Just Jane* and sold in aid of the plane. I've just checked: we've got one in the small fridge out in the barn (where we store sheep medicines) and another, already half-eaten, in the main, kitchen fridge. I know my wife and I are not alone in our liking for this cheese. *Just Jane*, both cheese and 'plane, had entered our lives.

The Fens of south Lincolnshire may be united by silty marine-deposited soils, but they are just as varied, in landscape terms, as their southern counterparts around Ely and the Lower Great Ouse. Admittedly there are fewer distinct 'islands' out in the wet-lands and the ones that do exist are much lower and less obvious than the ridges that run through Sutton and Haddenham. But one feature of the landscape is very striking and, if anything, has even more spectacular views of a great cathedral than the country around Ely.

Few British cathedrals can match Ely for architecture and setting and, apart from Durham, the only one I could name is, of course, Lincoln. This great cathedral was built on much firmer ground than its counterpart in the southern Fens and is therefore complete. Poor Ely lost one of its two very unusual west-end transepts when soft ground gave way at the end of the fifteenth century. But Lincoln is complete, and its soaring three towers dominate the surrounding landscape from the top of the hill at the centre of the city. The best views of the cathedral are from the Witham Valley, far below it, to the south and east. Sadly, the upper part of the valley will soon be traversed by the city's eastern bypass, which is under construction as I write. It has revealed a wealth of important archaeological remains, including three Bronze Age barrows, a late Bronze Age logboat, a likely Roman villa, Roman pottery kilns and a lot more.[10] Plainly this part of the Witham Valley was very heavily used and occupied in ancient times. But I rather doubt if the modern road, complete with its new bridge across the river, will do much to improve views of the cathedral (or the peace of the countryside).

The Witham Valley has a very distinctive character, with a broad, flat, peaty floodplain to the south and the gentle slopes of the Wolds foothills to the north. The original river would have had many courses through its expansive floodplain, but is now confined to a single, embanked northerly channel. I can't remember when I first encountered the Witham Valley, but over the years I have visited it many times, usually to view excavations. But one of my first encounters was during my morris dancing days and I was heading home after a gig in a pub on the outskirts of Horncastle, a charming market town about 5 miles (8 km) north of the Witham Fens. Originally a Roman walled town called *Bannovallum*, modern Horncastle is famous for its surviving walls and its many antique and junk shops. So it is something of a local Mecca for anyone interested in the past.

I was driving south from Horncastle, and for some reason, I found I had departed from the main road to Coningsby and was heading for the small fen-edge village of Revesby. And the reason I noticed my error was a large stone-arched gate, surmounted by a heraldic lion. I had never seen it before. I'd just passed through the village of Scrivelsby and as soon as I got home I pulled out my copy of Pevsner's *Lincolnshire*.[11] The gateway marks the entrance to the park of Scrivelsby Court, laid out by Humphry Repton in the late eighteenth century. The original manor house burned down in 1761 and was demolished, like so many others, in the 1950s. The Lion Gate was first built in the 1530s and was rebuilt in 1851. But the story behind it is extraordinary. The lion is the symbol of the Queen's Champion, and the man who holds the honour of this title is the feudal lord of the Manor of Scrivelsby.

The post of King or Queen's Champion dates back to the Norman Conquest and its possession replaces any payable rent. The Lord of the Manor of Scrivelsby is also the Standard Bearer of England. The champion's role was to defend the king or queen if challenged. He was also expected to ride into the coronation banquet in Westminster Hall, in full armour, to defend the new monarch against any usurpers. There were other splendid coronation rituals, including the throwing down of the gauntlet – several times. These rituals were discarded by Queen Victoria, but the office still lives on, and is held by the Dymoke family who have been royal champions since the coronation of Richard II in 1377. There is something so Lincolnshire about the way such rich history hasn't been trumpeted from the rooftops: there are no signs proclaiming you are now entering 'Dymoke Country'. I won't say the Lion Gate is taken for granted, but it certainly sits very comfortably, and modestly, within this gently undulating landscape on the edge of the Fens.

As soon as you leave the Wolds and venture out onto the flat floodplain of the Witham Valley, you are in another world. The modern landscape has been completely transformed by drainage and this transformation has been so profound that I still find it difficult to picture in my head. Today, the River Witham flows south-eastwards in straight lengths, between high flood banks. In its upper reaches, close to Lincoln, the parallel flood banks are raised remarkably high because the river needs to be confined to increase its pace of flow, for the long journey across the broad expanse of Holland Fen* to its outfall into the North Sea, at Boston.

---

* 'Holland' here probably refers to 'hollow land', rather than our neighbour across the North Sea.

Highly engineered modern drainage systems require constant updating and improvement and nowadays such work is always preceded by an archaeological assessment. In 2004, a series of trenches ahead of drainage improvements near one of the many pumping stations on the Witham banks, near Washingborough, about 2 miles (3 km downstream (east) of Lincoln, revealed clear evidence for Late Bronze Age activity. A dig was immediately commissioned and I had the very good fortune to visit it several times, because it was being filmed for a *Time Team* documentary.[12] Before the television programme had been proposed, Maisie had been made the project's wood consultant – and soon she found herself very busy.

At the first, or assessment, stage of the project, some of us thought that the new site at Washingborough was going to be another Flag Fen, largely, I think, because there were so many posts. The finds were also of about the same date. But we soon changed our minds when the larger, follow-up excavations began and a series of substantial trenches were opened up. These revealed that the site had been occupied between 1100 and 800 BC – in the Late Bronze Age. The dig produced quantities of pottery, a fine carved wooden bowl (shaped to resemble a pottery vessel, complete with a carved foot-ring on the base), and quantities of animal bone fragments, including sheep, cattle, pigs and a few horses, together with wild deer. Neither wildfowl nor fish were common, but there was good evidence for the grinding and cultivation of wheat and barley. The people who used this site were probably farmers from the surrounding uplands. This was not a permanent settlement on the wetland-edge, like, say, at contemporary Must Farm to the south, because there was no evidence for houses and for sustained, on-the-spot, domestic life. So what was going on?

To answer that question we must turn the calendar back to around 1500 BC when I have suggested there was a 'Domestic

Revolution'. Essentially, this was all about moving important ceremonies away from the region's specialized ritual landscapes, back to local communities – where people lived. This new pattern of religious observation was all about returning the ritual and ceremonial back to the farms and villages where it was needed, to mark and celebrate quite ordinary aspects of life: marriages, funerals, births, the transfer of land and the fixing of borders. Today we record these changes through wedding, death or birth certificates, or by paying lawyers to draw up deeds of entitlement to land or buildings. Even now, few of these things can be done entirely without ceremony or formality, in case other members of the community remain ignorant of the events. It matters if you live and work locally that somebody else now owns the meadow that leads down to the only ford across the river – or whatever. At a very basic level, the move from rather remote ceremonial sites to special places nearer people's homes was very significant, because it gave people greater control of their immediate surroundings. I think what we're looking at here are the origins of what much later we would call the parish system.

At Flag Fen we were given glimpses into some of the ceremonies that were taking place at wetland sites. These were places that were seen as being liminal – on the edge – of the ordinary domestic world and that of the gods and ancestors who ruled beneath the water and beyond the horizon. Flag Fen combined being a causeway and boundary with a role as a ceremonial site. Washingborough was rather different.[13] Many posts had been driven into the muds on the river's edge, but these were to support and reinforce a series of timber and brushwood platforms that extended out into the river, but never across it. Looking back, some aspects of it seem to anticipate the slightly later site at Must Farm.

Washingborough produced abundant evidence that the timber platforms were where people were carrying out ordinary tasks

*A reconstruction by the late David Hopkins of life on the Washingborough raised platform beside the River Witham, sometime between 1100 and 800 BC. Note the square tank in the foreground, possibly used for the brewing of beer.*

such as weaving fabrics, making bone and antler tools, wood-working, basket-making, leather-working and even coppicing. Rather surprisingly, given their watery setting, the platforms were the site of metalworking and there was also considerable evidence for feasting. The feasting and the metalworking hint at high-status activities, because there is now increasing evidence to suggest that Bronze Age metalworkers were quite highly regarded and would have had considerable social status. But the feature that was most revealing was a strange square wooden tank, carefully lined with hides to make it waterproof.

Similar tanks have been found at other sites in Britain and Ireland, and they are all accompanied by large numbers of burnt rounded stones. These stones were heated and dropped in the water to raise its temperature – and experiments have shown that this is a very efficient way of heating a large quantity of water. Various theories have been put forward about why so much water needed to be heated. Some people have suggested they were Bronze Age sauna baths. But for me the most convincing theory, backed up by some good evidence, is that these pits were the equivalent of a brewery's mash tuns, where water and malt were heated together as part of the brewing process. We know that barley, an essential ingredient of beer, was present at Bronze Age Washingborough. However, I think it would be a big mistake to assume that the platforms were prehistoric riverside pubs. There is abundant evidence from many pre-industrial tribal societies that the consumption of drugs and alcohol was never a leisure activity. The altered state of mind they brought about was seen as appropriate to religious rites and as an accompaniment to feasts that celebrated significant tribal ceremonies or political events.

I think it's also significant that the Washingborough platforms were placed on the side of the biggest river in the area. Almost certainly the Witham would have been a major territorial boundary, which was marked and emphasized by the ceremonies on the platforms. But as time passed and the population grew, so territories expanded and boundaries acquired fresh significance as places where communities could come together. And this probably explains what was happening later in the Iron Age, when the Witham produced a truly extraordinary object – and another very remarkable site.

We all take it for granted that an appreciation of architectural history will deepen our understanding of country houses and their parks, or of parish churches in their villages; but sometimes special objects have been found out in the open country, and these require history and context, too. The more we appreciate the details of such landscape settings, the better we will grasp the importance of the objects themselves. The Witham Shield, one of the greatest treasures of the British Museum, is just such an object.

It was found in the river near Washingborough and Fiskerton in 1826 and is an outstanding example of early Celtic art. It was made sometime between 300 and 400 BC, most probably in England, although it is inlaid with polished red coral beads, which most probably came from the Mediterranean. The shield is parallel-sided and rounded at top and bottom, and if used would have protected a man's chest and waist. Today, all that survives is the thin decorative bronze sheeting that once covered what was essentially a wooden shield. The wood was only a third of an inch (8mm) thick, so would not have been very strong in combat. The thin bronze would have added little, if any, additional protection. I am in little doubt it was a cere-monial shield – and a fabulously beautiful one, at that. The centre of the shield is decorated with three highly ornate bosses, linked by a raised rib. The central boss has the coral inlay and is positioned slightly above centre, but directly in front of the holder's hand-grip.

Celtic art has its origins across Europe, but it was taken to remarkable heights in Britain. I would suggest it was our greatest contribution to world art, prior to the development of the English style of parks and gardens in the eighteenth century. Essentially, Celtic art is about life and movement.[14] It makes use of formalized animal forms, scrolls and swirls, which are quite distinct from the static, balanced and symmetrical motifs of the classical world. Celtic motifs are often positioned off centre and slightly off balance, but in a competent, controlled way that gives the piece movement and energy. The Witham Shield was also decorated with an extraordinary wild boar with highly exaggerated long legs that dangle down on either side of the central boss. This boar was cut out in leather, which was riveted to the bronze sheeting. You can just discern the outline, if you know where to look, but fortunately for us it was accurately recorded in a fine drawing published in 1863. For me, that faint but superbly confident silhouette cartoon of a boar is great art, and the person who drew it possessed immense talent. That shield would have spoken volumes about the man who owned it. And there is something about that long-legged boar: I think the artist must also have had a wicked sense of humour.

We cannot be certain, of course, but it seems very likely that the Witham Shield had been offered to the waters of the river at a very special prehistoric causeway that was excavated in 1981, following the discovery there of a coral-inlaid Iron Age sword hilt by a metal detectorist. The new site was located just 750 metres (820 yds) downstream (east) of the Washingborough platforms. Essentially, the Fiskerton causeway was similar to Flag Fen, but it was later and shorter-lived.[15] If anything, however, the finds were even more high status. They included six swords and eleven spearheads and fragments of sword scabbards and probably shields, too. The site also produced six big axes, metalworking tools, files and an early metal saw. Other finds included complete

*The Early Iron Age shield from the River Witham (c.400–300 BC),
as drawn by A. W. Franks in 1863. Note the outline of a
long-legged boar, which is now very hard to discern on
the shield. In the collections of the British Museum.*

and fragmentary pots and a number of bronze rings. All in all,
the assemblage recalls what we found at Flag Fen and would
appear to represent ceremonies connected with life's rites of
passage: death, maybe marriage, and completion of apprentice-
ships. But the very high-status objects, such as the coral-inlaid
sword hilt and the Witham Shield, suggest that, unlike Flag Fen,
the River Witham was perhaps a major tribal boundary in the
final four or five centuries BC. We naturally tend to linger over
glamorous finds such as the shield and sword, but the Fiskerton
causeway had another secret up its sleeve. And it was only
revealed when specialists began to examine the tree rings of the
causeway's posts.

The causeway consisted of a double row of posts about 2.4 metres (8 ft) apart, with another row some 6 metres (20 ft) away. The causeway between the post rows was built up using horizontal timbers and brushwood, much the same as at Flag Fen, only the Fiskerton posts were very much taller – in one case (which had to be pulled from the ground by a mechanical digger), the post was 5 metres (16 ft) long. The posts were tall, but otherwise they seemed ordinary enough, as did their felling dates, which started in the winter of 457 BC and continued, on and off, for some 150 years until after 361 BC, when the last posts were replaced. The surprise came when the tree-ring specialists began to examine the pattern of post replacement and it was discovered that this had happened on at least nine distinct occasions. That was somewhat remarkable (at Flag Fen, for example, the posts seemed to have been replaced as and when they were needed), but when the dates were examined by a specialist in paleo-astronomy it was discovered that every one of the dates when posts were replaced (which occurred on a sixteen-to-eighteen year cycle) coincided with a year when the moon was in total eclipse.[16] It might be supposed that this was the mystical sign they were waiting for, before they felt able to fell the trees: but some of the eclipses would not have been visible from Lincolnshire. However, the people involved knew they were happening. Quite reasonably, the paleo-astronomers went on to suggest that in the Iron Age certain people had acquired the necessary knowledge of complex lunar and solar cycles to be able to predict lunar eclipses. This caused, and continues to cause, much controversy. Personally, I think the evidence speaks for itself and that they did indeed possess this knowledge. We sometimes forget that individuals with the minds of an Einstein or a Newton must also have existed in pre-literate societies – and sites like Fiskerton are their enduring legacy.

We noted at Flag Fen that people returned to make offerings

throughout the Iron Age and into Roman times, but by then I think it was becoming rather a faint memory. Something similar happened in Roman times at Fiskerton, where the site became a major and quite long-lived focus for ceremonial offerings from the later first century AD, through to the end of the third century. Interestingly, some of the Romano-British offerings included four top-quality whetstones made from Kentish ragstone. It is worth recalling here that at least one of the Bronze Age quernstones from Flag Fen was also quarried in Kent, which would suggest that trade along the North Sea coast was already an old tradition. The archaeological evidence suggests that it increased throughout the Iron Age, doubtless as sea-going ships improved, but the pace and frequency of cross-Channel contacts was to rise dramatically after the Roman conquest of AD 43. Roman influences would leave an enduring mark on the Fens, but not in a predictable manner. As we will soon discover, most of the 'Romans' didn't come from Italy, and many of the changes were largely home grown. But we are still living with their consequences.

# Castor:
# A Roman Palace with
# Saxon Prospects

*Tim Potter – Stonea Camp – Stonea Grange –
E. T. Artis and the Dairy at Milton Hall –
Durobrivae and Castor*

There's nothing like a winter dig to cement or sunder relationships. And that freezing cold site at Mucking, overlooking the Thames Estuary, where we trowelled the foundations
of Iron Age roundhouses back in 1966, was no exception. The
fellow student who found me the job was called Tim Potter. We
were both at the same college at Cambridge, although Tim was
a year ahead of me and had decided to specialize in the Roman
period. What I didn't know then, because we rarely discussed
such things, being more interested in the excitement of the here
and now, was that Tim Potter's father was the headmaster of
March Grammar School (now Neale-Wade Academy) in the
heart of the Cambridgeshire Fens. Tim and I became good friends
and I now realise that Tim's enthusiasm for the place where he
grew up was to have an effect on my life, very much later.

I frequently call in at March market on Wednesdays and

Saturdays and I love walking through the tall nave of the parish church, St Wendreda's, now on the edge of the modern town, where I always pause to look up at the sixteenth-century carved angel roof – one of the best in the area. Tim Potter had views on most aspects of life and I would have loved to have discussed his old parish church, but I hadn't discovered St Wendreda's when he was excavating at Stonea Camp. Sadly, dear Tim died in 2000, at the tragically early age of fifty-five.

After graduation, our paths diverged. Tim was very much an archaeological high-flyer. He got a very good degree and moved seamlessly from Cambridge to a research position in the British School in Rome and then to a curatorial job at the British Museum. It was while he was at the BM that he returned to his fenland roots and began to excavate a remarkable Roman site on an outlying 'island' at Stonea (pronounced 'Stony'), just a couple of miles south-east of March, the town where he had grown up. The gravel subsoil at Stonea doubtless explains its name (stones + water). Looking back on it, it was not surprising that our paths should have crossed again, if you bear in mind that many important Romano-British sites were often located on or near major Iron Age centres. And this is what happened at Stonea, where Roman Stonea Grange Farm is preceded by Iron Age Stonea Camp.

My interest in the Roman period of Fen history began to be aroused when we were excavating the Cat's Water farm, at Fengate. A few years later, during our researches at the Borough Fen Iron Age defended site, our attention was drawn to a smaller Romano-British farmstead a few metres to the east. By Roman times, the area occupied by the earlier enclosure was probably too wet for permanent settlement, but the presence of the Romano-British site does suggest that it hadn't been entirely forgotten.

It was the revelation of the Borough Fen fort's later Iron Age date that set me looking for similar sites elsewhere in the Fens.

I was curious to see what happened to them in Roman times –
something I was unable to do at Borough Fen, because of rising
water levels. Maybe I could find somewhere a bit drier? As a first
step, I turned to what is still the bible of Roman fenland studies,
a superbly comprehensive survey that should have become a
model for well-preserved Romano-British landscapes across
Britain. It was produced by the Royal Geographical Society in
1970 and is still one of the most thumbed books on my shelves.[1]
Like all good studies of the Roman landscape, *The Fenland in
Roman Times* pays due attention to what had gone before, in
the Iron Age. Indeed, its second plate is a remarkable air photo,
taken, I would guess, in the late 1960s, and complete with the
trailing edge of a wing, in the upper-right corner, of Stonea Camp.
Stonea Camp belongs to a slightly strange category of late Iron
Age sites known as *oppida*, this being the plural form of the
Latin word *oppidum*, meaning a town. Just like the term 'hillfort', this is extremely misleading.

*Oppida* were large defended enclosures that surrounded
a settlement, or settlements, together with open spaces. They
were never laid out as towns as we would understand the term
today, with a close network of streets and houses and a central
administration that supervised the disposal of rubbish, sewage
etc. True (i.e. self-governing) towns were a concept that arose
around the Mediterranean and were imported to Britain by the
Romans. They never really caught on as an idea and were largely
abandoned when Roman rule ended in the early fifth century
AD, only to return two or three centuries later, in Saxon times,
with the rise of new European trading networks, whose growth
was encouraged by the influence of the Emperor Charlemagne
in the eighth century. These later towns were based on trade
and were less rigidly laid out than their Roman antecedents, so
they became a fixture of the emerging medieval landscape. Well-
known early towns of this period in East Anglia include Norwich

and Harwich – the '-wich' part of their names refers to the Old English word 'wic' meaning, among other things, a trading or industrial settlement or harbour.[2]

*The Iron Age phases at Stonea Camp (near March, Cambridgeshire) have been described as Britain's lowest-lying hillfort. This photo shows some of the ditch-and-bank ramparts (foreground), which curl round to the left, in the middle distance.*

The ditched enclosure at Stonea Camp was far larger (24 acres, 9.6 ha) than Borough Fen and shows at least three clear phases of development.[3] Today it survives as a series of large ditches and banks that are well worth visiting, but it was very nearly destroyed in the 1970s when farmers were being strongly encouraged by grants and government agencies to rip out hedges, drain ponds or wetlands and smooth out any irritating humps and bumps that might get in the way of profitable ploughing. And that was what happened at Stonea Camp. Many of the surviving Iron Age earthworks of the camp had been bulldozed flat and an unusual late medieval house, complete with two rounded staircase towers, was demolished at Stitches Farm, also in the 1970s. The damage at Stonea was bad, but sadly it was by no means unique.

The main excavations of the pre-Roman Iron Age Stonea Camp took place in the early 1990s, when it was realized how much damage had been done to the site and that it would still be possible to stop it and maybe even to repair some of the worst depredations – at least visually, if not, of course, archaeologically: when ditches and banks are bulldozed, all the different layers and deposits become hopelessly mixed together. So a short, sharp campaign to halt the damage, to research and date the occupation of the site, and then to restore the earthworks was proposed by the County Council Archaeological Field Unit. Work would be spread over three seasons of excavation, between 1991 and 1992. The project was directed by another Tim, Tim Malim, who was well experienced in fenland archaeology.

Tim Malim and his team revealed that the supposed *oppidum* at Stonea Camp was certainly never a town or a heavily occupied settlement. But it was clearly a centre of some importance, because enormous efforts had been made to defend it with a series of very substantial ditches and banks, which were constructed in several phases during the late Iron Age, from about 100 BC, through to the mid-first century AD.[4] But there was nothing about the finds to indicate actual domestic occupation. Most houses and settlements produce lots of broken and abraded pottery, worn or damaged bone or flint tools, charcoal and burnt clay and large quantities of animal bone, some of it with butchers' marks. It would appear that the great earthworks at Stonea Camp were not protecting houses, certainly during the Iron Age, although there might have been a short-lived settlement there very early in the first century AD – more or less contemporary with the first decades of the Roman occupation, up until the Boudiccan revolt of AD 60. So what were the new ditches and banks protecting?

It's not known for absolutely certain, but it seems very likely that Stonea Camp was the original findspot of several hoards of coins and valuable metalwork, some of them revealed by metal detectorists. Tim Malim's excavations also produced two burials and evidence for many other human bones and there are good reasons to suppose that the small 'island' of Stonea was regarded as sacred in Iron Age times – and indeed earlier, to judge by the presence there of Bronze Age barrows. So we might see the earthwork defences as being erected to protect something even more valuable to members of the local Icenian tribe than mere dwellings. Stonea was where the souls of the ancestors resided and this spiritual strength was to ensure its survival into Roman times, despite the cruel repression that resulted from the Boudiccan revolt of AD 60/61. But by then Stonea had become a very different place.

I have warm memories of the year 1980. I had returned from Canada just two years previously and I was spending much of the time with Maisie driving around the Fens in ONK, my faithful Land Rover, looking for a house. It's amazing how those estate agents' signs stand out across a flat, treeless landscape. We got very good at spotting them from miles away. Being archae-ologists, we didn't have much money, but we were just able to scrape together the price of a down payment. I was also very aware that my job – indeed our entire Welland Valley Project – depended on the most fragile of annually renewable grants. But on paper at least I did have a 'real' job (with a contract, no less). That was important, because it meant that we qualified for a mortgage. Even so, it took some doing.

I walked into our bank and told the junior manager who interviewed me about the Welland Valley Field Officer's job: its prestige, its rock-solid security and superb prospects – ultimately leading to a professorship at Cambridge. And he lapped it up eagerly, even offered me more money than I wanted. Fortunately for me, the truth never emerged. Eventually we found a farmhouse, built in 1907, in the Parish of Parson Drove, Cambridgeshire, about a mile from the county border with Lincolnshire. And of course it needed much work to make it comfortable. So I set about insulating the roof and doing countless other jobs. I was so glad I had learned carpentry at school.

Parson Drove isn't far from March and we often passed through it while we were exploring the area. I was developing quite an eye for the subtleties of the Fen landscape and I can remember spotting the edges of Stonea 'island' as we approached it from the open fen. We'd already heard about the new dig at Stonea Grange Farm, and Tim Potter was very keen that we pay him a visit. He'd faxed me (remember them?) a map, which showed the site to lie about a quarter of a mile north of Stonea Camp, on the other side of the dyke, called Harding's Drain, that bisected the natural 'island'. When we got there we walked around the edge of the excavation to where we could see Tim working, on the far side of the dig. Incidentally, archaeologists never step into somebody else's trench, unless they are invited to do so. It's part of on-site good manners: you only walk where you know you can tread safely, without causing any disturbance; I have heard the eggshell crunch of a crushed human skull and I was so glad it didn't come from beneath my heel.

By now Tim had spotted us and was beckoning us over enthusiastically. He didn't leave what he was doing to greet us, because he was obviously very excited. We jumped down into the trench and hurried across to him. Tim and a small team of diggers were working in a large Roman ditch and had just got down to the wetter deposits. We knelt down on the edge of the ditch and looked closely at the filling, which was damp rather than wet, but had plainly been waterlogged until very recently.

The archaeologists were revealing quantities of wood and other organic material and Tim was plainly delighted. He was always a very enthusiastic person, but this time the width of his grin threatened to dislocate his jaw.

I don't think it was a coincidence that the new Roman regional authorities decided to build an administrative centre on Stonea 'island'. We know from similar sites elsewhere in Britain that they tended to make use of places that had been important in the late Iron Age and for fairly obvious reasons: people knew about them and it showed a respect for earlier traditions, which it was hoped would help communities come to terms with the new power in the land. And on the whole this policy worked: the Romans were nothing if not pragmatic. Aside from the fact that Stonea was a good, flood-free location in an otherwise very wet environment, the presence nearby of the huge earthworks of Stonea Camp was important too. We now believe that the Iron Age Camp had been a major centre for the dominant Iceni tribe and that it played a significant role in the Boudiccan revolt of AD 60/61. Indeed, Roman troops, hurriedly called in from the west to help suppress the uprising in East Anglia, probably marched along the Roman Fen Causeway, which crosses the natural 'island' of March (which includes Stonea as an outlier) a mile or so to the north.

We know that the Roman administration punished the communities who supported the rebellion and this would probably help to explain why work on the new small town and administrative centre at Stonea Grange was not begun for a couple of generations, only starting around AD 125.[5] The main feature of the new regional centre was a large square building whose walls were very substantial indeed at ground level. There were also the remains of a massive raft-like foundation made from courses of rough stone and layers of mortar. I'm no expert on stone-built buildings, but I can remember seeing the excavations in progress on several occasions and being very struck by how massive the walls were. Put another way, they seemed much more robust than they needed to have been. Tim explained his theory that those wall footings were not for an ordinary building – say a town hall equivalent – but for something much more substantial, such as a four-storeyed tower. A building like that would have dominated the surrounding landscape, almost as much as the later cathedral at Ely, which can just be seen on the horizon, far to the east.

Opinion is still divided about Tim's tower. I loved the idea when he first suggested it to me, but later, on reflection, I confess I began to have my doubts. Yes, I too could imagine such a grand structure dominating a large town, but with the best will in the world, the settlement at Stonea Grange was a *very* small town; indeed, I'm not sure the word 'town' is altogether appropriate, although the dig did produce clear evidence that land off the two excavated streets had been carefully laid out in neat squares, each of 50 Roman Feet (where one RF equalled 11.65 inches or 29.57 cm). I think it would probably be best to describe Stonea as a Roman administrative centre surrounded by houses and a settlement. But the people who lived and worked there were not short of cash: they seemed to drop coins out of their pockets with extraordinary frequency and they left behind a huge collection of Roman pottery – much of it made overseas – and a wealth of brooches, rings, ornaments and metal implements. Many of these items are in a form of bronze that by Roman times included added zinc, which gave it extra hardness and helped to resist decay; strictly speaking, it was more brass than bronze.

The settlement and centre at Stonea Grange lasted until about AD 220, when the whole character of the place changed from somewhere occupied by local government officers to a more conventional farming settlement. The big administrative building went out of use and was abandoned. Sheep appeared to have been the mainstay of this later economy. The Stonea Grange settlement continued through the third century and into the prosperous decades of the fourth century, when Romano-British culture developed its own distinctive character. This was the classic era of the Roman villa. During the third and fourth centuries AD, property boundaries that had been established early in the site's life continued to be well respected. The settlement was thriving at the end of Roman rule around AD 410 and continued well into Saxon times without any interruption. The people remained the same and were probably related to those Iron Age farmers who had helped to erect the nearby earthworks at Stonea Camp. There was absolutely no evidence for any incoming Anglo-Saxon migrants. We cannot be certain precisely when the Stonea Grange settlement ended, but it was probably sometime in the mid-seventh century AD when people decided they had to move elsewhere – probably towards higher ground near the modern village of Doddington, on March 'island'. This shift away from the lowest land was most probably due to rising groundwater levels.

There is some evidence to suggest that areas of the Fens may have formed part of an Imperial estate in Roman times. The farms and settlements on such estates were run for the benefit of retired soldiers or civil servants. One of the main arguments in favour of such an estate is the fact that some field systems in the Roman Fens appear to have been laid out on a grid-like plan, known as centuriation. Something similar happened with the block layout at Stonea Grange. Fields that are thought to exhibit signs of centuriation occur at Christchurch, a few kilometres east of Stonea, and also close to the Roman Fen Causeway. And there are other examples elsewhere along the Fen Causeway – for instance near Downham, in Norfolk. I must say I don't find these arguments particularly convincing: for a long time people believed that the Fengate Bronze Age fields were probably Roman, simply because they were straight-edged and regularly laid out. I'm inclined to think that if a Romano-British farmer had wanted to lay out some square fields, he did not have to be a civil or military surveyor to have done so. I have done it with two balls of string and some pegs. I'd like a bit more evidence from different sources to back the theory up.

There is a tendency to present the Roman period in Britain as one in which the rule of law, literacy and, yes, civilization was imposed on a constantly feuding Celtic population. Sometimes this treatment can go further: I can remember one of my schoolteachers drawing parallels between the Romans arriving in Britain and the British in Africa. On the surface this might seem like an easy analogy, but it also hides major oversimplifications and assumes that the people being colonized in both places were incapable of governing themselves. It also ignores their cultural complexity. And of course the arrogance of the colonialists always fails to make allowance for what will happen when the colonial era ends and the structure of native cultures has been eroded by years of imperial rule.

The fundamental lesson to be learned from this is that widely separated, simplistic historical analogies often conceal, rather than reveal, the truth. Indeed, the latest archaeological evidence now suggests that the end of the Roman era in Britain was far from chaotic, although it was probably unplanned. But it was never a simple picture of Britons versus Romans, rapidly followed by hordes of Anglo-Saxon incomers. The reality was far more culturally diverse and complex. And that diversity extended around and into the Fens. We have seen what was happening on one large 'island' in the central Fens. We will now turn our attention due west, to the other end of the Roman Fen Causeway where it leaves the prosperous Roman town of Durobrivae in the lower Nene Valley, just outside the modern city of Peterborough.

*

The lower Nene Valley was extensively quarried for gravel in the 1970s and '80s and the pits were subsequently converted into picturesque watery parks and gardens, which are now visited and enjoyed by hundreds of Peterborians, their families and children. But it was very different when I first arrived in the area in the early 1970s. I confess that even in my twenties I found my transatlantic commuting lifestyle difficult: jet lag can leave you exhausted for many days. It was always harder to adapt following the west–east crossing than after the return flight to Canada in the autumn. On one or two occasions, I even had to cross the Atlantic more than once in the spring. My problems were further complicated by the fact that I had nowhere permanent to live in Peterborough, so would have to commute from my parents' house near Baldock in north Hertfordshire, some 65 miles (105 km) to the south, until I could find somewhere local to rent – a process that took several weeks.

I was preparing myself mentally for my second period of Atlantic jet lag in the late winter of 1972 when an airmail envelope in my father's handwriting arrived at our Toronto flat. I was a bit surprised, because my father wasn't a great one for writing chatty letters – that was my mother's territory and she was much better at it. His news was, to say the least of it, unexpected. He had been to see his elder brother, whom I still think of as Uncle Johnny, at his house at the other end of the village, which had been substantially enlarged by my great-grandfather in the late nineteenth century. The heart of Weston Park was a small Georgian house, which had been almost completely submerged by my great-grandfather's 'extensions'. My great-grandfather and his son had liked to entertain a number of younger house guests – sometimes, but not always, relatives – who simply stayed at the park and socialized with their own children and their friends. I gather life at the park in late Victorian and Edwardian times was very free and easy. My great-grandfather was a Cambridge geological academic (part-time, I think) and my grandfather was a very liberal man who liked watercolour-painting and even found time to paint landscapes (with tanks and shell-shattered trees) during his four years in the trenches of the Somme.

One of the long-term guests at the park was a young man called Tom Wentworth-Fitzwilliam, who became a good friend of my Uncle Johnny and always had a soft spot for the Pryors of Weston Park. When Tom was staying at the park he was a charming young man from an old and noble family, but was never expected to inherit the title of Earl Fitzwilliam. Following a sequence of tragic and unexpected deaths in his family, however, Tom became the 10th Earl Fitzwilliam, inheriting the title from his second cousin in 1952. He and Lady Fitzwilliam lived at Milton Hall, on the outskirts of Peterborough near the modern suburb of Bretton. As I read my father's letter it became clear that Uncle Johnny had mentioned to his old friend Tom that I was an archaeologist working in Peterborough. I can imagine his reply: 'Excellent, well he'd better come and stay at Milton.' Although Tom died in 1979, I still have warm memories of him: tall, fair-haired and quite shy, but impeccably polite, very intelligent and with a remarkable ability to put people at their ease.

*The elegant mid-eighteenth century south front of Milton Hall, Peterborough by the leading Palladian architect Henry Flitcroft.*

My first glimpse of Milton Hall was unforgettable. I entered through the lodge gates off the Peterborough road and slowly drove through the elegant park, which had been remodelled by Humphry Repton in 1791. I immediately spotted several ancient oaks, which may well have been late medieval survivors. My father had mentioned that the house was very grand, but when I arrived outside what I now realize was the north door of the oldest (1594) surviving wing, I was completely lost for words. I hadn't yet found a copy of the then out-of-print Pevsner guide to the buildings of Peterborough, or I would have known that Milton was the largest house in Cambridgeshire.[6]

After a cup of tea, Tom Fitzwilliam took me round to the back of the house where we met the housekeeper, who showed me to a flat on the third floor, overlooking the drive and the park. With a window open you could just hear the faintest rumble of Peterborough traffic in the far distance. Meanwhile, somewhere out in the park, woodpeckers were tapping away and a few grey squirrels leapt from branch to branch in the tall lime trees that bordered the house. It was a wonderful flat with a large sitting room, kitchen, bathroom and two bedrooms. Yet it also felt strangely wild – like a child's dream tree house. And it was to be my English home for the next three years.

I hadn't been staying at Milton for very long when one day the phone rang and Tom Fitzwilliam asked whether I'd like to see the dairy floor. At this point I must confess that my research into the region's archaeology was still relatively sparse. I knew quite a lot about its prehistory, but was still very ignorant of its remarkable Roman story, although I had heard a lot from the members of the Nene Valley Research Committee – the local body responsible for my projects' academic standards. One of their principal members, Dr John Peter Wild of Manchester University, is a leading Roman expert and the acknowledged authority on Roman and other ancient textiles. As used to be the case in those days, John Peter acquired much of his practical hands-on knowledge through his family's involvement in the Manchester textile industry. John Peter was also fascinated by the archaeology of Castor, the village just outside the back entrance into Milton Park, and it was through listening to him and his colleagues talk that I learned just how important the lower Nene Valley had been in Roman times. One of the people they had often mentioned when we all got together in various local pubs was an early nineteenth-century archaeologist called E.T. Artis (1789–1847), who for some reason was rarely mentioned in the history of archaeology textbooks I had studied at university.[7] Yet he was undoubtedly a pioneer and a very meticulous one, even publishing his researches in a large illustrated volume, which appeared in 1828.[8]

I met Tom Fitzwilliam outside the front door and we started to walk through the park. I still couldn't quite believe what was happening to me: here was I, little more than a scruffy student, being treated as an equal by a senior English earl. Although on paper my background was quite posh (Eton and Cambridge), nearly all my friends were nice ordinary people who lived in places like Watford or Liverpool. Dare I say it, but some even spoke with regional accents. And yet here was I, strolling through a fabulous park, outside a jaw-dropping house, and being shown around by an earl. I had planned to tell everyone about it in huge detail when we met in the pub that evening, but for some reason I said nothing. It seemed somehow disloyal; Tom Fitzwilliam was such a kind, modest man.

As we walked, Tom told me about Edmund Tyrell Artis, who had worked for the Fitzwilliams as their house steward at Milton for some ten years, from 1816. Artis was a man of many talents and he was friendly with the local poet John Clare, who was also impressed by his wide-ranging abilities, memorably describing him as 'everything but a poet'. Perhaps his biggest interest, which seems to have verged on an obsession, was in archaeology. During his tenure as house steward at Milton, he would take other servants as a free labour force to man his excavations at Castor and elsewhere in the Nene Valley. This work revealed the huge palace-like building (known as the *Praetorium**) that enfolds the superb Norman church at Castor. It is still the largest building known from Roman Britain. This vast stone structure was closely associated with the prosperous Roman town of Durobrivae, which lay just outside modern Castor on the flatter ground of the Nene Valley. The modern A1 passes close by Durobrivae, near the village of Water Newton.

The dairy at Milton is a tiny building just off the walled garden. It contains picturesque niches for standing jugs of milk and pats of butter, but its principal feature is a beautiful Roman mosaic, with an elaborate border, which had been excavated by Artis from the Castor Praetorium. Some of it had plainly been restored, presumably by Artis himself, when he relaid it in the dairy, but it is far too grand for so seemingly mundane a setting. I can remember thinking it would have been more appropriate within Milton Hall itself. As an archaeologist I suppose I should have been wildly enthusiastic about the mosaic, but I'm afraid I don't remember it very clearly. The reason for this was the little building that enclosed it – which enchanted me.

The dairy was built and decorated in the late eighteenth century – maybe it was inspired or supervised by Humphry Repton himself, when he redesigned much of Milton Park and the gardens. It was a time when the upper echelons of society, together with the emerging middle class, had put rural life on a romantic pedestal. This was in part due to the rise of Romanticism, especially in France, under the influence of Jean-Jacques Rousseau (1712–78), who idealized the delights of a simple, rustic life.[9]

---

* Literally translates as 'a general's headquarters building'.

And you can see it in many pictures of the time: shepherdesses carried beribboned crooks and dairymaids had impossibly clean arms and wore dainty lace hats (if you've ever milked a cow by hand you'll know how impractical such hats would have been). This new view of rural life and the countryside had a powerful influence on the subsequent development of the English country house, its park and gardens. Although I have never been back to see it (maybe because I don't want my memory to be clouded by reality), I adored that picturesque little dairy with its delicate tiled walls. I could well imagine the sons of a Georgian Earl Fitzwilliam making repeated visits there, not so much to sip the milk as to admire the 'rustic' dairymaids in their floaty silken dresses. The scene still makes me smile.

Stonea seems to have been the only candidate for a Roman town within the Fens, but there were a number around the edge, including Cambridge, Godmanchester (on the other side of the Ouse at Huntingdon), Durobrivae, Great Casterton, Sleaford and, of course, Lincoln. The presence of these towns so close to the Fens is a strong indicator of the region's prosperity. They were linked to the wider Roman road network and had markets where local produce was sold for distribution across Britain. The final years of the Roman period are often portrayed as a rapid slide into something approaching chaos and darkness, which ended only with the gradual emergence of the earliest kingdoms of what would soon become Anglo-Saxon England. This is a theme I will return to, but for now I just want to have a closer look at what might actually have happened in the final years of Roman rule in and around the town just across the River Nene from Milton and Castor, where Lord Fitzwilliam's steward, E.T. Artis, had done so much pioneering research.

Like so many other towns of Roman Britain, Durobrivae was

sited on a major road, Ermine Street, which was the principal north–south route out of London (Londinium). It ran up the eastern side of the province, to Lincoln and York. Durobrivae was also close to where major east–west routes crossed Ermine Street, towards the Fens in the east (via the Fen Causeway) and the Midlands in the west. The modern road to Leicester (Roman Ratae), the A47, follows the course of the earlier route west for much of its length.

Durobrivae is something of an archaeological treasure because it has never been intensively farmed or built on.[10] Essentially, the entire town lies preserved beneath permanent pasture. The stone walls survive remarkably well and in several places you can see the outline of towers, or bastions, built at regular intervals along the wall's outer face. The towers would have added to the wall's defensive strength and would also have made the town's approaches appear far more impressive. The deep ditch that ran around the outside of the walls would also have added to the look and strength of the defences. Just like their medieval equivalents, Roman town walls were all about making visitors feel they were entering a really important place.

Because Durobrivae began its life as a *vicus*, the lowest level of Roman towns, its interior was not laid out on a strict grid of streets. Ermine Street forms the town's axis and runs across it in a dead straight line, from south-east to north-west. Ermine Street seems to have been lined with buildings on both sides and a number of streets and smaller lanes spring off it. By contrast with the main street, these gently curve and are rarely straight. They have the appearance of having been laid out with specific purposes in mind, probably to facilitate the building of workshops, because we know that Durobrivae was economically very successful. By the fourth century AD, it was upgraded from a *vicus* to a *civitas*, or regional capital. This would fit with the appearance, around then, of what on aerial photographs seem to be small temples. A larger stone structure nearby was probably a *mansio*, an official building used to accommodate travelling civil servants and governmental couriers. The outline of a second substantial building, not far from the *mansio* but aligned with the edge of Ermine Street, was perhaps another official structure, possibly to do with the administration of the Fens, if they were indeed part of an Imperial Estate, as many Romanists believe.

The story of towns in Roman Britain isn't particularly straightforward. I can remember learning at school that the Romans 'gave' us towns, which then grew and evolved over the centuries to become what we have today. Would that it were that simple. In reality, the Romans did indeed 'give' us self-governing towns because they were a concept that had developed around the Mediterranean over several millennia. The walled town of Jericho, in the Jordan Valley, was in existence around 9000 BC, when Britain was still emerging from the Ice Age. It was excavated by one of Britain's greatest archaeologists, Dame Kathleen Kenyon, who was a close friend and colleague of my boss in Canada, Doug Tushingham. The great lady visited Fengate in 1974 and she immediately grasped what I was trying to do in my large open-area excavations, which could not have been more different from the very deep trenches she had to sink to reveal the hidden walls of Jericho (which mercifully for her hadn't come 'tumbling down' – at least not where she was digging). Not all of the academic archaeologists who were supervising the work at Fengate approved of my approach and it was great to have her enthusiastic support.

True towns are not the same as large settlements, which had already appeared in Britain by the time the Romans invaded. A true town has to have a central controlling authority to oversee the layout of streets and the construction of buildings. This authority usually governs the collection of rubbish and the construction and use of sewers. It may well also supervise the siting of public buildings, the construction and manning of town walls and quite often, too, the running of fairs and markets – from which it will collect much-needed revenues. The towns of Roman Britain had all of these things. But they also had substantial extramural (i.e. 'outside the walls') or unofficial settlements beyond them. These tended to grow up in a rather higgledy-piggledy fashion, in marked contrast to the neat, gridded layout found within the walls of the larger towns. Similar informal settlements often grew up outside the walls or palisades of permanent army camps; Durobrivae had one of these, also close to Ermine Street, a short distance to the north-west.

The flat, well-drained land around Durobrivae was excellently suited for informal development and it soon began to acquire an industry of its own, which was based on local clay and the Romans' introduction of improved, higher capacity, permanent pottery kilns. Soon the area around Durobrivae was producing huge quantities of so-called Nene Valley Wares, which were widely traded across southern Britain, where they proved very popular and were soon turning up on many of the older farms and settlements that had been established in, or by, the Iron Age. Again, the picture is one of prosperity and continuity.

I confess that I normally prefer to excavate and study the remains left by ordinary people. 'Treasure' has never excited me. Yes, I admire the consummate workmanship of Roman silverware or Anglo-Saxon jewellery, but they don't fire my imagination – whereas a thumbprint I once spotted on the surface of a very ordinary Bronze Age loomweight took me straight back to life in a prehistoric roundhouse. I could imagine the family gathered indoors on a winter's evening with children playing and adults weaving and repairing clothes by the flickering light of the central fire. By the same token, grand buildings don't really move me. While I love visiting country houses and enjoy the elegance of Georgian interiors, as an archaeologist it's the evidence for the lives of ordinary people that I find inspiring. But there are exceptions, and one of these was the huge Roman building first investigated by E.T. Artis at Castor – and which probably provided the mosaic in the Milton dairy. This place fascinates me because it may be almost two thousand years old – but, as I discovered, its ruins don't lie completely hidden. It all depends on how you approach them.

When I first visited the stone-built village of Castor in 1970 I can remember thinking that its picturesque limestone houses would have looked more appropriate in a Cotswold setting than on the edge of Peterborough. The reason of course is that the limestones that formed beneath the sea in the Jurassic age, some 150 million years ago, provide the bedrock for a ridge of hills that run south from Lincolnshire, form the backbone of Northamptonshire and terminate in the Cotswolds. And Castor sits on the lip of this higher land, with the floodplain of the Nene Valley spread beneath. It's an extraordinary landscape of contrasts. Drive up the hill towards the church and you are immediately in a different world. Gone are the huge flat fields, gravel quarries and drainage dykes that make parts of the lower Nene Valley indistinguishable from the true open fen just 3 or 4 miles (5–6 km) to the east. Look at the stone walls on either side of you as you climb the gently curving lane towards the parish church of St Kyneburgha, with its superb decorated Norman tower against the sky and tall trees further along the slope. In a couple of places you will spot points in the stonework where the walls following the road are broken by short, wide walls that originally ran across the road and were subsequently removed. Have a closer look at them and the stonework is quite unlike anything nearby. Instead of being laid flat to form horizontal courses, the pieces of limestone are tipped up, on end – rather like books leaning one way, then another, on a bookshelf – to form alternating rows arranged in a regular herringbone pattern.

That form of zigzag stonework is distinctively Roman and those walls formed part of the great building at Castor. They date to the third century AD.

Castor has always been known as an ancient place: indeed, its name when it first appears in the Domesday Book of 1086 is Castre, meaning 'a Roman fort', from the Old English word *caester*.[11] This suggests that the ruins of the huge Roman building survived for some time after the legions departed. Castor Church is the only church named after Saint Kyneburgha, who was the daughter of King Penda of Mercia. Penda was a remarkable man: born a pagan, he converted to Christianity and defeated the rival kingdoms of Bernicia and the East Angles on several occasions, and eventually Mercia became the most powerful kingdom of Anglo-Saxon England. But it was not to last for long. Penda was eventually killed in battle by the Bernicians in 655. After her father's death, Kyneburgha founded a double monastery, most probably using the ruins of the large Roman building, and became abbess there, to be succeeded on her death, by her daughter. The bodies of mother and daughter were taken to Peterborough Abbey (now the cathedral) after the Saxon church had been destroyed by Viking raids in 1012.

The church that was built and dedicated to St Kyneburgha after the Norman Conquest is one of the finest in a region rich in great churches. It was started between 1100 and 1110 and the detailed decoration of the tower's stonework is truly exceptional. It may have been done to impress, because it's certainly very spectacular, but I felt there was something more to it than that, when I first saw it. I'm convinced that tower was constructed with something more profound in mind. Maybe it expresses love for the saint, respect for the people who died in the Viking raid of the previous century – or something else.

It has proved very difficult to gain access to excavate the huge Roman building that surrounds the church on its north, east and western sides, largely due to the presence of houses and gardens. But I remember visiting a small trench in a cottage garden where my old friend Dr John Peter Wild, of Manchester University, had excavated down to one of the great building's western rooms.[12] It was the first time I had ever seen a freshly exposed Roman flue, and I was very impressed by the quality of the stonework – which looked good enough to be modern. In Roman times, piped hot-water-based central heating systems had yet to be invented and large buildings were warmed by hot air (a system known as hypocaust), which was heated by an enclosed fire below ground level. The hot air then passed beneath raised floors, which became warmer. In a few grand buildings, ducts through side walls could take the hot air to higher floors.

The presence of such a heating system confirmed the Castor Praetorium's high status, which we already suspected from Artis's work, but we now knew the building was even larger than Artis had speculated. The room that was being excavated eventually proved to be 9 metres (30ft) wide and a minimum of 20

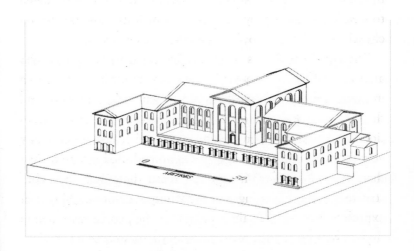

*A reconstruction by Donald Mackreth of the great Roman building (the Praetorium) at Castor.*

metres (65 ft) long. Closer examination of the heating system showed it to be of a type that was used in very much larger buildings than, for example, the usual Romano-British villas. Dr Wild's excavation was followed by a detailed examination of all the surviving evidence by the late Don Mackreth, who was both a field archaeologist and an architectural expert and draughtsman. He produced the superb reconstruction of the building, which frankly would not have looked out of place in Rome, or indeed Trafalgar Square. I have absolute confidence in Don's reconstruction, which is very firmly based on the evidence.

The great building in Castor has to have been closely connected both with the prosperous town of Durobrivae, which it overlooks, and the rich farms of the nearby Fens. It is such an impressive building that to call it a palace would be no exaggeration. We can only guess who or what it may have housed. Some have suggested it could have played a role in the regional military command structure. It was constructed around AD 300 when Britain was at peace and was starting to prosper greatly. If Durobrivae was indeed the capital of the Romano-British Fens, then one might see the Castor building as its Buckingham Palace. If nothing else, that palatial building must surely dispel any ideas that the Fens were even slightly backward, forgotten, or impoverished.

Not surprisingly, the great building had begun to fall into disrepair when Roman rule ended, around 410. But it was then used as an early Christian monastery – it wasn't torched or vandalized and there is absolutely no evidence for seething conflict or civil wars. Quite the contrary, in fact. So what did actually happen in Britain at the end of the Roman period – during the supposed Dark Ages – and how did it affect the Fens? This is quite a hot topic, which I will cover in the next chapter.

# Devil's Dyke and Reach Lode: Pre-Norman Boundaries that Shaped the Medieval Fens

*Steady Growth – Invasions and Migrations –*
*Movement and Land Management –*
*Devil's Dyke and the Lodes*

Traditionally, the early Fens weren't considered worthy of close study, because 'everyone knew' they were just tracts of wet, lonely, inhospitable landscape well beyond the reach of the law. Such entrenched views have proved hard to shake off. The first signs of changing attitudes came in the nineteenth century, when pioneering wildlife conservationists like Charles Rothschild pointed out the enormous richness of the Fens' natural environment. That was undoubtedly a major step forward, as was the creation of Wicken Fen and other nature reserves. But it was as if the worlds inhabited by nature and by human beings were on different planets. Yes, there was respect for traditional Fen lifestyles and practices – sedge-thatchers and wildfowlers, fishermen and eel-trappers were highly regarded. Much of this admiration was for the way they lived within the constraints imposed by their natural surroundings. They were seen as fine examples of what today we would describe as ecologically friendly lifestyles. But the reality of past fenland communities and their related economies wasn't given any close attention, because everybody assumed that the region had always been underpopulated, impoverished and marginal.

By the mid-twentieth century, well-preserved prehistoric sites on drier land out in the Fens had been discovered and were rightly seen as remarkable, but prehistorians still hadn't grasped that such sites could never have existed in isolation. Even the most resourceful and independent of Neolithic farmers required new bloodlines for their livestock and sources of fresh seed in particularly wet years. And of course we now appreciate that even the most lonely of migratory hunter-gatherers lived within networks of similar groups or small communities in order to avoid conflict and over-exploitation of sometimes quite fragile food resources. Humans have never lived in true isolation.

Research in the last three decades of the twentieth century began to reveal the true extent of prehistoric settlement in the Fens, and showed it to be as dense and as long-lived as anywhere else in Britain. It was also remarkably prosperous and well adapted to what could sometimes be quite a rapidly changing environment. We have also demonstrated beyond any doubt that this prehistoric prosperity extended into Roman times when naturally drier conditions allowed populations and farmed land-scapes to expand even further. Most prehistorians also agree that the wetter regions of low-lying, often peaty fen were never simply ignored. As we saw with those boats and fish-weirs at Must Farm, the wetter areas were a major resource of food, fuel and building materials and were carefully, and probably quite thoroughly, exploited. Such exploitation, however, does not happen haphazardly. The wetland area would have to have been apportioned into different areas to avoid unnecessary con-flict. Of course, we cannot prove that this actually happened, because *pre*history is just that: in pre-literate societies, all laws were spoken, not written down. But we can safely assume that the various communities surrounding the larger wetland areas would have convened regional gatherings to sort out any disputes over grazing rights and so forth. There are strong grounds to think that such tribal gatherings took place around the shores of the heavily exploited glacial Lake Flixton, in North Yorkshire, as early as 9500 BC, so to have broadly similar local political arrangements in the Fens, some five thousand years later, hardly seems far-fetched.[1]

We know that the population of the area that was to become fenland grew quite steadily during the ten or so millennia that followed the end of the last Ice Age. And the more we learn, the more we tend to play down ideas of 'abandonment' or desertion. We used to believe, for example, that the earliest (Mesolithic) inhabitants were confined to a few bands of wandering hunters. That may have been the case in the centuries around the close of the Ice Age (around 10,000 BC), but very quickly the population rose and by the dawn of the Neolithic, from about 4000 BC, the sites where we know farmers settled usually coincided with concentrations of Mesolithic worked flints. This would suggest that the earlier hunter-gatherers and the first farmers were in fact the same people. Yes, there was undoubtedly a proportion of incomers, but the vast majority of the population had been residing in the area for many millennia. Subsequently, Bronze and Iron Age communities extended their settlements, farms and fields to cover most of the Fens – and, as we have seen, even some of the wetter areas were exploited too.

The drier conditions that followed the Iron Age allowed the Romano-British population to continue the steady growth seen in later prehistory – and, if anything, even more rapidly. But now our story hits the buffers. Or rather, that is what received wisdom would have us believe. The conventional wisdom is that the Romans withdrew from Britain around AD 410, whereupon we enter the dreaded Dark Ages (and that is the second and last time I shall use that term). During this period, which was thought to extend until about AD 650, the light of Roman civilization was extinguished and Britain was invaded by hordes of Anglo-Saxon migrants from across the North Sea. The first Anglo-Saxons were probably mercenaries employed by the Roman Army from the fourth century AD. As a prehistorian and landscape archaeologist, I have always found the idea of mass migration on such a massive scale that it amounted to wholesale population replacement hard to accept – simply because there is no evidence for it on the ground: in the farms, villages and settlements of ordinary people. Buildings aren't abandoned, settlements don't die and field systems continue in use.

According to this theory, the native Celtic, or British, population migrated westwards. But again, there is absolutely no archaeological evidence for such a massive and disruptive change, either in the east or in the west, where people were supposed to have settled down. More to the point, there is no evidence for any conflict between incomers and 'natives': there are no battle sites, nor war cemeteries, and not so much as a hint at the genocide that often goes with wholesale population change. There is also no consistent evidence for a decline in population following the departure of Roman troops. The lights didn't go out. Things continued much as before – as indeed was the case at the start of the Roman period. But certain things *did* change – language, for instance. So what was going on?

The traditional version of the events that took place in the two or three centuries following the withdrawal of Roman troops from Britain was largely based on written historical accounts. *On the Ruin of Britain*, by the British monk Gildas, completed c. AD 540, is a prime early source, while *The Ecclesiastical History of the English People* (completed in AD 731) by the Venerable

Bede, a Northumbrian Benedictine, covers the latter part of the period. Neither writer was an historian in the modern sense of the word. Today, we expect our historians to offer objectively presented interpretations of the past, in which events that do not support the favoured interpretation are both mentioned and explained – even if they are, for clearly stated reasons, subsequently rejected. Neither Gildas nor Bede were bound by these conventions and although their histories contain a wealth of extraordinary and valuable information, they must not be interpreted too literally.

Another simplistic and misleading assumption was that post-Roman people were only capable of speaking a single language, which then somehow became their cultural identifier. So if I started to speak a version of Anglo-Saxon, I ceased to be a Celtic-speaking Briton and became transmogrified into a Germanic migrant – which would have been a terrible shock. But certainly by AD 400 a significant proportion of the British population would have been used to speaking at least two languages: Latin, together with the local variant of a Celtic tongue. In the fourth century AD, Roman Britain's increased prosperity led to greater contacts across the North Sea. Some Germanic people had already arrived in Britain, such as those mercenaries in various Roman Army camps. I can see nothing strange or sinister in this situation and we have already seen similar contacts in both the Bronze and Iron Ages when artefacts made in Britain were found overseas, and continental ones in Britain. The vast majority of imported or exported objects would probably have been accompanied by at least one person – and that was how long-distance contacts were both made and maintained.

When I was at Cambridge, the university was still buzzing from the award of a Nobel Prize (in 1962) to Francis Crick and James Watson, who had worked out the molecular structure of DNA nine years earlier, in 1953. It took nearly four decades for the characterization of DNA to become so sophisticated that scientists were able to trace evidence for past migrations by comparing the genetic material of ancient and modern populations. Historians of the post-Roman centuries were expecting to find significant DNA evidence for Germanic invasions of Britain, but while there were sometimes indications of considerable movements of people, they all took place within networks of existing relationships (i.e. complete strangers were not involved). Prior to the first DNA-based research, the available evidence did not suggest that the pre-existing Celtic and Romano-British population of eastern England had been forced to leave the Fens and East Anglia and make new homes much further west.[2] What DNA studies have revealed, however, is the great complexity and extent of movement and migration both into and out of Britain in the ancient past.[3] As we have seen, it was a process that intensified considerably in Roman times and there are no reasons to suppose it slowed down subsequently. What we still lack is good, clear evidence for folk movements and informal invasions by incoming Anglo-Saxon communities, or indeed anyone else, in late Roman and post-Roman times, prior to about AD 650.[4]

An excellent recent survey of Anglo-Saxon fenland by Professor Susan Oosthuizen has also concluded that the old view that 'one language equals one group of people' is also highly dubious and that most people were bi- or multi-lingual.[5] The author is in little doubt that the population who lived in the Fens were the same people who had been there in Roman times, and earlier – which I have to say I find a huge relief. The evidence from dozens of archaeological excavations and surveys is now in broad agreement with this reassessment of historical and DNA-based research.

The early historical records also provide interesting evidence of how the large areas of wetland that are so characteristic of the southern and central Fens may have been managed in pre-history. I have already suggested that the different communities surrounding wet areas of seasonal grazing and rich winter fishing and wildfowling would have shared out the wetland among themselves, but proof of just how complex and carefully thought-out those arrangements might have been is provided by some of the earliest legal documents that record grazing agreements. These date back to the AD 700s and 800s, and when they are studied in conjunction with early tax records, they reveal precisely how farmers in neighbouring villages divided up the larger wetland areas among themselves.

Susan Oosthuizen's study shows that these arrangements were very ancient and may have reached back to 'the early days of settlement', which we now know lie back in Neolithic and Bronze Age times – if not earlier.[6] Clearly, any laws and agreements would have changed as the wetlands themselves expanded or contracted. But the way they were organized and managed would have been flexible enough to cope with such changes – even in pre-literate societies. The idea that the Fens were a remote and lonely place, inhabited by gangs of brigands and bandits, is wide of the mark. The reality is that they were well populated by communities who had long known how to combine residence in the flood-free higher landscapes of the fen margins with regular exploitation of the seasonal resources of the large, lower-lying wetlands.

I like it when stories come together and start to make sense. As a prehistorian and archaeologist I could see that we were on the right track when we revealed that large tracts of fenland landscape, especially around the edges, had been farmed and managed for some four millennia before the Roman conquest. And the archaeology made it clear that those landscapes and the people living in and around them continued to prosper through the Roman period. We also knew from historical studies of the many fenland abbeys and priories that it was a very prosperous region in the Middle Ages. But then there were those six and a half centuries after the departure of the Romans and before the Norman Conquest. I didn't like the fact that they had gained a reputation for being a long period of chaos and anarchy when there seemed so little evidence for it on, or below, the ground.

On 18 October 1016, at a place called Assandun, the relics of St Wendreda were carried into battle by monks of Ely Abbey, hoping they would bring victory to the English army under Edmund Ironside against the invading Viking army led by Cnut. The saint's remains did not have the desired effect, Danish victory at this unidentified Essex location completing a process of reconquest that left all of England except Wessex under the control of Cnut. However bloody the events at Assandun, this was no sudden takeover by marauding strangers: the Vikings had long been established in England, their settlements concentrated in the areas known as the Danelaw, east and north of the line of Watling Street. Certainly there were periods of conflict and misrule, as we saw with the Viking attack on Castor Church in 1012 and the strange post-mortem 'life' of St Wendreda's remains four years later;* but these were relatively brief episodes and didn't seriously affect the local economy, the landscape or, far more importantly, the daily lives of fen men and women.

The Scandinavians who settled in England in the ninth, tenth and eleventh centuries have undoubtedly had a bad press, the word 'Viking' invariably being followed in short order by 'rape' and 'pillage'. But one needs to stand back from the vio-lence of war and take a longer view: that the Danes added to the cultural diversity of early medieval Britain. They blended rapidly into local society, but also contributed economically to many growing towns, such as York in the north of England and

---

* She is the patron saint of March parish church. See Chapter 10, p. 208.

Dublin in Ireland. Their outward-looking, expansionist attitude to life, which recognized few boundaries, must have come as a refreshing counterbalance to any British tendency to insularity.

Our next stop will be the Norman Conquest; but first I want to think about the state of the Fens in the centuries before 1066. We tend to see Britain's two great conquests as being cataclysmic events that changed everything profoundly. We saw that life in the Roman Fens was a logical development from what had gone before and the same could be said about the arrival of the Normans. If anything, the arrival of the Romans and the setting-up of towns like Durobrivae had a more profound effect on ordinary lives in the Fens, and elsewhere, than the coming of William the Conqueror and his Norman barons. Certainly the Normans had a drastic effect on the upper echelons of British society, but the majority of the population was far less affected. Besides, profoundly important changes had been happening out in the landscape long before the Battle of Hastings.

The early medieval landscape can be difficult to imagine, largely because very few upstanding buildings survive. While we now know that old notions of Britain reverting to impenetrable forest after the departure of the Romans are completely untrue, it can still be hard to picture the reality, which was probably a great deal more diverse than had been the case in later Roman times.

From about the seventh century AD, England had begun to form itself into small regional kingdoms, which expanded and coalesced as time passed. By the eighth century, it appears that England was divided into a series of major tribal groupings, some of whose names are still reflected in modern geographical nomenclature; the East Saxons gave rise to Essex, the South Saxons to Sussex, the East Angles to East Anglia, and so on. But the situation in the Fens was slightly less clear, because the complex nature of the landscape, with its areas of shared grazing, meant that this part of the territory of the Middle Angles, which extended to the south-west, through modern Northamptonshire, down to Bedfordshire and the Chiltern Hills, was subdivided into a series of much smaller tribal holdings, with names such as the Spalda and North and South Gyrwe. Spalda of course refers to the area around modern Spalding, whereas Gyrwe (from Old English *gyr*, meaning 'mud' or 'marsh') was an early name used to refer to the Fens in the area around and to the east of Peterborough.

*An 1853 engraving of the Devil's Dyke, looking towards Woodditton (just south of Newmarket), Cambridgeshire.*

Some of these tribal territories made use of rivers and catch-water drains to mark their boundaries. Major tribal kingdom borders could be emphasized on the ground by massive earthworks. The magnificent Devil's Dyke was probably built in early Saxon times – around a century or two after the end of the Roman period. It runs for 7½ miles (12 km) from Reach on the south-eastern fen-edge, some 12 miles (19 km) north-east of Cambridge, to Woodditton near the Suffolk county line. I used to take frequent walks along it when I was a student at Cambridge and it's certainly well worth a visit. It consists of a massive bank, some 5 metres (16 ft) high, with a deep ditch running alongside it, hillfort-fashion. The views from the top of the bank are superb. I revisited Devil's Dyke when I was writing the early medieval sections of this book, and I was struck by how many trees had been removed from the landscape since the 1960s. Most authorities agree that this massive earthwork marked the western edge of the kingdom of the East Angles – and there is an interesting footnote: the dyke still forms part of the western boundary of the Diocese of Norwich.

Some of the more remarkable early earthworks were dug to help manage water levels in the annually flooded wetlands that so many people depended upon for a living.[7] I know from personal experience that water standing on grassland into late spring can cause enormous problems. Not only does the grass refuse to grow when deeply flooded, but if you have made the mistake of already releasing your livestock to graze the land, the damage they will do to the soft, waterlogged turf will set the pasture back for the next couple of seasons. Turf and root systems can be badly disturbed by being trampled, even by quite light animals such as sheep and goats. The damage horses and cattle could inflict is even more significant. So it is important to try to ensure that pastures are drained promptly – by mid-March, ideally – and, just as importantly, once they are free of water, they must then remain dry. This requires drains, pipes, skill, knowledge and experience. It also requires people in different communities to work together closely, because even a temporary blockage at one spot can cause a major flood further up the dyke.

If you follow the line of Devil's Dyke north-west, out into the open fen, you will find you are following the straight course of

Reach Lode,* which runs for some 3 miles (5 km) before draining into the River Cam, near Upware. The lodes are now popular with boaters and holidaymakers, and I can understand why. With their grassy banks, and often slightly higher than the surrounding drained peatlands, these raised rivers are a world apart and very peaceful. There are also some pleasant rural pubs and places to moor the boat and go for walks and bike rides. The main lodes draining into the Cam in this most southerly region of the Fens are, to the north, Burwell Old Lode, Wicken Lode and Reach Lode; and, further south, the Swaffham Bulbeck and Bottisham Lodes.

In the Middle Ages the flooded pastures drained into the lodes through hollowed-out tree trunk pipes, known as 'gotes'. (I particularly enjoy the name given to smaller gotes: 'pisgotes'.) The gotes were often fitted with a hinged clapper door (known as a 'clow') that allowed water to flow out of the pipe, but closed when water levels began to rise in the lode itself – thereby stopping water from re-flooding the dried-out land. Gotes were employed extensively in the Fens and there was a major complex of four drains, each with a gote and clow, at Tydd St Giles on the Cambridgeshire–Lincolnshire border, quite close to where I now live. The tiny hamlet that grew up near them is known as Four Gotes and the earthworks and dykes are still clearly apparent in the landscape.

Today, however, the landscape around Tydd St Giles and Four Gotes is dominated by the huge dykes that feed into the massive tidal channel of the new alignment of the River Nene outfall. This had started to silt up badly in the eighteenth century, leading to the temporary demise of Wisbech as a shipping port. The great civil engineers John Rennie (1761–1821) and somewhat

---

* The word 'lode' derives from Old English *lad*, meaning a watercourse or drainage channel.

later (1821) Thomas Telford (who based his scheme on many of
Rennie's ideas) proposed a new, self-scouring straight channel
for the Nene's outfall into the Wash. Strangely, this was initially
opposed by Wisbech Town Council, who eventually gave in and
even contributed to the project, following an Act of Parliament
in 1827.

I drive along the new cut of the Nene, past the big gas-fuelled
power station at Sutton Bridge, almost every day and I am
always impressed by the width and depth not just of the main
river, but of the subsidiary dykes that feed into it. They must be
some of the largest hand-cut artificial watercourses ('drainage
ditches' somehow doesn't do them justice) anywhere in Britain.
I also like the ironwork on the smaller structures around the
great channels: the footbridges, the handrailings and the supports beneath the pathway. You get the same delicate work
on railings and bridges at Clough Cross sluice gate, just north
of Parson Drove on the Lincolnshire–Cambridgeshire border.
Again, Telford was the engineer in overall charge of the North
Level Main Drain. A few years ago, when I was in North Wales
doing research for *The Making of the British Landscape* and was
walking around Telford's pioneering Menai Strait suspension
bridge, I was delighted to notice, as I walked along the footpath
leading up to the world's first suspension bridge, that the fences
and railings that prevented me from dropping hundreds of feet
into the angry sea below were identical in every detail to those
that Telford would use some five years later on the vastly more
modest structure at Clough Cross. A good engineer never wastes
a successful design.

We tend to think that large-scale water management schemes
are a modern phenomenon, but there is now increasing evidence
that the lodes of the southern Fens, and indeed other watercourses
in fenland, were much earlier than we once believed. Many have
antecedents that date back to the refoundation of many early

monastic estates and institutions that took place in the later tenth century – about a century prior to the Norman Conquest. It's not impossible that some Roman catch-water drains may have been maintained during early Saxon times, although this is difficult to prove. But there is now a wealth of evidence to suggest that systems of lodes and the catch-water drains that feed into them were being laid out and maintained prior to the later tenth century. The problem with fixing such dates with any precision is obvious, when one pauses to think about it. Drains and ditches have to be maintained, as do pipes and sluices. Every time you scrape sludge from a ditch you probably deepen it very slightly and thereby remove all archaeological evidence for what happened in and around the ditch prior to the last time it was cleaned out. As a consequence of this, only the most recent silt deposits survive – and they usually formed after the drain's abandonment. The trick is to find early versions of the ditch that were abandoned with their deposits intact.

Susan Oosthuizen has shown that wooden pipes and sophisticated water-management systems existed in late Iron Age Germany, and my own excavations at the Cat's Water site at Fengate have revealed an early precursor of pipes – known as a 'brush drain' – along the bottom of a drainage dyke.[8] As their name suggests, brush drains consisted of bundles of brushwood that were placed along the bottom of a ditch to catch and hold any loose material that might erode or wash out of the ditch sides. Material would then accumulate on top of them and they would form, in effect, an informal duct, or pipe.

I could find very little archaeological or historical evidence for brush drains in the distant past, when we were digging the late Iron Age example we had found at Cat's Water. But two recently retired local farmers, who had called in at the dig, knew all about them. Indeed, they told me about the term 'brush drain' – and one was of the firm opinion that they had a useful life of ten

*Fengate excavations, 1975: two bundles of long, straight osiers (of willow or alder) laid along the bottom of an Iron Age ditch to form a 'brush drain'. Note the hole left by a modern (1950s?) clay pipe land drain in the far baulk.*

to twenty years, before needing to be dug out and replaced with new brushwood. The other was absolutely convinced that the example we'd just excavated was modern, as its preservation was so good. Fortunately, we had overwhelming archaeological evidence for its antiquity. And there's a final twist to this story. We widened the trench to take in some other ditches and in the process came across the fired clay pipes of a land drain that was probably laid in the 1950s. This drain was running slightly above, parallel to, and alongside its Iron Age precursor. Clearly that part of the Cat's Water site had been giving farmers a drainage problem for over two thousand years. It has since been destroyed by a towering waste-processing facility.

The lodes of the early medieval Fens and the brush drain of Iron Age Fengate demonstrate that, before the modern era, 'fen drainage' was about water management and sometimes even maintenance. Water wasn't seen as an evil, to be removed at all costs, as tends to be the modern view. It was water – and the fertility it washed onto the land every winter helped to give the region the considerable prosperity it enjoyed in the Middle Ages. As a sheep farmer, I sometimes wish we could turn the clock back and reverse some of the massive over-drainage that has been such a feature of fenland agriculture over the past two centuries. Sadly, this would be impossible in areas of deep peat in the southern and western Fens, where ground levels have shrunk to what they were two or three thousand years ago. But in the silt lands around the Wash it's already very noticeable that livestock farms are on the increase. These farmers rely on grazing, which in the hotter, drier summers of the twenty-first century require good irrigation. So maybe there are a few reasons to be optimistic.

Close study of the early medieval fenland reveals a substantial population, with many farms and settlements. These people were direct descendants of earlier residents in the area. They had developed subtle and well-regulated systems of governance and communication, which allowed local communities and the farms within them to manage and manipulate seasonal flooding and drainage to everyone's advantage. Over the past half-century, modern excavations of Anglo-Saxon burials have clearly demonstrated that communities living around the Fens enjoyed economic prosperity that was the equal of any in Britain. The recent discovery of a small seventh-century settlement and graveyard at Trumpington, near Cambridge, included the grave of a young woman (aged sixteen to eighteen) buried on a decorated plank-built wooden bed joined together with iron fittings. She wore gold ornaments, including an exceptionally fine cross, inlaid with garnets and was accompanied by a purse (a chatelaine), ornamental pins, a knife and a comb. Such wealth reflects the considerable prosperity of communities living in and around the Fens before the Norman Conquest, and if anything that economic success was to gather pace in the centuries that followed the Battle of Hastings in 1066.[9]

# Ely Abbey and Cathedral Church:
# The Ship of the Fens

*The Luttrell Psalter – Ely and Peterborough*
*Cathedrals – Thorney Abbey and Village – Croyland*
*Abbey and Crowland town*

I am writing this in early April 2018, during the second week of lambing. I have just returned to my desk after checking the barn for any new births. Thankfully, there weren't any. Earlier in the morning, sometime around 5.00 am, I had found two sets of twins and three ewes fighting for possession of them. It took me half an hour to resolve the situation. But after it was all over, I have to confess I was feeling a little stiff and tired. So I did a few stretches, while leaning against the Aga, whose all-pervading radiant warmth can be as effective as a resident physiotherapist. Then I poured myself a cup of tea and was about to sit in my comfy armchair when my eye was caught by the spine of the biggest volume on our bookshelves: a superb facsimile of the Luttrell Psalter. We'd bought it for ourselves a few years ago, as a joint Christmas present. It certainly isn't the fluffiest of light reading for someone who needed to relax, but it wasn't text that I was after. No, I planned to lose myself in the superb illustrations, which were beautifully painted, in extraordinary detail, by someone who plainly had first-hand experience of farming and sheep-keeping and loved the animals.[1] He also had a wonderfully vivid and sometimes tortured imagination and knew the Fens well – to judge by the frequent appearance of fish, eels and men with scaled fishtails or stilt-like legs.

The psalter was created between 1325 and 1335 for Sir Geoffrey Luttrell of Irnham, Lincolnshire. The village of Irnham lies in gently undulating country about 7 miles (11 km) north-west of Bourne and some 5 miles (8 km), as the crow flies, from the wetland-edge at Hacconby Fen, so it probably depicts life in the region in the final few decades before the horrors of the Black Death arrived in 1348. The farming scenes are more like a series of snapshots placed along the bottom of the page, done in superb detail, with wonderfully eccentric perspective, but always packed with movement and action. Even if you know nothing about country ways, you can immediately understand the precise actions needed to launch a hawk, or spread grain for chickens. Nothing seems sacrosanct. We are even treated to a quick shot of a highly decorated coffin, with its lid partially off, revealing the tightly shrouded corpse, more like a bundle than a body, within.

The arable scenes show details of how pre-tractor farmers worked in muddy conditions, with toothed grips fixed to the rim of their cart wheels. Today we would add an extra pair of driving wheels or double-width tyres, but as a child and young man I can remember many tractors – especially Fordsons, for some reason – being fitted with toothed metal wheels that closely resembled those shown in the Luttrell Psalter. It is clear how important these everyday tasks were to the men and women doing them. You can read the concentration on the faces of people spreading seed corn or driving waggons – even if, as in the case of the waggon-driver, he has been given the body and head of an ape.

*A scene from the fourteenth-century Luttrell Psalter showing a pen of tightly packed ewes, one of which is being milked. The shepherd is holding another ewe, which is ready to be milked. Two women carry a jug and a cream/butter churn back to the dairy or farmhouse kitchen.*

One of my favourite vignettes is a detailed drawing of a small hurdled enclosure, containing nineteen or twenty ewes, closely packed together. Being so closely packed, the sheep would remain calm and could be handled with ease. If I have a few sheep to inject or de-worm, this is the way I would do it. The detail is superb, even showing how the hurdles were joined together at each corner, with rings made from a stout twisted cord of some sort. And make no mistake, those hurdles would have been under considerable strain – I have known cheap metal ones bend under such circumstances. Also inside the hurdles with the sheep are a man and a woman. He is standing, semi-crouched (a position I am very familiar with), holding the front legs of a sheep, which he has turned over – probably to examine her hind legs or, more likely, her udder, or 'bag', as shepherds refer to it. I wouldn't be at all surprised if the sheep he is worried about didn't have mastitis, which is readily treated today with antibiotics. The woman is sitting, probably on a specially made and very low three-legged stool, and milking the ewe beside her.

She is obviously an old hand at this because she is milking both sides of her bag at the same time. Whenever I've had to do this job (which may become necessary after a ewe loses her lambs and you cannot persuade her to adopt any others), I find it much simpler to milk off each side separately.

Just outside the hurdles are two young women who are starting to walk back to the house or dairy. Both are carrying vessels full of milk on their heads, which they steady with one hand. One vessel is a tall green-glazed single-handed jug (of a type you find frequently on earlier medieval sites), the other is a wooden butter churn. The jug, the churn and the scene in general leave me in absolutely no doubt that the sheep shown in the Luttrell Psalter were bred for their milk. The breed we keep, Lleyns, were also bred for their milk, which is rich and very tasty. Personally I prefer it to goats' milk, which can sometimes taste a bit goaty.

The Luttrell Psalter paints a picture of everyday rural life around the edges of the Lincolnshire Fens in the mid-fourteenth century. The animals and the people tending them all seem to be well nourished and thriving, but the 1340s would witness the arrival in England of the Black Death. The impact of successive waves of plague was exacerbated by the prevailing demographic conditions of late thirteenth- and early fourteenth-century England. At this time the population had reached such a high level that local rural economies were struggling to maintain food supplies, and certain parts of the country experienced episodes of hunger and famine. This would have weakened resistance to the disease, especially among people of working age, who would have been most adversely affected by a reduced diet. By the late medieval period farming had become a major industry, producing quantities of food, wool and leather – and, of course, profits. Today, the beneficiaries of such commerce might display their wealth by acquiring fast cars or large yachts. In the Middle

Ages, however, people worried about their eternal souls, so the wealthy and materially successful put much of their cash into the building and improvement of churches and chapels. Their funding of such ventures has proved to have an enduring legacy, indeed, one that we can all enjoy today – particularly in the Fens, which were made very wealthy through the expanding trade in wool.

Ely is synonymous with the Fens. The island on which the town is sited is spectacular and would undoubtedly have been a focus of some interest, even if the cathedral had never been built; but that vast Norman building has transformed the entire region for over almost a millennium. I go there as often as I can, but even though you now have to pay to enter (something I am not entirely happy with, as it reduces such transcendental buildings to mere visitor attractions), I still always try to pop in, if only to take a slow walk up that inspiring nave. It puts everything into proportion. I find my worries and anxieties are laid to rest. As I approach the transept, I lower my eyes to the rood screen that separates the choir from the main body of the church. At this point I mustn't look up. Then as I pass beneath the soaring arch at the east end of the nave I allow my eyes to travel up, higher and higher. Impossibly high. And there, directly above me, is the octagonal lantern whose distant supports resemble eight delicate, painted posts, but are, in fact, the carved trunks of entire, massive oak trees. By now my head is beginning to swim and I must look down at the ground, or risk fainting. At this point I will often sit down and remain quiet, in a deep peace. No other place on this planet affects me in quite the same way as Ely Cathedral.

I strongly suspect that many of the holiest places in Britain – places later dignified by the building of cathedrals or abbeys

– have roots that extend back into the remote past. In prehistory there is some evidence that it was the places themselves that were special – something that we still see in many cultures today. I suspect Bronze and Iron Age communities living in the Ely region might have regarded the hill that was later to be host to the great church as something comparable to what we used to refer to as Ayer's Rock (Uluru is its correct Aboriginal name), which is regarded as a place of profound, transcendental importance by the native communities of Australia. In Britain, many locations that were later occupied by henges and other great ritual sites had been venerated in Neolithic and Mesolithic times, too. Right back, in fact, to the reoccupation of Britain after the last Ice Age, over eleven thousand years ago. I suspect that direct evidence for Ely as a prehistoric sacred site has been destroyed by the construction of the town, but we know the area around was quite heavily occupied in prehistoric times, and I would be very surprised if those religiously aware communities did not treat the great hill as a very special place.

I have long been fascinated by religions, both ancient and modern. An aspect of great churches like Ely, Lincoln and Durham that I find especially interesting is the fact that they completely dominate their settings in a way that their prehistoric predecessors never did. Indeed, Neolithic and Bronze Age sacred sites were often deliberately positioned to be just off a hilltop – as if they were somehow subservient to their setting. To the ancient mind, the landscape and the spiritual powers within it were more important than anything else. This leads me to believe that they were always well aware that the monuments they used, such as Stonehenge, were indeed their own creations and were not the 'works of giants', as some earlier authorities had supposed.[2] By way of contrast, the great cathedrals I have just mentioned (and many others too) show no such restraint. It's a perception of faith that goes beyond the landscape and indeed ordinary life – and as such it leaves me feeling somewhat uncomfortable. I suppose you could say that the experiences I value so much when I walk slowly down the nave at Ely are somehow otherworldly. But I would disagree. I find Ely to be so powerfully moving because I am aware of when and how it was built and of the extraordinary carpentry that produced the domed roof that supports the timber lantern over the transept. It's the human vision, skill and effort that makes the interior of Ely so magical. Meanwhile, the exterior is rooted in the place, which I concede it does dominate, but it doesn't diminish the hill, which is still very prominent. And yes, it is an enormous cathedral, but it is flawed too: the north-west transept tower collapsed at the end of the fifteenth century and has never been replaced. I am sure many can see the hand of God in the construction of Ely Cathedral, but to me it is more about the aspirations, and indeed the human frailties, of men and women over a very long time. I don't think that something has to transcend reality to be transcendent – which Ely most certainly is.

I became more interested in Ely when I discovered I had several cousins who lived in the town, or farmed the land immediately outside it. I particularly remember one large farmhouse on the north slopes of a quite steep small island, known as Quanea (pronounced 'Quainey') Hill, about half a mile south of the cathedral. It had magnificent views of that building across the open, low-lying and peaty fen. Sunlight would catch it in the morning and early afternoon and at sunset it would be silhouetted against the orange glow of what Fenman have called 'the Old Golden Ball'. The Fens have the finest sunrises and sunsets of anywhere in Britain, but I can't think of even a fenland sunset that could match this one for sheer awe-inspiring and all-enveloping magnificence. No wonder people thought that the hill on which the cathedral sits was so special.

When I started working in the Fens on my return from Canada in 1978, I found I was seeing more of my cousins in Ely and I naturally began to read more about the town* and its cathedral. Also during the mid-1970s I realized that I would never be able to fully appreciate how the regional economies of the prehistoric Fens would have functioned if I didn't also study similar aspects of life in later times. And you cannot possibly come to grips with the complex world of the medieval Fens if you don't pay close attention to the early monasteries.

Most people are probably aware that many famous English cathedrals were originally abbey churches of large, and usually prosperous, monasteries. Westminster Abbey is an obvious example, but the two principal cathedrals of the southern Fens, at Ely and Peterborough, were also abbeys of the ancient order who followed the Rule of St Benedict, which was probably written sometime in the 590s. The Benedictine Order was founded in the early sixth century and spread rapidly through western Europe, often encouraged by powerful and influential people, who had good reasons to be more worried than normal folk about their souls' avoiding the fires of hell in the afterlife. A fine fenland example of this was Peterborough (then known as Medeshamstede) Abbey, which was founded around 655 by Peada, king of the Middle Angles. Peada was son of the powerful King Penda of Mercia. Earlier we saw how Peada's sibling, St Kyneburgha, established the original church at Castor.

The abbey at Ely was founded in 673 by St Etheldreda.† She established a double monastery of monks and nuns, as quite often happened in the Anglo-Saxon church. At first glance you might suppose that Etheldreda was a saint, pure and simple. But no. In reality she was the daughter of an East Anglian king

---

* Technically, of course, as Ely possesses a cathedral it is a city.
† Also known as St Æthelthryth.

and was married to a King of Northumbria. It is said that Etheldreda based her foundation on an older church that had been destroyed by one of King Penda's Mercian attacks and if that is the case, this church would have had very old roots – certainly in the British or Celtic tradition and possibly extending as far back as Roman times.[3] If true, this would support the idea that the isle and hill of Ely had been sacred for a very long time.

St Etheldreda's foundation thrived for some two centuries until it was sacked in a Viking raid around 870. It was refounded a century later by Aethelwold, Bishop of Winchester, as a Benedictine abbey for monks alone.[4] Although founded on an isolated fenland 'island', the new abbey soon became one of the most prosperous in England, on a par with Glastonbury and Winchester. Of course, this strongly suggests that the region was far from impoverished. Indeed, I would see the abbey and later the cathedral as a towering symbol of the region's economic success, over the ages.

Following the Norman Conquest of 1066, a new abbot of Ely, Simeon, who was related to William the Conqueror, embarked on a massive rebuilding of the abbey. The post-Conquest period saw the creation of many new castles (the Tower of London being the best-known example), which are seen as powerful symbols of Norman rule. The same can also be said for many Norman-style churches, with their distinctive round-topped arches, which were refurbished, or completely rebuilt, in the late eleventh or early twelfth centuries.

I suppose it's because I'm an archaeologist, who likes to discover how things were built or constructed, that I've always taken a somewhat oblique view of ancient buildings and places. So I love the atmosphere of somewhere like Stonehenge, but I'm far more interested in how and why they sought exotic stones from South Wales – and why on earth they chose Salisbury Plain?

Happily, we are beginning to answer both of those questions. And as we do so, I find the mystery of the place is enhanced, not diminished. Knowledge, especially detailed knowledge, adds an extra dimension to even the most highly scrutinized of places. And that may be the reason why I am intrigued by an aspect of cathedrals that doesn't always make it into the guidebooks. But before we look at that, we need to make a very quick diversion back to Flag Fen.

When we found the first few timbers at Flag Fen we were inclined to think that they would probably have been cut from trees that had been growing round about. But we were wrong, because it soon became apparent that many were far more substantial and almost certainly came from managed woodland on much drier ground. The oaks in particular could not have grown on the wet fens of Fengate. This was great news for Maisie, our woodworking consultant, because she had always wanted to tackle a site with real prehistoric carpentry, as opposed to a few sharpened stakes and the occasional chopped wattle stick. And the more we dug, the more the great timbers proliferated: huge split oak planks, shaped beams with carpenters' joints and evidence for the use of a variety of axes, chisels, awls and other heavy-duty Bronze Age tools.

Over the winter that followed the discovery of Flag Fen, back in 1982–83, Maisie lent me her copy of the woodworking historian's bible: *English Historic Carpentry*, by Cecil Hewett.[5] Textbooks tend to leave me rather cold, but not this one. Not only was it well and clearly written, but it had a terrific narrative, which was wonderfully illustrated by the author's own drawings. Most importantly, it had a message: that England's greatest contribution to the world of architecture was its carpentry. Sadly, this is a message that still needs to be proclaimed. We love our church spires, especially around the Fens, but we rarely think about the timber frames and scaffolding that made and make

them possible. I have to say I devoured Cecil's book and I still
dip into it frequently.

So you can imagine how we felt when the great man came
to visit our excavations at Flag Fen in the mid-1990s. He had
just recovered from a stroke, so his movements were stiff, but
his mind was very sharp and he had the sparkly eyes of a lively,
humorous intelligence. In those days the dig was protected by a
large steel shelter, clad with plastic sheeting. I remember escort-
ing him through the narrow doorway onto the scaffold-plank
viewing walkway that ran along the edge of the dig. He took
one step inside, then stopped, looking down at the students and
diggers working silently below him. They, and he, were rapt in
concentration. And I have to say the site that day was looking
very good, with plenty of large, well-preserved timbers, many of
them with the heavy carpenters' joints that he understood so well.
He said nothing for several minutes and was clearly very moved
indeed. Later, over a cup of tea in our visitor centre, he said that
Flag Fen showed that carpentry skills were not all imported to
Britain by Viking shipwrights – as some have suggested – nor
that we acquired them from visiting Angles, Saxons or Romans,
because – as he firmly believed – we had always possessed them.
By now, I had studied his great book and was familiar with
structures like the spire at Salisbury, the lantern at Ely and the
roof of Westminster Hall. I said something to the effect that they
all had roots in places like Flag Fen, back in the Bronze Age – and
earlier. And he nodded. A shy man of few words. I think that visit
meant a great deal to him. Cecil died a few years later, in 1998.[6]

It was through reading *English Historic Carpentry* that I first
came across what has to be the glory of Ely Cathedral, the soaring
timber lantern set in an octagon, which lights up the centre of
the transept from high, high above the ground. According to
records that survive from the time, it was built between 1328
and 1342 under the direction of Master Carpenter William of

Hurle (today we would call him William Hurley) at an annual cost of £8 (approximately £20,660 in modern money).[7] William of Hurle was widely regarded as the Master Carpenter of England, and he provided his services with the approval of King Edward III. In medieval times the top carpenters and masons also designed their projects and were, in effect, architects too.

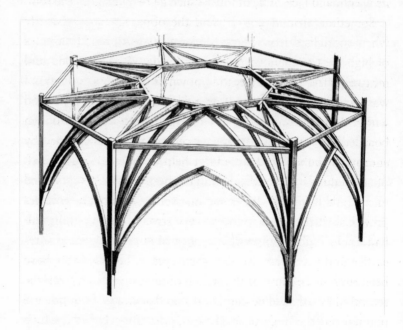

*Cecil Hewett's drawing of the timber framework of the Ely Cathedral Octagon, or transept tower. This structure, based on a dome, is one of the greatest achievements of medieval carpentry.*

The great octagon at Ely was designed and built during the Decorated phase (*c.*1250–1350) of medieval architecture, when English architecture was 'the most forward, the most important and the most inspired in Europe'.[8] Hewett was quoting Nikolaus Pevsner, who was writing from a deep knowledge of architecture as exhibited by finished stonework, but who had no experience of carpentry. It was Hewett who revealed that the carpentry that lay under the stonework and supported it was even more advanced and remarkable. Hurle based his design for Ely on masons' stone vaults and in the process he created what is, in effect, the largest domed roof in medieval Europe north of the Alps. Stonework would have been impossible, simply because of its weight and lack of flexibility at such a great height in the roof.

Sometime around 2005, I had the opportunity to visit Ely when specialists from English Heritage were taking samples of high roof timbers to be accurately dated by counting and measuring tree rings (a method known as dendrochronology).[9] I was escorted up innumerable narrow spiral staircases concealed within the walls and eventually emerged onto a rough wooden boarded floor above the transept ceiling. I was surrounded by enormous timbers and I couldn't help thinking that the smell of stone dust and wood would have been what Hurle's skilled men would have been breathing in, over six and a half centuries previously. I then recalled how very strongly freshly split oak had smelled when we made a replica of Seahenge* a few years earlier, and I realized also that their eyes would probably have been running because of the stench of tannin released from the recently hewn oak. The cathedral's archaeologist alongside me pointed out the huge posts that supported the lantern, which they had also examined closely. It would have been a major feat of engineering simply to have raised these straight oak trunks to this great height, let alone to have shaped and fitted them in place. Then he opened a little hatched window and we were given a superb view down into the transept far below. Of course I've been in tall modern buildings, but one never gets the chance to look down from directly overhead and the experience was both scary and absolutely transfixing. I don't think

* See Chapter 2, pp. 35–39.

the overused phrase 'bird's eye view' has ever been quite so appropriate. We were eagles looking out of our lofty eyrie at the tiny world below.

The transept at Peterborough Cathedral was built and rebuilt, after various collapses, early in the Perpendicular phase of English Gothic architecture, a few decades after the Decorated period. The dendrochronologist Ian Tyers has dated the start of work to 1371, the year the trees were felled.[10] Originally, Peterborough had an octagonal structure, which included a lantern similar to that at Ely, over the transept, but this was supported on the arches of the two transepts, the nave and the chancel. There was no need for the lofty timber dome. Sadly, the lantern was taken down in the early nineteenth century and you can only appreciate the elaborate timber work if you go into the roof space – which I have done, when restoration work was being carried out following severe fire damage to the nave roof (caused by an arson attack in 2001). Peterborough Cathedral boasts many glories, but its superb painted nave ceiling, built and decorated sometime between 1230 and 1250, is one of the finest in Gothic Europe. The nave ceiling at Ely is also magnificent, but sadly nothing like as ancient as Peterborough. It was begun in Victorian times and completed in 1855. Unlike some Victorian 'improvements', I think this one works very well; it enhances the view both along and up the nave. It looks particularly good on a bright, sunny day and I know it contributes to my mood whenever I treat myself to that special walk up the nave.

Conventional wisdom would have us believe that the proliferation of monastic estates right across fenland in the early Middle Ages came about because the Fens were remote and isolated: suitable places for hermits and impoverished monks to sit in their cells and ponder the supernatural. And it's a very persuasive vision: the perfect atmospheric backdrop for a creepy sci-fi film or a bleak M.R. James ghost story. The trouble is, it doesn't fit with our current understanding of the Fens, nor with the way that many early Roman Catholic monastic houses, such as the Benedictines, were organized. Mendicant (begging) monks, belonging to the indigenous British Celtic tradition, did indeed inhabit lonely cells in remote corners of Ireland or northern Britain during the fifth and sixth centuries, but the Synod of Whitby, in AD 664, led to England moving away from the Celtic to the Roman Catholic tradition, in which solitary monks and hermits were not encouraged. At their foundation, monastic houses were often granted extensive and productive tracts of land, and they were expected to put these to good use and thereby to function self-sufficiently. It wouldn't have made sense to set up monasteries in impoverished landscapes, where they would have very little chance of surviving independently. So I am firmly of the opinion that the proliferation of early medieval monastic foundations in the Fens was a reflection of the region's richness, rather than its loneliness or poverty. Of course it made sense to disseminate the notion that monastic life in the Fens was all about hardship and austerity – because that would encourage generations of donors and legacies.

The Benedictine abbeys at Ely and Peterborough were both very wealthy. Indeed, the town of Peterborough was known in the twelfth century as Gildenburgh, or City of Gold, because of the region's prosperity. Most of the abbey's extensive land-holdings stretched along the Nene Valley into what is today Northamptonshire, whereas Ely's large estates were positioned in and around the Fens that surrounded it, as well as further afield in East Anglia.[11]

The ruins or reused churches of smaller monastic houses also continue to form an important part of the Fen landscape. On my way to work at Flag Fen, I used to drive through the charming village of Thorney, in Cambridgeshire, which is home to a splendid medieval abbey church.[12] Every time I passed through Thorney, which in those days was cut in half by the heavy traffic of the A47, I saw something new and interesting. Today, Thorney has been bypassed, but there are still archaeological traces of its previously congested existence, such as numerous speed cameras and a set of completely unnecessary traffic lights, which I could swear went red whenever a family of ducks crossed the now almost empty road.

The monastery at Thorney has the usual colourful early history, starting as a colony of anchorites (monks and nuns who observed strict religious isolation), which was raided by the Danes in 870. It was refounded in 973 by our friend Bishop Aethelwold of Winchester (refounder of Ely), who granted it care of the relics of St Botolph, a seventh-century abbot (and patron saint of travellers). This would have attracted pilgrims to Thorney and thereby guaranteed the foundation an income. Built in the 1080s and finished in 1110, the church was massively larger than the current parish church of St Mary and St Botolph (whose name is also commemorated in the parish church of Boston, in Lincolnshire), which was partly demolished after the Dissolution, reputedly to provide stone for the building or enlargement of Cambridge University buildings, probably including my old college, Trinity. I was in two minds when I first discovered this. My initial reaction was one of horror: how could they demolish a fine Norman church? But over time my views have changed. Yes, it was a pity that they did what they did, but vast monastic buildings were relics of a past, medieval way of life. And besides, sources of good-quality building stone were hard to find in and around the Fens. So as I saw it, and am still inclined to see it, superstition was slowly giving way to something more progressive – and ultimately more humane. When I walk beneath the lime trees around Thorney Church, I calm my slightly uneasy conscience with the thought that maybe some of Sir Isaac Newton's extensive researches took place in rooms built from stonework taken from walls whose foundations still lie in the earth beneath my feet.

Following the Dissolution of the Monasteries, the abbey's lands were granted to the first Earl of Bedford. (During the following century, the fourth earl, Francis Russell, would undertake an ambitious project to drain the Fens, which I will consider in Chapter 15.) Thorney thus became the centre of the Bedford family's vast fenland estates and you can see this in almost every building away from the very centre of the village, around the church, where the quite large houses are older than the estate cottages, most of which are Victorian.

In the seventeenth and eighteenth centuries, Thorney became home to large numbers of French Protestant refugees, known today as Huguenots.[13] French names are still common in the area, although of course they have become completely anglicised: for example, a large firm of truck operators called Thory (a place name in France) can be seen on many local roads, especially during the sugar-beet harvesting season. Huguenot settlers were welcomed to Britain by Oliver Cromwell, who granted them certain tax advantages and freedom from foreign military service for forty years. They were also encouraged into the region by the dukes of Bedford, who were looking for labour for their newly drained fenland estate. There is a memorial to them in Thorney Church and a display in the Thorney Heritage Museum, housed in the old Bedford Estates water tower. This is the tallest building in the village. It has a single stair turret on the roof above the tower that can be seen as a nod of respect to the neighbouring ex-abbey church, especially when viewed from across the fen to the north – or indeed from the new bypass.

There is at long last a growing realization that many of the landed estates of the eighteenth and nineteenth centuries were innovative and surprisingly enlightened.[14] Yes, they were managed for profit, but by no means at any cost. Most of these estates were well, and humanely, run and their workforce was usually accommodated in good housing. The Russell family, the earls and later the dukes of Bedford, have left us a wealth of fine Georgian streets from their London estates centred around Bloomsbury – their names (Russell Square, Bedford Square etc.) providing a clue to their ownership.[15] The family also owned land outside London, including their headquarters at Woburn, Bedfordshire (Woburn Abbey is the family seat) and major holdings around Tavistock in Devon, Thornhaugh, near Peterborough, and at Thorney. The Bedford estate employed its own architects and builders and you can see many similarities between the estate buildings in Tavistock, Thornhaugh and Thorney. Some of the most successful estate buildings in Thorney, including the village school, a small terrace of shops and the old water tower, were by the estate architect S.S. Teulon, who was employed by the 7th Duke of Bedford to draw up plans for the village's development. Particularly fine terraces of some sixty estate houses, each with a substantial garden at the back, line the north side of Wisbech Road.

The Thorney estate pioneered some innovative community schemes, including gas lighting and purified water, supplied from a tank yard near the water tower. The plots behind each terrace house were originally ⅓ acre each. This was enough land for a family to grow its own food and keep chickens and maybe a pig. Each plot also included an outhouse equipped with a copper for boiling water for washing clothes and a flush toilet (an innovation for the time). You can still see traces of all of this in the overgrown land behind the terraces. I only hope the local council doesn't decide that this is a 'brownfield' site, sweep it all away and replace it with an unsightly sprawl of vast executive homes.

★

My second abbey site is about a twenty-minute drive north-west of Thorney, across the county line, in Lincolnshire. It lies closer to the edges of the Fen, and although it might seem more remote in the modern landscape, it was never cut off and isolated, despite what some chroniclers would have us believe.

I don't think I'm unusual in not liking to drive to and from somewhere, following precisely the same roads in each direction. For me, driving is a great opportunity to view the landscape, so I always try to vary my journeys. I usually drive to Leicester along the mostly Roman course of the A47, as that is guaranteed to get me there promptly. On my way back, I start out along the A47, then head off northwards towards Stamford. Stamford must surely be one of the most perfect towns in Britain, with the outline of the Viking age burgh intact at the centre and superb architecture, all constructed from the finest limestone, mostly quarried at Barnack, just outside the town.*

I often take the Barnack Road (the B1443) eastwards, out of town. We drive along a tree-lined road, pass by the back door to Burghley Park and House, which you can glimpse through Capability Brown's landscaped park, then into the village of Pilsgate, passing by a disused quarry where in the 1970s I took a small team of diggers from Fengate and we spent an enjoyable sunny afternoon excavating a Bronze Age cremation, with a complete urn.[16] Then it's on into Barnack, past the fine church with its superb Saxon tower, before heading out into the flatness of the Welland Valley, which gets rapidly wider as one heads east.

Soon I'm in familiar territory at Maxey, where the vast gravel pits still seem as busy as they have ever been. From Maxey I

---

* See Chapter 4, p. 73.

hop across the county boundary into Lincolnshire at Market Deeping, where I might stop for fish and chips (the town has no less than two award-winning shops) and then it's time to head even further east to Deeping St James, the home of the last quarries in the Welland Valley and where I exposed an intact Bronze Age landscape in the late 1990s.[17] The landscape around the disused quarries in Deeping St James features many tall trees, which are home to birds who need high nests: rooks, birds of prey and herons. Those trees stand in contrast with the vastness of Deeping Fen, which extends away to the north, with east–west dykes forming a regular arrangement, dividing the peaty soil into large, rectangular fields. I have to say I find this late-drained landscape rather bleak and cheerless and it always comes as a relief when the road climbs up onto the top of the high flood bank that retains the waters of the River Welland.

*A distant view of the ruins of Crowland Abbey,*
*as seen from the River Welland bank.*

I love this part of the journey. From a height – and make no mistake, this is a tall bank (maybe 8–10 metres?) – even the vast flatness of Deeping Fen looks attractive, with water gleaming in dykes, isolated farms and barns and glimpses of the higher fen-edge in the background. But the grass-covered Welland bank is grazed by flocks of sheep and there are occasional willows, often bent and broken by the ruthless winds of winter. The river itself is rich in wildlife, with crested grebes, mallard, teal, moor-hens and huge numbers of swans, often accompanied by cygnets or young adults, still with their pale brown plumage. Often I pull over and get out, just to enjoy the stillness of the place, which is further enhanced by a tractor ploughing three fields away and the frantic beating of wings on water as two swans take off on their way to visit friends and relations on larger washes elsewhere.

If I look across the river and beyond the sheep-lined flood bank on the other side I can see the tower of Crowland (more cor-rectly Croyland) Abbey a couple of miles to the east. From this far away, the little town around the abbey still lies hidden by the riverbank, but as I drive further I come to a tall white-painted water tower with a pub at its feet. This is where I turn right and cross the river into an entirely different landscape. I am now in a small and controlled wash, with sluice gates and weeping willows, which, despite being shady and pleasant in summer, have always struck me as inappropriate. I suspect they were planted by well-meaning county officials keen to improve the amenity value of the area sometime in the 1960s, but they certainly aren't fen trees. The willows most commonly encountered in the Fens are the smaller shrubby goat willow and the much taller white and crack willow, which are often pollarded about 10 feet (3 m) off the ground to prevent cattle and sheep browsing the growing shoots. I drive by picnic tables and litter bins, complete with the obligatory glaring red one for dog poo. Then the road swings

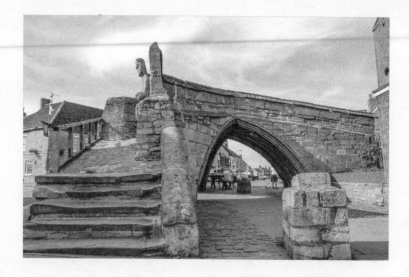

*The late fourteenth-century Triangular Bridge, in Crowland.
Although now on dry ground, this bridge originally crossed three
streams. The much weathered medieval stone statue of Christ
probably originally came from the abbey's west front.*

high onto the flood bank that has long protected the town of
Crowland. At this point we turn sharp left.

We follow the bank for a few yards and then turn right and
swoop down into town on one of two roughly parallel roads
that run alongside a long-drained river whose course is now
grassed over. The houses to left and right are mostly eighteenth
and nineteenth century and quite small. After a short drive, the
two roads join the marketplace, at the end of which is a unique
medieval three-way stone bridge. Trinity Bridge (also known
as Triangular Bridge), which dates from the fourteenth century
and is constructed of Barnack stone, originally spanned the
Welland and one of its tributaries, but these rivers have now
been rerouted, leaving the bridge high and dry. It is made up of
three pointed half-arches in the form of a triangle. On its southern arm is a seated figure of Christ, probably removed from

the nearby abbey after the Dissolution. The eyeless face stares into infinity with haunted serenity. I turn left at the Triangular Bridge and head towards the abbey down a shop-lined street that retains a distinctly Georgian atmosphere. Many of the houses in Crowland are brick or masonry fronted, but have earlier timber-framed interiors – something one also sees in Stamford, where a high proportion of the seemingly Georgian buildings are in fact seventeenth century, or even late medieval.

*The partially ruined mid-thirteenth-century and later west front of the Benedictine Crowland (or Croyland) Abbey. The damage took place in the aftermath of the Dissolution of the Monasteries and during the English Civil War of the mid-seventeenth century.*

The abbey church still dominates the little town, despite being a mere fragment of its once magnificent self. Today, the body of the parish church was originally a side aisle of the monastic abbey, with a two-storey porch. It's well worth walking into the church, but I always like to have a stroll around it first. The west front is superb, with statues – many original – in niches and a fine doorway with scenes from the life of St Guthlac in the tympanum over the doorway beneath the large glassless window, where all the tracery has been smashed out. Pass through the door arch, beneath the mid-twelfth-century carvings, and then walk towards the high rounded Norman chancel arch, just one stone-width thick, which seems to hang, unsupported, in the sky, and pass to the rear of the church, at the east end. Here, the stonework has been reddened by fire. I mentioned in the Prologue what I was told when I was first shown around the abbey, namely that this burning happened during the Civil War, when Cromwellian troops were stationed nearby. But Pevsner suggests[18] the damage was actually done by successive squires' sons, who would light an ox-roasting fire against the wall. Having met a few squires' sons in my life, I am inclined to believe this rather less colourful version of the story.

In the next chapter we are going to visit some more fenland monasteries in the northern part of the region – in the Witham Valley – and look at how the influence of such institutions made the Fens socially and economically different from the neighbouring Midlands, where the more highly structured feudal manorial system held sway. We'll also visit the towns of King's Lynn and Boston, which have much to tell us about the medieval history of the Fens and about the succeeding period, from about 1550 to 1700, when modern Britain began to find its identity – a process in which the Fens were to play a significant part. But first let's head north, and deeper into Lincolnshire.

# Tattershall Castle: The Saving of England's Past

*Witham Valley Monasteries – Lord Curzon and*
*Tattershall Castle – King's Lynn – Boston*

Landscapes are about time, people and places coming together. Sometimes the results create a delightful harmony, occasionally a dissonance; but most landscapes present a mixture of both. And of course the balance of this blend is constantly changing, and patterns of settlement shifting, as land and people adapt to the evolving environment and economy. For reasons that I don't fully understand, but are probably due to the size and scale of landscapes in the regions concerned, these relationships are particularly clearly visible along the valley of the River Witham, as it flows slowly south-eastwards to join the main spread of the Fens a couple of miles south of Coningsby.

I have long enjoyed visiting and travelling through the Witham Valley, usually on my way to Lincoln from the Fens of South Holland, where I live. It's an area quite unlike any other part of the Fens, because it can change over quite short distances.[1] There are the regulation flat, often treeless stretches of river floodplain with deep dykes, but the edges of the valley are quite distinct and here the landscape soon alters, with hedges, spinneys, pasture and sometimes extensive areas of woodland. This is particularly true of the northern side of the valley, which also marks the course of the modern, canalized river. Here the valley slope is steeper and the transition from floodplain to upland is quite abrupt. By contrast, the southern approach to the valley seems gentler as it blends into the wide floodplain, with the artificial banks of the Witham visible in the middle distance.

The Witham Valley floodplain is well known to prehistorians for at least four buried prehistoric and Roman timber causeways that divide it into roughly equal segments, each about 4 miles (6 km) long. These ancient divisions continued to be respected into early medieval times, even though the causeways themselves had long been abandoned. This was when the valley was to become host to a number of abbeys and priories, belonging to various orders. The monastic communities, many of which were founded in the eleventh and twelfth centuries, were regularly spaced along the valley at Bullington Priory (where sadly nothing survives), Barlings Abbey (ruins), Stainfield Priory (earthworks), Bardney Abbey (ruins), Tupholme Abbey (ruins), Stixwold Priory (no remains), Kirkstead Abbey (ruins). The final, southern, step in the Witham 'ladder' might have been provided by the castle at Tattershall (first built in stone, in 1231). I also suspect there is another prehistoric causeway between Tupholme and Stixwold, but it still lies hidden.[2]

The intricate ladder-like arrangement of causeways and monastic sites along the Witham Valley hints at the complexity of each foundation's relationships with other, religious and non-religious, communities in the immediate vicinity. These arrangements have been closely examined in an ambitious recent study of Barlings Abbey,[3] which describes how relationships changed as time passed and strongly suggests that monastic communities played an active part in supporting farms, villages and the rural economy of the region. They have sometimes been portrayed as parasitical and corrupt and a few of them may indeed have become lax in their latter years, prior to the Dissolution, but for much of the medieval period, monastic foundations played an essential role in local life, both as an economic force and as providers of health services, social care and education. Without them, many rural communities would have been seriously diminished.

Over the years I have taken friends and colleagues to visit the Witham Valley. There is something stark and sad about the remaining monastic earthworks and ruins, especially given the size, longevity and success of the original foundations. Some monastic churches were reduced in size before taking up a new role as parish churches, as we saw at Thorney and Crowland, but many of the examples in the Witham Valley had suffered too much after the Dissolution: walls and pillars are all that survive. You can see this very vividly at Kirkstead and Barlings, where the bare stone ruins seem to stand to attention, like an aged sentry, gaunt and defiant. I find them very moving. Happily, all the sites are either listed as Historic Buildings or are protected by being scheduled as Ancient Monuments. This was an important legal process whose inspiration lay nearby, and also in the Witham Valley.

I mentioned that the castle at Tattershall (or a predecessor) may have formed the most southerly 'rung' of the Witham ladder. Today it is one of the earliest and finest brick-built buildings in England, the original stone-built castle having been largely reconstructed in brick in the 1430s.[4] And what a superb building it is! Its setting is wonderful, too – the castle, the moat, the grounds and the church alongside it together make an excellent

*Tattershall Castle. This remarkable and very early brick-built tower dates to the mid-1400s. The buildings surrounding the tower have mostly gone, but the moat survives. It was built by Lord Ralph Cromwell, who was Treasurer of England from 1433.*

day out. It was, however, *very* nearly destroyed – and not by a besieging medieval foe, but by modern ignorance. Its preservation has had a huge impact on the protection of ancient building everywhere.

I have vague memories of somebody at school declaiming a so-called Balliol rhyme about George Nathaniel Curzon:

My name is George Nathaniel Curzon,
I am a most superior person.
My cheeks are pink, my hair is sleek,
I dine at Blenheim once a week.

It didn't make me laugh then, as I had no idea who on earth it was about, but I gather it had been popular a generation or two earlier. Indeed, George (Lord) Curzon had been very important, first as Viceroy of India, where, among other things, he organized the restoration of the Taj Mahal. He returned to England in 1905 and became active in English politics, serving in Lloyd George's war cabinet during the First World War. He was foreign secretary from 1919 to 1924. But despite playing these major roles in politics, he had always had an interest in historic buildings and ancient monuments and was very concerned indeed when, in 1910, the Fortescue family, who owned Tattershall Castle, sold it to an American consortium, who promptly ripped out the fine fireplaces, which they intended to sell to rich compatriots for their new homes in America. They then planned to demolish the castle. In 1911, the local vicar contacted Lord Curzon and begged him to help them save the castle, which he did, single-handedly – by stepping in and buying it.

Curzon then tracked down the missing fireplaces and had them reinstalled in the castle, which, having been abandoned for some two centuries and treated as a romantic ruin, was in a pretty terrible state. Curzon repaired the roof and carried out extensive restorations, but sensitively, following the well-established conservation principles of the Society for the Protection of Ancient Buildings.* I particularly like the stained glass in the windows, which Curzon decorated with the coats of arms of the castle's past owners. Curzon opened Tattershall to the public in 1914 and on his death, in 1925, he bequeathed it to the National Trust, who still own it.

Much influenced by his experiences with Tattershall, Lord Curzon was one of the principal sponsors of the Ancient Monuments Consolidation and Amendment Act of 1913. Prior to this act, owners could do what they chose with their buildings, no matter how important they might be architecturally, or to the nation's history. The act gave legal protection to a list of historic structures and by 1931, when the original act was replaced by a new Ancient Monuments Act, there were more than three thousand listed buildings and some two hundred had been taken into public ownership. Few ancient buildings can have had such an important modern history as Tattershall.

I suppose there's a geeky, somewhat obsessive side to many archaeologists. You can see it in the way we compulsively mark and label all our finds – a process that sometimes continues into the tea shed, where mugs can be labelled (and nowadays sandwich boxes in portable fridges carry their owners' details). Everything on an archaeological excavation should be labelled and have its correct place. If you see chaos in the tea shed, you'll probably find it in the site database and the Finds' Register as well. I'm aware that I too have a geeky side, which in my earlier career manifested itself in the compulsive measurement of the length : breadth ratio of flint tools – among other things. This often involved days of work measuring thousands of flints to

---

* The Society for the Protection of Ancient Buildings (SPAB) was founded in 1877 by William Morris and others.

within a tenth of a millimetre. As a reward, I was able to tell the readers of my reports whether the flints in it were Early or Late Neolithic, Bronze or Iron Age. So it was a compulsion that also served a purpose.

My obsession with detail began at school when I was studying for A Levels and was learning about the small changes that happened when plants and animals mutated and evolution advanced by a tiny step. I can remember it being pointed out to me that such changes can rarely be identified shortly after they happen, but when mutations proved successful they would soon become apparent – and would often be statistically provable. This was when new species and subspecies became visible. The process of speciation fascinated me. Also around this time, I was starting to be interested in archaeology and the physical remains of the past. My grandfather had recently died and my father inherited his house, a manor, high on a chalk hill in north Hertfordshire. It was an old house, in need of extensive repairs, with a late medieval core and successive additions in the seventeenth, eighteenth and nineteenth centuries. I can remember walking slowly through it, listening to my father and the architect discuss the various periods of rebuilding. The architect pointed out how the brick sizes changed through time – and this appealed to me. I liked being able to measure things for a purpose.

When I returned to Eton for my final year I headed straight into School Yard to measure some of the bricks, which I found were significantly smaller than any of those discussed by the architect in what would soon be our new home, or indeed in the Victorian building where I boarded. I did further research and learned that the non-ecclesiastical buildings around School Yard had been built in the first half of the fifteenth century and were completed by 1450.[5] Brick technology was still in its early days in England and the buildings of Eton purportedly involved the import of over a million of them, probably from the Netherlands. I can remember being enthralled by the vision of brick-filled barges being towed up the Thames to Windsor and Eton (which lie on opposite sides of the river). Then my life moved on and eventually I became a prehistorian – a world where bricks are unheard of. But somehow they still retained a hold on me, which they have never relinquished. And then – Glory Be! – like Lord Curzon (another Old Etonian) before me, I discovered the great brick-built tower of Tattershall Castle.

As we have seen, the original castle was built in 1231, probably from earth, timber and stone. Elements of the earlier fortification can be discerned in the complex of earthworks at the foot of the great tower, which include flooded moats that define two fortified areas, known as the inner and outer baileys. The castle tower dominates the inner bailey, and indeed everything around it, but in a way that nobody would have recognized in the fifteenth or sixteenth centuries, soon after it was built. In those days, the great tower would have soared above a dense complex of buildings, which is hard to imagine when one visits the site today. The tower was built by Ralph Cromwell, who became Treasurer of England, to Henry VI, in 1433. Henry VI is always portrayed as a weak and ineffectual king, but even so, his reign has left us some of England's finest buildings, including the Chapels of Eton and King's College, Cambridge, both of which he founded.

Cromwell's great tower was built between 1430 and 1450, out of brick, which was an unusual choice at the time, because bricks were softer than stone and more prone to damage during attack. But it does look very spectacular indeed, which was probably Cromwell's intention from the outset. In the fifteenth century, power was becoming as much about the display of wealth as anything else. The practice of brickmaking was originally introduced to Britain by the Romans, who made flat, tile-like bricks.* Brickworking was reintroduced by Flemish weavers and merchants in the Middle Ages. Initially, as at Eton, bricks were actually brought in, but soon it was found to be more cost effective to employ skilled Flemish brickmakers using local clays. The tower at Tattershall used some 700,000 bricks, which were made by one Baldwin Dutchman (sic), ably assisted by his bricklayer colleague Peter Lyndon, who also hailed from the Netherlands. According to surviving accounts, in twelve months between 1445 and 1446, Baldwin's kiln produced some 322,000 bricks. It could not have been an easy life.

*Holy Trinity Church, Tattershall, as seen from the roof of the castle. This fine church is all of one period, the late Perpendicular, and was built in the later 1400s, with work starting in 1469. It contains important memorials, including a brass commemorating Lord Cromwell. It was originally built to serve an ecclesiastical college.*

---

\* You can see reused Roman bricks in the superb Anglo-Saxon parish church at Brixworth, Northamptonshire, which is one of the oldest and finest buildings in Britain, but not often appreciated as such.

If you climb all the staircases through the four storeys above the entrance level at Tattershall Castle, you will see, among other things, a selection of the wonderful rescued fireplaces, on each floor. Eventually you will find yourself on the roof, where the brickwork was extensively and competently restored by Lord Curzon's team. You can step onto a high ledge, and if you turn your back on the Witham floodplain and look instead towards the north-east and the foothills of the Lincolnshire Wolds, you will see the large late Gothic Church of the Holy Trinity. Like many other English churches in the Late Perpendicular style (and I am thinking here of the two college chapels I mentioned earlier), this church was designed and built with enormous verve and confidence. The large windows don't so much let light in, but seem to capture and even to retain it. I was very surprised when we first visited to be dive-bombed by solitary bats, which would sometimes swoop down on us from high in the roof. It was delightful, but not a little unnerving.

The church, like the nearby brick castle, was built by Ralph Cromwell, but a few decades later. Building work began in 1469 and the tower was completed in 1482. Holy Trinity Church, Tattershall, is built from stone and contrasts wonderfully with the castle's brickwork. I remember thinking, however, as I walked around its interior, that there was something odd about it – apart from the diving bats, that is. It wasn't until I reread Pevsner that I realized the church is almost undecorated. The windows, for example, lack the ornamental curved projections – known technically as cusps – that are such a feature of the windows at King's College Chapel. Somehow this decoration manages to soften the outline of the huge windows that are so characteristic of English Late Gothic, but it also cuts out light. Thus the lack of decoration makes Cromwell's new church at Tattershall one of the best-lit medieval buildings in Britain (another reason why I found those bats so surprising). Holy Trinity served an

ecclesiastical college, whose gatehouse and other buildings originally stood north-east of the church.

The huge church and the improbable brick tower stand in a
very English setting of mown grass and tall, elegant lime trees in
the churchyard. Tattershall has a confidence and serenity that I
always find very relaxing. So I try to visit on weekdays and outside the summer holidays. Certain places do not benefit from
being crowded. Like the nave at Ely, they require tranquillity.

The Fens along the north Norfolk coast are confined to a very
narrow belt of coastal marshes that extend down the eastern edge
of the Wash, north and west of King's Lynn. Geographically
speaking, the small seaside town of Hunstanton, some 12 miles
(19 km) north-west of Lynn, might be considered to be a fenland
town, but as a nineteenth-century resort it has much more in
common with the other, mostly later, Victorian, resorts along
the north Norfolk coast, such as Cromer.

But is King's Lynn *truly* a fenland town? It's a very good
question. King's Lynn is certainly unlike any other fenland town,
but it would be fair to describe most of the larger fen towns
as having strong individual identities, too. My own feeling, and
this tallies with the views of many of my Norfolk friends and
relations, is that Lynn is more fen than Norfolk, although the
voices of many local people have that distinctly Norfolk soft
way of speaking, where o-sounding syllables are smoothed out,
so that words like 'beautiful' are pronounced 'bootiful'. I suspect
that the town's identity has changed as the local economy has
developed and that, in turn, has depended very closely on the
drainage patterns of the River Great Ouse and the fluctuating
shoreline of the Wash. King's Lynn is a beautiful but also
unspoiled and relaxed place. We go there often, simply because
we like it and the people who live and work there. It also helps

that our approach to the town is across water, not on a bridge, but in a small boat that crosses the choppy waters of the Great Ouse (and believe me, it truly *is* great by the time it passes through the town) in all weather: wet, dry, cold or windy.

We normally park the car in South Lynn and then take the regular ferry across the wide expanse of the mouth of the Great Ouse.[6] When I first took it, back in the mid-1990s, I was astonished to discover that there has been a ferry service operating continuously between King's Lynn and South Lynn since 1285. Currently, newspapers are reporting that the local authority will soon replace the boat with 'an amphibious craft'. I'm sure it will be safer and more comfortable and passengers won't have to pick their way along slippery planks at low tide, or battle with a pitching deck in rough weather, but will it be the same? I love the way the skipper stands among the other passengers as he steers the outboard motor towards the landing stage with enormous skill. I've never known him get it wrong – and sometimes the mouth of the Great Ouse can get very turbulent indeed. But there are compensations: quite often we get to glimpse a passing seal who might deign to give the small boat a casual glance. Their faces are very dog-like; every time I see one it reminds me that our Labrador is descended from a long line of water dogs – which explains her huge appetite and seal-like ability to accumulate an insulating layer of fat below the skin.

During the Middle Ages, King's Lynn belonged to the Hanseatic League, which traded widely across northern Europe and brought the town great prosperity, and with it some fabulous buildings, including two fine churches. Although much damaged since the war, architecturally speaking King's Lynn is in the same league as Stamford.[7] But my favourite place in King's Lynn isn't a great church, or a civic building. It's much humbler than that. And it isn't even original.

The railway reached King's Lynn in 1846. Today the Fenland Line is mostly single track and I can recite the stations from Lynn to Cambridge by heart: Watlington, Downham Market, Littleport, Ely, Waterbeach. From Cambridge you can go to London (King's Cross or Liverpool Street stations). The big stations in London, Cambridge and even to an extent in Ely have been modernized and their coffee shops 'baristafied', if I may coin a phrase. But that doesn't apply to the stations of the Fenland Line. Until very recently, Downham Market station hosted what is probably the smallest pub/bar in England. At King's Lynn the station, and particularly its buffet, are an absolute delight, and I never tire of going there – even if I'm not catching a train.

*The distinctive passengers' buffet at King's Lynn railway station. Rebuilt in 1877, the entire station has recently been sensitively restored to how it might have appeared in the heyday of British Railways, in the 1950s. The food and coffee served are, however, very much better.*

The original station buildings at King's Lynn were wooden, and by all accounts rather ramshackle, but they were rebuilt, in brick, in 1871. More recently the station has been very sensitively restored and modernized, using paintwork that recalls British Railways in the 1950s. It was reopened by Michael Portillo in 2014. When work started, many of us were concerned that the restoration would involve the sweeping away of the old buffet. But happily it did not. Some of the woodwork was repaired and restored and the place was given a fresh coat of paint. While the restoration was underway, a customer brought in two water-colours of the buffet interior, painted in the 1920s. They feature the original Victorian décor, which has been carefully restored. The result is a little odd: slightly jazzy, but hugely appealing and obviously authentic. The two watercolours are displayed in the buffet, high on a wall, away from sunlight that might fade them. Incidentally, my favourite table, which is barely large enough for two, occupies the centre of a small curved-glass bay window, which overlooks the booking hall and main entrance, with the excellent Fenman pub visible across the street outside.

The Fens have always been productive, working landscapes and this is reflected in the region's two principal ports, positioned on inland corners of the Wash: King's Lynn, in Norfolk, to the south and Boston, in Lincolnshire, to the north. I mentioned that Lynn's story was heavily influenced by the changing course of the River Great Ouse. The biggest change happened in the mid-thirteenth century, when it was diverted from a more northerly outfall into the Wash via Wisbech, to its present course through, or rather past, King's Lynn – which would have been known as Bishop's Lynn at the time (the name was changed during the Reformation). The town has a very complex early history, with various areas growing under different leaderships at separate times, but driving everything in the Middle Ages was the prosperity of the southern Fens and north Norfolk. Prior to about 1300 the region was exporting wool, salt, corn and fish in exchange for Baltic timber, furs, wine (from France) and cloth (from the Low Countries). After 1300, England's prosperity increased rapidly and its ports, especially Lynn, Boston, London and Southampton, were able to compete with their continental neighbours on an equal basis. By now the principal items being traded were wool and cloth, but wine, timber and corn continued to be brought in. It is sometimes a mistake to exaggerate the importance of the 'wool trade' on its own.

Fundamental to these trading arrangements was the Hanseatic League, a confederation of German towns that possessed the power and influence of a nation state (Germany, of course, had yet to be united). The Hansa was granted special privileges in Lynn in 1271, a process that undoubtedly helped encourage increased trade with Germany and the Baltic states in the subsequent two centuries. By the late fourteenth century, the port was still very prosperous, but trade was becoming more diverse, with the Netherlands becoming increasingly important. Coastal trade with Newcastle, Scottish ports and London was growing, too. Building stone, for example, was being mined at the Holywell Quarries in Rutland, taken to Lynn along navigable fenland waterways and then exported to London, where it was loaded onto Thames barges and shipped upstream to build Windsor Castle.[8]

By the later Middle Ages, Lynn began to decline in the face of increasing competition from London and southern ports, such as Bristol, all of which were able to export cloth from the growing English textile industry of the south-west. Lynn was able to export textiles from the expanding East Anglian industry and from as far inland as Coventry, but it could not compete with London or the more southerly ports in either scale or volume. But the town was still very prosperous: by 1600, Lynn was doing four times the volume of trade as its ancient rival, Boston, across the Wash. Corn was now the town's main export and, very surprisingly, Kirkcaldy, in Scotland, its principal 'foreign' partner. In 1600 the skyline of the warehouses and other buildings along the river front would have been broken by the late sixteenth-century six-storey brick-built tower of Clifton House, which enabled merchants to spot incoming vessels in comfort, through large windows. It was also a centre where deals were made and debts were paid.[9] Clifton House pokes up between the roofs of contemporary and later structures clustered along the old waterfront. King and Queen Streets follow the line of this, but now stand a good hundred yards back from the water's edge.

During the 1990s, Maisie ran a small but very successful archaeological contracting company, which was given the task of excavating some medieval buildings close to St Nicholas' Church, whose spire still dominates the northern townscape. The excavation unearthed large quantities of pottery and other finds, but Maisie became particularly excited when the trenches hit waterlogged deposits. Medieval ports had worked out a foolproof, simple and completely secure method of recording a ship's cargo. In many respects it was just as effective as modern digital records, but it was far cheaper to run and install, and it didn't require any specialist knowledge. Many of the people who helped it function efficiently were probably illiterate. Not surprisingly, it had a profound effect on the developing economy. I am referring, of course, to tally sticks, which Maisie's excavation began to reveal in considerable quantities.

The system works on the simple principle that when a piece of wood is split in half, the two split pieces join together perfectly when held edge to edge. You could try to create an identical stick, but split it in half and it will never join with the first one. In other words, pieces split from different tally sticks will never match. Using this principle, early medieval shipping clerks developed a system of recording cargoes that involved notched pieces of wood, where the notches represented the cargo – say, a notch per ton of wheat or bag of wool. When the ship had been loaded and the cargo recorded on the notched tally stick, it was then split in half. The ship's captain retained the bit that had been split off and the cargo's owner, or more probably his agent/merchant, retained the 'stock' or larger part of the stick, complete with identical notches.

As time passed and merchants started to develop futures markets in cargoes that were still at sea, the stocks of tally sticks were traded at stock exchanges. When the vessel eventually docked, the new owner of the cargo would present his stock to the vessel's captain, who would compare it with his fragment of tally stick, and when the two matched, it proved that the man claiming to be the new owner was genuine. And here we were, excavating the remains of thirteenth-century tally sticks from

*The Customs House, King's Lynn, is a symbol of the port's past prosperity. This fine stone building was designed by Henry Bell and built in 1683.*

a building close by the medieval waterfront at Lynn. That little piece of split wood in my hand might well have caused grief to a medieval corn merchant who had overextended his credit in the 1250s. Having overextended my own resources when setting up the public site at Flag Fen in the late 1980s, I knew what credit and cash flow was all about, and how they could cause me repeated sleepless nights. Those tally sticks had given me a memorable glimpse into a vanished way of life that I can still identify with. As archaeology so often teaches us, in all sorts of fundamental ways, people in the distant past were no different from us.

King's Lynn is so full of fine historic buildings that it is difficult to know where to start. If you can, I suggest you visit the town on one of the annual Heritage Days, when you can plan your visit to coincide with open houses.[10] One of the remarkable things

*The South Gate, King's Lynn. This is the only surviving medieval town gate. The south side (seen here) was built by Robert Hettinger in 1437. Although capable of being defended, this gate was clearly intended to impress visitors to the town.*

about Lynn is that many of its residential dwellings and other buildings were not over-maintained and constantly modified to keep up with changing fashions, as happened in many places that continued to be prosperous after the Middle Ages. As a result, most of its interiors remain remarkably well preserved. Some of the finest streets and buildings are found along the river and in the three or four blocks back from it – the area around the Tuesday Market, to the north, and St Margaret's Church, in the south, being particularly fine, as is the area around the Customs House midway between them. You can follow published perambulations, or just wander. I prefer the latter.

Sadly, parts of King's Lynn were devastated by Nazi bombing in the Second World War and by appalling redevelopments in the 1960s and '70s. You will soon realize when you are entering one of these areas and my advice is to turn around – unless of course you need to go shopping. Other noteworthy early buildings in Lynn include the two guildhalls and Clifton House, Hampton Court, the South Gate and Thoresby College. The urban park known as the Walks, with its superb fifteenth-century Red Mount Chapel, is a beautiful place for a more extended wander.

The magnificent Greenland Fishery House, one of the last built of the town's many timber-framed buildings, sits in solitary splendour, having been saved from demolition. While its isolation has removed its context, it has also lent it an air of defiance. Lynn still boasts a small fishing community that provides local shops, inns and markets with cockles, mussels, brown shrimps, crabs and samphire, together with the more usual whitefish. When I find myself walking down Ferry Lane on my way to the ferry and back to my car, my thoughts often turn to fish. So when we have crossed the river, I frequently make a small diversion to a nearby industrial complex that houses Cole's fish merchants, who supply the local hotel and restaurant trade, but also have a fine shop near their large cold stores.

I recall one visit – I think it was the first time we had ever taken the ferry and found ourselves in Cole's. Besides ourselves, there was one other customer, an impeccably dressed man, from whose well-informed conversation with the fishmonger it was evident he was chef and butler to a very rich and influential local nobleman – and was plainly planning quite a large dinner. In the end, having looked closely at several boxes of fish, he went off with a dozen Dover Sole. After his departure, I said something about the cost of Dover Sole. 'Yes,' replied the fishmonger, 'I didn't know he wanted sole. I knew his boss liked turbot, so I'd kept a special fillet back for him.' He glanced up at the clock and shrugged his shoulders with resignation. 'Oh well, I'll never sell it now. We close in five minutes.'

There was a short pause as he tidied the counter.

'Would that turbot fillet be *very* expensive?' Maisie asked with, I thought, slightly too much shy reticence.

But it worked. He stopped what he was doing. His eyes had lit up.

'For you, my dear: a fiver.'

The fishmonger wrapped and handed over an enormous fillet worth many, many times what Maisie had paid. And it was delicious. Turbot is still my favourite fish: superb texture and sublime flavour. And it always reminds me of King's Lynn.


When the Seahenge timber circle at Holme-next-the-Sea on the Norfolk coast was being excavated, I would come down to the beach to help Maisie and the team carry timbers from the site to the trailer behind our four-wheel drive, which would tow them to Flag Fen for washing, drawing and photography. Later they would go to a conservation laboratory for long-term preservation in PEG, a water-soluble wax.

One clear sunny afternoon I can remember standing on Holme

beach and staring out towards the horizon, not looking for anything in particular, but my gaze was drawn there: there's something fascinating about seeing the curvature of the Earth – it's one of the things I like about the flatness of the Fens. When I checked later on my computer, I discovered that for somebody of my height standing at sea level, the horizon is actually quite close: just 2.9 miles (4.7 km away.[11] So I was not altogether surprised to see something that looked a bit like a ship's mast on the horizon. I thought nothing of it, and we were having a mug of the now rapidly cooling tea I had made at Flag Fen that lunchtime, when I glanced up at the horizon again. And there was that mast thing – in precisely the same place. Holme-next-the-Sea is famous for its RSPB bird sanctuary and one of the archaeologists standing beside me was a keen birdwatcher. So I asked if I could borrow the large binoculars he had slung round his neck. I focused them on that spot on the horizon and there could be absolutely no doubt: it wasn't a mast at all, but the tower of St Botolph's Church, known universally as the Boston Stump, on the other side of the Wash. I checked the distance on a map: it was 23 miles (37 km). Again I checked on my computer and I was probably seeing about two-thirds of the tower, which is some 272 feet (82.9 m) tall, above the far horizon.

A few years later I was looking around the Stump and bought a copy of the church guide, which quoted the great antiquarian and archaeological pioneer Dr William Stukeley (1685–1765) as saying that the tower of the Stump was 'an excellent seamark, seen about 40 miles (64 km) distant'.[12] I could now vouch for that. Stukeley was born in Holbeach, and although we don't know his precise birthplace, the house where he grew up is now occupied by a school. From Holbeach he went to Cambridge and later practised as a medical doctor in Boston.[13] He is principally known for the detailed notes to his many antiquarian travels, where he provides important descriptions of churches, barrows and other ancient monuments. Thanks to Stukeley, we are in a far better position to judge how well our greatest monuments have been treated in recent times. He is also famous for his early investigations at Stonehenge and Avebury.

*Boston Stump, the tower of the parish church of St Botolph's, Boston, was built between 1425 and 1520. The stone came from quarries in Barnack, on the western edge of the Fens, near Stamford. It is one of the largest medieval parish churches in England and is a symbol of the port of Boston's great prosperity in the Middle Ages.*

Normally it's great cathedrals that dominate a townscape, as at Salisbury, Durham, Lincoln or Ely, but in Boston, it's the tower of the parish church, St Botolph's.[14] The tower, sometimes called a spire, dominates the countryside and can be seen right across the open Fens, almost as far as the western fen-edge around Heckington, over 11 miles (8 km) away, as the crow flies. I have heard various derivations of the word 'stump', as applied to St Botolph's tower, most authorities believing that it reflects the shape of its highest storey, which sort of resembles a cut-off branch, or stump. As explanations go, it is more than somewhat literal, and it also completely fails to grasp the irony of fen humour. I'm in no doubt that the name stuck (whatever its actual origins) because the magnificent tower is so high and soaring – and entirely *unlike* a chopped-off tree trunk. It's what fenman call a joke; but I'm afraid ecclesiastical historians can sometimes be a bit introverted and serious-minded, and are unlikely to get it.

St Botolph's is the largest medieval parish church in England. Inevitably, people tend to spend most time examining its splendid tower, but that would be a big mistake. If anything, the main body of the church is even finer, being slightly earlier and built in the Decorated style. Work began in 1309 and finished around 1390. The lowest storey of the tower was mostly built in the following, Perpendicular style, with massive foundations and construction starting around 1425–30, being completed some ninety years later, about 1510–20. As at Ely, the stone came from Barnack, via fenland waterways.

Work on the tower took place after the arrival of the Black Death in 1348. That initial, terrible epidemic was followed by successive waves of plague throughout the tower's period of construction. Apart from the plague, construction of the tower also coincided with a downturn in the port of Boston's early period of prosperity. I have always seen that extraordinary structure, erected on the less-than-stable soils of a Wash port, as more than an architectural and engineering feat, or a soaring expression of religious beliefs. I also see it as a strong symbol of defiance, erected in an age of faith and pestilence.[15] For me, the Boston Stump is a fenman's stone finger jabbing up angrily towards the heavens, whence came successive waves of disease and human misery. Long may it continue to soar skywards.

Lincolnshire seems to specialize in fine churches that were built in a single period. While it is intriguing to see how a building developed over time, it can also be rewarding to see an architectural creation from the Middle Ages still intact, in more or less the same state as when it was first built. It is particularly pleasing when such churches were built in prosperous areas that could afford the finest masons and carpenters. One of the best of these single-period churches, which was built on a large scale and seemingly regardless of expense, is the church at Heckington, due west of Boston, on the very edge of the Lincolnshire Fens. The parish church of St Andrew's has been described by Pevsner as: 'A large town church in a village, in fact one of the dozen or so grandest churches of Lincolnshire.'[16] Like Boston, the church at Heckington exudes confidence, and it fairly bristles with extraordinary carved heads and grimacing grotesques. It was built for Edward II's chaplain, who was rector from 1308 to 1345 and whose monument is still in the church, together with a stupendous Easter Sepulchre.[17] The carvings (which are generally not over-restored) are so fine that I've made several visits to the church, and for some reason always in the depths of winter, when the poor light seems to give the interior an added air of antiquity. I gather that Edward II never visited St Andrew's, but his far more successful son Edward III did, in August 1330.[18] I can remember discussing this with somebody who understood church architecture far more profoundly than I ever will. He was firmly of the opinion that the interior and exterior of the current church would have been almost identical to what Edward III would have seen on his visit there, nearly 700 years ago.

I don't want to compare the interior of the Stump with Heckington, as the two churches are very different and such comparisons aren't always very productive. But I would recommend visiting both of them and allowing enough time to appreciate the wealth of detail in each. I can think of few places where humour and the daily lives of ordinary people are captured more vividly. At Heckington, it's the carvings on corbels and bosses that repay close attention, and in St Botolph's it's the carving of the misericords in the choir.[19] Misericords or 'indulgence seats' were provided by the medieval church to support the creaking joints of elderly priests, who might find the long periods of standing upright during services increasingly hard on their anatomy. Essentially, misericords were similar to those high, firmly padded seats that you can sort of perch or lean against, near the doorways in London Underground trains. But instead of being fixed, misericords consisted of carved ledges on the underside of tipping seats, usually in the choir. When the congregation rose to chant or pray, infirm priests could support their bottoms on the ledges carved into the tipped-up seats, and their legs would be more or less straight, so they would be technically standing – as demanded by the Church's liturgy.

The carvings on misericord seats remained hidden when the seat was down and when it was tipped up they would only have been briefly glimpsed by the priest using them. So they were often rather saucy and even a bit daring. St Botolph's has one of the finest collections of them in Britain. Some of my favourites include a baboon wearing a hood and sitting cross-legged, about to pour a fox a bucket of water (or, more probably, ale). Another shows two jesters, each squeezing a cat under his arm, while biting its tail (a joke at the expense of bagpipes?). I particularly like the unsuccessful hunter with a bow and two arrows, but nothing for the pot. He has raised his right hand to protect his face from his furious wife, who has grabbed him by the chin and is about to whack him with a stick. Wonderful scenes to be hidden beneath robes draped over a tired priest's bottom.

Not many parish churches in England can still claim to house a library. In the Fens, many of the books owned by parish churches were removed 'for safe keeping' to Cambridge colleges. But Boston managed to retain its library, and it possesses a fine collection of some 1,200 books, housed in a room over the south porch. Most of these books were printed in the sixteenth and seventeenth centuries, but a few are even earlier. Medieval chained libraries (where the books are attached to the shelves by long chains that dangle below them) can be somewhat daunting places, and I have to say that while the two I have visited (at Winchester and the Old Library at Trinity Hall, Cambridge) were gorgeous as rooms and as buildings, they didn't really feel like places where you could put your feet up and relax with a good book. But the room over the porch at St Botolph's was different. It was very welcoming and pleasantly informal. Maybe this is because it was actually fitted out shortly after 1634, in post-medieval times, when scholarship was already being regarded with a more open mind.

But old libraries still contain hints of somewhat darker earlier practices. My first visit to an ancient library was around the age of fourteen, when I was at school. I crossed School Yard and entered College Library, where we were shown some of the treasures in the collections, including a Gutenberg Bible, which I can remember as being huge, but not much else. This was because next to it was a smaller, but still very thick, 1,800-page volume written by a man called John Foxe, whom I have subsequently learned was born in Boston in 1516 or 1517. Foxe was a scholar, but also a keen – I am tempted to say fanatical – Protestant and his book contains accounts of the deaths of religious martyrs, with special attention being paid to the English Protestant martyrs and their often grisly, tortured hours of final agony. The illustrations made me feel physically sick and I can understand why this book, *Actes and Monuments* – more usually known as *Foxe's Book of Martyrs* – was so influential. It was published in two editions (the first in 1563, the second in 1570) and was owned by many English Puritans. It played a major part in the growth of anti-Catholic feeling, which contributed to the tensions leading up to the English Civil War (1642–51) and persisted into the following two centuries. The library at St Botolph's has a copy of *Foxe's Book of Martyrs*, but I didn't dare take a look – it might have rekindled the nightmares that woke me so often when I was a boy.

The port of Boston enjoyed a long period of prosperity in earlier medieval times, when, like Lynn, it was linked with the Hanseatic League and was the port from which wool from the Lincoln region was exported to the Continent.[20] For a few years it was even more successful than London, before business slowly began to decline. However, the town's fortunes picked up quite dramatically in the later eighteenth century, when many of the large neighbouring Silt Fens were drained and enclosed – a process that gathered pace in 1760 with the canalization and embanking of the River Witham. At about the same time, the town acquired enlarged sluices, which protected it from tidal floods off the Wash and from rivers in spate further inland. Boston became a major market in livestock, grain and other food products that were then exported, either down the coast, south to London, or along fen waterways and later, via turnpikes, to the expanding industrial centres of the Midlands, Yorkshire and Lancashire.

Sadly, much of the town's architectural heritage was destroyed by some very insensitive road building in the late twentieth century, but a number of warehouses have managed to survive and the vast central marketplace of Wide Bargate – in the nineteenth century it was one of the biggest sheep markets in Britain – still survives, almost intact. I'm very fond of an engraving, made in the 1840s, of a sheep market there. Having attended dozens of such markets, I can recognize much of what is going on, with buyers feeling the muscle conformation on a fat sheep's hindquarters while its owners look on anxiously.

Throughout the later medieval and early post-medieval periods, life in most of the towns and rural regions of fenland continued in a traditional way, largely based around trade and hard work. We are going to see a few more of these towns – and enter their often wonderful churches – in the next chapter. But we are also going to touch on some of the political and cultural developments of the sixteenth, seventeenth and eighteenth centuries, when people began to appreciate that there was more to life than work alone. These ideas were to have a profound effect not just in the Fens, but across the nation as a whole.

# Small Towns and the Gentlemen of Spalding

*Long Sutton and Holbeach – Moulton and Mills –*
*Spalding Town and Ayscoughfee Hall –*
*The Spalding Gents*

The Fens are principally known for watercourses, flat fields and nature reserves. Nobody ever pays much attention to the smaller fenland towns, which is a great shame, as many of them are charming, but in a businesslike, non-chocolate-box way. Three of my personal favourites are Long Sutton, Holbeach and Spalding.

All three of these places have beautiful churches that are testament to the region's considerable prosperity in the Middle Ages. But they are each very different, too. The church at Long Sutton, for example, looks like a fine, but otherwise fairly standard, late medieval 'wool' church from the outside, but as soon as you open the door and look inside you are in another, much earlier, world. It's my local church and every time I visit I am struck afresh by that contrast. From the outside the architecture is mostly post-1300, in other words Decorated and Perpendicular, but with the usual Victorian restoration. The interior is Norman and done to a very high standard. But one of the two greatest delights of Long Sutton church is its churchyard, which looks green, lush and peaceful all year round. Tall trees provide cool shade in summer and in spring the graves, paths and the base of the church walls are lit up with a fine array of naturalized bulbs. And the gravestones are still in position, often complete with headstone and footstone. Maintenance is still done by local volunteers and the whole churchyard feels as though it is well loved.

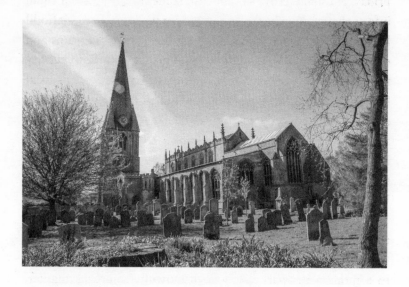

*The Church of St Mary, Long Sutton. The magnificent thirteenth-century tower carries a timber-framed lead spire, said to be the earliest of its type in Britain. When first built, the tower stood on its own, but was joined to the main body of the church during alterations, which were probably funded by John of Gaunt (1340–99), who owned the manor of Sutton.*

The greatest delight of the church is undoubtedly its fine thirteenth-century tower with superbly detailed exterior stone-work. This is capped by one of the earliest lead-covered timber-framed spires in England, which is 162 feet (49 m) tall and appears to be anchored to the tower by four miniature spires (technically spirelets), which all lean inwards slightly. The west door of the tower leads out into Market Street, lined with Victorian and Georgian buildings, including a late eighteenth-century coaching inn, the Bull Inn, which as I write is still abandoned. Like many country towns in Lincolnshire, Long Sutton isn't particularly prosperous and many of the shops are empty or are run for charity. The market, however, which takes place every Friday, is usually crowded and still sometimes features a small informal auction, where you can bid for walking sticks, daffodil bulbs, old hat stands, bookcases, egg boxes, watering cans and even second-hand Wellington boots. I go there every week. My first, and main, port of call is the fish stall, which offers local kippers, cockles, whelks, mussels and marsh samphire, all freshly caught – or harvested – in the Wash. I like the family who run it and I always enjoy meeting and chatting to the customers: there is so much more to market-stall shopping than merely buying things. So far, there are no plans to build a major supermarket in Long Sutton.

About 3 miles (5 km) west of Long Sutton is the small market town of Holbeach. Here the market takes place on Thursdays, but it has been removed from its traditional site near the church to a modern car park close to the town's large supermarket. Within weeks of the supermarket's opening, the greengrocer and two butchers had closed, together with many other shops. Even today, years later, shops are continuing to close and the departing shopkeepers blame the supermarket. Their contempt for the local politicians who inflicted the superstore on them in the first place is unrepeatable. More local businesses seem to be closing every week, and market-stall holders tell me that trade in the new 'marketplace' is very slack. Talking to people in Holbeach, one gets the impression that the place is losing the will to survive.

It is very sad. The buildings in the town reflect this: many of them are in a poor state of repair and some, like the abandoned hotel opposite the church, are frankly dangerous. But the fine church seems to offer a spirit of defiance.

The Wash towns between King's Lynn and Boston were built along the landward side of a continuous ridge of Iron Age and later tidal silts that had accumulated along the southern fringes of the Wash. They all possess very fine medieval churches, which, being built of stone, have survived much better than contemporary timber domestic and commercial buildings. The church at Holbeach, like its neighbour at Long Sutton, is magnificent and sits within a graceful tree-lined churchyard. All Saints Church is a large fourteenth-century (Decorated) building, with an imposing porch that faces on to the main street. The door into the porch is framed by two towers that are very un-church-like and were probably 'borrowed' from a castle or defended manor, sometime in the 1700s.

The interior of the church is very fine, albeit rather Victorianized in places. Normally I would like to walk down the centre of the nave, as at Ely, and pay my respects to the chancel. But not in Holbeach. Here I have something far more important to do. And I like to do it several times a year, if I possibly can. I walk straight into the body of the church and then turn right, towards the tower and the dangling bell ropes. Just before I reach them, there's a superb late fourteenth-century tomb and memorial to Sir Humphrey Littlebury, who I assume was a Crusader, and is shown in armour lying on his back, on top of his tomb, his hands pressed together in prayer. His head is resting on his helmet, which has a man's face and head as a crest. The crest was very important in medieval times as it was, in effect, a personal trademark, or identifier, especially during the heat of battle, when nobody would have had the time to read something as long-winded as 'Sir Humphrey Littlebury'. But just one glance at that crest would have been enough to tell you who was beneath it. In this instance, however, I detect rather more than mere personal identification. We need to take a closer look at the image beneath Sir Humphrey's head.

*The late fourteenth-century tomb of Sir Humphrey Littlebury in All Saints Church, Holbeach. Sir Humphrey's head rests on a carving of his helmet, which has as its crest a remarkably lifelike Saracen's head. Sir Humphrey had fought in the Crusades.*

For a start, neither Sir Humphrey nor the Saracen were too severely damaged during the Civil War, as happened to so many other church monuments in the area, when many Puritans did terrible damage to church interiors. (The defaced angels around the nearby font are an example of such vandalism.) The device on the crest of Sir Humphrey's helmet is conventionally described as a netted Saracen's head – a motif that became popular in heraldry during the Crusades, and was used as an easily recognized inn sign, too. In an age when most people could neither read nor write, this was a pub sign that told potential customers much about the landlord: that he was an ex-soldier and that the inn was his project in later life. It also suggested that he could be trusted as a loyal military pensioner.

But the bearded face beneath Sir Humphrey's head carries messages more complex and profound than these. I find it so extraordinary an image that I have always been surprised that people can walk by it unaffected. It is remarkably lifelike and unlike many images of Saracens it isn't caricature, either. Yes, it represents the severed head of an enemy, but it is carved with remarkable skill and lightness of touch. I would suggest it was done from life and that the model was an Arab, and possibly a friend or colleague of the sculptor or craftsman (who may have worked in Bristol around 1368).[1] The face of the Saracen would be considered a portrait of the highest quality in any other context. It somehow manages to convey inner peace, dignity and humanity in a way that transcends the intervening centuries and tells us much about people's attitudes in the Middle Ages. The Saracen's head portrayed in Holbeach church suggests that some returning soldiers respected their opponents and maybe even sympathized with them: they had all shared the same traumatic experiences. I detected a similar attitude when I talked to my grandfather about his years in the trenches of the Somme in the First World War. He never said much, but he always spoke of the Germans with respect – and I never detected a hint of hatred. I would suggest that Sir Humphrey, who would most probably have been involved in the commissioning of his own tomb, felt much the same about the men he had faced in battle.

The area around Long Sutton and Holbeach is known as 'The Saints'. Long Sutton was originally Sutton St Mary, with the parishes of Sutton St James and Sutton St Edmund to the south and west. These were daughter settlements that were extended into the neighbouring wetlands, as drainage reached inland, back from the Wash. The chronological progress of drainage and subsequent settlement is reflected in the ages of the local parish churches. Sutton St James is closest to Sutton St Mary and has a later medieval church (albeit much collapsed). The church in Sutton St Edmund, some 4 miles (6 km) further into the wetland, was probably first built in the late seventeenth or early eighteenth century and was rebuilt in 1795.[2] Holbeach has an even larger clutch of sister parishes, all with much later (nineteenth century) churches: Holbeach Drove, Holbeach Hurn, Holbeach St Johns, Holbeach St Marks and Holbeach St Matthew.

If you stay on the higher silt lands around Holbeach and head due west, you will drive past the magnificent church of Whaplode, which is mostly Norman, with a superb tower and clerestory and with a wonderfully light interior. I first visited Whaplode church during its flower festival, maybe ten years ago. This whole region is noted for such festivals, which were originally an attempt to use the area's many great churches to attract visitors and thereby to acquire funds for their maintenance. The first flower festival was held in 1954 at the church of St Peter at Upwell, a fine late medieval church close to the Old River Nene, on the Norfolk side of the county line, some 4 miles (6 km) south-east of Wisbech. Commercial-scale flower-growing is a major part of the agricultural/horticultural economy of the silt-lands and many of the growers donate surplus flowers to the parish church, where they are incorporated into themed displays, put on by local charities and community groups.

So far I have stressed the glories of fenland church architecture, but landscape history is not just about the great buildings. It must also include the less flamboyant and humbler structures that gave meaning to the lives of people in the past. Not far from where I live is the small village of Whaplode Drove. One day I noticed a small, unassuming and rather run-down building, which caught my attention because I had recently learned about a series of very early prefabricated churches, sometimes known as Tin Tabernacles.[3] These became very popular in the late nineteenth century, as they were cheap, light and required shallow foundations. They were made of galvanized corrugated iron. The St John the Baptist Church Rooms in Whaplode Drove is a particularly good example of a small, unembellished Tin Tabernacle.

*The St John the Baptist Church Rooms, at Whaplode Drove, near Spalding, Lincolnshire. This is a prefabricated Victorian 'Tin Tabernacle', of a type that was very popular in the later nineteenth century. This photograph was taken in 2009, before the building's recent (and very sensitive) restoration.*

Many people, from pensioners to youngsters at primary school, go to a lot of trouble for the parish flower festivals, and as a result they attract many visitors and raise substantial sums of money for charity. Most of them last for three or four days, but some of the larger ones can remain open for over a week. They begin in late April and are held throughout the summer. I enjoy the look and the smell of the flowers, but the main reason I visit the festivals is to see ancient buildings being used as they would have been in the Middle Ages. Instead of being occupied by tiny congregations of very elderly parishioners, these often magnificent fen churches resume their rightful place as centres of local life, in which people chat freely, children play – and glum veneration is replaced by smiles and laughter. And you get to sit down with a hot cup of tea and a thick slice of home-made cake. I remember leaning back in my pew and looking up at Whaplode's high medieval nave ceiling and imagining that the stonemasons and carpenters who built it were sitting beside me, quietly enjoying tea and cake.

If you continue along the gently winding medieval road out of Whaplode, the next village you encounter is also set back a short distance to the south. You turn off the road and follow the signs to Moulton, past a modern housing estate on the right and a very pleasant landscaped country park on the left. The road jinks right, then left, and suddenly you are in another world – the tranquil rural village of Moulton. All Saints Church has a superb tower capped by a tall Lincolnshire-style steeple, complete with flying buttresses, and is set in a large, picturesque graveyard edged with trees. In front of the church is a triangular green, also with mature trees. The wide main street is lined with fine late eighteenth-century and Regency houses, and starts to taper towards the south, closer to the more recent, deeper fen. Over the years, I have watched progress being made on restoring the windmill, which is set back from the street behind Mill House, another fine Georgian building. The approach to the mill from the main road used to be past a large semi-industrial agri-horticultural business, which has since moved elsewhere. I hope this hasn't led to the loss of local jobs, but it was something of a noisy eyesore, so close to the centre of the village. But what about the mill?

The northern Fens are well known for their huge windmills, which are used for grinding corn. Many of the windmills of the southern Fens were much smaller and were built around wooden post frames, often in rows. These were pumping 'mills' – more correctly wind-driven 'engines' – that used scoop-wheels to lift water out of the dykes and up into the embanked rivers that took the water to tidal outfalls. One is preserved at Wicken Fen. But as the peats continued to dry out and the land surface fell, the distance between the bottom of drains and the top of the riverbanks gradually increased and more power was required to raise the water. In the early nineteenth century the wind pumps were slowly replaced by steam pumps, based around beam engines.[4] Then in the twentieth century, steam gave way to diesel power. Today most pumps are electric, but there is nearly always a diesel back-up, kept in full working order, should a power cut take place during a major flood or tidal surge. The mill at Moulton was never about pumping, it was about grain and flour, but that didn't mean it wasn't very powerful. Far from it, in fact.

The grain windmills of the northern Fens are some of the tallest and finest in Britain. There is a superb eight-bladed mill at Heckington, a few miles north on the fen-edge near Sleaford. The Maud Foster five-bladed mill, which sits beside the Maud Foster Drain in north-eastern Boston, is 80 feet (24 m) tall and provides the only rival to the massive tower of the Stump. But the mill at Moulton (built c.1822) is said to be the tallest in Britain and marginally taller than the other two, being 80 feet to the top of the brickwork, but 100 feet (30 m) to the top of the wooden cap, which turns its four sails into the wind.[5] All three of the great fenland mills, at Heckington, Moulton and Boston, now produce their own flour, which Maisie frequently bakes into bread for our table. At this stage, I cannot yet say whose flour I prefer, but as I have to continue to live in the region, such things are perhaps better left unsaid. The flour from all three mills makes delicious bread.

*The brick tower windmill at Moulton, near Spalding, Lincolnshire. This is the tallest windmill in Britain. It is a major local landmark and was built c.1822. Pevsner memorably describes it as 'looking like a giraffe'.*[6]

★

After tea and cakes at Moulton Mill, I would normally return to the main road and head for Weston, but the nearby village of Weston Hills is not, as its name implies, a scene of rolling chalk downland. Like other villages in the Fens that include the word 'hill', it appears absolutely flat to the modern eye. Shippea Hill in the southern Fens is another good example. These 'hills' would in fact have been low ridges, humps and bumps that would have stayed dry in times of flood or in very wet winters. In one or two instances the word might refer to a sharp corner or 'heal' in the configuration of the local drainage. This may apply to the village of Gedney Hill on Lincolnshire's southern boundary with Cambridgeshire.

The road to Spalding passes Baytree, a nursery where I have bought some rare and beautiful wet-loving plants for the garden. I particularly treasure some swamp cypresses, natives of Louisiana and South Carolina, and a golden variety of the wet-loving Dawn Redwood (*Metasequoia glyptostroboides*), which now extend high above my head when I stroll along the main border. I can remember when Reinhard Biehler was setting the place up in the 1970s, using funds he had raised by being a rose-grafter for local growers. He came to England from his native Bavaria in 1964. I've watched him graft a rose and his fingers move faster than a concert pianist's. I wonder what will happen to similar start-up businesses when and if Britain leaves the European Union? The horticultural industry in the Silt Fens around Spalding relies heavily on our European neighbours, especially the specialist flower markets in the Netherlands.

A couple of miles after Baytree, the road reaches Spalding, where it crosses over the Coronation Channel, which, as its name suggests, was opened in the autumn of 1953, the year the queen was crowned. This is a flood-relief channel off the River

Welland, particularly designed to protect the town of Spalding. The nature reserve at Arnold's Meadow is on your left as you cross the new channel and enter the town.* The more usual way to approach Spalding is from the west along the original course of the Welland, which is entirely delightful and architecturally echoes the grace and charm of Wisbech,† with some beautiful Georgian and Regency houses. Heading north past the High Bridge at the centre of town, you enter an area of Georgian and Victorian warehouses, many of which have been converted to housing, but in a sensitive way. The appearance of the centre of Spalding has been damaged by some horribly insensitive modern development between the fine parish church of St Mary and St Nicolas and the Welland.

I visit Spalding frequently and park my car in Love Lane alongside the low brick wall that bounds the churchyard to the east. We're very fortunate with our churchyards in the Lincoln-shire Fens: none of them have been 'rationalized', as so many have in the prosperous south-east, where gravestones are moved to the fringes to allow contractors' huge mowers to further reduce the interest of the place. As forms of cultural vandalism go, the blitzing of graveyards scores very high, destroying at a stroke both family history and the record of social relationships (preserved in the placing of graves of different trades and classes of people) at various periods, while also wiping out insect life and plant variety. Happily, the gravestones in Spalding are still in situ, as they are in the other small towns and villages we have just visited: Holbeach, Long Sutton and Moulton.

I often stroll through the trees and gravestones of the church-yard and look up at the magnificent church, mostly built in the thirteenth and fourteenth centuries in close collaboration with the

* See Chapter 18, p. 392.
† See Chapter 17, p. 351.

town's priory, which has since, sadly, largely disappeared. The tall interior always feels hugely spacious and somehow remains cool in summer. Once I have walked clear of the church's west end I look resolutely ahead so as not to see what lies on either side. To the north is a post-war pub, now empty and semi-derelict, which urgently requires demolition and the site planted with trees. To the south is the Town Hall, a building one might kindly describe as nondescript, yet intrusively ugly. It was built in 1960– 62 to replace Holyrood House, a building designed by William Sands, the architect of the gardens (c.1730) of neighbouring Ayscoughfee (pronounced 'Ascoffee') Hall. Holyrood House was demolished by Spalding Corporation to make way for their new Town Hall, whose presence is an insult to the two magnificent buildings – the church and Ayscoughfee Hall – on either side. Next to the church is the church hall, a building of the mid-1960s that is almost, but somehow not quite, as offensive as the Town Hall. I sometimes wish that a few of John Betjeman's 'friendly bombs' could be diverted from Slough to other selected targets.

Modern Spalding is the centre of the English flower industry. In the past you would see field after field of screaming red, yellow or white tulips. From the 1950s until the 1970s, coaches would set out from towns and villages across eastern England and head towards Spalding for the annual Tulip Parade, where they would see floats filled with displays of tulips culminating, of course, with one for the Tulip Queen, whose smiling face would then grace the inside pages of many national papers. Sometime in the later twentieth century, the tulip fields were struck by viruses and other diseases. As a result, the flowers grown in these fields are now far more varied: daffodils seem to be the most popular, but farms around where I live grow delphiniums, eremurus (foxtail lilies), gladioli and even peonies.

In the past, products from the region's productive farms were despatched from quays and warehouses along the River Welland in Spalding, which was also host to merchants and bankers living in stylish houses along the river, but slightly further upstream.[7] Among these buildings are two late-Georgian terraces, Welland Place and Welland Terrace, which probably dates to 1813. They would look elegant in Bloomsbury.

*The river front of Ayscoughfee Hall, Spalding. This remarkable late medieval hall was originally built in 1429, but little survives of that date. Most of the building was rebuilt in the late fifteenth and early sixteenth centuries and the river front was Gothicized in 1729 and again in 1845. Recent work has shown that some of the roof timbers have been smoke-blackened from the central hearth in the medieval hall below.*

Almost opposite the two terraces, on the other side of the river, is a much earlier merchant's house, in fact the most distinguished non-ecclesiastical building in the area: Ayscoughfee Hall. Today this late medieval house is the town museum and it includes some excellent displays on drainage and other fen themes. The main hall is believed to have been originally built in 1429. Having said that, there are no features that would seem earlier than the late fifteenth century. As its name would suggest, it is laid out on the medieval hall plan with a large central space and a wing for kitchens and accommodation for the family. It was recently subject to extensive restoration. I remember seeing smoke stains on the inner surfaces of the roof, directly above the hearth, which was nearly always positioned at the centre of a medieval hall.

Ayscoughfee Hall was well maintained throughout its long life and although there were many additions and alterations, these were generally done sympathetically. The garden features a huge yew and box hedge that is almost as high as the hall. I love this hedge, which over the decades has been shaped to accommodate the steadily growing box trees. You can comfortably walk between the trunks and look up high into the branches, inhabited in winter by a loudly chirping population of wrens and robins. From the outside, the swirling, tightly clipped contours of the hedge resemble the puffing smoke trail of an accelerating steam engine. Just beyond the hedge is a war memorial by Edwin Lutyens, complete with a long rectangular pond that reflects its simple but elegant pillars to great effect. Ayscoughfee Hall is a beautiful house, in a unique garden, accompanied by a moving tribute to the dead of two world wars. But that is not all it has to offer. It has also played a significant part in the early development of archaeology, science and rational thought, thanks to its perceptive owner in the early eighteenth century, then a young banker called Maurice Johnson.

When I first started researching into the ancient Fens, I discovered that it was not enough merely to examine individual sites. Entire landscapes had to be worked out: how the various communities developed through time and how they parcelled up the fields and wetlands around them. I soon realized that we were learning about people whose past was as rich and diverse as any in prehistoric, and indeed Roman, Britain. Then I turned to the Fens in post-Roman times, where I came across an altogether different narrative of deserted landscapes, monastic isolation and mass migrations from abroad into the supposed fenland wastes. The picture of the apparently impoverished fens continued into the Middle Ages, despite a wealth of evidence to the contrary (including some of the finest buildings anywhere on Earth). Thanks to the work of Susan Oosthuizen and others we can now debunk the deserted, doom-and-gloom view of the Fens – hopefully for good. And we have to do so if we are to understand how the towns and villages of the later Middle Ages and early post-medieval period evolved into the thriving and enlightened communities of Stuart, Georgian and later times.

To accept that the Fens were prosperous and diverse in the Middle Ages and sixteenth century is one thing, but we must also come to grips with the way rural life was organized. In the neighbouring East Midlands, parishes followed the open field pattern of farming, which was firmly structured around manorial courts, the Church and a tightly controlled system of rights and obligations. The lord of the manor controlled everything and individual parishioners would rent their properties from him, in return for rights to use his land and the parish's communal assets, such as heavy ploughs, harrows and the means of pulling them. Open field farming is still practised in the parish of Laxton in Nottinghamshire.[8]

The parish was the basis of the feudal system. The next rung consisted of noblemen, responsible to the crown, who could raise armed men from the parishes under their control. The feudal system never became as firmly established in Britain as it did in France and Germany, where it persisted for much longer. It was also weakened by the arrival of the Black Death in the mid-fourteenth century and by successive waves of plague thereafter.

Put crudely, shortage of labour moved power away from the lords of the manor and back to the workforce.

The feudal system of the English Midlands did not extend into the regions to the east or west, where the land was not suited to such rigid control. In these areas local variations evolved, usually involving less manorial control and more rights for parishioners and small, owner-occupier farmers, known as yeomen. Manors did exist in the Fens and many were part of large monastic estates, but the open field system only became established around the edges of the wetlands. This lack of feudal control undoubtedly gave rise to an independence of spirit in fenland communities, which of course were not as cut off and isolated as had previously been supposed. In fact, neighbouring and more distant villages would have been in constant communication about grazing rights and other shared interests, such as fishing, salt-extraction and wildfowl. This may explain why Oliver Cromwell, who was born and raised in Huntingdon (in 1599) and became its member of parliament, was so popular in the Fens. You could say that many of the people there disliked controlling authorities and were predisposed to accept his radical Protestant views.

Although some of what I have just said is probably an over-simplification, the later evidence for free-thinking across the Fens, from Spalding to Wisbech and of course to Cambridge, does suggest that there were antecedents in the area. Such things don't just happen overnight. Maybe, to put it another way, fen people were naturally more inclined to reject received wisdom and to think for themselves.*

So the cultural climate in prosperous, working fen towns such as Spalding in the early eighteenth century, when young Maurice

---

* It could lead to problems too, such as the Ely and Littleport Riots of 1816, when rising unemployment and collapsing farm prices following the Napoleonic Wars brought about a popular uprising.

Johnson took possession of Ayscoughfee Hall, would have been an intellectually progressive one. Johnson was only a year older than William Stukeley, who was born and raised in nearby Holbeach. Stukeley had finished reading medicine at Cambridge and had gone to London to further his medical career with a leading doctor at St Thomas's Hospital. He moved in exalted circles in London, but decided to return to Lincolnshire in 1710, and joined a medical practice in Boston. In 1713 he was made a freeman of the town of Boston. These were the years when he developed his interests in the past and made at least two tours researching antiquities, including Stonehenge. Not surprisingly, given their age, proximity and shared education, Stukeley and Johnson became good friends. Stukeley had returned to the Fens at the same time (1709–10) that Johnson was setting about founding a new local society: the Gentlemen's Society of Spalding, which he ran with great skill and energy for its first thirty-five years. It is still in existence and can claim to be one of the oldest learned societies in the land, albeit significantly younger than the Royal Society, which was founded in 1660.[9] The Spalding Gents (as they are generally known in the area) are still thriving and lately – and at long last – have admitted women as members. Their museum and headquarters are in Broad Street.

In its early days, the Spalding Gents had some remarkably distinguished members, apart from Stukeley and Johnson.[10] They included the scientist Sir Isaac Newton, the poet Alexander Pope, the composer Samuel Wesley (called by some 'the English Mozart'), John Gay, librettist of *The Beggar's Opera*, and finally one of the leading sculptors of the day, John Rysbrack. That isn't a bad list for a medium-sized market town (whose population would then have been about 2,000), and it suggests that distinguished people were happy to travel there because they knew they would hear interesting discussions and meet stimulating company. As someone who has tried to run local organizations, I have great admiration for some of Maurice Johnson's basic rules, which included the following:

*'The Society must meet or assemble at four.*

*There must be a Pot of Bohee Tea of ½ oz. to Twelve dishes.*

*There must be Twelve clean Pipes and an Ounce of the best Tobacco.*

*There must be a Chamber Pot.*

*Then a Tankard of Ale holding One Quart and No More must be set upon the Table.*

*The President must always sit on the Right-Side of the Chimney and take care of the Fire.'* [11]

Those rules neatly sum up what it would have been like to have attended one of the early meetings of the Spalding Gents. These eighteenth-century gatherings would have been rather more relaxed than they were to become in Victorian and modern times, when pipes of best tobacco and quarts of ale would not have been welcomed. It is interesting to note that similar societies also arose in the early eighteenth century in two other towns on the edges of the Fens, at Peterborough and Stamford, although neither lasted for very long.[12] But again, it suggests that there was a considerable appetite for learning and enquiry among many people in the region. It was a trend that was gathering pace.

# Cambridge: Rationality and Fen Drainage

*Cambridge, Town and Gown – Rational Thought and*
*Fen Drainage – Vermuyden and the Bedford Levels –*
*Fen Formation*

Cambridge is internationally regarded as a world-class university and we tend to forget that it was, and still is, a fen town. In some ways its early history is quite ordinary and typical of the area. It was the site of numerous prehistoric settlements and the Roman town that grew up there was, in Pevsner's words: 'never a place of grandeur, but a workaday place...'.

I suppose Pevsner was right, but I am not altogether sure: great places of learning, like the early industrial centres of the West Midlands, don't just pop up out of the ground unexpectedly, mushroom fashion. If you look closely, you will often find something pre-existing in the region that attracted people. There is historical evidence for monastic learning in the Cambridge area in the decades following the Norman Conquest, but for me the best archaeological evidence is to be seen in two pre-university churches that would have been exceptional buildings when they were first built. The earliest church in the county is St Bene't, in Bene't Street, opposite the Eagle Inn, famous for the ceiling of the front bar, which has candle-smoke graffiti put there by bomber crews between raids, during the Second World War. (How stressful it must have been to be drinking with crew and girlfriends one night, then being in a Lancaster bomber dodging night-fighters the next.) From the window in the bar you can see the Saxon tower of St Bene't, which was built before the Normans introduced large, rounded arches.[1] The tower's corners feature so-called long-and-short work, where the vertical masonry forming the corners is tied into the body of the tower by horizontal pieces. Much of the interior is early, too, and the scale and size of the church suggests it was something out of the ordinary.

My other example of a pre-university church is also decidedly unusual. The Round Church (more correctly the Church of the Holy Sepulchre) is across town, about twenty minutes' walk away, just beyond St John's College in Bridge Street.[2] Today it sits beside a multistorey car park, which doesn't exactly add to its charms. The Cambridge Round Church is just one of five English churches of this plan, all of which were built in the eleventh and twelfth centuries, in the Norman style. I'm always rather careful about writing off Victorian restorations, because in many instances they did save buildings, but Anthony Salvin's work on the Round Church in 1841–45 was rather drastic. Even so, it is well worth visiting, because the space within the central, domed nave feels quite unlike that of any other church. I cannot believe that the monks who built this remarkable structure, sometime after 1130, had selected the site at random. People locally and farther afield must have believed that Cambridge was a special place – and probably for some time, too.

The university was famously founded by a migration of students from Oxford in 1209, who came to the town and stayed there. In actual fact it wasn't quite as simple as that, as Stamford

*King's College Chapel (1448–1515), Cambridge, as seen from the
Backs. The classical building to the right also belongs to the college:
the Gibbs' Building (1723–9) by the architect James Gibbs.*

was also involved, and Cambridge already had a history of
religious education. But whatever the details, the town became
a university, organized along collegiate lines. The earliest college
was Peterhouse (founded 1280). During the Middle Ages the
university grew steadily, but it never achieved the medieval
status of Oxford, which produced more scholars and, more
importantly, a larger quantity of bishops and men of influence.
But in the fifteenth century new things were starting to happen,
and the greatest symbol of that change is the superb chapel for
the college founded in his own name by King Henry VI: King's
College.[3] The king specified its proportions (289 feet long, 94
feet high and 40 feet wide/88×29×12 metres) in a document
known as his will, which was produced in 1448 (though Henry
died much later, in 1471). This was the year that work began on
the site next to the River Cam. Owing to budgetary problems
and a succession of royal sponsors, construction of the building was a drawn-out process. King's College Chapel wasn't

completed until *c.*1515 – and further furnishing and glazing work continued until about 1540: it had taken almost a century to complete. Perfection takes time.

King's Chapel is a building in a class of its own. It soars majestically above the floodplain of the River Cam. I know it's a cliché, but it does genuinely seem to defy gravity – and not just from the inside. Even when I stand outside and look up at the windows and the buttresses that separate them, I still find it impossible to suppose they could ever stand a stiff breeze, let alone a storm. But they have, and for some five and a half centuries. And now I will have to stop. Any description of such a perfect symbol of grace, elegance and soaring imagination must fail. The only way to appreciate is to visit. It photographs very well and its acoustics are familiar to most listeners to the Festival of Nine Lessons and Carols, broadcast every Christmas Eve. But nothing can better the real thing. One small suggestion, if you do manage to pay a visit: try to approach from the west end, via the Backs, those expanses of lawn and meadow that line the River Cam behind the colleges. This approach from a distance, with nothing to distract your view, is the best way to prepare yourself for the great treat you are about to enjoy.

Cambridge came into its own as a university from the mid-sixteenth century, especially following Henry VIII's Dissolution of the Monasteries, from 1538. The Dissolution allowed the king to grant monastic lands to Cambridge colleges, which thereby acquired not just wealth and land, but new security and financial independence. With the weakening of the Church as a major force in political life, and with the new financial independence, came a degree of intellectual and academic freedom. Some of the older, smaller colleges were combined by Henry VIII to form new institutions such as Trinity College.[4] I am of course biased, being a graduate of Trinity, but its Great Court demands to be seen, along with the huge hall of 1604–05 and the fine late Gothic (1555–65) chapel, containing Roubiliac's superb statue of Sir Isaac Newton. I try to pay homage whenever I'm in town.

*Nevile's Court, Trinity College, Cambridge. This view is dominated by the Wren Library (named after its architect, Sir Christopher Wren), with a small part of the north range (rebuilt 1755–8) to the right. The Wren Library was built in 1676–91, some sixty years after the completion of Nevile's Court.*

Nevile's Court (named after Thomas Nevile, Master of Trinity from 1593 to 1615) seems to lie hidden behind Great Court and is too often ignored by visitors. This is a shame, because with the obvious exception of King's Chapel, it is possibly the greatest set of buildings in Cambridge. One end is formed by the College Hall and the two long side ranges, perched above delicate cloisters, are very elegant. But the whole assemblage is completed by Christopher Wren's majestic library, which forms the west side of the court – and looks equally good from punts on the River Cam, beyond. As you might expect, the library includes treasures, such as Newton's books, annotated in his own hand. But for me the real treasures are the superb carvings in lime wood that adorn the ends of the library's bays. These are all by the master sculptor and carver Grinling Gibbons (1648–1721). I've tried my hand at carving, but I could no more achieve what Gibbons did, than fly – which is what I think his carvings so often seem to do. They have a deft lightness of touch that is out of this world.

Wren's Library and King's Chapel are best seen from the Backs, looking across the smooth waters of the River Cam with the tourists and students punting along it. It's a view that seems never to change in its essentials. Yes, the river has flooded and sometimes it may fall slightly in a dry summer, but these are very occasional events. The Cam, like so many other rivers in fenland, has been controlled by the hand of man. At this point we need to pause and take stock, because our story is about to change gear. I am referring, of course, to the widespread drainage of the Fens. We have seen that water levels had been controlled and that limited de-watering schemes had been in place locally, especially on the higher marshland around the Wash, since at least Saxon times. There were also some notable improvements to rivers and dykes in the Middle Ages, but larger-scale drainage didn't take place until the seventeenth century. It was a process that was made simpler by the Dissolution of the Monasteries and the transfer of their lands to more entrepreneurial landowners. The funds and other capital assets once owned by monasteries were also used to pay for the new works. But I think there was another, perhaps even more important, factor involved too.

By the early seventeenth century, the domination of religion and theology in universities was gradually beginning to be challenged. Science was thriving in the rapidly expanding colleges of Cambridge University. I would suggest it was the analytical thought behind the scientific method that was to prove so important in the process of Fen drainage. The principle is simple:

a problem is defined, a solution devised – which is then tested empirically in the real world. But it is rarely a straightforward process either in pure or indeed applied situations. In astrophysics the presence of Dark Matter complicates the study of the universe's composition; in Fen drainage, another Dark Matter, namely peat, and its shrinkage (plus sea level change), make the seemingly simple business of removing water extremely difficult. These are problems that cannot be resolved by faith or intuition. They require rational thought.

I quite often drive along the twisting road from Wisbech (Cambs) into Downham Market (Norfolk), via Outwell, Nordelph and Salter's Lode – all names steeped in fen history. It's a history that can be frustratingly complex for those, like me, who are interested in the region's past. You look out of the car window at a straight river, dyke or ditch and assume that it was necessarily quite recent – simply because it is so straight and geometrical. But nearly always, you'd be wrong. Take the longest, straightest river of all, the first artificial course of the River Ouse (or Old Bedford River), which starts its canalized course from Earith on the south-western fen-edge, a few miles east of Huntingdon. It then runs dead straight, more or less due north-east, across the Fens to Salter's Lode, near Downham Market, in Norfolk, a distance of 21 miles (34 km).[5] It is 70 feet (21 m) wide and was entirely dug by hand, from about 1630 to 1637. Efforts were made to keep the workings dry while the digging took place, but even so, many men would have had to have excavated in very wet conditions, up to their knees or waists, or even higher, in water. Much of the ground they dug through was peaty and quite soft, which may have made the digging easier, but when such light soil was used to build up the flood-protection banks – even if efforts were made to use heavier clays for the bank core – it would always have been prone to dry out and become porous, especially if the summer was unusually hot or dry.

The large-scale draining of the southern Fens was an immense enterprise that was undertaken using funds released earlier from the Dissolution of fenland monasteries, together with money provided by the crown and government and what today we would call venture capital advanced not by hedge funds but by 'Gentlemen adventurers' who 'adventured' the money in return for promises of land, or 'adventurers' grounds' in the newly drained fen. And it was by no means easy money. Many of the adventurers faced considerable financial hardship while the work was taking place. They had a somewhat easier time once the work was finished, but further problems soon arose. When the land surface shrank, either of its own accord or sometimes as a result of the newly dried-out peat blowing away, flooding episodes became more frequent. If you want to watch peat shrink, put the growbag that raised your summer greenhouse tomatoes in a dry, sunny spot. Then leave it for a few weeks. When you return, the peat will have shrunk to a quarter of its volume and most of the bag will be occupied by the dry roots of your old tomato plants.

In the early seventeenth century, the maintenance of the Fens was entrusted to various boards of local landowners, known as commissioners of sewers. It was a system that was used in other wetland areas of England, such as in the Essex marshes, where in the early 1620s the commissioners had appointed a new head engineer, called Cornelius Vermuyden, a young Dutchman, who had arrived in Britain in 1621. Various attempts were made to get work started in the Fens, but the sheer scale of what it would entail must have been daunting. King James I wanted something to be done, but then failed to do anything. Charles I came to the throne in 1625 and in 1629 told the commissioners of sewers meeting in King's Lynn to get things moving – which they did. The following year they approached Vermuyden to draw up proposals, but had to abandon them because of strong local opposition.

This opposition is generally portrayed – as it was by the proponents of drainage in the seventeenth century – as a conservative reaction to a progressive development. The reality was far more complex. Fenland ways of life were very ancient and well-attuned to a delicate and difficult environment, with intricate rights and obligations between neighbouring communities. The new proposals drove a coach and horses through these long-lived, and carefully balanced, agreements. So I find it completely understandable that there was intense opposition to them. Indeed, I would have been out there with the protestors, every night, digging into flood banks and sabotaging new sluices. They had a lot to lose.

Later in the year 1629, a group of local landowners approached the largest landowner in the Fens, the 4th Earl of Bedford,* and in 1630 he agreed with them to drain all the fens south of (and including) his Thorney and Whittlesey estates. This huge area, which included most of the peat soils of the Fens, was later named the Bedford Level. The following year, the earl was joined by thirteen co-adventurers and together they appointed Cornelius Vermuyden to draw up plans for the immense drainage scheme. In addition to the Old Bedford River, the new project required three other major drains, north and south of Peterborough, together with two medium-sized drains. It also involved the re-engineering of an earlier drain, known as Morton's Leam, which had been cut by men working for the Bishop of Peterborough in 1478. This drain still runs for about 12 miles (19 km) from Peterborough to Guyhirn. Bishop Morton was one of the first people to appreciate that water flows fastest when it passes along straight channels.

---

* The earls of Bedford were promoted to dukes of Bedford in 1694. See also Chapter 12, p. 265.

Things started to go wrong with the drainage of the Bedford Levels in the years leading up to the Civil War. There were problems in the silty fens of the north and east, around the Wash, but they were as nothing compared with what was happening in the Bedford Level further south, where there was civil unrest and an increasing realization that the new system of dykes and drains was failing to cope with the issues caused by peat shrinkage and other effects of drainage itself. Then the Civil War intervened and most people had other things to occupy their minds. But Vermuyden still had his eye on the ball. He may not have been very popular with local people, or indeed with many of his co-adventurers and colleagues, largely because he was one of the few people who understood the full extent of the problems facing them. And of course it didn't help that he was always asking for money, which was now in very short supply. The world of English politics was growing increasingly tense, but Vermuyden continued single-mindedly to analyse the problem facing him in the Fens. I think that tells us much about his intellect, his persistence – and his personal courage.

In 1642, the year the Civil War broke out, he published a 'Discourse Touching the Draining of the Great Fennes' in which he proposed that the problems in the Bedford Level could only be addressed if the region's natural drainage was used to rationalize it into three smaller levels, which survive to this day. Boundaries have shifted a bit since Vermuyden's times, but the North Level extends from the River Welland to the Nene; the Middle Level from the Nene to the Old Bedford River; and the South Level from the Old Bedford River to the fen-edge.

Each one of these Levels had its own problems of drainage, some of which would not be sorted out until the nineteenth and even the twentieth century, when, for example, the Maxey Cut was dug (1954–56) to prevent flooding in Deeping Fen. Extensive improvements were also made by the different Levels to the tidal

*The boundary between the North and Middle Bedford Levels is formed by the canalized River Nene, seen here immediately downstream of Dog in a Doublet Sluice, between Whittlesey and Thorney. This is the point (some 25 miles/40 km from the Wash) where the Nene becomes tidal. This photograph was taken close to low tide.*

and outfall arrangements of their major rivers, especially in 1954, following the catastrophic floods of 1947. Vermuyden's diagnosis of the Fens' drainage problem has proved to be both perceptive and effective. Many of the changes he proposed should have been adopted earlier than actually happened. I remember hearing a drainage engineer in the 1970s describe how a new catch-water drain to the south of Peterborough was more or less precisely following the line originally suggested by Vermuyden, three hundred years previously. But Vermuyden's biggest idea couldn't wait, because something simply had to be done about the problems associated with the recently dug Old Bedford River.

Vermuyden's big idea of 1642 was to cut an even wider (100 foot) river about half a mile to the east of the Old Bedford River, running parallel to it for its entire 21 miles (34 km) across the peatlands. The outer bank of the Old Bedford River was to be made the same height as the outer bank of the new river (the New Bedford, or One Hundred Foot River). The land between the two rivers could then be used as a wash, or reservoir, to contain excesses of floodwater in times of high rainfall, especially in spring and autumn when higher than usual tides blocked or slowed the outfall of river water into the Wash. The new river was constructed in the last year of the Civil War, 1651. Flow into the Old and New Bedford rivers was controlled by sluices at either end, at Earith, near Huntingdon and at Denver Sluice, near Downham Market, in Norfolk. The Denver Sluice still controls flow into the Wash. It has always been a major engineering challenge since it was first erected in 1652 and its long history reflects the changing drainage environment of the Fens. It was improved in 1682, but then collapsed in 1713, to be rebuilt in 1750 and reconstructed in 1832; it was further enlarged in 1923 and was the subject of major improvements and modifications in 1954. Whenever I visit Denver, there seems to be work going on there – which is a relief to anyone, such as myself, who lives a metre or two above sea level. Today, Denver Sluice is an enjoyable day out. The gigantic sluice gates are scarily impressive, as are the big pumping houses and the various high banks, all of which are kept in impeccable condition, with mown grass and surprisingly few moles (which again I found strangely reassuring – not that a tiny mole could do any real damage to a well-made, modern civil engineer's flood bank).

The last improvements to Denver Sluice were made in the 1960s. These involved the cutting of a new flood-relief channel that runs close by, and parallel to, the Great Ouse, on its way from the Denver Sluice to its outfall north of King's Lynn. While this work was underway, it was realized that the Great Ouse might provide a way of supplementing the growing water shortages in London and the south-east. There had to be a special Act of Parliament, in 1968, but the work of constructing the complex of necessary sluices and new pipes and channels was completed by 1972. It involves being able to block the flow of water into the flood-relief channel by a wonderfully sounding 'impounding sluice'. This raises the water level and reverses the flow into a new channel, which feeds various pumping stations and a substantial tunnel on the long journey south to Essex and London.

Accounts of fen drainage pay great respect to the many banks, sluices, dykes and ditches, as works of civil engineering, alone. Indeed, the wide man-made channels and the complex, often multiple, sluices at Denver Sluice (or more correctly, sluices) are always presented in that way. But surely there is more to them than that? Setting aside the practical benefit of providing millions of Londoners with a reliable and plentiful source of good clean water, very little regard is paid to how such engineering works look in the landscape. This is a great pity, because many of them have a presence and, yes, a beauty that can equal the finest contrived, artificial landscape in a great country house park. I find the massive sluices and channels at Denver strangely moving: it's about control of the forces of nature, which can never be absolute, nor entirely predictable. Such places can also induce feelings of humility as well, of course, as huge admiration for the engineers and visionaries, such as Vermuyden, who had the temerity, knowledge and experience to propose them.

Views along the wide washes of the Ouse, and further north, the Nene Washes east of Peterborough, can be just as stirring as the finest Capability Brown landscape, but with the added attraction of massive scale. Washes are an essential part of fen water management, where surplus water is stored until conditions are right to release it into the North Sea. Today they are also used to provide shallow meres for waders and other wildfowl. The shallow washes of the Nene can be home to flotillas of geese and swans.

*Dog in a Doublet Sluice on the River Nene, some 5 miles (8 km) east of Peterborough. In this view, taken from downstream (the tidal side), the sluice gates are lowered, allowing freshwater to accumulate and then be released at low tide. The slightly flooded Nene Washes are to the left. The pillbox in the foreground was built in 1940 as part of the GHQ line. The sluice was regarded as strategically important.*

The slow-flowing, embanked rivers also provide a few surprises. I was once heading along the narrow road that fringes the Nene to the west of Dog in a Doublet Sluice (the Nene's tidal equivalent of Denver sluice), on my way to record an interview at Flag Fen. I'd had to make an early start, and I confess I wasn't feeling very lively or wide awake. The sun was rising and I was driving the Land Rover quite slowly, almost on autopilot, when I found I was looking into the wide, inquisitive eyes of a seal, who was swimming parallel to the road and giving me strange looks, as if to say: 'What are you doing out here, at this hour?' I saw him twitch his whiskers as he swam his dog-like way upstream. Then he dived, and that was the last I saw of him. That back road from Whittlesey to Peterborough, via the

Dog in a Doublet pub and sluice, has some of the finest views in the Fens.

Archaeologists and palaeobotanists have been researching into the prehistory of the Fens since before the war and their studies have been greatly helped by the advent of radiocarbon dating in the 1950s. The result of all this work is that we now understand how and when the Fens began to form. It didn't happen in one place and at one time. The underlying process that caused rivers to silt up and salt water to flood low-lying land was the gradual rise in sea levels after the Ice Age that is continuing to this day. Ultimately that was the process that caused the North Sea to spread ever further southwards. But it wasn't just a simple process of water inundating land. All sorts of complex things started to happen as sea levels rose. In the flat landscape around what is now the Wash, the rivers couldn't drain efficiently into the sea and their waters ponded further to the south-west in low-lying landscapes, such as the Holme Fen basin. These ponded waters gave peats an opportunity to form, a process that seems to have begun between six and seven thousand years ago and which continued, at various rates, according to local conditions, until 1851, when drainage of the deepest peatlands stopped all peat growth instantly. We are still feeling the effects of this momentous change.

# The Holme Fen Post: The Drainage of the Deepest Peatlands

*The Holme Fen Post – Fens and Bogs – Holme Fen and Whittlesey Mere – The Draining of Whittlesey Mere – Lord Orford's Voyage*

Holme Fen is a National Nature Reserve about 4 miles (6 km) south of Peterborough. It is undoubtedly best known for a mysterious cast-iron post that lurks within it, beside a long drove, in a clearing in birch woodland. I can remember first hearing about the Holme Fen post at university. The story I learned then was slightly simpler than the truth as we now understand it, but it's absolutely fascinating and shows what can happen when responsible developers think about the future. The developer in this case was Mr William Wells, who owned much of the land beneath Whittlesey Mere and around its fringes. He was also the member of parliament for Peterborough from 1852 until 1874.[1] He decided to drain what remained of the mere, which had shrunk a great deal thanks to widespread drainage all around it, but in a moment of inspiration (as I imagine) he first decided on a remarkable experiment, about half a mile back from the mere's edge. In 1848, he had a deep hole dug through thick

accumulations of peat, down to the underlying Oxford Clay.
This stiff blue clay forms both the low hills around Peterborough
and the natural 'island' around the town of Whittlesey and
is still used in the area's commercial brick industry. Much of
nineteenth- and twentieth-century London was built from bricks
made near the then village of Fletton, today an industrial suburb
of Peterborough.

*The Holme Fen posts. The top of the post on the right was level with
the surface of the peat in 1848. The original post was made of wood,
but was replaced with the iron pillar in 1851. As peats continued
to shrink the 1851 post required supports and was eventually
joined by another, more securely anchored post.*

Oak piles were driven into the clay and another wooden
post was bolted to them in such a way that its top was precisely
level with the surface of the surrounding peat. That was in 1848.
By 1860 the peat surface had sunk by 4 feet 9 inches (1.44 m).
By 1932 the post stood 10 feet 8 inches (3.25 m) above the
ground. It now (2015) stands proud by an amazing 13 feet 1 inch

(about 4 m).[2] In 1851, the original wooden post was replaced by a cast-iron pillar. A century later, it had become unstable and had to be propped up by steel supports. At the same time, for added security, a second, and larger, pillar was driven into the ground alongside it, a few metres away. Today, the land surface at the feet of the two Holme Fen posts is at 9 feet (2.75 m) below sea level – probably the lowest point anywhere in Britain.

Peat growth rates vary enormously according to local conditions, but it is probably fair to say that in most places it accumulates at very roughly a millimetre a year. By way of contrast, the process of erosion is far more rapid and is even faster directly after drainage – again, with variations depending on location. Peat wastage had been clearly demonstrated – but the rate of erosion revealed by the Holme Fen post is startling, nevertheless. It suggests that in this far from typical area (for a significant part of its life it has been a protected nature reserve), peat erosion has taken place at the rate of about 2.4 cm (nearly an inch) a year.[3] That's very high. For example, the average rate of peat wastage, following drainage, in East Anglia is about 1.37 cm per annum.[4] The important point behind these very general figures is that peat, which takes millennia to grow and accumulate, can be destroyed in decades. And there are no short cuts to replacing it, either: if peat can be persuaded to start growing again, it will do so at the rate it grew thousands of years ago. So the damage has already been done. And if, or more likely when, climate change and the associated underlying rise in North Sea levels continue their seemingly relentless upward trend, the Fens will flood again – and in many areas of ex-peatland, to a depth of several metres. My guess is that this will happen sooner rather than later. People write about the brooding darkness of the Fens, but this uncertain future gives reality to that gloomy vision.

A growing public awareness that the commercial digging of peat is causing irreparable damage to the environment has led many people (myself included) to avoid using peat-based composts in their gardens, and it has largely ceased to be used as a fuel, as was the case in the nineteenth and earlier twentieth centuries. Indeed, we burned squares of dried peat on the sitting room fire in a holiday cottage my family rented near the coast in County Galway in the 1950s. The fire was stoked by a blast of air powered by a wheel that my mother encouraged me to turn. Which of course I did, to excess, but even so, the fuel didn't seem to give off much heat. Looking on the positive side, peat extraction has ceased in the Fens, although sadly it still continues in the Somerset Levels and in Ireland.

I first came face-to-face with the Fens in their wild, natural state at Holme Fen and it wasn't at all what I had expected: no open, bleak expanses of boggy nothingness, punctuated by the occasional stand of rushes and reeds. The reality was very different: a huge and sometimes quite open birch woodland with alders and willows; reeds and rushes, yes, but bracken and lush grasses too. I knew that Holme Fen was close to the edge of Whittlesey Mere. So there would have been boggy areas and open water too, but it was a far richer and more varied environment than I had once imagined. My first visit must have been in June, because I can remember being completely bowled over by the luxuriant, shoulder-high stands of the stately yellow flag irises that fringed the edges of Holme's lake and the dykes around it. And everywhere were the sounds of reed warblers, moorhens, grebes, ducks, ducklings and – in the background – woodpeckers. It was a watery paradise: just the sort of place where one might have expected to encounter Adam and Eve.

Holme Fen lies at the western edge of the Fens, within clear sight of the limestone uplands of northern Northamptonshire. At this point, the underlying geology dips away to form a natural basin that soon filled with water after the Ice Age, because the River Nene (correctly styled the River Nen upstream of Peterborough, despite what Google Maps and iMaps would have you believe) enters the low-lying fenland basin a short distance to the north, at Peterborough. So this is classic peat or Black Fen country, where the fen deposits accumulated entirely because of freshwater flooding. But the peat here isn't the spongy, uniform stuff you can still, regrettably, buy at garden centres. That peat is mainly dug in Ireland and Somerset and it mostly consists of a wet-loving moss known as sphagnum. Sphagnum moss, in common with carnivorous plants such as honeydew and Venus fly traps, likes to grow in an acid environment where there is very little natural nutrition. Such environments are usually known as bogs. They are mostly fed by slightly acidic rainfall and they form large areas of acid peat that grow into so-called raised bogs, which are then mined for your garden compost.

It is not generally appreciated, but fens are completely different from bogs. They tend to occur in areas of slightly lesser rainfall and rely for their water on rivers, many of which in Britain flow through chalk or limestone country and are consequently rich in calcium carbonate – which of course is alkaline, not acidic. So the peats that form in them contain no sphagnum moss. Calcium carbonate allows the water to retain minerals and the nutrient-rich river waters that feed the Fens give rise to an abundant and diverse natural flora. Take a walk through Holme and Wicken Fens today and you will find reeds, rushes, sedges, water irises (the yellow flag iris, *Iris pseudacorus*), water lilies and wet-loving trees and shrubs, such as alder, sallow and willow. The peat into which the roots of the current crop of plants are growing contains the seeds and pollen together with the compressed and blackened stems and leaves of plants that grew there earlier.

By analysing this pollen under the microscope, palaeobotanists can produce an accurate picture of how a fen developed and changed over the centuries. Radiocarbon dates can help us work out when these changes happened and how long the peats took to form.

From earliest times, people living on the edges of the wetland appreciated that the Fens were a diverse natural larder and that they also provided a rich source of fats and protein (from fish, eels and wildfowl) during the otherwise lean months of winter. But as time passed and techniques of farming improved, peripheral areas of wetland were drained and these peaty soils were often found to be exceptionally fertile. So the long drawn-out process of drainage began. It didn't happen as a single event. The Dutch didn't suddenly arrive and drain the Fens in the seventeenth century, as some people still believe. It was a long, difficult and often very dangerous process that happened at different times in each region of the Fens. I have heard it said that the Romans started the process, but that's not strictly true: they took advantage of naturally dry climate conditions to settle in areas that had previously been too wet. The earliest evidence for true drainage on any scale goes back to early medieval times when large areas of the less low-lying fens around the Wash, in Lincolnshire and north Cambridgeshire, were embanked, drained and farmed.[5]

The story of the late draining of Whittlesey Mere is fascinating. I have to confess I have always seen it not so much as a heroic saga of mankind's ascendency over the forces of nature, but as a rather sad tale of what happens when you allow short-term goals to take charge. The draining of Whittlesey Mere was a victory of sorts, but many of us regret that it ever happened. I feel that way very strongly when I find myself driving across the bleak, treeless black fields south of Whittlesey that would still have been under water when the railway engineers started building the East Coast Main Line, just a short distance to the west. But by then, the seemingly unstoppable process of drainage, of improved pumps and wider, deeper dykes (the name given in the fens to drainage ditches) had already caused the once-great mere to shrink substantially.

In its heyday during the Middle Ages and early modern times, Whittlesey Mere was one of the largest natural lakes in England, but in common with other fenland meres, it was never particularly deep (roughly 6 feet or 2 metres) and would change in size and depth every season, depending on the amount of rain that was falling in the Midlands, the catchment area of the Nene and its tributaries. So it was very much smaller in summer than winter, when it expanded from just below some 2,000 acres (750 ha) to 3,000 acres (1,200 ha).

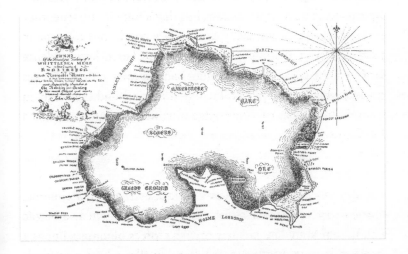

*Map of Whittlesey Mere, 1786. This map of what was one of the largest natural lakes in England was made by a talented local map-maker, John Bodger, in 1786. He intended it to be seen and used by the 'Nobility and Gentry'.*[6]

The draining of Whittlesey Mere involved a very remarkable engineering achievement, which was masterminded by the foresighted landowner William Wells, who bequeathed us the Holme Fen post. Britain is of course celebrated as the country that gave the world modern steam engines, but other British inventions have been just as revolutionary, if less celebrated. Work on emptying the mere began in 1851 and took two years to complete. It would have been an ambitious project, even with the advanced technology available today, but it would have been virtually impossible in 1850, or earlier, simply because the scoop-wheel pumps that were then the norm were not sufficiently powerful, nor efficient. All of that changed in 1851 when the inventor John Appold came up with the idea of a curved vane centrifugal pump, which he first displayed at the Great Exhibition of the same year.

Drainage of the mere began in the conventional way, by cutting breaks in flood banks and allowing water to flow naturally, by gravity, into the river that drained the land to the north. But it soon became apparent that they would also need pumps, because the bed of the mere was lower than much of the surrounding land. So one of the new centrifugal pumps was installed. It was a substantial piece of kit, capable of lifting 16,000 gallons a minute to a height of 6 feet (2 m). It was driven by a twenty-five horsepower steam beam-engine. Progress was rapid and by the summer of 1852, the authorities were laying out roads, digging dykes and apportioning land for new farms. Then, in the autumn of 1852, disaster struck. It had been a very wet season and on 2 November the riverbanks burst and within a few hours Whittlesey Mere had reformed, with some 1,000 acres (450 ha) flooded under 2½ feet (0.75 m) of water. But now comes what I have always regarded as a remarkable fact: the new pump was run flat out for three weeks and by the end of that time, the land was dry again.[7] Such an extraordinary feat would have been impossible just two years previously – and it was all down to those curved vanes on Mr Appold's centrifugal pump.

We can acquire some sense of how Whittlesey Mere was in its prime – before it was drained and bisected by the railway – by looking at a little book entitled *Lord Orford's Voyage round the Fens in 1774*, which was first published almost a century later, in 1868.[8] George Walpole, the 3rd Earl of Orford, was in his mid-forties when he decided to take his voyage, which happily for us involved at least nine days on Whittlesey Mere. He liked to travel in considerable style, using a string or 'gang' of five shallow-hulled barge-like vessels. The leading boat, in this case the *Whale*, had sails and provided the towing power in open water. The *Whale* also accommodated female servants and had been fitted with an enlarged galley to provide food for the party. In confined waterways and on still days, a horse would be taken from the last boat of the gang, known as the 'horse-boat', and in this case she was called the *Cocoa Nut*. The towing horse had the wonderfully apposite name 'Hippopotamus' – the classically educated Lord Orford had come up with a name that, when translated literally from ancient Greek, means 'river-horse'. Behind the lead vessel, the *Whale*, were two accommodation barges for Lord Orford's party, with substantial quarters; these were the *Alligator* and the *Shark*. Behind them was the *Dolphin*, which housed the crew, with the horse-boat, *Cocoa Nut*, taking up the rear. In addition to the main gang of five, there were a

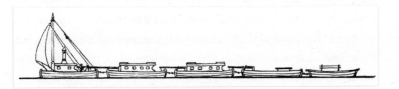

*In 1774 Lord Orford (George Walpole) organized an expedition to explore the Fens. It was based around a tethered 'gang' of five shallow-hulled boats.*

number of other smaller vessels that looked after and serviced the party. It was quite an undertaking.

The ships' company, as listed by Lord Orford, consisted of Frank, John and Sam ('belonging to the family'), Harry and William ('Watermen'), Will ('a boy who rode Hippopotamus'), Long Robin, Charlotte and, finally, the cook. Judging by Orford's detailed account of the journey, the three (probably younger) male members of the family were in effect volunteer crewmen – as were two other gentlemen, Thomas Roberts and George Farringdon, both of whom kept journals of the voyage. The other main passenger was Martha Turk, Orford's long-term mistress – who bore him several children. Many people visited the party, but the most important by far was Orford's old friend from their days in the notorious Brotherhood of Medmenham, or 'Hell-Fire Club', as it is known today. Lord Sandwich was then First Lord of the Admiralty, and lived at Hinchingbrooke House (the building survives and is now a secondary school) on the approaches to Huntingdon, a few miles to the south. Sandwich spent several days with the flotilla – he had his own yacht, of course – during their five-day stay on Whittlesey Mere.

I won't attempt to summarize the near-three-week voyage, which began near Peterborough on Sunday 17 July and ended at Denver Sluice, Norfolk, on 6 August. This short extract from Lord Orford's journal is taken from day 17, 1 August 1774, their last day on Whittlesey Mere. Shallow waters can develop large waves very quickly, as sailors on the Wash know only too well, and this certainly applied to the mere, where a 'storm had arisen quite suddenly, and in a few minutes [had] thrown the Meer into... fermentation'. Lord Orford's party joined the fleet, which was anchored offshore:

...and found those on board moving from the great consternation they had been thrown into by this violence of the water, during which they had assembled a council to debate upon the means of preserving themselves, and resolved, if the wind increased, to quit the Fleet to the waves, and, getting into the Cocoa Nut, run her ashore to save their lives. This alarm had been increased by one of the tenders breaking her hold, and driving with the wind across the Meer, which was fortunately recovered by the longboat before she foundered.'[9]

*A Regatta on Whittlesey Mere, 1842. This image was first published in J. M. Heathcote's 'Reminiscences of Fen and Mere' (1876).*

The recent republication of Lord Orford's journal uses as its cover illustration a view of a regatta on Whittlesey Mere in 1842. As with Lord Orford's 'voyage', people seem more intent on having a good time than in doing what they are supposed to be doing, which I would imagine is racing, to judge by the two dinghies in full sail at the centre of the picture. Again, it paints the mere as a pleasant, sometimes even joyful place. But we also know the Fen meres were very productive, too. Lord Orford's expedition cooked fish caught by members of the party, as did other visitors to the Fens, such as the late seventeenth-century traveller Celia Fiennes, who visited Whittlesey Mere in 1697. She notes (and I shall translate into modern English) that:

'Whittlesey Mere is 3 miles broad and 6 miles long, in the midst is a little island where a great store of wildfowl breeds, there is no coming near it in a mile or two, the ground is all wet and marshy, but there are several little channels run into it which by boats people go up to this place; when you enter the mouth of the Mere it looks formidable and it's often very dangerous by reason of sudden winds that will rise like hurricanes in the Mere, but at all other times people boat it round the Mere with pleasure; there is abundance of good fish in it...'[10]

Fenland history has often been portrayed as a simple contrast between the 'haves' who profited from drainage and the 'have nots' who protested, sometimes violently, when they saw the wetlands with their rich natural resources shrink and then largely vanish. But by the eighteenth and nineteenth centuries, the towns of fenland were also home to a growing middle class, who provided banking and other services to expanding local economies. Contacts with the regions that surrounded the Fens – with Lincolnshire, the East Midlands and East Anglia – were improving, as were roads and, later, railways. But even in a period of rapid social and economic change, the towns and villages of the Fens managed to retain their identity and even to increase their distinctiveness.

We've already seen that, architecturally speaking, the region is blessed with some of the finest townscapes in Britain: places like Spalding, Boston and King's Lynn. And we've also seen how a prosperous town like Spalding played an important part in the growth of free-thinking, liberal attitudes and social enlighten-ment. Another fen town whose history embraces both material affluence and progressive thought is Wisbech, on the banks of the tidal River Nene. It is time to head north-east from Whittlesey, to a port in Cambridgeshire's far north.

# Wisbech: Enlightened Bankers on the Brinks

*Wisbech Port and Town – The Peckovers, Octavia Hill
and Thomas Clarkson – Norman Cross – Rise and
Near Fall of the Railways – The Future*

Many townscapes are best appreciated from a distance: often across a square or along a street. One of the best urban views anywhere in England is to be found on either side of the River Nene, the North and South Brinks respectively, in Wisbech. Many of the mostly Georgian buildings are architecturally fine, but it's the way they seem to sit so comfortably, and yet with grace and elegance, that gives this view its immense charm. Of course you can examine the individual buildings, but every time I see the North and South Brinks together I find my spirits lifted.

Over the years I've tried to pin down exactly why it is always so appealing. It's not a particularly carefully planned townscape. It certainly isn't like Georgian Bath: there are no arranged vistas, nor grand end-stops. One or two buildings, such as Peckover House, stand out, but no more than, say, a slightly taller person in a team photograph. And then it slowly dawned on me: the buildings that line the river are indeed like people. They are both friendly and in harmony, they have presence and charm, like members of a church choir. So although they were never planned, they present a remarkably uniform whole. And being mostly built in the eighteenth and early nineteenth centuries, they take advantage of the Georgians' inability to erect an ugly or unattractive building. Even the materials used in their construction – the different coloured bricks and stone – blend together and add the textural variety that is so often lacking in the formal terraces of Georgian houses in places such as Bloomsbury.

*View along the (tidal) River Nene at Wisbech. The two streets on either side of the river are the North (right) and South Brinks. Both are famous for their Georgian buildings and the North Brink is widely regarded as one of the finest river frontages in Britain. Note the high flood walls, which have to be heightened every few years.*

The great Nikolaus Pevsner was a don at Cambridge when he wrote the first edition (1954) of the Cambridgeshire volume in his pioneering *Buildings of England* series. Reading between the lines, it is quite clear that Pevsner shared my fondness for the buildings that line the two Brinks on either side of the Nene. He describes the North Brink as 'one of the most perfect Georgian streets in England'. He goes on to state that the individual houses are mostly subdued in design, which again, cannot be denied. He describes the South Brink as 'the perfect foil to the North Brink... but more subdued and less ambitious'. Taken together, he sees the view as 'decidedly Dutch in its setting, but the houses are as English as only the Georgian century could make them'.[1] Inevitably, the Brinks on either side of the river command attention, but there are also some fine buildings in the Old Market Place and in Ely Crescent, which encloses Wisbech Castle – today a Regency house, not a medieval castle.

Sadly, like Spalding and Holbeach to the north, the town of Wisbech has also fared very badly since the war, mostly in the period from the 1950s to the 1970s. Insensitive road construction destroyed many warehouses and other buildings along the river and the course of the old Wisbech Canal (built 1794–7), which linked the town to Upwell, has been taken up by a new road. The buildings alongside it are fairly uniformly modern and drab. Many older buildings in the town were also seriously damaged or destroyed by a great storm and tidal surge in 1978. So the description of Wisbech in the second edition of Pevsner is more downbeat and less enthusiastic.

I completely agree with the revised Pevsner (2014) about the recent damage to the town, but there is also an upside: the recent problems have drawn attention to the town's surviving historic buildings, which are now better appreciated by local people – in part thanks to a very active local conservation organization, the Wisbech Society and Preservation Trust, founded in 1939.[2] One of their projects has given the town what is essentially a new park. A hitherto largely forgotten and very early civic town cemetery, the Wisbech General Cemetery, was leased to the society by the local authority in 2014, for thirty years, and is now actively being restored. Like many old urban cemeteries, it is an excellent place to enjoy a quiet, reflective stroll and escape the hassles of daily life. Thanks to this newly reactivated sense of civic pride, the townspeople of Wisbech will never allow a repeat of the wholesale destruction we witnessed in the three decades after the last war.

As we saw in Chapter 14, Spalding's historic success as a port and as a market for agricultural produce gave rise to a new class of professional people who were interested in many subjects and played an important part in the formation of a very early and influential archaeological and historical society. Similar developments were to happen in Wisbech, but these were to have an even bigger impact, not just on the world of archaeology, history and ancient buildings, but on mainstream politics in Britain and across the world.

Like Spalding, Wisbech was an important inland port and market town in an area of high agricultural productivity. As the town's economy grew throughout the eighteenth century, so did the population, which in the first census of 1801 numbered some 4,700.[3] There were problems with the silting-up of the Nene in the decades on either side of the transition between the eighteenth and nineteenth centuries, which effectively cut off the port and led to stagnation, but eventually a reluctant town council allowed the digging of the new Rennie/Telford outfall, in 1827–30. Thereafter, things improved dramatically. Wisbech is still Cambridgeshire's only maritime port.[4]

The Religious Society of Friends, generally known as the Quakers, became a major presence in Wisbech when the Peckover family moved there, from Norfolk, in 1777.[5] Quakers were widely trusted throughout the country as being honest folk who would not abscond with people's money, nor water down their beers and ales – which we forget were an important source of liquid nourishment to many working men and women. Soon, Quakers became a driving force in many rapidly growing industries, including banking, brewing, chocolate-making and malting. The Peckovers were bankers, but bankers with a conscience. They lived at Peckover House on North Brink (then known as Bank House). Peckover House is now, very appropriately as we will soon see, owned and operated by the National Trust. Jonathan Peckover established the Wisbech Working Men's Institute in 1864 and Priscilla Hannah (an old Quaker name) Peckover was a leading philanthropist, who was nominated for a Nobel Peace Prize no less than four times, between 1903 and 1913. Peckover's Bank became part of the larger Quaker bank, Barclays, in 1864.

Some enlightened bankers came unstuck, however. One of these was James Hill, father of Octavia Hill, who was born in the family home on the South Brink in 1838. Two years later, her father was declared bankrupt and her mother, a remarkable woman in her own right, moved the family to a cottage in Finchley, then on the rural outer fringes of London, where she educated Octavia at home – she couldn't afford a school. Octavia devoted her life to reforming the circumstances of poor people and through her love of nearby open spaces, such as Hampstead Heath, she understood the benefits of fresh air and exercise to people living in inner cities. Ultimately these interests led her to become one of the three co-founders of the National Trust, in 1895. A museum, the Octavia Hill Birthplace Museum, has been established in the house on the South Brink, where she was born.[6]

I come now to perhaps the greatest of Wisbech's many philanthropists, Thomas Clarkson, known today as the co-founder, together with William Wilberforce, of the anti-slavery movement. In fact, this is a misunderstanding of what actually happened. And here I must introduce some of my own family history. The Pryors were originally a Quaker family and, like other Friends, they tended to marry fellow Quakers. So I have many distant cousins in Norfolk and elsewhere in East Anglia, which had a huge population of Quakers. My four-greats grandfather was a Quaker banker named Samuel Hoare. Incidentally, his biography – and it's an excellent read – was edited by my namesake, Francis Pryor, in 1911.[7] By the later eighteenth century, word was reaching London Friends, from their North American colleagues, about the appalling conditions endured by African slaves on plantations in the American South. Samuel Hoare had been one of six London Quakers who in 1783 had set up an informal committee to abolish the slave trade. Unfortunately, in the eighteenth century Quakers were not allowed to enter parliament, so they soon realized the committee would have to be extended to include Anglicans (who as members of the established Church were of course allowed to be MPs).[8] Five of the original committee of six (including Samuel Hoare) became members of the new twelve-man committee, which was set up in 1787. Thomas Clarkson was one of three Anglicans invited to attend this enlarged group.

Clarkson was born in 1760 and brought up in Wisbech, the son of an Anglican priest and the headmaster of Wisbech Grammar School – one of the oldest schools in the country (founded in 1379). After Wisbech Grammar School, he attended St John's College, Cambridge and in 1785 he entered a Latin essay in a competition organized by the university. The topic to be considered was the legality of enslaving people against their consent. He read widely for his research and his essay won the competition. It also changed his life. From now on he knew what he had to do – he gave up plans to become an Anglican vicar and devoted himself full-time to the anti-slavery campaign that was then being organized by the first Quaker committee. This campaign culminated in a petition to parliament in 1783, signed by 300 Quakers.

Following his inclusion on the enlarged committee of 1787, Clarkson became the principal campaigner and it was he who worked with the MP William Wilberforce to present the first bill to end the slave trade, in 1791 – which was defeated by a large majority. But they persisted and Clarkson worked hard to spread the word throughout Britain. Wilberforce and Clarkson made regular attempts to have anti-slavery bills passed into legally enforceable Acts of Parliament and the various campaigns began to have an adverse effect on Clarkson's health. The outbreak of the Napoleonic Wars brought further delays, with the result that the Slave Trade Act was not passed into law until 1807. But that was not the end of the story. Slavery continued to be legal in British colonies until 1838, and was only ended by Clarkson and Wilberforce's successful campaign to pass the Slavery Abolition Act of 1833. Clarkson is commemorated in Wisbech by the erection, in 1880–81, of the Clarkson Monument on the south side of the town bridge. The monument resembles a slimmed-down version of the much larger Albert Memorial, which was also designed by the Victorian architect Sir George Gilbert Scott. Clarkson is further commemorated in Wisbech by the naming of two schools, a pub and a road in his honour. He was undoubtedly a very great man.

Some places seem always to have been there. And for me, one of them is a little hamlet called Norman Cross. It lies on the A1, just south-west of Peterborough, and I have memories of driving past it as a young child in the 1950s. I remember looking out of the back-seat window as we drove past a bronze eagle atop a stone column. 'What's that?' I asked my father. 'Oh,' came the immediate reply, 'that's a memorial to the men who died there, when a Zeppelin was shot down in the First World War.'[9] I should have realized from the swiftness of his response that it was something he had just pulled out of thin air. Doubtless the poor man just wanted peace, after an hour of 'Are we nearly there yet?' And it certainly set me thinking. Maybe my father came to regret what he'd said, because I immediately started researching airships and that terrible crash of the R101, which was built at Cardington, Bedfordshire, not far from where we lived. The vast hangar still survives (it is a listed building) and I nagged him so much that one Sunday afternoon he had to take me to see it. And I've been back there several times since – it is so huge and so unlike any other listed building.

My second introduction to Norman Cross came in 1970 when I spent much time in the reserve collections of Peterborough Museum, going through box after box of prehistoric pottery in preparation for my excavations at Fengate the following year. Sometimes, the interesting aspects of Iron Age pottery, which are few at the best of times, failed to hold my attention and I knew I would have to do something else, before I screamed, or went mad. So I'd take a walk through the galleries, which in those days still included many Victorian displays. The curator at the time was – how should I put it? – rather conservative and very little had been altered or modernized. Some of the cases contained a remarkable collection of hand-made models carved out of the bones of cattle. They included detailed warships, complete with cannons and rigging. There were also smaller vessels, a guillotine, domino boxes and many tools and other items. The models were absolutely superb. But then came the bit that really interested me: they had been entirely made by amateurs in the early nineteenth century, Napoleonic prisoners of war in the large camp at Norman Cross. Then I thought of that eagle on the roadside, and it all made sense: it was the Imperial Eagle, as carried into battle by troops of Napoleon's *Grande Armée*. It had nothing to do with Germans or Zeppelins.

During the three decades that I excavated and researched

into the landscapes of the fen-edge near Peterborough, I rarely strayed beyond the medieval period. It wasn't until I became interested in more general landscape history that I lifted my eyes beyond the horizon imposed by the hills of the fen-edge and started to glimpse the richness of what lay beyond. Tight academic discipline is essential if you are to make progress in a particular, and often quite narrow, field of research, but it does blinker your imagination, too. In hindsight, I can also appreciate that it does remove a lot of the enjoyment of actually making new discoveries. I think I began to look beyond the conceptual box labelled 'Prehistory' sometime around 2000, when I started writing books for a wider audience.

Prehistory and archaeology only make sense to a general reader if you can set them in context. It was then that I discovered that something as simple sounding as 'setting in context' actually takes a lot of research in itself. You cannot make use of a topic if you don't understand it quite thoroughly yourself. It took me ten years before I was able to publish the results of my contextual research as *The Making of the British Landscape*, in 2010. And one of the places I visited was the Napoleonic prisoner-of-war camp at Norman Cross. Sadly, I couldn't discover sufficient information to include it in the book, but at the time I was working regularly for the Channel 4 series *Time Team*, who were always looking for interesting places to investigate, and in 2009 they devoted an episode to Norman Cross and I was the dig director. I was delighted – and it turned out to be one of our most successful projects. It also made an excellent film.

We know from historical records that building work on the camp at Norman Cross started in 1796, and it opened as soon as it was finished, in 1797.[10] It remained in use as a POW camp until the summer of 1814, when people believed the Napoleonic Wars had finished. Waterloo happened the following year, but Norman Cross wasn't reopened. One of the things about

*The Agent's House at Norman Cross Napoleonic prisoner-of-war camp, near Peterborough. The agent was responsible for the administration of the camp. It was built in 1798 and converted into an elegant country house in 1816. Part of the high prison external wall is still attached to the front of the house.*

*The only remaining part of the Norman Cross prison external wall (built in 1807), with the gateway leading to the agent's office within the prison.*

Norman Cross that amazed me was its sheer size: it was built to accommodate about 7,000 men and was, in effect, a small town. During its seventeen years of use, some 1,770 men died there, mostly of infectious diseases. An outbreak of typhoid (or 'enteric fever') in the autumn, winter and early summer of 1801–2 claimed 848 of those victims. Aside from this one major outbreak, the death rate at Norman Cross seems about average and suggests that the medical care in the camp was generally good. Typhoid continued to be a major problem in Britain until the second half of the nineteenth century, and it provided an incentive to build the first modern sewers and sewage works.

Norman Cross was sited at the top of an escarpment that overlooks the village of Yaxley with superb views across the Fens towards Holme Fen. This site was chosen because it was quite close to London but its location on the edge of the Fens was thought to be daunting to men wishing to escape across the North Sea to France and the Netherlands, where the majority of prisoners originated. One or two men did manage to escape the camp, but very few left the region; most were recaptured. So maybe the planners were right. Prior to Norman Cross, prisoners of war were housed in redundant warships, known as 'hulks', which were mostly moored along the Thames Estuary. Exercise within these confined spaces was almost impossible and when diseases struck, the consequences were dire. So the authorities in Britain decided that a new approach was needed and the result was the world's first purpose-built prisoner-of-war camp, at Norman Cross.

The prisoners were housed in large barrack blocks and slept in hammocks. The camp was surrounded by high walls and there was a central blockhouse with an overhanging octagonal upper storey manned by guards with mounted guns. Contemporary watercolours by a French officer, one Captain Durrant, show life in the camp, which wasn't as harsh as the central blockhouse might suggest. There was a camp market and the men had access to ovens and were able to wash and dry their laundry. Some kept pet dogs and others practised fencing or played skittles. To judge by the quantities of debris we revealed in the *Time Team* excavations, carving wood and bone was a popular pastime. These were sold through intermediaries in local fairs or markets, and were also bought by visitors to the camp. They were an important source of ready money.

Time Team *excavations at Norman Cross, 2009. Geophysical survey found a likely location for the prison's cemetery, whose whereabouts was lost. Excavation revealed a number of graves, including the two bodies exposed here. They were not disturbed and remain in situ.*

The PoW camp is now a scheduled ancient monument, but it survived remarkably well prior to its statutory protection. The large, elegant Regency Agent's House survives, facing across to the A15, Peterborough Road, which has just left the Great North Road and is heading north towards Peterborough. Some of the camp's external walls (built in 1807) survive, including the elegant rounded-arch entrance leading from the Agent's House to his office in the camp. The interior has never been deeply ploughed, so archaeological preservation is generally quite good. But the big missing item was the exact location of the camp's cemetery, which many people, including of course the French government, were naturally keen to locate: it's harder to honour your dead soldiers if you don't know where their graves are. Happily we were able to employ geophysical survey to detect them. I recall looking at the geophys plots, which showed an area to the north-east of the camp where there were possible grave outlines. We opened a number of small trenches there and revealed the bodies of men, mostly in their twenties – skulls can be aged with reasonable accuracy without lifting them. Then we back-filled the trenches and the graves, leaving the bones undisturbed. During the excavations we were honoured to receive a visit from the French ambassador, who was suitably moved by what he saw. We know the names of some of the men buried in the cemetery: Phillipe Gauthier, Denis Godart and Pierre François Molin. They and their fellow countrymen can continue to rest in peace, protected by the knowledge that their remains will be looked after, now that we know their final resting place.

I have to confess that I find abandoned railway lines intensely irritating. I concede that they can be used as footpaths and walks, but just imagine – if we could somehow have retained the railway network of the early twentieth century, and we had then modernized it (as happened in many countries of mainland Europe), we wouldn't now be facing the vast petrol and diesel bills that are part and parcel of rural life, and air quality in our towns would also be very much better. And when it comes to line closures, I am convinced the Fens have fared far worse than other regions: the major city of Lincoln enjoys a terrible service, as does Spalding. Towns in the southern and central Fens aren't too badly served, but those in the north mostly remain isolated. But it wasn't always that bad. Indeed, there was a time when the region was excellently served.

It all happened remarkably quickly. *Fowler's Railway Traveller's Guide* of 1845 includes a map that shows no railways anywhere in the Fens and with Peterborough only served by a short spur of track from the London–Leicester main line. Just seven years later, H. G. Collins's map of 1852 shows the main line from London King's Cross to Peterborough, which had opened two years earlier, in 1850. That line was still being constructed north of Peterborough, to Grantham and Newark, where it would join with the already existing line to Doncaster, York and ultimately to Newcastle. From Peterborough the line goes to Spalding and Boston, where it branches, with one line to Tattershall and Lincoln and another to the coast, and ultimately Grimsby. To the east, the line from London to Cambridge continues north to 'Lynn Regis' (I had no idea the old name continued in use so late), with branches that link Wisbech and March to Peterborough, or Huntingdon, further south. But that was not the end of it. Railway growth continued. The total mileage of Britain's growing railways give an idea of the speed of the process. In 1830 there were just 100 miles (160 km), in 1852 there were 12,000 miles (20,000 km) and by the year Queen Victoria died, in 1901, there were 19,000 (30,500 km).[11] Today, the total, of 10,072 (16,210 km), has fallen well below the figure for 1852.[12]

I don't want to get into the whys and wherefores of railway closures, but I think the main problem in the 1950s and '60s, when most of the decisions were taken, was short-termism. It never occurred to people that the role of railways could possibly change from being movers of goods or materials in bulk to being a reliable way of moving people to and from their place, or places, of work. So much of the 'rationalization' that took place, mostly under Dr Beeching's supervision in the post-war decades, has effectively prevented the diminished railway network from ever being able to adapt to changing circumstances. This was particularly true in the Fens, where many old railway lines were used as the basis for new roads. A particularly good example is the A141 March bypass, where sharp-eyed drivers can spot old sheds and other railway furniture still in situ on the roadside.

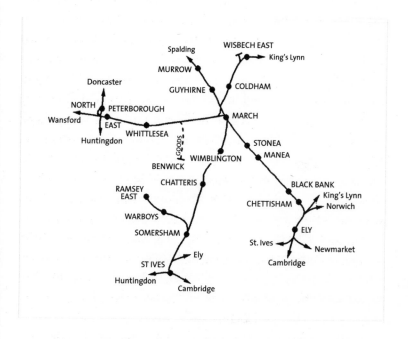

*Railways around the fenland town of March, as they existed in the 1930s. This layout is sometimes called the fenland 'spider'. Today only one line survives, that from the East Coast Main Line in Peterborough, via March, to Ely and Cambridge. All the others were closed, mostly in the 1950s and '60s.*

The flat landscape of the Fens, although not without its problems caused by soft ground and many dykes and watercourses, was ideally suited to the construction of railway lines, which

soon proliferated. One example should illustrate what came
and went in slightly over a hundred years, between about 1845
and 1965.[13] Just in my lifetime, the changes have been so fast.
Our first house in the Fens was outside the village of Murrow,
which had been well-known in the pre-war years as a railway
junction where two branch lines had crossed. By the time we
moved there, in 1980, the line from March to Spalding had
closed to passengers, but was still very occasionally used by
goods trains. Eventually this line closed in May 1983. There was
no announcement, nor clear reason given, and it caused a good
deal of local suspicion, because even in the early 1980s people
(apart from politicians, that is) were starting to appreciate the
potential of railways in the future.

The nearby town of March had been something of a railway
hub in its heyday before the war and some of its extensive and
fine station buildings (built in 1885) with at least four platform
buildings survive, albeit with reduced canopies and a fine roofed
footbridge. An active friends organization is helping preserve this
historic station. Because it stood at the junction of five separate
lines, March developed a huge set of goods marshalling yards
that would not have looked out of place in a major railway hub,
such as Crewe or Doncaster. They are now very much reduced
in size and the land where the old yards stood has now been
used to build the new high-security Whitemoor Prison, which
opened in 1991. Today, March is just another stop on the Ely–
Peterborough line. Sadly, the many towns and villages in the
area around can only be reached by road.

The Fens and fen-edges were also host to some very unusual
lines, including Lord Willoughby's private railway, also known
as the Edenham Branch, near his stately home at Grimsthorpe
Castle. Its route was exceedingly rural and it was built to help
the estate and local farmers move produce to market. It opened
in 1855 and closed in 1873.[14] It was just over 4 miles (6 km)

long and throughout its short life was run by Lord Willoughby's agent. It appears to have come about not through any local demand, but because of his lordship's great interest in steam traction. Lord Willoughby tried hard to have his railway adopted by the Great Northern Railway, who operated what is now the East Coast Main Line, nearby. But sadly, they were never interested. I can't think why.

*A postcard dating from the 1950s, showing a goods train of three wagons and a guard's van on the Wisbech to Upwell tramway. Note the British Railways insignia on the side of the locomotive.*

The Wisbech and Upwell Tramway was, quite literally, a tramway, with lightweight engines that looked more like an old-fashioned guard's van than a conventional steam locomotive.[15] The tramway ran alongside the Wisbech to Upwell canal, which was in decline. It was cheap to build and run and was very successful. Eventually it put the canal out of business. The lightweight track also ran alongside the Wisbech–Emneth–Outwell road (today the A1101) to the point where it met the Well Creek. Here there were quays where goods that had been moved from farms and orchards in Norfolk were transferred to the tramway for transport to Wisbech, where there were vessels that crossed the North Sea, but most were again transhipped to trains bound for markets in London. The line opened in 1883 with an extension from Outwell to Upwell a year later. Some passengers were carried in two coaches, but most of the trade was in produce and vegetables, with coal from the port of Wisbech being carried in the opposite direction. This was neatly summarized by the phrase of the day: 'coal in, fruit and potatoes out'. The tramway was taken over by the much larger LNER (London and North Eastern Railway) in 1922. The new owners ceased passenger services in 1927, because of competition from cheaper motor buses. It continued to make money in the 1930s, and during the war it played an important part in moving much-needed produce from the Norfolk Fens down to London, where fresh food was in very short supply. The tramway continued to carry freight until 1966, when it was closed down completely by Dr Beeching.

During the last war, the Fens became the nation's vegetable growbag, encouraged by money from the government, which was becoming increasingly anxious about the destruction of merchant shipping by German submarines.[16] The importance of self-sufficiency was emphasized by the Dig for Victory campaign, which encouraged people, from the king and queen downwards, to dig up their roses and plant cabbages in their stead. Whether or not this was actually very productive has long been questioned, and it certainly did a lot of damage to important historic gardens, but it did undoubtedly help people come to terms with their situation and allowed them to focus their efforts on doing something everyone considered useful. Personally I consider the campaign was a considerable social, if not an economic success.

In the open Fens, away from railheads and stations, the less accessible fields were now reached by Dig for Victory concrete roads, which consisted of two parallel strips of concrete for tractors' and waggons' wheels. An old farmer once told me that as many carts were still horse drawn, the central band of earth was kinder to his horses' feet than a harsh surface of concrete. Dig for Victory tracks still survive in more remote parts of the Fens, and many were simply covered over with a layer of tarmac directly after the war. Subsequently, further layers of tarmac have been added, but this has not overcome the fundamental weakness of the two-strip shallow foundations. Modern 20- and even 30-tonne trucks and trailers have caused many rural fen roads to 'break their backs', down the middle, between the two underlying concrete strips, like a vast chocolate bar, with at least one side starting to subside into the drain, or drains, along the roadside. The current local authority 'remedy' is to erect warning signs, which promptly get bent over or knocked flat by the first passing 20-tonne trailer. Some roads, including the one to our farm, have become almost impassable.

The fenland railways did sterling service during the war, but in the 1950s trucks and lorries were undercutting British Railways' prices and many branch lines were closed down, including the still locally much-missed Wisbech and Upwell Tramway, where the last tram ran on 20 May 1966.[17] It seems so strange that such a naturally flat landscape as the Fens should be served by such a tiny railway network.

# Wicken, Welney and Willow Tree: Modern Attitudes to Fen Conservation

*A 'Fen Blow' – Woodwalton Fen and the Great*
*Fen Project – The Southern Fens – Wicken Fen*
*– Floodplains and Washes – Welney Wash –*
*Lincolnshire Silt Fens – Arnold's Meadow –*
*Willow Tree Fen*

The Holme Fen post is the abiding monument to the erosion of peat, following drainage. Various factors are at work, but one of them is simple physical erosion – the result of wind action on light, dried peat. Anyone who has lived in the Fens for a few years will have experienced a 'fen blow'. These usually happen in spring and autumn when the soil is bare but recently cultivated. The wind gets up and soon collects a dark, swirling cloud of dry peaty topsoil. Very often these 'blows' are quite small and local. But not always.

We were excavating at Fengate on the eastern outskirts of Peterborough, in April, sometime in the early 1970s. The dig had started a couple of weeks previously and large earth-moving machines had just finished removing topsoil from several acres of ground. We were scraping with hoes to clear the surface to reveal the faint traces of prehistoric field boundary ditches. It was slow, tiring and, to be quite frank, very boring work, but we all knew it had to be done. Every so often we would pause to allow aching arms and shoulders to recover. The archaeologist working alongside me had just stopped to catch breath and was looking across the fen, towards the tall smoking chimneys of the Whittlesey brickworks. This was where the wind was coming from and we could all detect the distinctive sulphurous smell given off by the kilns.

'Good grief, look at that: looks like a kiln has blown up!'

I looked at where she was pointing, and yes, there was a dark cloud forming at the base of one of the chimneys. By now the hoeing had stopped and we were all staring out towards the brickyards. Then somebody said:

'I think it's closer than that, and I'm not sure it's smoke.'

And he or she was right. The cloud was actually forming out in the open fen, north of Whittlesey. I guessed it was still 3 or 4 miles (5–6 km) away. But it was certainly growing. By now it had extended above the horizon, and as I watched, I slowly realized it could be only one thing: a 'fen blow'. And it was turning into quite a big one – then suddenly it seemed to veer slightly to the left – and was heading directly towards us. Or was I imagining things? I glanced across at the other diggers, who were all looking anxiously in the same direction. I was the director of the dig, so I knew I would soon have to make a decision. On the other hand, I didn't want to be seen to panic, but I had no idea what it would be like to be caught up in such a strange storm. Indeed, one or two people were already glancing anxiously towards me. Then I had a very English idea:

'Let's take an early tea break!'

You cannot offer professional diggers and students a tea break lightly. These things matter. So they now knew I was taking the approaching storm seriously. Everyone quickly cleared up the loose soil at their feet, which was barrowed away to a nearby spoil heap. I told the rest of them to head straight across to the tea shed, while I waited for the two people with their barrows, which we upended over the tools to keep them dry. By now, I could see that the storm had developed a vaguely teardrop shape, with quite a distinctive spike or stalk at the top. It was a mini-whirlwind. As we approached the shed we could all feel the breeze suddenly increase in strength, but this time it had changed direction and had started to pick up some of the finer sand and grit at our feet.

We three were the last into the site hut and I shut the door behind us firmly, and then turned the key in the lock. Normally at this time of the year the windows would be open to let steam out and fresh air in. But not today. We could hear the sand and grit starting to hit the walls and then, quite suddenly, it grew darker and for a moment, as the wind speed increased, I wondered whether the shed roof would blow off, as it had done the previous season. Then I remembered: a month ago we had screwed it down with coach bolts, which I knew wouldn't please the company we'd hired it from, but now I didn't care. I glanced around me: nobody was talking, everybody was looking and listening. Next it began to hail, or at least that's what it sounded like, but there were none of those hailstones that slowly slide their way down the windows as they melt. It was all very odd. Finally, even faster than it began, it ended: a bird sang; the sun came out.

It was like somebody had turned the lights on. The wind dropped. The gritty hail noise stopped. Quickly I got up and tried to open the door, which I'd forgotten I'd locked. The key dropped out. I retrieved it, opened the door and was transfixed: the site had been transformed. It wasn't the same place we had left just fifteen minutes ago.

What had been pale-coloured gravel right across the site now looked much darker. I bent down and brushed the surface with my hand to reveal a very thin skin of fine black, peaty dust. But what were these strange white grubs that seemed to be nestling in it? Sandy, a professional digger from Scotland, was standing alongside me, also examining a sample of the black dust in his hand. We both looked up at the same time and our eyes met:

'That's grain,' he said.

I looked more closely at the small white granules that were interspersed with the grub-like seeds of corn.

'Yes,' I replied, 'And that's Nitram.'

I recognized the small white grains of nitrate fertilizer from my time doing farmwork as a student. And then it became clear what had happened. It had been a very dry season indeed, and the newly drilled (planted) spring barley had failed to germinate. Normally the artificial fertilizer would have dissolved after a shower or two, but not this year. And then a passing 'twister', or mini-whirlwind, had simply picked up everything on the field's dry surface and dumped it on our site – and it must have cost some poor farmer a fortune. It was seed corn and fertilizer that had struck the tea shed roof, not hail.

After a breezy weekend, we returned to site and everything had reverted to its normal colour, but the leeward sides of the spoil heaps that surrounded the stripped area had not been wind-cleaned and three weeks later they were all shrouded by a thick green cloak of freshly germinated barley seedlings. I remember thinking that the spoil heaps looked like they had grown a head of luxuriant green hair. Later in the season that hair turned blonde and, towards autumn, a rather sad, broken grey. We all agreed: there was something strangely human about the site that summer.

The experience of being caught up in a 'fen blow' shows that soil erosion, especially in drained wetlands, is likely to become a growing problem as farm mechanization advances and as climate change gathers pace. But most of the land surface shrinkage demonstrated by the Holme Fen posts happens more quietly and unseen. Essentially, it's the same process that iron goes through when it's exposed to the air and gets damp: it's a sort of rusting or oxidation, which causes the peat to disintegrate. It's also a process that sees the release of much carbon into the atmosphere, so it contributes in a large way to climate change, whereas the formation of fens and bogs does the precise opposite and actually traps carbon. I don't want to sound like a prophet of doom, but if the release of carbon were not bad enough, fen drainage has other, perhaps even more immediate implications for the near future.

My first visit to Woodwalton Fen, a nature reserve a couple of miles south of Holme Fen, was in the mid-1970s, when I was digging in Peterborough, ahead of the then expanding New Town. In those days, I was employed by The Royal Ontario Museum in Toronto and would spend half my time in Canada and half in Britain. Even on a junior academic's modest salary, the rate of UK income tax was horrendous, so I made sure I stayed overseas for just over six months, every year. I would use local contacts to find somewhere to stay when I was in Britain and in 1975 I found lodgings in a cottage in the little village of Ashton, near Oundle, a short distance to the west of Peterborough. Ashton had been, and still was, the estate village of the Rothschild family and it was famous for its lovely thatched pub, the Chequered Skipper, named after the rare butterfly that only (I believe) occurred there. The inn sign was an anatomically accurate picture of the butterfly.[1]

Ashton was a very friendly, if somewhat eccentric place to live. Just down the road, also facing the village green, was the cottage where Ginger Baker, famous drummer of the band Cream, lived. Only when I saw him collecting the milk did I realize he was named Ginger because of his wonderful hair. Through various contacts I soon got to meet and know Dame Miriam Lane (née Rothschild), who was the daughter of the great conservationist Charles Rothschild and a very distinguished entomologist in her own right. She lived in the big house at Ashton, which was surrounded by a large but restrained garden and wildlife park – both of which have influenced my own garden. Miriam was a wonderfully humorous, unassuming person and the greatest living expert on fleas, particularly the human flea.

Even at the height of late Victorian enthusiasm to drain the Fens, certain visionary people realized that something had to be done to preserve areas of wetland for future generations to study and enjoy. Charles Rothschild was a banker and business-man, but he was also a renowned entomologist and is widely regarded as 'the father of modern conservation'. He bought part of Wicken Fen in 1899 and gave it to the then young National Trust.* Ten years later, in 1910, he bought Woodwalton Fen, a mile or so south of Holme Fen. Rothschild understood only too well the importance of preserving different types of habitat: it was all about the survival of diversity.

Although I was living at Ashton at the time, I didn't know of the link between the Rothschilds and Woodwalton Fen. So it came as a wonderful surprise when I was walking through dense woodland on my first visit there to come across the Rothschild 'Bungalow'. This charming thatched and timber-clad single-storey Arts and Crafts house was originally built on wooden piles driven deep into the peat, by Charles Rothschild, in 1910. It was where he used to entertain his friends and it is

---

* The National Trust for Places of Historic Interest or Natural Beauty was founded in 1895 and given statutory powers in 1907.

*Charles Rothschild bought Woodwalton Fen in 1910 and built this small wooden house, known as The Bungalow, where he could entertain his friends and family. It has excellent views of the nature reserve from the balcony.*

clearly designed to be a building that looks outward, with large windows and a wonderful veranda. I can well imagine lazy weekends when he relaxed there with his rich and influential friends, sipping glasses of champagne and enjoying the diverse sights and sounds of the natural world around them. And this rural/ landed hospitality would have had more than a purely hedonistic purpose. Rothschild knew only too well what he was doing. Yes, he was entertaining himself and his rich friends, but he was also gently converting them to more important things than money and finance alone. He understood that the causes he believed in so passionately needed, in effect, to be sold to the lawmakers and other powerful members of society, who would normally only view such a tract of countryside from a much narrower, landowner's, perspective, which was then all about field sport or profit – or both.

In more recent times, the gathering pace of climate change and global environmental impoverishment have meant that Charles Rothschild's first steps have been taken much further. Many people interested in and involved with fenland conservation have long wanted somehow to unite the neighbouring nature reserves at Holme and Woodwalton fens. Eventually, in 2001, these dreams came to fruition in a fifty-year grand plan, known as the Great Fen Project.* The aim was to create a very much larger wetland of some 3,700 hectares (9,143 acres) that would surround and unite the two original areas and allow their wildlife to spread out into a far larger and more diverse wetland landscape. Water levels will be raised, but at the same time flooding needs to be carefully controlled. Knowing a little about the problems involved, I can appreciate the enormity of the task. But in its first two decades, huge advances have been made, with some 2,140 acres (866 ha) of land in restoration and 3,750 acres (1,519 ha) already in active conservation. It's the scale of the project that I find so inspiring: just as in archaeology, conservationists have moved away from single and often quite isolated and site-specific projects to a fresh approach, involving entire landscapes. And I'm quite convinced they're right: you have to think far more broadly if you want diverse and complex ecosystems to survive into a future that global climate change is making increasingly uncertain.

---

* The Great Fen Project is still under development and there are bound to be funding problems in the future, given the national and geo-political uncertainties that are such a sad feature of British life in the later second decade of the twenty-first century. The project has an excellent website (www.greatfen.org.uk) and if ever you happen to be passing by on the nearby A1, take the B660 (the junction is between Stilton, to the north, and Sawtry, to the south) and head east, towards Ramsey. After about 4 miles (6 km), you will pass the New Decoy Farm information centre and car park on your left. This is the best place to start or plan a visit.

I suppose you could say that the damage has already been done, that land surfaces have fallen too far and if you want to reverse the effects of fen drainage you must somehow turn the clock back to the mid-nineteenth century. But short of such an impossibility, it seems to me the Great Fen Project is a remarkably imaginative venture in practical conservation. And for the next few decades it will be going through a period of rapid change, as plants and animals move into their newly emerging habitats. It's not often that one is given the opportunity to witness such an extraordinary surge of emerging ecological diversity. If wetland drainage could be spectacular – and I gather it was – then I suspect wetland re-flooding will be even more so. But this time the changes will be entirely positive.

While researching Fen history and writing this book, I have had to change many long-held ideas, one of which was that nature takes a very long time to change. My views began to alter when we planted our own wood and meadows in the mid-1990s. I was astonished, for example, by the speed with which black poplars moved from being rootless cuttings to saplings and young trees in less than five years. Today my poplars are host to great spotted woodpeckers, who can be heard hammering away at them every morning, like numerous machine guns. But the biggest influence on how I have always regarded the development of wetland landscapes has been the reinstatement of new fens around Woodwalton Fen and, of course, the Great Fen Project. Recently my eye was caught by a new walk, or ramble, that has just been opened and does sound very inviting indeed.[2] It has all happened – and is happening – so very fast.

But now it is time to travel further south, where we will find landscapes of sharp contrasts, with real hills on the 'islands' and dramatic views across peat-filled floodplains and basins. These are the landscapes that most people think about whenever the Fens are mentioned. They are glimpsed from the city of Cambridge and they are symbolized for many by the towering cathedral at Ely. But for anyone interested in conservation they are home to one of the oldest and most revered of all Britain's great nature reserves, Wicken Fen. My idea of heaven is a weekend spent at Ely and Wicken. But these are also surroundings where the sun can be hidden by clouds and where views are shrouded by impenetrable mists. Light can give way to dark, hope and optimism to a harsh reality. These landscapes have never been straightforward, nor predictable.

*A view across the sedge wetland at Wicken Fen Nature Reserve, near Soham. The only operating scoop wind pump can be seen in the background.*

While Holme Fen may be most familiar to me, as it is close to Peterborough where I have spent most of my professional life, it is certainly not the best-known nature reserve in the Fens. That honour undoubtedly belongs to Wicken Fen, which lies in the deep peaty landscapes some 8 miles (13 km) north-east of Cambridge and 5 miles (8 km) south of Ely. I used to visit quite often when I was a student at Cambridge, largely because my cousin, the late Norman Moore, who I admired enormously, was very active there. Norman was one of the principal pioneers of environmental conservation and the leading expert on dragonflies – which thrive in wetlands.[3] One day, around 1990, Norman visited and advised us on how to make the new park we were then laying out at Flag Fen friendly to dragonflies, and the smaller damselflies – and less than five years later I was able to tell him that his advice had paid off handsomely: every summer the air around the mere positively seethes with their shimmering wings and glistening bodies. I always think of these large insects as a direct, living link to a very remote past, some 300 million years ago, during the Carboniferous era when, as its name suggests, the exuberant population of plants that were eventually to form the coal measures were still growing.[4]

I wasn't aware that dragonflies were such an important part of the environment when I first visited Wicken Fen, as a Cambridge student, in the late 1960s. I wasn't an ideal student and I preferred spending my time with girls rather than books. Most of my male student friends (and my college, Trinity, went co-educational only in 1976, nine years after I had graduated) envied the fact that I lived relatively locally and so had friends in the town who were not part of the university. I had also had the very battered Austin A40 in which I first visited Ely. I shouldn't have taken the car to Cambridge as such things were not allowed to students and in retrospect it was a dangerous, dirty rattletrap. People were less obsessed in those days about visiting the car wash regularly – and it's a tradition I'm still proud to maintain. But to cut to the chase, I thought I could impress one potential girlfriend with my illegal car, which I kept (without their permission) at the end of a private drive of a religious order on the outskirts of town. I arrived at her flat and she seemed quite impressed by my strange little car.

It certainly made her smile. I think she thought we were going out for lunch, but instead we drove to Wicken Fen. To this day I can't think why I chose to take her there on that particular day in mid-January. I was well wrapped up, my companion rather less so.

It was pleasant enough when we set out: bright, if not actually sunny. But the drive was not a great success: the heater, which was useless even when it worked, had failed and the passenger-side front window wouldn't close properly. So the car was freezing. I think the mizzle began just north of Cambridge and continued for the rest of the morning, on and off.

In those days Wicken Fen didn't have much of a visitor centre and even if it had, it wouldn't have been open in January. We got out of the car and traipsed down a short drove to the site. By now, my self-confidence was beginning to flag and I was having doubts about the whole outing. But as we stood there at the edge of the great wetland, my spirits suddenly lifted. Before us was a huge expanse of recently mown sedge fen, with water-filled dykes and alders in the middle distance. Herons were everywhere, as were grebes, moorhens and ducks. It was fabulous. Then I glanced at my companion and saw the place through her cold, disapproving eyes: it was a large, flat, wet field with nothing whatever to commend it. Even the herons looked depressed. She indicated the view disdainfully, then turned, looking me full in the face, and asked:

'So is *that* it?'

After all these years I still can't be absolutely certain, but I think it was the last thing she ever said to me.

I have returned to Wicken Fen many times since, and have watched as the place has grown and subtly changed over the years. The thing is that landscapes – even those of such scientifically sensitive places as Wicken Fen – can never be preserved, as it were, in aspic. They have to be actively maintained or else they will lose that unique combination of factors that make them so special. If nothing else, they have constantly to be protected from 'progress', as the modern world around them changes.

Wicken Fen has had a complicated history but in essence it was always a difficult place to drain, since it was very low lying and on the edge of Soham Mere, the largest of the southern meres around Ely. It also served a very useful purpose as the place that provided the large quantities of sedge that make the best ridging material for thatchers. We used sedge to form the apex cones of our reconstructed prehistoric roundhouses at Flag Fen. We were helped by a local thatcher, and I was lucky enough to spend a couple of days with him. He had great respect for sedge, which is essentially a wet-loving reed-like grass.

Large areas of the Fens are distant from sources of permanent building materials, such as stone or slate. And in some of the poorer rural communities even locally produced bricks were hard to come by and expensive. So people had to make do with what they could find. In Lincolnshire, for example, cottage walls were made with mud and stud, which involved the careful filling in of a timber framework, or stud, with a special mud, prepared from wet earth and chopped vegetation as a binder. A very few mud-and-stud cottages still survive.* Roofs were generally thatched. Over the past three or so centuries, as areas of arable land increased, what we would regard today as conventional straw thatching became increasingly popular, but before that reeds and sedge, which still grew abundantly in the Fens, were more usually used.

You will still sometimes see sedge thatching in the villages

---

* The technique was also successfully employed by settlers from Lincolnshire in the new colony at Jamestown, Virginia, on the other side of the Atlantic. See Rodney Cousins, *Lincolnshire Buildings in the Mud and Stud Tradition* (Heritage Lincolnshire, 2000).

around Wicken to this day, but it is no longer used as a complete covering. Instead, it forms a slightly raised ridge that covers the apex of the roof. After my short time working on the roof of the roundhouse at Flag Fen I had acquired huge respect for sedge. And I could fully, and painfully, understand how it had acquired its common name: sawtooth. When dry it's extremely tough, and the edges of the leaves are unbelievably sharp. Wicken Fen was, and still is, a major producer of sawtooth sedge, which is still much sought after by thatchers, although today production is controlled and managed by the National Trust. Modern garden centres are packed with miniature and variegated varieties of sedge, which bear about as much resemblance to thatching sedge, *Cladium mariscus*, as poodles do to their close relatives, wolves.

Modern Wicken Fen is evolving, but harvesting and managing the sedge is still central to its existence, as indeed are the dragonflies, which are magnificently displayed and explained in the dragonfly centre there.[5] The story of nature conservation in the peat fens is essentially a tale of enlightened people and some near disasters. Indeed, as I well recall, things looked very bleak indeed in the 1980s and '90s: decades of farming subsidies had encouraged ever-deeper draining; the few surviving hedgerows had been seriously depleted and orchards were being grubbed up in favour of more lucrative arable fields. We were also becoming far more aware of climate change and the lurking menace of rising sea levels, which were brought home to me by the opening, in 1984, of the Thames Barrier at Woolwich. A documentary film on television showed how the barrier would close – and save London. That was great – and of course to be welcomed – but the film made no mention of how those coastal and low-lying communities along the surge's path from the north would cope. It was also hard to avoid the conclusion that they didn't matter, which probably isn't entirely fair, but that's how it seemed to me at the time.

\*

The more we understand about the evolution of past environments in the Fens, the more we appreciate their subtlety and complexity. Earlier I drew a clear distinction between acidic bogs, which are mostly based on rainwater, and fens, which use nutritionally richer river water. But detailed research into the peats at Wicken, Holme and Woodwalton fens (among many other places) has shown that even fen peats can turn acidic when the thickness of the deposit has built up.[6] So it's not a simple matter. The same blurring of seemingly clear distinctions can also apply to the Black (or peat) Fens, to the south and west, and the salt-water Silt Fen, to the north and around the Wash. The zone where the two types of fen meet is rarely simple and will often involve a complex succession of layers of silts, clays and peats – and to further complicate matters, quite often the peats might not actually have grown there, but may have been washed in from somewhere else.

You will find a similar complex mixture of peats, clays and silts, but this time mixed with sands and gravels, along the lower floodplains of the larger rivers that drain into the fenland basin. Sometimes this transitional fen/river valley land is known as 'skirtland'. In certain areas, especially around the lower reaches of the Ouse Valley around St Ives, Over and even further out into the Fens, at Earith, these layers of gravel have proved to be commercially important.

In the past, disused gravel workings were simply abandoned, along with old cranes, derelict conveyor belts, collapsing Nissen huts and rusting ironwork. But today things are different, if perhaps a little less characterful: old pits are now landscaped and planted with the appropriate fen vegetation, to provide nature reserves and even, in some cases, archaeological reconstructions – Bronze Age barrows and suchlike. Recent excavations around

Over have revealed some fascinating insights into the way that landscapes developed in prehistory. It was an extraordinarily dynamic process and far from random, or unplanned.[7]

As an archaeologist I'm always very interested in the nature of the ground beneath my feet; when I drive or walk around the country I like to look into ditches or stare at building sites, or roadworks. I'm always picking things up in ploughed fields. I suppose you could call it my trainspotter side and I don't suppose I'll ever lose it. But sometimes one needs to take a broader view if one is to get the most from the landscape – and this certainly applies when it comes to the distinction between the peat and silt fens. By and large the Silt Fens were being settled from later Roman and early medieval times – long before the peatlands were drained. As a consequence of their earlier settlement, the Silt Fens of southern Lincolnshire tend to occur in a far less regimented fashion than the Black Fens further south. Yes, fields are large, but roads generally wander and have gentle corners; villages often have medieval churches. By contrast, the peat Fens along the western fen-edge in Lincolnshire are arranged like steps in a ladder, with parallel dykes and dead straight roads. Fen parishes like Deeping, Haconby, Rippingale and Billingborough Fens are laid out immediately to the east of the dry, medieval fen-edge villages that gave them their names. In my experience these later fens can be particularly cold, open and exposed during winter.

Peats can form very differently in contrasting environments and the same can be said for the mineral deposits that characterize the Silt Fens, which range from the fine-grained, muddy and clay-like to grittier, sand-like silts. The former owed more to the flooding of rivers, whereas the latter were a direct result of marine and tidal flooding. From as early as the fourth millennium BC, many marshes formed behind the dunes and mudbanks along the low-lying shores of the North Sea and the Wash.[8] Although strictly speaking it is more coastal than fen, the superb nature reserve at Gibraltar Point, which extends from Skegness to the Wash, shows how diverse and rich such environments can be. I like to go there in late winter or spring, to look at and listen to the waders, including the improbably attractive avocets, and to clear my head in the often rather traumatic run-up to lambing, towards the end of March. Those of us lucky enough to live in the Fens take clean air for granted, but nothing can touch Gibraltar Point for deep breaths that seem to purge the blood and soul. I try to get my fix at least once a year, if not more often.[9]

*A view of Welney Washes Nature Reserve, shortly before feeding time. This photo of the flooded Ouse Washes was taken in January. The wildfowl include the yellow-billed whooper and Bewick's swans and teal, among other species of ducks and waders.*

On the other side of the Wash, but further inland, is the RSPB reserve at Welney Wash, in western Norfolk, close to its border with Cambridgeshire. We have seen that washes are areas that have been set aside for regular flooding and are an important part of fenland water management. The Ouse and Nene Washes were recognized as good wildfowling areas in the eighteenth and nineteenth centuries and more recently became National Nature Reserves. I particularly enjoy visiting the wooded areas of the Nene Washes and Holme Fen because they provide a wonderful glimpse of what the deeper fens might have looked like in prehistory. These are just the kind of places people would have visited to fell trees for their raised platforms, causeways and palisades.

*Alder woodland in the Nene Washes Nature Reserve, near Whittlesey.*
*This picture was taken in February and some of the alder trees show*
*signs of having been coppiced (i.e. chopped off at ground level)*
*a long time ago – maybe thirty to fifty years previously.*
*Alder recovers well if coppiced in late autumn or winter.*

We live just under 20 miles (32 km) north of the River Ouse Washes and every late autumn we hear the sound of whooper swans wheeling southwards over our small farm and heading down for the nature reserve at Welney Wash, which floods every year.[10] The birds do the same, but in reverse, the following spring, when they return to their summer feeding grounds. We spoke to some ornithologists at Welney who told us that as the rivers and dykes around our farm made a particularly recognizable pattern when seen from the air, the swans might well use it as a navigation point. I find it fascinating that something as transient, in the greater scheme of things, as a man-made drainage pattern can affect the long-term behaviour of wildlife.

I gather that when the first astronauts orbited the Earth, two, if not *the* two, man-made features that could be seen from space were the Great Wall of China and the Ouse Washes. A cheaper alternative is to see them from the ground. You can get excellent views from the A1101, the Littleport to Upwell road, which, unlike many a fenland road, actually wiggles as it crosses the great Hundred Foot Washes between the new and old Ouse rivers. There are plenty of places to get out of the car and have a look around. But my favourite view by far is from the train between March and Ely, which crosses the washes about three miles (5 km) upstream of the A1101 via a rail bridge that is higher than the road causeway. I often find myself travelling south to London or Cambridge in the winter, when the trees are bare and the washes are flooded. I've even been known to plan my journey to coincide with sunset. I know of no more spectacular and atmospheric a sight than the vast expanse of the Ouse Washes ablaze in the setting sun, with mists rising and geese coming home to roost. The Fens are never truly dark in winter. Moon and starlight seems to be brighter. I suppose this could be an illusion caused by low horizons, but there seems to be far more ambient light here than elsewhere in Britain. The cold and dampness can be a bit oppressive, but I find the spectacular fenland sunrises and sunsets more than make up for the chill. A full moon rising through the mists can be truly magnificent, too, and I often wonder what prehistoric people would have thought about such things.

*

It always used to be the peat fens, at places such as Wicken, Woodwalton and Holme, that attracted the most public interest and concern, but recently people have started to become more aware of the subtle attractions of the Silt Fens, especially in Lincolnshire. Again, the popular misconception is that the Fens are mostly a phenomenon of Cambridgeshire (which today includes the old counties of Huntingdonshire and the Isle of Ely*), but the Norfolk Fens are almost half their size and there is a substantial area of Suffolk fenland, too. The less celebrated Fens of Lincolnshire are of comparable size to those of Cambridgeshire, but their character is somehow quite distinct. And it's not something that is easy to define. There is certainly no sharp change as one crosses from Cambridgeshire's Fenland District into Lincolnshire's South Holland. Traditionally, people who grew up in the southern Fens were known as Slodgers, whereas those from further north were Yellowbellies. And it has taken me some forty years to appreciate their mutual subtle distinctiveness – and it's real, I'm sure of that.

I think it's fair to say that there is a growing pride in being a Yellowbelly. Indeed, it's a label I would be proud to bear, had I been born where I have been living for over two decades. Over the years I have grown increasingly attached to the distinctively open landscapes of the Lincolnshire Fens. To the south, the great cathedral at Ely dominates the landscape all around, but so too does the vast tower of Boston's parish church of St Botolph. But

---

* Huntingdonshire was an administrative county from 1889 until 1965, when it was merged with the Soke of Peterborough. Huntington and Peterborough became part of Cambridgeshire in 1974. The Isle of Ely was an administrative county from 1889 to 1965, when it became part of Cambridgeshire.

even the Stump and, dare I say it, Ely too are eclipsed by the magnificence of Lincoln's three towers, which seem to transcend the laws of gravity, first propounded, of course, by Sir Isaac Newton, who was born and raised nearby, in the family home at Woolsthorpe Manor, near Grantham.[11]

This growing appreciation of the beauty, variety and distinctiveness of the Lincolnshire Fens has been mirrored by the establishment of a number of new nature reserves, some of which are still quite young and are evolving fast. It's fascinating to observe these changes, which again remind me that the natural state of nature isn't as static as we once believed: evolution only works because imbalances have to be corrected and new opportunities taken. It's a dynamic and far from chaotic process that contrasts strongly with the orderly Creation of earlier, religious thinkers.

The fenland landscapes of Lincolnshire are set off by, and in turn enhance, the rounded limestone hills of the Lincolnshire Wolds. The fen/wolds area is one of the least densely populated regions in England, with few large towns and very widely separated villages. My favourite fen view is from the top of the wolds escarpment overlooking the Fens at East Keal, a couple of miles south of Spilsby, on the A16. They may be thinly populated, but I have never found these landscapes lonely or hostile. Quite the contrary, in fact: the pubs often serve Batemans beer (brewed locally in Wainfleet) and the welcome is always warm.

The unique character of the region was evocatively captured by the artist Peter De Wint (1784–1849), who is particularly celebrated for his atmospheric portrayals of Lincoln Cathedral. My father had a large collection of his watercolours and, being a fairly rebellious youth who disliked all paternal authority, I naturally took against his choice of paintings, which in those days I regarded as underwhelming: too restrained and English for my taste. I now realize I was wrong in seeing restraint as being bad; on reflection, I now appreciate that it's the best way to trigger the viewer's own imagination, which is needed if you want to capture the latent power, majesty – and, yes, magic – of flat or gently undulating landscapes. Peter De Wint's paintings are on permanent display in the Usher Gallery, Lincoln.[12]

I have always been a keen photographer and rather to my surprise over the years I have discovered that the landscapes of southern Lincolnshire make wonderful pictures, providing, that is, you can reveal or discover a good foreground subject. Nobody does this better than Jon Fox, whose wonderful book *The Lincolnshire Landscape: An Exploration* includes some truly breathtaking images.[13] You can almost cut their clarity and crisp freshness with a knife. Wonderful stuff.

The new Lincolnshire nature reserves are mostly distributed between the towns of Bourne, on the edge of the Fens, and Spalding, towards the Wash.[14] As a boy I loved racing cars and my father used to tell me about the legendary Raymond Mays who built and drove ERAs (before the war) and BRMs (in the 1950s). May's firm was based in Bourne and he used to test-drive ERAs at phenomenal speeds along the dead-straight road that leads to the outlying fenland village of Twenty – a remote spot, if ever there was one. I know the Twenty straight well: the fields around are often full of bog oaks and there are deep, wet drainage dykes on either side. Those drives in the hard-suspension pre-war racing cars must have been hair-raising.

Spalding, of course, is a famous centre for the horticultural trade and especially for the production of tulips, although nowadays the fields in the area also include vast areas of daffodils and potatoes. The nature reserve at Arnold's Meadow is within walking distance of the town, on its south-eastern side. If you saw its location on a map, you would not rush to visit, as it appears to be sandwiched between a massive artificial river cut and the A16 Spalding bypass. In the recent past, Spalding was notorious for flooding and the problem wasn't solved (finally?) until 1953 when the new Coronation Channel of the River Welland was diverted around the centre of the town. Arnold's Meadow is what it says it is: a meadow on land that was first grazed in medieval times. It is surrounded by wet-loving trees, hedgerows and ponds, flag irises, meadow buttercups and spotted orchids – not to mention frogs and grass snakes. It isn't very large (almost 6½ acres, or 2.60 ha), but it is substantial enough to feel remote and timeless – which is all the more remarkable, given the fact that the land in question was a bare field in 1968. You can just hear the bypass, but it's not intrusive. If anything, it enhances your sense of peace.[15]

*Willow Tree Fen Nature Reserve, near Spalding, Lincolnshire. This was drained arable farmland until 2009 when it became a nature reserve and carefully managed areas were allowed to flood. This photograph was taken in November 2018 and shows the rich natural vegetation that has grown around a long-abandoned borrow pit (pits dug to quarry material for nearby riverbanks).*

One of the most recent of the newer reserves was established at Willow Tree Fen, Deeping St Nicholas.[16] It is wonderfully remote, making even Wicken Fen seem positively metropolitan. Willow Tree Fen lies to the south of the River Glen, one of the larger of the secondary rivers that drain into the Wash, and is reached off the long and bumpy Slipe Drove (a *slipe* is the local name for a wash). It was bought in 2009. Although it consists of land that has been drained, it is subject to regular flooding, especially in late autumn, winter and spring. At 274 acres (111 ha) it's much larger than Arnold's Meadow, and not surprisingly it's also more open, but the intention is to use the new land as an extension to two smaller neighbouring reserves. With luck, the presence of a new and long-term flooded area should encourage migratory geese, swans, waders and other species to move in. If Arnold's Meadow is anything to go by, Willow Tree should look remarkable in ten years' time, because it's certainly well worth visiting now. I really like to see, monitor and experience the way that nature changes and adapts. If nothing else, it offers hope for the future.

# Epilogue:

# Farewell to Boston

This has been a book that I have always wanted to write, because it's about a region I have grown to love dearly. I'm working on this epilogue in my office on the ground floor of our house, just a little above sea level. It's late October 2018 and in the faint light of dawn I can just see a V-shaped skein of some twenty whooper swans flying inland from off the Wash, heading towards their winter roosts on the Nene or Ouse washes. Migrating geese and swans have become old friends and I have seen them arrive and depart over many autumns and springs. Every year I get to look forward to their distinctive warbling sounds as they pass over our garden. There are so many signs of the changing seasons here in the Fens: the dark ploughed soils of autumn, the vegetable-picking gangs in winter, the seed drills of spring and harvest of late summer. I feel profoundly at home here, with the people, the animals and the landscape. But I am becoming increasingly anxious about the future of the Fens.

Our journey into fenland history has been about the passage of time and how it affected the way people lived and continue to live their lives. It has been about the past as seen from the perspective of the remembered present. I want now to move the clock forward and address two of the phenomena we have been considering as background themes throughout this book. The first is the relentless rise of North Sea levels since the end of the last Ice Age, around twelve thousand years ago. We can document its steady, if fluctuating, rise through the Neolithic, Bronze and Iron Ages, then (after a brief slow-down in Roman times) it resumes in the Saxon, medieval and post-medieval periods. The pace of sea level rise around Britain has varied through the centuries and has been complicated by other factors, such as the local lifting of land levels (in parts of north-eastern Scotland), but the underlying process continues to this day. Furthermore, there is now strong evidence to link it to the global climate changes brought about by the increased release of carbon into the atmosphere that was a direct result of the industrialization of the mid-nineteenth century.[1] Current predictions suggest that sea levels will rise by 'at least' a metre in just eighty years – i.e. by the end of the present century.[2] Flood defences will need to be very much higher if they are to contain such hugely raised sea levels.

The second factor is the drop of land levels in the peaty Fens brought about by widespread drainage – as recorded so memorably by the Holme Fen post. I still find a visit to that post a humbling experience. The mark showing the ground level in the 1850s is so far above my head: if I were in my garden pruning shrubs, I would need my tallest stepladder to reach up to it – and even then it would still be well above me. So-called bog oaks used to be a common sight in the Fens, especially before the war. Essentially, these were trees that had been growing in prehistoric wet woodlands, that had died, toppled over and been preserved in the wet peaty soils around them. After drainage the soils would dry and shrink, thereby exposing the 'bog oaks' – many of which were often pine, alder or birch. Today, bog oaks are becoming rare, but not because soil erosion is slowing down. Sadly, their rarity reflects the fact that peat deposits are now very thin and there are few remaining bog oaks preserved beneath the surface.

A 'bog oak' in an arable field in Holme Fen, November 2006. The East
Coast Main Line is at top right, with the trees of Holme Fen Nature
Reserve just beyond. More bog oaks can be seen in the ploughed field,
middle distance. These are stumps and roots of trees that were growing
on the drier peats in the past. In the early twentieth century, bog oaks
were probably of medieval or slightly earlier date. Today they
are usually prehistoric. These 'oaks' are almost certainly pines,
to judge from their pale colour and distinctive bark.

So is it inevitable that the Fens will flood again? Sadly, I have
come to the reluctant conclusion that it's a process that cannot
be delayed forever. We can go on raising sea walls, but eventually
the waves must break through them.

During the course of this book I have had to refer to flooding
– it would be impossible to write an account of the Fens without
doing so. But I have avoided describing individual events in any
detail because I have been concerned with long-term processes
rather than individual events. I am too young to remember the
devastating floods of 1947,[3] but I do recall my parents' shock
and horror as my father read out newspaper accounts of the
1953 floods at the breakfast table. I still wonder whether that

flood, which affected the entire southern North Sea basin, will prove a model for some future event. Most of the east coast of Britain (including Scotland) was affected, with the Fens and the low-lying land of the Essex coast being hardest hit. More than three hundred people died in England; the toll in the Netherlands was over two thousand.

Of course, we can only guess how and when the truly catastrophic, irreversible flood, or floods, will happen. Most winters we receive flood warnings of one sort or another. Indeed, I have lived through several major tidal surges – and happily the sea defences more or less held. Usually the damage was confined: Boston, for example, was badly hit in 2013 and 2018 – when King's Lynn also experienced significant problems. Often the most severe tidal surges happen when tides are at their highest due to the alignment of the Earth, sun and moon. These highest tides are known as spring tides.* Neap tides, which are almost as high, occur the week following a spring tide. In winter the effects of high spring and neap tides can be greatly exaggerated by the strong northerly gales that blow down the east coast.[4] This is precisely what happened in the terrible flood on the night of 31 January and 1 February 1953.

We have now come to that 'when or if' moment. Had I been writing this twenty years ago I would have said 'if', but ten years ago it would reluctantly have been 'when'. Today, I am in no doubt whatsoever: it's a firm 'when'. So when at some time in the future the Fens are eventually allowed to flood, I suspect that, like most aspects of the modern world, it will have to be managed in some way. Indeed, one could see this management as a campaign that has already started. From 2015, all the major roads around us started to display strange little red signs

---

* The term 'spring' is historical and does not refer to the season. It probably derives from references to the tide 'springing forth'.

that made no sense at all when I first saw them.[5] They feature just two letters: 'ER', which for many months I thought was something to do with Her Majesty, or a royal anniversary (with Sandringham just up the road, such things are not unheard of). I have since discovered that they refer to 'Evacuation Route' and are intended to help in times of flood. Knowing the way Fen roads block up at the slightest hint of congestion, I shall stay well clear of them when the crisis happens.

Quite recently, new areas of tidal mudflats, marsh and water were created as part of a programme of 'managed retreat'. The term isn't used very much today, largely I suspect because the word 'retreat' is synonymous in many people's minds with 'defeat'. One of the largest of the managed retreats took place just 4 miles (6 km) east of Boston in a region known as Freiston Shore.[6] This is a delightful site of banks, marshes and open water, which also includes a number of unusual wartime structures. It occupies some 163 acres (66 ha) and to flood it, in the year 2000, the authorities had to demolish a short length of the Wash sea defences. I recall that when the bank was taken down, much was made of the fact that the new breach would take pressure off the rest of the bank, which was then beginning to show its age. I would imagine that similar things would take place when the main fens are allowed to flood. Such management is likely to play a key part in avoiding any future casualties.

I must now briefly consider the possible political justification for the flooding of the Fens, surely the ultimate managed retreat. Obviously, the rapidly escalating expense of maintaining and increasing flood defences would be the principal issue. The Wash has a long shoreline, broached by major estuaries, all of which require large-scale protective measures. Rivers flowing through the deeper fens have very high banks, too. As banks get higher, they get weaker and the expense of their construction and maintenance rises disproportionately. So future costs are likely to be immense. There would also be some very substantial ecological benefits, as Freiston Shore and the Great Fen Project are continuing to demonstrate. Indeed, their success would make it easier to argue in favour of a programme of planned flooding. Another major factor, which would prove politically popular among the tens of millions who reside in Greater London and along the Thames Estuary, would be that flooding the Fens would take pressure off the capital. Such a huge expanse of marshy ground would absorb much of the energy of future tidal surges along the east coast. The Woolwich barrier, and its successors, would certainly be more secure, as would the people living behind them.

A managed flooding of the Fens would almost certainly be handled in stages. It would probably begin with further Freiston Shore-like areas closer to the coast. Maybe the existing river washes would be extended. I would suspect that much of the higher Iron Age and Roman tidal deposits of marshland that surround the Wash would escape flooding until very late in the process. These are the parishes with some of the finest medieval churches. Eventually some towns, or urban areas on their fringes, would be inundated. Most of Ely, being raised on a substantial island, would escape, as would places like March, Haddenham, Sutton, Chatteris and Wilburton in the Cambridgeshire Fens. I fear Boston and Spalding would fare very badly, as would Fengate and much of eastern Peterborough, but Thorney and Whittlesey, both on natural islands, would largely survive. Sadly, the beautiful town of Wisbech would be an early casualty. The inundation of the higher-lying silt fens of Lincolnshire would be a gradual process that could be managed quite effectively. But I have serious concerns about the later-drained peaty lands of the southern and western Fens. Their eventual flooding strikes me as inevitable and I am worried that when it happens, the water will be marine – and this could have a devastating effect on the rich, freshwater-based wildlife in the conservation areas, such as Woodwalton Fen.

So when will this happen? The answer to that question is simple: it has already begun. And it will be an irreversible process, even in the unlikely event that in the near future measures are agreed at an international level to limit carbon emissions. In the case of the Fens, much of the damage has already been done and sea level rises are longer term and are not a direct consequence of man-made climate change alone. I concede that this has been a catalogue of gloom and doom, but I have deliberately omitted one crucial element: Fen people.

So will the people of the Fens be able to halt the process? I don't think that would be physically possible, but I do believe that their collective imagination will produce ideas that some-how transcend the physical changes to their surroundings. The builders of the Boston Stump did just that when they erected that soaring symbol of hope and resistance in the terrible years of the Black Death. Maybe the Fens in the future will become a European centre for migrating birds and for wildlife conser-vation? In an overcrowded world, the region's hugely enlarged conservation areas might provide the leisure and educational experiences that their urban populations would be demanding. And all these visitors would require accommodation, food and entertainment – and stimulation. Perhaps we will see a revival of the arts, of painting, theatre and music? I don't know: you can never second-guess the future, but if the past is any sort of a guide, the shift away from intensive farming towards a more diverse and ecologically sustainable future can only be for the good. And who knows, maybe we will be able to preserve the Stump from the encroaching tides of the North Sea? For me, it is the ultimate symbol of the Fens. I would hate to see it come crashing down.

# Notes

## Prologue: Everything Comes Out in The Wash

1   Simon Jenkins, *England's Cathedrals* (Little, Brown, London, 2016) selects Lincoln and Ely (together with Wells) as his 'Three Graces', the finest cathedrals in England.

2   It's a topic I discuss at length in *The Making of the British Landscape*, (Penguin Books, London, 2010), pp. 3–18.

## Chapter 1: Cambridge: My Introduction to the Fens

1   I highly recommend Richard Muir's excellent *Landscape Encyclopaedia: A Reference Guide to the Historic Landscape* (Windgather Press, Macclesfield, 2004). 'Assart' is defined on pp. 6–7.

2   Sadly, the school no longer exists.

3   Brian Fagan, *Grahame Clark: An Intellectual Life of an Archaeologist* (Westview Press, Oxford, 2001).

4   Grahame Clark's two books that had a profound influence on me were: *Archaeology and Society*, 3rd edition (Methuen, London, 1957) and *World Prehistory, An Outline* (Cambridge University Press, 1962).

5   I discuss those early days in 'When Francis Dug the Fens', *Current Archaeology*, no. 300, March 2015, pp. 26–33.

6   Royal Commission on Historical Monuments, *Peterborough New Town: A Survey of the Antiquities in the Areas of Development*, (HMSO, 1969). The 'trackways' shown in fig. 1, nos. 3, 4 & 5, were quite reasonably believed to be Roman on the basis of pottery found nearby.

7   David Thomas Yates, *Land, Power and Prestige: Bronze Age Field Systems in Southern England* (Oxbow Books, Oxford, 2007).

8   Ibid., p. 141.

## Chapter 2: Fengate: Approaching the Wet from the Dry

1   G.W. Abbott, 'The discovery of prehistoric pits at Peterborough', *Archaeologia*, vol. 62, 1910, pp. 332–52.

2   For a summary of earlier Fengate research, with references, see: F.M.M. Pryor, *The Flag Fen Basin: Archaeology and environment of a Fenland Landscape* (English Heritage Archaeological Report, Swindon, 2001) pp. 7–9.

3   Royal Commission on Historical Monuments (England), *Peterborough New Town: A Survey of the Antiquities in the Areas of Development* (HMSO, London, 1968).

4   Ibid., fig. 1.

5   C. Evans, G. Appleby and S. Lucy, *Lives in Land. Mucking Excavations by Margaret and Tom Jones, 1965–1978: Prehistory, Context and Summary* (Oxbow Books, Oxford, 2016).

6   I discuss the Fengate drafting race in *Farmers in Prehistoric Britain*, pp. 100–107 (Tempus Books, Stroud, 2006).

7   C. Evans, *Fengate Revisited: Further Fen-edge Excavations, Bronze Age Fieldsystems and Settlement and the Wyman-Abbott/Lees Archives*, fig. 3.9 and p. 78 (Cambridge Archaeological Unit, Dept. of Archaeology, Cambridge University, 2009).

8   Francis Pryor, *Seahenge: a quest for life and death in Bronze Age Britain* (HarperCollins, London, 2001). For the detailed final report see: M. Brennand and M. Taylor, M, 'The Survey and Excavation of a Bronze Age Timber Circle at Holme-next-the-Sea, Norfolk, 1998–9' *Proceedings of the Prehistoric Society*, vol. 69, 2003, pp. 1–84.

## Chapter 3: Haddenham: Prehistory Pickled in Peat

1   T. Lane and J.M. Coles (eds.), *Through Wet and Dry: Essays in Honour of David Hall* (Heritage Trust for Lincolnshire and WARP, Heckington, Lincs and Exeter, 2002).

2   David Hall, *The Fenland Project, Number 6: The South-Western Cambridgeshire Fenlands*, East Anglian Archaeology, No. 56 (Cambridgeshire County Council, 1992).

3   We now know that the Stonehenge landscape can be dated back to about 8000 BC. See my *Stonehenge*, pp. 39–43 (Head of Zeus, London, 2016).

4   C. Evans and I. Hodder, *A Woodland Archaeology: Neolithic Sites at Haddenham* (McDonald Institute Monograph, University of Cambridge, 2006).

5   I have written a non-specialist account, 'The Ritual Landscapes of Pre-Roman Britain', in *The London Magazine*, Dec/Jan, 2016, pp. 105–110.

6   Ibid., figs 1.1 and 1.2.

7   Francis Pryor, *Excavation at Fengate, Peterborough England: the Fourth Report*, burials 1, 4, 5 and possible 6 (pp. 116–22).

8   Francis Pryor, *Excavation at Fengate, Peterborough, England: the Third Report*, figs. 23 and 27.

9   Some of the best examples in Europe come from Britain and are on permanent display in the British Museum.

10  C.A.I. French and F.M.M. Pryor, *The South-West Fen Dyke Survey Project 1982–86*, East Anglian Archaeology Report, No. 59 (Fenland Archaeological Trust, Peterborough, 1992).


## Chapter 4: Cropmarks and the Welland Valley

1   H.C. Bowen and R.M. Butler, *A Matter of Time: An Archaeological Survey of the River Gravels of England*, Royal Commission on Historical Monuments (England), (HMSO, London, 1960).

2   Ibid., p. 36.

3   https://www.directenquiries.com/information/Barnack%20Hills%20and%20Holes%20National%20Nature%20Reserves/103006/internal/information.aspx

4   F. Pryor and C.A.I. French, *Archaeology and Environment in the Lower Welland Valley*, Vol. 1, East Anglian Archaeology, Report No. 27 (Cambridge, 1985)

5   Jonathan Bate (ed.), *John Clare, Selected Poems* (Faber and Faber, London, 2003).


## Chapter 5: Etton: Perfect Preservation

1   For example: E. Beadsmoore, D. Garrow and M. Knight, 'Space, Time, and Material Culture Within a Causewayed Enclosure in Cambridgeshire, *Proceedings of the Prehistoric Society*, Vol. 76, 2010, pp. 115–134.

2   A. Whittle, F. Healy and A. Bayliss, *Gathering Time: Dating the Early Neolithic Enclosures of Southern Britain and Ireland*, Vol 1, p. 324 (Oxbow Books, Oxford, 2011).

3   R. Palmer, 'Interrupted ditch enclosures in Britain: the use of aerial photography for comparative studies', *Proceedings of the Prehistoric Society*, vol. 42 (1976), pp. 161–186.

4   For a superb reassessment of the Etton bone assemblage by Pip Parmenter, go to: http://www.tandfonline.com/eprint/Yf9TUtbtS6kh4k7Zu2gG/full

5   B. Taylor, B. Elliott, C. Conneller, N. Milner, A. Bayliss, B. Knight and M. Bamforth, 'Resolving the Issue of Artefact Deposition at Star

Carr', pp. 37-9, *Proceedings of the Prehistoric Society*, vol. 83, 2017, pp. 23–42.

## Chapter 6: Flag Fen: Wetlands Revealed

1   C.A.I. French and F.M.M. Pryor, *The South-West Fen Dyke Survey Project 1982–86*, East Anglian Archaeology Report No. 59 (Fenland Archaeological Trust, Peterborough, 1993).
2   https://www.cam.ac.uk/museums-and-collections/collaborative-projects/my-museum-favourite/docky-bag
3   I describe the discovery of Flag Fen, at greater length and with pictures, in: *Flag Fen: Life and Death of a Prehistoric Landscape*, pp. 107–118 (Tempus Books, Stroud, 2005).
4   M. Robinson, 'Late Bronze Age Coleoptera from Flag Fen', in F. Pryor, *The Flag Fen Basin*, pp. 384–89 (English Heritage, Swindon, 2001).
5   It is the principal theme of my *Home: A Time Traveller's Tales from British Prehistory* (Allen Lane, Penguin Books, London 2014).
6   *Britain AD*, (HarperCollins, 2004), p. 18.

## Chapter 7: Must Farm: At Last, a 'Lake Village'

1   F. Pryor, *The Flag Fen Basin: Archaeology and Environment of a Fenland Landscape* (English Heritage, Swindon, 2001).
2   E. Henton, 'The Application of Oxygen Isotopes and Microwear from Cattle Tooth Enamel at Fengate and the Flag Fen Basin', in F. Pryor and M. Bamforth, *Flag Fen, Peterborough: Excavation and Research 1995–2007*, pp. 105–14 (Oxbow Books, Oxford, 2010).
3   R. Bradley, *The Prehistory of Britain and Ireland* (Cambridge University Press, 2007). D.T. Yates, *Land, Power and Prestige: Bronze Age Field Systems in Southern England* (Oxbow Books, Oxford, 2007).
4   D.T. Yates, *Land, Power and Prestige: Bronze Age Field Systems in Southern England*, pp. 107–133 (Oxbow Books, Oxford, 2007).
5   See, for example, T. Malim, 'The Ritual Landscapes of the Neolithic and Bronze Ages Along the Middle and Lower Ouse Valley' in M. Dawson (ed.), *Prehistoric, Roman and Post-Roman Landscapes in the Great Ouse Valley*, pp. 57–88 Council for British Archaeology, Research Report No. 119 (York, 2000). C. Evans and M. Knight, A Fenland Delta: Later Prehistoric Land-use in the Lower Ouse Reaches, ibid., pp. 89–106. C. Evans and M. Knight, 'The 'Community of Builders': the Barleycroft Post Alignments', in J. Brück (ed.), *Bronze Age Landscapes: Tradition and Transformation*, pp. 83–98 (Oxbow Books, Oxford, 2001)
6   *Britain BC*, (HarperCollins, London, 2003), fig. 62, pp. 290–1.

7   F. Pryor, *Excavation at Fengate, Peterborough, England: the Third Report*, plate 16.

8   S.P. Needham, D. Parham and C.J. Frieman, *Claimed by the Sea: Salcombe, Langdon Bay, and Other Marine Finds of the Bronze Age*, Council for British Archaeology Research Report (York, 2013).

9   For an excellent blog about Must Farm go to: www.mustfarm.com The site has also featured in the popular archaeological journals *Current Archaeology* (Issues 263, 312 and 319) and *British Archaeology* (Nos. 147, 148, 149 and 150).

## Chapter 8: Borough Fen: A Hillfort Lurking Beneath the Surface

1   We have long known that hillforts like Danebury and Maiden Castle were settlements, but recently geophysics has revealed some unexpected new ones: D. Stewart and M. Russell, 'Iron Age Interior Design: Mapping the Inside of Dorset's Hillfort Enclosures', *Current Archaeology*, Issue 336, March 2018, pp. 28–35.

2   H.C. Darby, *The Changing Fenland*, pp. 202–27 (Cambridge University Press, 1983).

3   I am grateful to my wife, Maisie, who first pointed this out to me.

4   F.R. Hodson, 'Some pottery from Eastbourne, the 'Marnians' and the pre-Roman Iron Age in southern England' *Proceedings of the Prehistoric Society*, vol. 28, 1962, pp. 140–55.

5   The Cat's Water site is fully described in F. Pryor, *Excavation at Fengate, Peterborough, England: The Fourth Report* (Northants Archaeological Society Monograph 2/Royal Ontario Museum Archaeology Monograph 7, 1984).

6   Ibid., Structures 3, 16, 20 and 54.

7   H.C. Darby, *The Changing Fenland*, pp. 139–41 (Cambridge University Press, 1983).

8   W.A. Cook, 'The Number of Ducks caught in Borough Fen Decoy 1776–1959', The Wildfowl Trust 11th Annual Report, 1960, pp. 118–22.

9   The site (Site BoF 7) is written up in C.A.I. French and F.M.M. Pryor, *The South-West Fen Dyke Project 1982–86*, East Anglian Archaeology Rep. No. 59, pp. 68–76 (Peterborough, 1993).

10  Ibid., pp. 76–9 (Site BoF 1).

11  See my *Farmers in Prehistoric Britain*, chapter 8 (Tempus Books, Stroud, 1998).

12  T. Lane and E.L. Morris (eds.), *A Millennium of Saltmaking: Prehistoric and Romano-British Salt Production in the Fenland*, chapters 1 and 2 (Lincolnshire Archaeology and Heritage Reports Series, No. 4 (Heckington, Sleaford, 2001).

## Chapter 9: Billingborough Iron Age: Salt and Farming in the Northern Fens

1   http://www.caitlingreen.org/2016/05/a-note-on-evidence-for-african-migrants.html
2   C. Evans and I. Hodder, *Marshland Communities and Cultural Land-scapes from the Bronze Age to the Present Day: the Haddenham Project Vol. 2* (McDonald Institute Monograph, Cambridge, 2006).
3   Ibid., pp. 313–5.
4   N. Pevsner, J. Harris and N. Antram, *The Buildings of England: Lincolnshire*, pp. 258–9 (Penguin Books, London, 1989).
5   https://en.wikipedia.org/wiki/Morris_On
6   E. Porter, *Cambridgeshire Customs and Folklore*, pp. 103–4 (Routledge and Kegan Paul, London, 1969). For information about the current Straw Bear festival go to: http://www.strawbear.org.uk/history-whittlesea-straw-bear-festival.html
7   P. Chowne, R.M.J. Cleal, A.P. Fitzpatrick and P. Andrews, *Excavations at Billingborough, Lincolnshire, 1975–8: A Bronze-Iron Age Settlement and Salt-Working Site*, East Anglian Archaeology, Report No. 94 (Wessex Archaeology, Salisbury, 2001).
8   Ibid., p. 95.
9   www.lincsaviation.co.uk
10  C. Taylor and R. Moore, 'Beside the Witham: Lincoln Eastern Bypass', *British Archaeology*, No. 156, August 2017, pp. 18–25.
11  pp. 630–31.
12  https://youtu.be/_hzNokvhQlM
13  Carol Allen, *Exchange and Ritual at the Riverside: Late Bronze Age Life at Washingborough, Lincolnshire*, Pre-Construct Archaeology (Lincoln) Monograph Series No. 1 (Lincoln, 2009).
14  For a good introduction see I.M. Stead, *Celtic Art* (British Museum Publications, London, 1985).
15  N. Field and M. Parker Pearson, *Fiskerton: An Iron Age Timber Causeway with Iron Age and Roman Votive Offerings* (Oxbow Books, Oxford, 2003).
16  A.T. Chamberlain, 'Lunar Eclipses, Saros Cycles and the Construction of the Causeway', ibid., pp. 136–148.

## Chapter 10: Castor: A Roman Palace with Saxon Prospects

1   C.W. Phillips (ed.), *The Fenland in Roman Times* (Royal Geographical Society, London, 1970).
2   A.D. Mills, *A Dictionary of English Place-Names*, p. 384 (Oxford University Press, 1991).

3   T. Malim, *Stonea and the Roman Fens* (Tempus Books, Stroud, 2005).

4   Ibid., pp. 79–81.

5   R.P.J. Jackson and T.W. Potter, *Excavations at Stonea, Cambridgeshire, 1988–85* (British Museum Press, London, 1996).

6   C. O'Brien and N. Pevsner, *The Buildings of England: Bedfordshire, Huntingdonshire and Peterborough*, pp. 562–68 (Yale University Press, 1968, revised 2014).

7   S. Tomlinson, 'Edmund Artis, Antiquary' *Durobrivae*, vol. 2, 1974, pp. 22–3.

8   https://www.royalcollection.org.uk/collection/1076192/the-durobrivae-of-antonius-identified-and-illustrated-in-a-series-of-plates

9   *The Making of the British Landscape*, (Penguin Books, London, 2010) p. 401.

10  D. Mackreth, 'Durobrivae', in *Durobrivae: A Review of Nene Valley Archaeology*, 7, 1979, pp. 19–21.

11  A.D. Mills, *A Dictionary of English Place-Names*, p. 68 (Oxford University Press, 1991).

12  D.F. Mackreth, 'Castor', in *Durobrivae: A Review of Nene Valley Archaeology*, 9, 1984, pp. 22–25.

### Chapter 11: Pre-Norman Boundaries that Shaped the Medieval Fens

1   F. Pryor, *Paths to the Past*, pp. 13–18 (Allen Lane, London, 2018).

2   The authoritative report on the Fenland Survey of 1981–88 was reduced to stating (p. 131): 'As with the remainder of England, the exact fate of the Roman population is something of a mystery.'

3   For an excellent summary see: 'The ancient British genome: writing new histories', *British Archaeology*, No. 151 (Nov/Dec 2016), pp. 14–25. For a detailed critique see S. Oosthuizen, *The Anglo-Saxon Fenland*, pp. xii–xiv (Windgather Press, Oxford, 2017).

4   I discuss this in chapter 1 of *Britain AD* (HarperCollins, London, 2004).

5   S. Oosthuizen, *The Anglo-Saxon Fenland*, pp. ix–x (Windgather Press, Oxford, 2017).

6   Ibid., chapter 4.

7   Ibid., chapter 7.

8   Francis Pryor, *Excavation at Fengate, Peterborough, England: The Fourth Report*, pp. 112–14 (Toronto and Northampton, 1984).

9   Carly Hilts, Sleeping by the riverside: Trumpington's Anglo-Saxon bed burial', *Current Archaeology*, no. 343, October 2018, pp. 20–28.

## Chapter 12: Ely Abbey and Cathedral Church: The Ship of the Fens

1  *The Luttrell Psalter: A Facsimile* (British Library, London, 2006).

2  C. Chippindale, *Stonehenge Complete*, chapter 1 (Thames and Hudson, London, 1983).

3  https://www.elycathedral.org/history-heritage/the-story-of-ely-cathedral

4  S. Bradley and N. Pevsner, *The Buildings of England: Cambridgeshire*, pp. 480–91 (Yale University Press, 2014).

5  C. Hewitt, *English Historic Carpentry* (Phillimore, London and Chichester, 1980).

6  www.independent.co.uk%2Farts-entertainment%2Fobituary-cecil-hewett-1201460.html&usg=AOvVaw2fBB1WWn-bKO0-vEJi_5zp

7  C. Hewitt, *English Historic Carpentry*, p. 161 (Phillimore, London and Chichester, 1980). I have taken the quoted figure of £1,000 in 1960 and increased it to the 2017 value, allowing for inflation.

8  Ibid., p. 169.

9  A.J. Arnold, R.E. Howard and C.D. Litton, *Tree-Ring Analysis of Timbers from the High Roofs of the Cathedral of the Holy and Undivided Trinity, Ely, Cambridgeshire*, Centre for Archaeology Report 19/2005 (English Heritage, London, 2005).

10  R. Bond, *Peterborough Cathedral Vault of the Tower Crossing,* Historical Analysis and Research Team Reports and Papers No. 82 (English Heritage, London, 2003).

11  http://www.british-history.ac.uk/vch/cambs/vol2/pp199-210

12  C. O'Brien and N. Pevsner, *The Buildings of England: Bedfordshire, Huntingdonshire and Peterborough*, pp. 699–703 (Yale University Press, 2014).

13  http://www.fensmuseums.org.uk/page_id__25.aspx

14  J. Finch and K. Giles (Eds.), *Estate Landscapes: Design, Improvement and Power in the Post-Medieval Landscape*, Society for Post-Medieval Archaeology Monograph 4, 2007.

15  http://www.british-history.ac.uk/survey-london/vol36/pp37-40

16  F. Pryor, 'Two Bronze Age burials near Pilsgate, Lincolnshire', *Proceedings of the Cambridge Antiquarian Society*, vol. 68, 1974, pp. 1–12.

17  F. Pryor, *Farmers in Prehistoric Britain*, chapter 8 (Tempus Books, Stroud, 1998).

18  N. Pevsner and J. Harris, *The Buildings of England: Lincolnshire*, 2nd Ed., p. 241 (Penguin Books, London, 1989).

## Chapter 13: Tattershall Castle and the Saving of England's Past

1  S. Catney and D. Start (Eds.), *Time and Tide: The Archaeology of the Witham Valley* (Witham Valley Archaeology Research Committee, Heckington, Sleaford, Lincolnshire, 2003).

2   The Witham Valley monastic sites are listed in N. Pevsner and J. Harris, *The Buildings of England: Lincolnshire*, 2nd Ed., pp. 446–7 (Penguin Books, Harmondsworth, 1989), as follows: Bardney (pp. 112–15), Barlings (p. 117), Kirkstead (pp. 417–18), Stixwold Priory (no ruins, p. 719), Tupholme Abbey (p. 770), Stainfield Priory (p. 683) Nocton Priory (earthworks, p. 578). They are also individually included in R.W. Morant, *Abbeys and Priories of Lincolnshire: Past and Present*, 2nd Ed. (www.impressionpublishing.net, 2013).

3   P. Everson and D. Stocker, *Custodians of Continuity? The Premonstratensian Abbey at Barlings and the Landscape of Ritual*, Lincolnshire Archaeology and Heritage Reports Series, No. 11 (Heckington, Lincolnshire, 2011).

4   N. Pevsner and J. Harris, *The Buildings of England: Lincolnshire*, 2nd Ed., pp. 743–50 (Penguin Books, Harmondsworth, 1989).

5   https://www.etoncollege.com/OurHistory.aspx

6   https://www.west-norfolk.gov.uk/info/20007/people_and_communities/441/public_transport

7   Paul Richards, *King's Lynn* (Phillimore, Chichester, 1990). N. Pevsner and B. Watson, *The Buildings of England: Norfolk 2: North-West and South*, pp. 459–506 (Yale University Press, 1999).

8   Richards, ibid., p. 24.

9   Ibid., p. 25.

10   https://www.heritageopendays.org.uk/

11   https://en.wikipedia.org/wiki/Horizon

12   M. Spurrell, *The Stump: Boston Parish Church, St Botolph's* (RJL Smith & Associates, Much Wenlock, Shropshire, 2001).

13   S. Piggott, *William Stukeley: An Eighteenth-Century Antiquary*, 2nd Ed. (Thames and Hudson, London, 1985).

14   N. Pevsner and J. Harris, *The Buildings of England: Lincolnshire*, 2nd Ed., pp. 153–71 (Penguin Books, Harmondsworth, 1989).

15   F. Pryor, *Paths to the Past*, chapter 10 (Allen Lane, London, 2018).

16   N. Pevsner and J. Harris, *The Buildings of England: Lincolnshire*, 2nd Ed., p. 375 (Penguin Books, Harmondsworth, 1989).

17   There is a good photo of the Easter Sepulchre in S. Jenkins, *England's Thousand Best Churches*, p. 380 (Penguin Books, London, 2000).

18   http://edwardthesecond.blogspot.co.uk/2016/07/st-andrews-church-heckington-lincs-and.html

19   J. Orange, *A Ten Minute Guide to the Choir Stalls and The Misericords including some information about Boston Parish Church* (Photocopy compiled in 1980).

20   N. Wright, *Boston: a Pictorial History* (Phillimore and Co., Chichester, 1994).

## Chapter 14: Small Towns and the Gentlemen of Spalding

1  N. Pevsner and J. Harris, *The Buildings of England: Lincolnshire*, 2nd Ed., p. 384 (Penguin Books, Harmondsworth, 1989).

2  I have based my guess at the original building of Sutton St Edmund Church, on the presence nearby of Guannock House.

3  See my *The Birth of Modern Britain*, pp. 226–7 (HarperCollins, London, 2011).

4  https://www.prickwillowmuseum.com

5  N. Pevsner and J. Harris, *The Buildings of England: Lincolnshire*, 2nd Ed., pp. 568–69 (Penguin Books, Harmondsworth, 1989).

6  *The Buildings of England: Lincolnshire*, 2nd edition, p. 568 (Penguin Books, London, 1989).

7  K. Seaton, *The River Welland, Shipping & Mariners of Spalding* (The History Press, Stroud, 2013).

8  I discuss Laxton, with references, in *Paths to the Past*, chapter 12 (Allen Lane, London, 2018).

9  https://royalsociety.org

10  S. Piggott, *William Stukeley: An Eighteenth-Century Antiquary*, 2nd Ed., pp. 33–36 (Thames and Hudson, London, 1985).

11  Ibid., p. 35.

12  R. Sweet, *Antiquaries: The Discovery of the Past in Eighteenth-Century Britain*, pp. 114–15 (Hambledon and London, London and New York, 2004).


## Chapter 15: Cambridge, Rationality and Fen Drainage

1  S. Bradley and N. Pevsner, *The Buildings of England: Cambridgeshire*, pp. 287–88 (Yale University Press, 2014).

2  Ibid., pp. 284–86.

3  Ibid., pp. 132–46.

4  Ibid., pp. 215–30.

5  I draw heavily on H.C. Darby, *The Changing Fenland* (Cambridge University Press, 1983) in the following account of early drainage.


## Chapter 16: The Holme Fen Post and the Drainage of the Deepest Peatlands

1  https://www.theyworkforyou.com

2  http://www.greatfen.org.uk/holme-fen-posts

3  In broad terms, 4 metres/13 ft over 165 years.

4  http://onlinelibrary.wiley.com/doi/10.1111/j.1365-2389.1977.tb02256.x/full

5   David Hall, *The Fenland Project, Number 10: Cambridgeshire Survey, The Isle of Ely and Wisbech*, East Anglian Archaeology Report No. 79 (Cambridgeshire County Council, 1996).

6   http://www.greatfen.org.uk/heritage/whittlesea-mere/map-location

7   H.C. Darby, *The Changing Fenland*, p. 179 (Cambridge University Press, 1982). Richard L. Hills, *Machines, Mills and Uncountable Costly Necessities*, pp. 139–43 (Goose and So, Norwich, 1967).

8   I use the 2nd revised edition (Cambridgeshire Libraries Publications, 1993) with an excellent introduction and notes by H.J.K. Jenkins and Mary Liquorice.

9   Ibid., pp. 33–4.

10  Christopher Morris (ed.), *The Illustrated Journeys of Celia Fiennes c.1682–c.1712*, p. 82 (Webb and Bower, Exeter; Michael Joseph, London, 1982).

## Chapter 17: Wisbech: Enlightened Bankers on the Brinks

1   N. Pevsner, *The Buildings of England: Cambridgeshire,* p. 694 (Penguin Books, Harmondsworth, 1954).

2   http://www.wisbech-society.co.uk/

3   N. Pevsner, *The Buildings of England: Cambridgeshire,* pp. 412–14 (Penguin Books, Harmondsworth, 1954).

4   See also N. Scarfe, *The Shell Guide to Cambridgeshire*, pp. 208–15 (Faber and Faber, London, 1983. D. Abel and D. Thurman, *Wisbech: Forty Perspectives of a Fenland Town* (The Wisbech Society, 1998).

5   http://www.wisbech-society.co.uk/peckovers.html

6   http://www.octaviahill.org/

7   F.R. Pryor, *Memoirs of Samuel Hoare* (Headley Bros., Bishopsgate, London, 1911).

8   https://en.wikipedia.org/wiki/Society_for_Effecting_the_Abolition_of_the_Slave_Trade

9   I quote this anecdote in the foreword to P. Chamberlain, *The Napoleonic Prison of Norman Cross*, p.9 (History Press, Stroud, 2018).

10  I draw extensively on Ibid. in the following account of Norman Cross.

11  M. Freeman, *Railways and the Victorian Imagination*, pp. 1–4 (Yale University Press, 1999).

12  https://en.m.wikipedia.org/wiki/Transport_in_the_United_Kingdom

13  V. Mitchell, K. Smith, C. Awdry and A. Moot, *Branch Lines Around March* (Middleton Press, West Sussex, 1993).

14  R.E. Pearson and J.G. Ruddock, *Lord Willoughby's Railway: The Edenham Branch* (Willoughby Memorial Trust, Bourne, Lincolnshire, 1986).

15  P.W. Swinger, *Railway History in Pictures: East Anglia*, p. 79 (David and Charles, North Pomfret, Vermont, 1983).

16  The definitive account of wartime farming: B. Short, C. Watkins and J. Martin (Eds.), *The Front Line of Freedom: British Farming in the Second World War* (British Agricultural History Society, Exeter, 2007).

17  https://www.lner.info/co/GER/wisbech/wisbech.php

## Chapter 18: Wicken, Welney and Willow Tree: Modern Attitudes to Fen Conservation

1   According to a leading butterfly website, the Chequered Skipper became extinct in England after 1976! http://www.ukbutterflies.co.uk/species.php?species=palaemon

2   https://www.theguardian.com/travel/2018/apr/22/a-wild-walk-in-the-fens-marshland-fen-edge-trail

3   For an excellent semi-autobiography see Norman Moore, *The Bird of Time: The Science and Politics of Nature Conservation* (Cambridge University Press, 1987).

4   https://en.m.wikipedia.org./wiki/Meganeura

5   https://british-dragonflies.org.uk/content/dragonfly-centre

6   See, for example, Harry Godwin, *Fenland: Its Ancient Past and Uncertain Future*, pp. 113–123 (Cambridge University Press, 1978). For more recent research see Martyn Waller, *The Fenland Project, Number 9: Flandrian Envionmental Change in Fenland*, pp. 102–5 East Anglian Archaeology, Report No. 70, 1994.

7   Mike Dawson, *Prehistoric, Roman, and Post-Roman Landscapes of the Great Ouse Valley*, Research Report 119 (Council for British Archaeology, York, 2000).

8   David Hall and John Coles, *Fenland Survey*, fig. 15, p. 29.

9   http://www.lincstrust.org.uk/gibraltar-point

10  http://www.wwt.org.uk/wetland-centres/welney/

11  https://www.nationaltrust.org.uk/woolsthorpe-manor

12  https://en.m.wikipedia.org/wiki/The_Collection_(Lincolnshire)

13  Hardback published in 2015 by Green Plover Books, 21 Cambridge Avenue, Lincoln, LN1 1LS.

14  There are five: Arnold's Meadow, Pinchbeck Slipe, Willow Tree Fen, Baston Fen and Thurlby Fen Slipe. Go to: http://www.lincstrust.org.uk/

15  http://www.lincstrust.org.uk/reserves/arnolds-meadow

16  http://www.lincstrust.org.uk/Willow-Tree-Fen/

## Epilogue: Farewell to Boston

1   I discuss the effects of climate change on the landscape in *The Making of the British Landscape*, pp. 667–75 (Penguin Books, London, 2010).

2   https://www.bbc.co.uk/news/science-environment-45983260

3   https://ousewasheslps.wordpress.com/2014/02/07/flooding-in-the-fens-1947-floods/

4   There is an excellent account of tidal surges in H. C. Darby, *The Changing Fenland*, pp. 220–21 (Cambridge University Press, 1983).

5   https://www.lincolnshire.gov.uk/lincolnshire-prepared/news/red-flood-evacuation-signs-introduced-to-lincolnshires-coastline/127416.article#content

6   https://en.wikipedia.org/wiki/Freiston_Shore

# Acknowledgements

This book has benefitted from almost half a century of living and working in the Fens and I cannot possibly thank everyone who has helped me over the years. I would, however, like one or two special names to be remembered. The late Dermot Bond and Boyd Dixon helped maintain the morale of the Fengate team, often in difficult times. I have always depended very heavily on the special skills of our team as the sites we worked on were often very fragile: Bill Moss, Sarah Lunt, David Cranstone, Bob Bourne, Janet Neve and Jane Downes. Chris Evans worked at Fengate before taking on the running of the Cambridge University Unit (CAU) and we have remained in close touch ever since. My wife, Maisie Taylor, Professor Charly French, David Gurney and Dave Crowther formed the nucleus of the remarkable crew that excavated at Etton and Flag Fen simultaneously. The late George Dixon was our on-site accountant and David Bath eased all negotiation with the authorities at Peterborough New Town. The late Eric Standen was a staunch supporter for many decades. Nearly all our projects were funded by Historic England or its previous incarnations and we all owe copious thanks to the late Dr Geoff Wainwright, Chief Archaeologist. Some of our more notable Inspectors included Tony Fleming, Philip Walker and Professor Mike Parker-Pearson. Many volunteers helped us at Flag Fen and chief among them are Linda Ireson, Frank Rowley, the late Freddie Kramer, Dr John Fuller and Tony Hirst. Flag

Fen was run by Fenland Archaeological Trust, which owed an enormous amount to its two Patrons, the late Peter Boizot and HRH The Duke of Gloucester. Day-to-day running was in the capable hands of many, including Toby Fox, Neil Hart, Garner Roberts, Richard Rigg, Jacquie Lawson, Nyree Ambarchian and Brenda Hirst. Michael Bamforth was Maisie's right-hand man at Flag Fen and helped me assemble and edit the report on the excavations of 1995–2007.

The production of this book was a most enjoyable experience. It was ably edited by Richard Milbank, design was by Adrian McLaughlin and copyedit by Claire Cock-Starkey. The excellent index was compiled by Geraldine Beare.

Finally, I would like to thank Maisie for reading early drafts of this book and pointing out numerous occasions when my memory was playing tricks. Despite her vigilance, some errors are bound to have found their way into print. They are, of course, my responsibility alone.

# Image credits

The images on pp. vii–ix, 12, 29, 32, 36, 44, 66, 76, 94, 97, 102, 108, 121, 124, 145, 146, 147, 152, 153, 162, 174, 175, 187, 210, 219, 245, 268, 270, 271, 276, 281, 285, 289, 290, 294, 302, 305, 308, 311, 315, 331, 334, 338, 352, 360, 362, 367, 380, 387, 388, 393 and 397 are the authors' own.

p. x Map of the Fens / © Chloe Watson.

p. 64 Frontispiece of *A Matter of Time*, H. C. Bowen and R. M. Butler / © The Crown Estate.

p. 199 Life on the Washingborough raised platform, David Hopkins / © PCAS Archaeology Ltd., Lincoln.

p. 203 The Witham Shield *c.* fourth century BC / © Werner Forman / Getty Images.

p. 229 A reconstruction of the Praetorium at Castor / © Donald Mackreth.

p. 250 A scene from the Luttrell Psalter *c.* fourteenth century / © British Library Board / Bridgeman Images.

p. 260 A drawing of the timber framework of the Ely Cathedral Octagon / © Cecil Hewett / Every effort has been made to secure permission from the copyright holder.

p. 323 King's College Chapel, Cambridge / public domain.

p. 325 Nevile's Court, Trinity College, Cambridge / public domain.

p. 343 Map of Whittlesey Mere, 1786 / public domain.

p. 345 A tethered 'gang' of five shallow-hulled boats / public domain.

p. 347 A regatta on Whittlesey Mere, 1842 / public domain.

p. 365 A re-drawing of the branch lines around the fenland town of March / © Middleton Press.

p. 377 The Rothschild bungalow at Woodwalton Fen Nature Reserve / © Michael David Murphy / Alamy.

Every effort has been made to trace copyright holders and gain permission to reproduce images. We apologise if there are any errors or omissions and would be happy to make any amendments in future editions.

# Index

## ABOUT THE AUTHOR

FRANCIS PRYOR is one of Britain's most
distinguished living archaeologists, and the excavator
of Flag Fen. He is the author of *Home*, *Britain BC*,
*Britain AD*, *Seahenge*, *The Making of the British
Landscape* and *Stonehenge*.